Dr Michael
Carrera

Sex

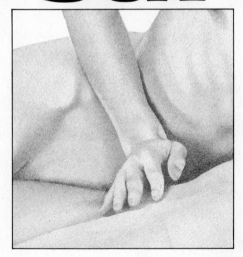

Dr Michael Carrera

Sex

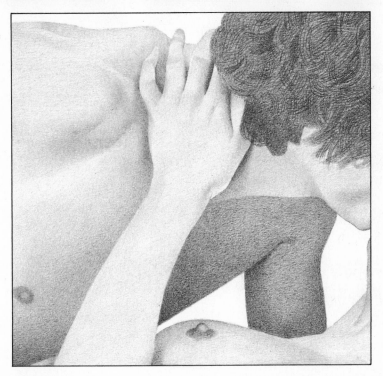

The Facts, The Acts and Your Feelings

MITCHELL BEAZLEY

Sex: The Facts, The Acts and Your Feelings was edited and designed by
Mitchell Beazley International Ltd, 87/89 Shaftesbury Avenue,
London, W1V 7AD

© Mitchell Beazley Publishers 1981
Text © Michael Carrera 1981
ISBN 0 85533 346 4

Composition in Ehrhardt by Filmtype Services Limited, Scarborough,
North Yorkshire

Origination by Adroit Photo Litho, Birmingham
Printed and bound by Morrison and Gibb, Edinburgh

Art Editor: Len Roberts

Designers: Anne Braybon

  Jane Owen

Researcher: Nicholas Law

Editorial Assistant: Margaret Little

Illustrators
HOWARD PEMBERTON: pages 1, 3, 20–21, 52–3, 56, 146, 148–9, 206–7, 210–11,
212–13, 250, 260–61, 281, 367, 370–71, 378-9, 386, 400–401, 404–5, 410–11, 414-15,
416-17, 420–21, 422–3, 428–9, 434

BILL PROSSER: pages 107–8, 218, 221, 225, 231, 328, 331, 364, 375
RORY KEE: pages 381, 392–3, 419, 437
TERRI LAWLOR: pages 11, 214–15, 275, 382–3, 391, 432–3
ANDREW McDONALD (diagrams): pages 58, 59, 69, 83, 85, 222–3, 229, 230, 235,
239, 242–3, 334, 358
CHRIS NEAVES (Kee Scott designs): pages 258–9, 272–3, 282, 338, 348–9
TONY GRAHAM: pages 55, 60, 62–3, 250–51, 365
PETER GUDYNAS: page 345.

CONTENTS

CONTENTS

Acknowledgements

Many people — teachers, students, professional colleagues, co-workers in sex education programmes — have helped shape my thinking and have encouraged me in writing this book. I am grateful to all of them. For their particular help in reading and commenting on sections of the book I would like to thank: Dr James Bevan, Richard Bennett MD, Derek Calderwood PhD, Carol Cassell PhD, Wendy Chavkin MD, Takey Crist MD, William Granzig PhD, Lorna Littner, Mel Littner, Michael Perelman PhD, Stephen Roos, Leah Schaefer EdD, Julie Spain PhD, Ann Welbourne PhD, Barbara Whitney, and Shirley Zussman EdD. I would also like to thank Trish North for her research assistance and Judy Cohen, Irwin Cohen and Millie Becerra for their patient help in typing the manuscript.

I would also like to record my appreciation for the enthusiasm and encouragement of James Mitchell, Adrian Webster and the staff of my publishers, Mitchell Beazley. To Frank E. Taylor I offer my thanks for much wise and friendly counsel, and I owe a special debt of gratitude to my editor, Roger Hearn, for his guidance, unstinting support and friendship throughout the preparation of the book.

On behalf of my publishers I would like to thank Dr J. L. Scheuer, Dr Katharina Dalton, Betty Westgate of the Mastectomy Association, members of the staff of the Family Planning Association and members of the staff of the Health Education Council. I am indebted to Dr David Smith for permission to quote from his work on the sexological aspects of drug use and also to the Masters & Johnson Institute and Little, Brown & Co for permission to reproduce the diagrams from *Human Sexual Response* on pages 93 and 94.

A number of individuals and bodies offered much helpful advice in the preparation of this English edition. In recording my appreciation I do not mean to imply their approval of the content; all faults of omission and commission remain mine. I would however like to thank: Dr Peter Schiller and Dr Michael Rogers; Jonathan Walters, Gay Switchboard and the Campaign for Homosexual Equality; Mr Peter Houghton and the National Association for the Childless; Michael Stephenson and Melissa Brooks; Ms Toni Bellfield and the Family Planning Information Service; the National Marriage Guidance Council; the Well Woman Clinic; Mr Terry Thompson and Physically Handicapped and Able-Bodied; Sexual Problems of Disabled People.

I also owe large debts of thanks to many friends and relatives: to Gilbert M. Shimmel for his unfailing confidence and support; to the Flexner family who have always encouraged me; to Janice, Toni, Kim and Alyssa, to my brothers Sal and Jimmy, and especially to my parents Jim and Grace, whose unconditional love and understanding have taught me the true meaning of family. My son Chris and my daughter Courtney have both been remarkable in their encouragement of me in this work, and I am deeply grateful for their unfailing support and affection. Finally, I would like to acknowledge the largest of all my debts of gratitude: to my wife, whose encouragement, love and understanding have made this book possible.

Preface

Many people equate sexuality with genital acts only, and there are many books that describe exciting, fulfilling approaches to them. The purpose of this book is however much broader. It seeks to deal with whole people — thinking, feeling people who need, have and seek relationships. Genital expression may play a part in some of these relationships, but sexuality plays a part in all of them. This book is about an integrated, joyful, informed, creative expression of sexuality.

It is my belief that all people have a right to express their sexuality as a dignified, positive source of personal enrichment and happiness. Unfortunately, many people accept unnecessary limitations that prevent them from realizing their full potential. There are two reasons for this, and it is the purpose of this book to explore them both.

The first reason is that sex and sexuality are areas in which irrational fears thrive, fed by myths and misinformation. This book therefore sets out the facts so that each person may make informed decisions about the expression of his or her sexuality, both as an individual and as a family member.

The second reason is that we regard sexuality as something separate from the rest of life. Sex, to many people, means genital acts, either with a partner or alone. But this is to deny the completeness of our sexuality. Sexuality has to do with being male or female, and is vitally conditioned by the cultural and religious views of the societies in which we live; sexuality has spiritual, intellectual, cultural and emotional dimensions as well as the biological. Genital activity is a very important way of expressing our sexuality, but it is only one aspect of a much wider expression. How we feel about ourselves conditions all our contacts with other people; what we think are appropriate ways of behaving for males and females of all ages does the same.

This book sets out to explore all the dimensions of sexuality. For that reason, every subject it contains has been considered under several different headings, though not all of them are appropriate to all subjects. These headings — the dimensions of sexuality — are: Facts: the foundation without which no broader understanding of sexuality can be reached; Myths: a description of irrational fears and misinformation; Age: our stage in the life cycle is an essential qualifier of how we express our sexuality; Feelings: the private convictions and concerns that also condition our behaviour; Relationships: some of the rewards and some of the problems of sharing our sexual expression with others; Culture and Religion: the major social and religious forces that determine what is approved behaviour and what is not; and Problems: what may go wrong, why, and what may be done about it.

Fulfilling our sexuality is a lifelong opportunity. We may choose to explore our thoughts and feelings about sexuality and sexual acts or we may not. We may seek to change some of our attitudes or we may be happy as we are. Either way, this book respects absolutely the right of individuals to make their own decisions for themselves and in their relationships according to their own beliefs and values. A true understanding of sexuality can only occur when the aspects of sex and self, sex and feelings, sex and intimacy, sex and religious beliefs and sex and cultural context are fully explored and integrated.

M.A.C.

To my wife, June

FACTS AND FEELINGS

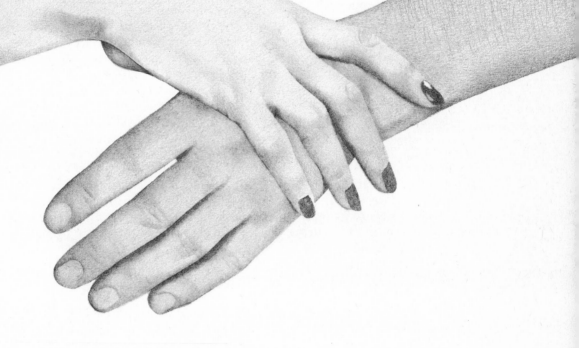

AGES AND STAGES

Both sexual learning and sexual expression start from the moment of birth and continue throughout the life cycle. Each stage of a person's life shows different aspects of sexual expression. These are the stages discussed in the following pages: **1 Infancy; 2 Toddler and Preschool; 3 Childhood; 4 Preadolescence; 5 Adolescence; 6 Adulthood; 7 Mid-Life; 8 Later Years.**

1 Infancy

Infancy is the phase from birth to the toddler period (around 16 to 18 months) when the most profound emotional and intellectual development takes place. It is clear that the degree of proper caring by the parent(s) and the child's establishment of basic trust and security in his or her environment are crucial to the child's development of a healthy emotional life. Improper bonding between parent(s) and child and deprivation of nurturance and security frequently result in the development of insecure, dependent behaviour, sometimes characterized by an insatiable search for affection. Inappropriate sexual behaviour in adolescence and adulthood may be connected to this early deprivation but we have no way of establishing this connection for certain.

Infants are both sensual and sexual. Baby boys can have erections from the moment they are born (they have even been observed to have them while still in the womb). Similarly, vaginal lubrication has been observed in baby girls within 24 hours of birth. Rhythmic body movements and sensual and erotic body exploration by infants of both sexes sometimes result in orgasm. As infants move past their first year this body exploration and pleasuring becomes less diffuse and appears to be concentrated on the genitals.

Several recent studies on the meaning of infantile genital and nongenital sexual expression suggest that those infants whose sexual and sensual behaviour was accepted as a natural part of development grew to adulthood with less guilt and anxiety about affection, intimacy and sex than those whose sexual and sensual behaviour was met with anger and prohibition. It must immediately be pointed out here that in general these connections are made by adults who recollected and reconstructed their early days. They are not the result of studies following people through from infancy to adulthood, though this type of long-term study is now underway.

During this early stage of development, the behaviour and attitudes of the adult(s) providing nurture for the young girl or boy are crucial. Overreaction or punitive attitudes towards touching the genitals or the body in general may set the stage for similar parental behaviours throughout the child's development. These may have a negative influence on the young person's feelings about his or her body image in general and about the genitals in particular. It is, incidentally, a myth that babies who touch their genitals a great deal will be sexually hyperactive when they grow older.

Q: "Can infants really have orgasm?"
A: "Yes. Kinsey and others have reported obvious orgasm among infants of both sexes during the first year of life — even during the first month."

Q: "A social worker I know keeps referring to the importance of the 'oral phase' in child development. What is that about?"
A: "The term 'oral phase' comes from the psychoanalytic theory which stresses the importance of sucking and the use of the lips and mouth during infancy. In the oral stage, the mouth is not only necessary for feeding and therefore physical survival but it is also seen as the principal site of pleasure, security and well-being. Those who accept oral phase theory believe that proper development during this period sets the stage for oral pleasuring later in life.

"It is obvious that sucking is important in the early development of children, but the connection between the importance of oral pleasure in infancy and sexual development later on is only speculative."

Q: "Lately, we have been reading that it is important for us as parents not to get excited or anxious if our infant touches her genitals. The authors write that it is natural and good for her to do that. It certainly sounds good but it's awfully difficult for us to do. Will we permanently damage our daughter's sexuality if we can't be as relaxed as we are advised?"
A: "I don't believe so. Your attitude about the whole matter seems to be sensitive and concerned, and that is the most important consideration in your relations with your daughter and will have a positive influence on her sexuality. It seems to me that it is your involvement with and care for your daughter that are really crucial to her proper emotional development; not being able to follow what sounds like reasonable advice to the letter will not damage her sexual development permanently.

"It is important to do what you and your husband feel comfortable and natural doing; behaving in some prescribed, artificial way would be likely to create unhelpful tensions between you and your child. Incidentally, you make an excellent point about the difficulty of acting on things that look reasonable in print. This is a common concern of parents who struggle with behaving in ways that may be so unlike their own. Doing things that sound good but are contrary to what comes naturally is difficult and not always rewarding in the long run."

2 Toddler and Preschool

After the infancy stage, children begin to walk and talk. The child moves from total dependency towards a kind of interdependency, develops confidence and begins to exercise some initiative. The adults in the child's life start to place limits on the child's acts, and they begin to have some expectations of the child as well. Toilet training is one of the developmental tasks of this phase and may present a problem for some parents, but most children are toilet trained by the age of three.

During the toddler and preschool state the child's sexual identity takes on a new sharpness. Children are likely to be fascinated with their own bodies — particularly their genitals — and very curious about the way others are made. Parents are often confused about how to respond to this, and the way they respond will influence the young person's sexual learning. Intense negative reactions, as well as seductive, inappropriate discussions of genital exploration can both have a guilt- or anxiety-producing effect on the child's concept of his or her sexuality. A relaxed, accepting attitude in keeping with the naturalness of the child's own exploratory behaviour is likely to have a more positive influence, allowing the child to develop more naturally.

It is at about this time that some parents get to be anxious about nudity in the home. The rule is that parents should do what *they* think proper and what is consistent with their own attitudes and feelings. Changing customary patterns of behaviour may lead to self-consciousness and nervousness — not the best example to set a child. If parents are used to being nude at home some of the time, there is no good reason to change. On the other hand, if they are not in the habit of being nude there is no reason why they should change their habits for the child's sake — whatever other people tell them they ought or ought not to do.

Q: "What can a child learn by seeing a parent nude?"

A: "Our own children told us that seeing us nude on occasion helped them understand what they might look like when they grew up. Our son, for example, said it made him feel more comfortable about his own body and he felt less self-conscious about changing at school with other young boys.

"In general, parental nudity communicates an attitude about the body which may be picked up by children and may make them feel more comfortable about their own bodies."

Q: "A psychologist whom we know told us it was important to be nude in front of our children. We are uncomfortable about that. What do you think?"

A: "Don't let a stranger tell you what to do in your own home. Certainly there is something to be said for parental nudity — it shows children that bodies are perfectly normal things that don't always have to be wrapped up in clothes, that bodies are nothing to be ashamed of. But children will not get that message if they sense that their parents are uncomfortable about being nude. *It must feel right for you.*

"Remember that your own values about privacy and modesty are important childrearing guides too — I imagine you want to convey these attitudes to your children and it is right and proper that you should do so. If you both feel more comfortable changing and bathing in private it is generally better for you and for your children if that is how you continue to act."

Q: "I just don't want my child fiddling with his penis when he is with other children, or when he is in the presence of friends and family. Am I being too dogmatic about this?"

A: "No. Inform your son gently that playing with his penis is not a public activity. Children need to learn that there are some things that just aren't done in public — brushing your teeth and undressing are in the same category. It is important that you should make it clear to your son that there is nothing wrong with touching his penis — it is not a bad act, but it is not a proper public act."

3 Childhood

When boys and girls are between the ages of about four and seven, they tend to be interested in reproduction, pregnancy and birth. Answering their questions simply and straightforwardly is usually the best approach. If they do not understand what you mean, they are likely to ask again. Don't get into very detailed, scientific explanations about simple questions, and don't sexualize the question. It seems to me that many young people discover that when they ask a sexual question, or a question that turns out to be sexual, mum and dad act strangely about it. They probably wonder if the embarrassed overreaction was because of them or the question and sometimes decide not to ask questions like that again. Unfortunately, they don't know it has nothing to do with them at all.

During this stage of development the child generally shows a strong affection towards the parent of the other sex and may talk about marrying daddy or mummy. Some parents are concerned about this, but they need not be; it is a commonplace occurrence and not a sign of a problem.

Autoeroticism in general and masturbation in particular usually increase during this period, although many adults seem to have little or no recollection of these acts in their own childhood. No physical harm results from this type of sensual and sexual behaviour and it is not a sign of a sexual identity or emotional problem. When a child is touching his or her body parents have another opportunity to act in an accepting manner and thereby influence the child's self-image in a positive way. Such a circumstance also offers parents the opportunity to discuss the meaning of private and public acts with their children. This kind of guidance helps young children, and it is important that parents should be clear about it.

Children with positive feelings about their own bodies and respect for the bodies of others are less likely to become involved in self-destructive acts, or in acts that hurt other people when they are older.

Q: "Our five-year-old walked in on us when we were having sex. We were just so surprised and embarrassed that we didn't handle it very well. Will that incident cause an emotional disturbance later on for him?"

A: "Lasting damage is unlikely, though parental embarrassment in such a situation is almost guaranteed. In the future, you could close your door as a sign to your child that you don't want to be disturbed. If he comes in anyway, ask him to leave and then explain later on in the simplest way what you were doing. Do make sure that he understands that neither of you was being hurt or angry."

Q: "We discovered our four-year-old son playing doctor with a friend. Is that uncommon, and should we be concerned because the friend was also a male?"

A: "The answer to both questions is no. It is common for young-sters of that age to explore and examine their own genitals and to do the same with other boys and girls (this is not, by the way, the first step toward intercourse). Curiosity is natural and healthy at this age and the adult sexual meanings so frequently attached to certain behaviours are overreactive and unhelpful. There is probably no connection at all between the play you observed and his future sexual orientation.

"Parents who 'discover' their child ('observe' might be a better term) in genital exploration might do well to ask what the child learned during his or her play. Similarities and differences between boys and girls can be discussed sensitively and parents can use that opportunity to establish an attitude toward the body and the proper time and place for particular behaviours. Ex-pressions of parental alarm or disgust are not helpful during these discussions."

Q: "My six-year-old daughter asked me how was it I had breasts and she didn't. In my embarrassment I avoided the question. Is what I did harmful to her?"

A: "Usually no single event of this kind makes a long-lasting impact on a child. However, if your avoidance of this particular question is part of an overall pattern of silence or evasion about sexual matters, the cumulative effect may be to cause problems in your daughter's psychosexual development.

"In the future you could say: 'You do have breasts and they will grow to be like mummy's when you get to be older like mummy. Just like my hands, feet and head are bigger than yours are now, so are my breasts — as your body grows, so will your breasts.'"

Q: "We've noticed our five-year-old is much more interested in sex now than when she was younger. Should we begin some sex education this early?"

A: "You have been providing sex education for your child from the moment she was born. The way you and your husband held her and touched her during her infancy and the way you both interacted with her was laying the foundation of her sexual learning without your ever talking about a genital sexual issue. Making her feel loved and lovable was a profound influence on her sexuality during that early period. Now that she is older, the ways you relate to each other and to her continue this never ending sexual learning or sex education process. Through your everyday behaviour you affect her feelings and beliefs about gender roles, family roles, body image, affection, love, intimacy and relationships, all of which contribute to her developing sexuality. All of these things are infinitely more important than a discussion of how babies are born, even though many parents erroneously believe that is what sex education is all about."

Q: "Isn't it true that boys always show more sexual interest and get into more sexual acts than girls?"

A: "This seems to be the case, but there is an important qualification. In our society we have a double standard by which boys' interest in sex is encouraged and girls' interest is discouraged. In other cultures, where the double standard does not apply, there does not seem to be as great a difference between the sexes in this regard."

Q: "What is an Oedipus complex?"

A: "From three years of age to approximately five or six, psychoanalysts who follow Freud believe the child passes through an important developmental phase called the Oedipal period. The name comes from the Greek myth in which Oedipus killed his father and married his mother.

"During the Oedipal period, the young boy is said to hate his father because he is a rival for his mother's affection. The boy fears his father will retaliate by cutting off his penis (he suffers castration anxiety). Eventually this competition for the mother and fear of the father subside. The resolution of this period is thought to be of crucial importance for the proper emotional development of the male child.

"Girls go through a similar stage, frequently referred to as the Electra complex. The young girl begins this period by recognizing she has no penis (she suffers penis envy), feels cheated and blames her mother. Accordingly she competes with her mother for the affection of her father. The theorists believe that the resolution of this phase is not as complete as the young boy's resolution.

"This is a much simplified explanation of a rather complex psychoanalytic theory to which many child development professionals do not subscribe."

4 Preadolescence

Between the ages of about eight and 12, young people are likely to make a rapid social development and their exploration of their own sexuality also gathers pace.

Socially, the major development is in forming friendships — "best friends" become very important at this stage. Boys tend to have a group of friends, whereas girls are likely to have just one or two special friends. This new pattern is a further stage in the movement of young people away from total dependency on their parents and towards a system of relationships with their contemporaries (their "peer group"). Some parents do not accept the normality of this behaviour. They construe it as a rejection of themselves and make the young person feel guilty.

Sexually, young people in this age group continue the process of self-discovery that has been going on since birth. They are also increasingly likely to masturbate. Kinsey found in his studies of 1948 and 1953 that 21 percent of boys and 12 percent of girls had masturbated by age 12. In 1974 Hunt found that 63 percent of boys and 33 percent of girls had masturbated by age 13. Kinsey also found that boys who were maturing younger masturbated more frequently than those who matured later; he did not, however, find a similar correlation for girls.

Homosexual acts such as exploring a friend's body or masturbating with others may now be more common than before. They do not of themselves tell us anything about the adult sexual orientation of the young person. The reasons for preadolescent homosexual experiments are probably curiosity, strong affections for best friends, the desire to experiment with growing sexual interest and maybe a defence against a growing attraction to members of the other sex.

Heterosexual contacts appear to be increasing among the 10 to 12 age group in most western countries. Group dating, parties and kissing games tend to increase in response to peer pressure and the expectations of society. Intercourse occurs among a small minority of young people during this period, but it appears that the size of the minority is growing. Incidentally, heterosexual contacts at this age do not predict with certainty an adult heterosexual orientation any more than preadolescent homosexual acts predict an adult homosexual orientation.

Q: "My wife says I should talk to our 12-year-old son about wet dreams. Is that a good idea?"

A: "It is an excellent idea for either or both of you to discuss this with your son. First ejaculation can be a frightening and confusing experience, so a low-key, caring discussion about the naturalness of it, and how it is one of the signals of the entry into a new phase of development, is very important. A discussion of this sort is a wonderful opportunity to open or continue communication about some of the other issues that emerge during adolescence when your son will still need understanding and guidance.

"Incidentally, a recent study showed that only two percent of fathers talked with their sons about nocturnal emission. Although a mother can properly discuss them with her son, a man has the advantage of having had experience of wet dreams; this can add a special dimension to the discussion, just as a woman's experience can when she discusses menstruation with their daughter."

Q: "Aren't young people getting most of their sex information from their parents?"

A: "No. Recent studies indicate that young people get approximately 40 percent of their sex information from their peers. Only 12 percent report their parents as the principal source of their sex information. When I ask young people where they would like to get their sex information from, they generally identify their parents as their first choice. This is further evidence of the enormous responsibility parents have in this important area."

5 Adolescence

Adolescence, which broadly means the teen years, has almost as many descriptions as there are adolescents. Adolescence is expressed differently from one culture to another and even from one subgroup to another within the same cultural system. A number of very important physical changes will occur anyway, but the emotional developments that run alongside them will be profoundly affected by the adolescent's social environment.

Of particular importance to the adolescent, and of particular interest to the adults around him or her, are the dramatic body changes and feelings about these changes that occur during this period. The period of observable, rapid change is called puberty and is marked by some particular events:

* onset of menstruation (current average age is 12.7 years)
* breast development and pubic hair growth in girls
* enlargement of the labia and clitoris
* growth in body height in both girls and boys
* growth of testes and penis
* development of pubic hair and facial hair in boys
* first ejaculation, frequently during "wet dreams"
* voice changes in both boys and girls
* body shape changes toward characteristic adult patterns
* gain in muscular strength for boys
* skin problems (acne) for some boys and girls
* concern on the part of both girls and boys about how their bodies appear to others and sensitivity to remarks by parents and peers about their changing appearance.

These changes in adolescents are triggered by an enormously increased production of testosterone in males and oestrogen and progesterone as well as other hormones from the pituitary gland in females. When some adolescents observe that their physical development is not in step with that of their peers, they feel inadequate and inferior. Sometimes these feelings produce defensive behaviour that make adolescents' lives painful and also affect their parents and other adults in ways that make living together stressful. Parents must be very understanding and supportive of their children during this period and can do much to alleviate the extreme stresses that young people generally suffer through this time. Descriptions of adolescent ego development, personality development and general psychological development are beyond the scope of this book, but suffice it to say that the evolution and consolidation of those aspects of the person, combined with the natural biological changes mentioned, make the

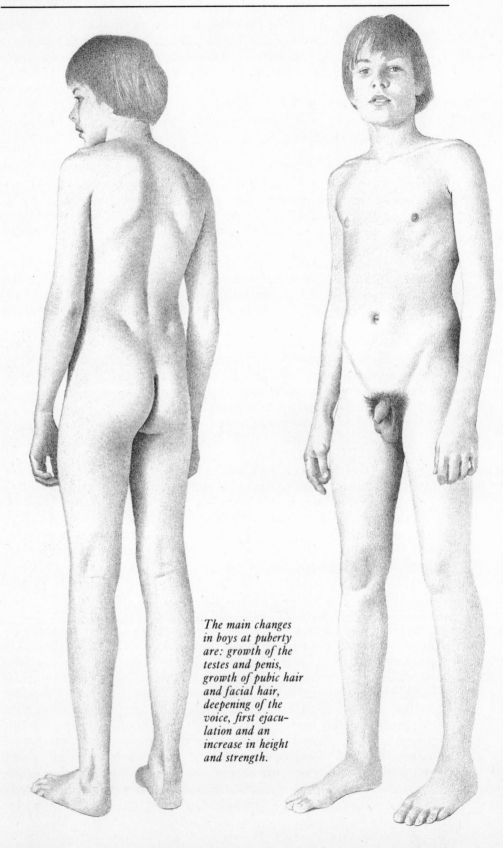

*The main changes
in boys at puberty
are: growth of the
testes and penis,
growth of pubic hair
and facial hair,
deepening of the
voice, first ejacu-
lation and an
increase in height
and strength.*

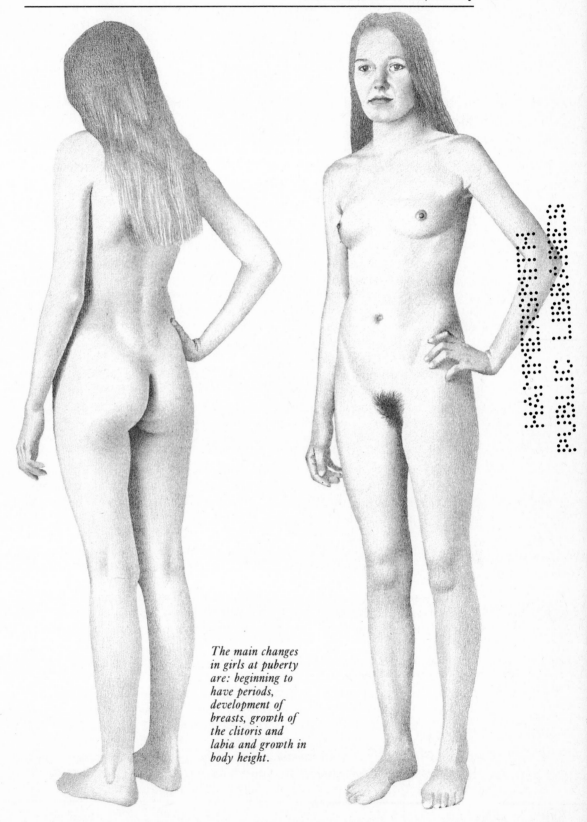

The main changes in girls at puberty are: beginning to have periods, development of breasts, growth of the clitoris and labia and growth in body height.

adolescent period an exacting developmental phase both for the young person and for the adults around her or him.

During adolescence movement away from the family continues. Identity formation and developing autonomy are tasks that must be faced during this period. The degree to which an adolescent does this will affect his or her capacity to develop intimate adult relationships. The task is complicated, though, because while adolescents must go through a process of disengagement from their families they still need guidance from their parents. Not surprisingly, parents and young people often have a great deal of difficulty managing this seeming paradox. I raise this issue here because parents sometimes feel that their adolescent sons or daughters are beyond the time when they need or will respond to the opinions or wishes of their parents about sexual behaviour. However, adolescents want and need this guidance and parents need to maintain their own equilibrium during this period and to continue to support their adolescent sons or daughters.

Sexual interest and desire increase markedly during adolescence and this may lead to difficulty, since approved sexual outlets for young people are not plentiful. During adolescence masturbation increases dramatically among both sexes. By the end of adolescence most males and two-thirds of all females have masturbated to orgasm. Kissing, hugging and petting are popular forms of sexual expression during adolescence and it is quite common for a couple to know what the limits of their behaviour should be so that difficulties resulting from different expectations are avoided. These dating, necking and petting relationships are trivialized by some adults, but they are crucial steps in the establishment of adolescents' sexuality, increasing their confidence in their ability to form relationships and helping to establish erotic and social patterns outside the family.

As to sexual intercourse during adolescence, it is clear that the number of teenagers having intercourse has increased. Kinsey found in 1948 and 1953 that 20 percent of girls and 45 percent of boys had had premarital intercourse by the age of 19. In 1964 in the UK Michael Schofield reported that 16 percent of 15–19 year olds said they had had intercourse, and by 1974 he found this had increased to 51 percent. In 1978 Christine Farrell found that 54 percent of the boys and 42 percent of the girls she questioned said they were sexually experienced before they were 19 and nearly half before they were 16 years old.

"Adolescent sexuality" has become a code phrase to mean adolescent genital sexual behaviour. Unfortunately, today's adolescents are being defined by what adults believe they do sexually. Therefore, the common discussion on adolescents today is about the high rate of unintended pregnancies among 15- to 19-year-olds and the growing number of teenage parents. Indeed these are important issues, but most adolescents are not becoming pregnant or being parents and it is unfair to regard them all in this way. By no means all adolescents are irresponsible or acting in ways that are destructive. Adolescents now have to face all sorts of social and cultural factors that previous generations were not aware of, but they still have to go through the same struggle that their parents and grandparents did to establish their emergent adult identities. If the young person is to develop into a mature and responsible adult then the challenge of this struggle must be accepted.

Q: "Shouldn't something be done about adolescents today? Everything I read indicates that they are really sexually promiscuous and getting out of hand."

A: "What needs to be done is to get the story straight about the majority of adolescents and their behaviour. The generalizations made about today's adolescents come too much from the population of adolescents with problems; case studies tend to focus on adolescent girls who are pregnant or who are teenage parents, with the implication that they make up the majority of cases when in fact they are a minority. Very little attention is paid to teenage boys other than to suggest that they impregnate girls and then leave the scene; not enough is said about the typical adolescent who negotiates this period without any particular disasters to self or others and who moves into adulthood without leaving a trail of out-of-wedlock babies.

"Yes, some young people are experiencing difficulty, as adolescents from each generation always have, but the majority of today's teenagers are responsible to themselves and to others, and that needs to be recognized by adults."

Q: "What is your opinion about a 13-year-old having sex?"

A: "I don't think a 13-year- old can appreciate the full meaning and fulfill the responsibilities of such an intimate act. Intercourse should involve a degree of maturity which, on the whole, 13-year-olds have not yet attained. Teenagers are in a stage of their lives when important personality and emotional characteristics are developing and moving toward consolidation; intercourse would therefore probably take place against a background of needs that are not particularly unifying and integrative to the personality or to the couple.

"In my opinion intercourse fits best in a relationship that is loving and caring, where both the joy and the consequences of the act are fully appreciated and accepted. Teenagers, with the possible exception of older teens, generally are not able fully to meet these standards for intimacy and may by routine premature sexual activity affect their ability to form intimate relationships in the future."

Q: "The number of teenagers having sex may be increasing today but I want to make sure our daughter knows that we don't approve of intercourse until marriage. Is this too old fashioned?"

A: "No. It is important for you and your wife to communicate your values to your daughter and the reasons for them. Young people want direction and guidance and it is the parental responsibility to provide it consistently. You must also understand that providing guidance is no guarantee that it will be followed. However, even though young people make important decisions — such as the decision to have intercourse — without consulting with the important adults in their lives, it is crucial for them to understand in advance the principles underlying such decisions."

Q: "I'm 16 and I don't want to have sex. What do I say to someone who says everyone is having sex so we should too?"

A: "Say 'No!' If your friend really cares for you, your views and desires will be respected. Incidentally, despite media reports not everyone is having sex in their mid-teens, or even in their later teens for that matter."

Q: "I told a friend of mine that discussing birth control with her daughter was giving her approval to have intercourse. Do you agree?"

A: "No, I do not. I believe a parent can discuss the facts about birth control and pregnancy prevention with a daughter or son and at the same time indicate that they do not approve of them having intercourse until they are older or are in a certain type of relationship. It is not contradictory to say: 'I believe it is better for you to wait before having sex, but if you choose to do so anyway it is crucial that you behave in a responsible way and take the proper steps to prevent a pregnancy.' An open, honest discussion of this kind can only help a teenager to appreciate the value of trust in a relationship."

Q: "I'm a single parent and haven't talked to my teenage son about sexual topics yet. There are so many things I want to say and to ask him. Is it too late?"

A: "Absolutely not. It's never too late. Let him know you are interested and that you value his views and feelings about things. Let him know you have some opinions too.

"Remember too that even though you may not have discussed these issues directly with your son, his sexual learning has been influenced by your attitudes and the nature of your relationship all the years you have been together. He has been learning about sexuality from you even though you have never formally discussed the subject."

Q: "Our 16-year-old daughter doesn't go out with boys yet. Is that a sign of a problem? Should we encourage her to do so or arrange a date for her?"

A: "No to all the questions. Some young people are not interested or ready to begin dating at 16 years old. Everyone's social and emotional timetable is different, and it is best to let young people develop their relationships naturally. It is not wise for parents to rush their children; suggesting dates or even going so far as to arrange a date is putting on undue pressure.

"Parents in this situation need to examine where their anxiety comes from and ask themselves who would be the beneficiary of their 16-year-old's dating. What teenagers really need from their parents is reassurance, understanding and support that they are OK and that their development is not a source of concern. Trying to make your daughter conform to the timetable you think is right for her is unlikely to help her in any way."

Q: "Isn't there a great deal of homosexual activity among today's teenagers?"

A: "I don't know what you mean by 'a great deal.' However, the few studies that have addressed this important topic do not show any dramatic changes in the percentage of the adolescent population having some homosexual experience.

"Kinsey, Hunt and Sorenson have shown that more teenage boys than girls have some homosexual experience — between 11 and 20 percent of boys, and between six and ten percent of girls. However, the percentage of the adult population that has a homosexual orientation has remained the same, regardless of the higher frequency of homosexual acts in the second decade of life.

"One dramatic change that is apparent among adolescents is their acceptance of homosexuality as valid. They appear to be less judging of homosexual men and women than adults in our society. If this trend continues, the numbers of those with a homosexual orientation will probably remain the same, but acceptance by heterosexuals that a homosexual orientation is a proper expression may increase as today's young people become tomorrow's adults."

Q: "I heard that once a young person has had some homosexual experience they tend to stay that way. Is that true?"

A: "No. It is not uncommon for adolescents to have one or more homosexual experiences during their teen years, but these are not predictors of their adult orientation. In general these homosexual acts are the results of strong affection for friends, or they may be the result of wanting to try a new experience, or they even may be a response to the anxiety many adolescents feel about being attracted to the other sex. If adolescents continue to express themselves with someone of the same sex, they may indeed have a homosexual orientation. However, for the majority of adolescents, homosexual acts during their teen years are simply experiences which are appropriate at that time in their lives.

"The percentage of adult men and women who have a homosexual orientation has remained fairly constant since such statistics have been recorded."

6 Adulthood

Around the end of the second decade of life a person leaves adolescence and moves into adulthood. There are various phases of adulthood, but like those periods that preceded it, adulthood contains some major tasks which must be faced and negotiated. Forming relationships, their nature, duration, meaning and termination are crucial parts of the adult experience. Decisions about single living, living together, marriage and children are some of the important threads which comprise the sexual fabric of the adult experience. The main choices are discussed on the following pages.

Living As A Single Living as a single woman or man has become a more acceptable life-style today than at any other time in American and European history. Indeed the trend toward single living seems still to be increasing. Although obviously some proportion of singles live alone by force of circumstance rather than free choice, and some are adults who are delaying forming a partnership of some kind with another person, there does seem to be a definite trend toward the single life as a choice and not as the result, say, of having bad luck in relationships.

Despite the fact that the choice to live as a single is a perfectly proper one, society as a whole is suspicious of singles and often puts them under pressure. "Old maid," "confirmed bachelor" and "spinster" are all terms with a negative connotation. All too frequently singles are suspected of being homosexual (or of being "repressed") — as if it mattered. Society encourages and rewards marriage and children, even to the point of preferring that people divorce several times rather than never marry at all.

Not all singles want to be single; on the other hand, getting into a relationship just to win society's approval is not an adequate solution. No relationship at all, many people believe, is better than a wrong relationship.

The great difficulty for many single people is meeting enough other people. As men and women move through their 20s toward their 30s, more and more of their contemporaries get married and the number of people available to choose from decreases. The social structures that provided numerous contacts early on — neighbourhood, school, university — are less effective as they recede in time. One solution to this problem is the "singles scene" — clubs, or groups — but many people find this a forced environment in which they are subject to undue pressures. Another solution is to panic and acquire a partner somehow before the magic 30th birthday, compromising personal standards to relieve the debilitating anxiety of being left "on the shelf."

A very common complaint from singles is that they are expected to have intercourse with any new person with whom they start to form a relationship. Some find this demeaning and a limitation of choice — they are not properly free to decide when it would be appropriate for them to have sex with someone. Acting on their personal values has put some singles up to ridicule for "saving it for their one and only."

Q: "I'm single and I want to stay that way. I have a few close friends and a few relationships where I can get sexual gratification when I need it. When I discuss this with some people they look at me as though I'm strange. Is my situation so unusual?"

A: "I don't think you are strange at all. You are someone who sounds clear about your needs and preferences. People may see your life-style as different, but different does not necessarily mean inferior. As long as your life-style meets your needs that is the way you should continue to live. It would be a big mistake to change just so you will meet with the approval of others."

Q: "I'm single and I don't mind having sex with someone if they appeal to me, even if we have just met. Sometimes their reaction is to want immediately to get into an intense emotional relationship, but that's not what having sex means to me. I would like to have some fun and not make a big thing about it. Do you have any suggestions?"

A: "Tell your partners what your views are about sex. Be clear so they understand that for you sex is fun and enjoyable, but it is not the signal of the beginning of a deep emotional relationship. And tell them before you have sex, because it is a lot more complicated to do afterward and it's not fair to let them build false hopes."

Q: "I'm single and would like to meet someone, but I just can't stand the singles groups. Am I being too fussy, and what could I do instead?"

A: "No, you are not being fussy, but you are cutting down your options. Many single women and men find going to singles clubs degrading because it seems to be advertising, in a blatant way, their vulnerability. The superficiality of the interactions combines with the desperation that is apparent in many of these settings to produce strong feelings of repugnance.

"The problem is that finding acceptable alternatives is difficult; but things are changing. Cultural, intellectual, recreational and religious activities are being organized with an emphasis on singles participation. Singles travel clubs and adult education programmes are also being developed. If you can take the initiative in one of these contexts you will certainly be increasing your chances of forming a relationship."

Q: "I've heard a great deal about single parents lately. Are they increasing in number?"

A: "Yes. Death of a partner and divorce are responsible for some of them but there are increasing numbers of women and men who choose the role of single parent. Single men and women are adopting babies. An extremely high percentage of unmarried teens who have a baby choose to keep the child. Some single women beyond their teenage years are deliberately getting pregnant and have no intention of ever getting married. This is further evidence of changing perceptions of family systems, child-rearing concepts, and the re-examination of the nature of relationships between men and women.

"Clearly, many women no longer see the necessity of marriage to establish their identity as a person or their financial security. In keeping with that evolving sentiment, they feel that separating parenthood from marriage is for them both honest and proper."

Living Together Living together ("cohabiting") and not getting married is a situation chosen by more and more people who do not want to live alone but are reluctant to involve themselves in marriage. Some people object to marriage as an institution, finding it inherently sexist or arbitrarily limiting. Others decide to live together because they are very close indeed to someone but are not sure that in the long run they wish to marry them. Cohabiting for some people may take the form of a "trial marriage" or it may be regarded as the most intimate and satisfying way of having a relationship.

Living together as a life-style has become particularly popular at universities and colleges. Between 20 and 30 percent of students now cohabit at some time during the years of their further education. Such relationships are not usually regarded as trial marriages, are based on deep emotional attachments and routinely include sex. They are commonly sexually exclusive.

In society at large, significant numbers of people who start a relationship find that living together makes better sense than maintaining separate apartments; it is more convenient and less expensive. Most such couples present themselves as a couple, and many of them claim their relationship is at least as strong as marriage since it depends on the constantly renewed choices of two individuals rather than on a marriage contract. They also claim they can split if they need to with a minimum of family and financial disruption.

One special context in which cohabiting appears to be occurring more frequently is after a divorce. Divorced people may be disenchanted with marriage but still believe in long-term live-in relationships. They may be particularly likely to set up home with a lover if there is a child to care for, on the grounds that it will be better for the child to live with two adults than with one, but this is a situation that requires careful handling. It is important for the child (or children) to know the extent and meaning of the parent's new relationship. Issues of sexual behaviour must be clarified lest the child become confused about the meaning of adult sexual relationships and how they relate to parenthood. Issues of roles and authority which are important in any relationship become doubly so when the child spends time with the other parent as well. Having two mothers or two fathers is not easy for a child.

Q: "We've been living together happily for the past year but our parents, who live a long way away, aren't aware of our situation. Should we just leave well enough alone?"

A: "As you must already know, keeping your situation secret has disadvantages. Hiding your secret can be wearisome, and because neither of you can invite your families for a visit your contacts with them are cut down significantly.

"It is true that many parents do not approve of living together outside marriage, but sometimes parents surprise their children with their understanding and acceptance. In the end you must make the decision together, but it seems to me that openness is to be preferred. Perhaps after an initial trauma your resolve to be together and the quality of your relationship will be recognized by your parents. This may lead them to be at least neutral, maybe accepting, and perhaps happy for both of you; their reaction does not have to be hostile.

"There is something else that you ought to think about: if your parents did disapprove strongly when you told them you were living together, would that affect your relationship with each other? Is your relationship really strong enough to meet that disapproval head on, or are you disguising a weakness in your relationship behind your anxieties over your parents' reactions?"

Q: "Is it true that a couple who live together before marriage have a better marriage than those who do not live together before marriage?"

A: "There is no evidence that this is so."

Marriage and Other Long-Term Relationships The majority of adults in our society become involved in long-term relationships. Many, of course, marry. In some countries the relationships of men and women who live together without marrying for a certain number of years are granted legal status called common law marriage. No legal status is granted to long-term homosexual relationships, though many of them constitute bonds as strong as any marriage.

Despite increasing rates of divorce throughout the Western world, people remarry or enter other long-term relationships at a very high rate (in the UK, for example, 50 percent of all divorced people remarry within five years). Not only do such relationships provide for most people the most comprehensive way available of showing their love for another person but there is also a strong cultural pressure to be part of an accepted social unit — the couple.

The study by Morton Hunt and the *Redbook Report* in America both indicated that people who reported their sex lives as good also reported their marriages as good. Although there is other evidence that doesn't connect sexual satisfaction and marital happiness so closely, it seems fair to assume there is some connection between satisfying sex and a satisfying relationship.

Sexual satisfaction in a long-term relationship does not occur solely because of the commitment the couples have to each other. Prior experience, the meaning of sex to each person, their expectations from their sexual acts, the roles each fills in a relationship and expects the other to fill, their cultural and religious beliefs about sex — all these are important elements in determining the degree of sexual pleasure and satisfaction the couple achieves. There are many couples in long-term, committed and caring relationships who do not nearly reach the level of sexual fulfilment of which they are capable because of ignorance, irrational fears, misinformation and unrealistic expectations about themselves and their partners. The "doing what comes naturally in bed" school underestimates the number of barriers that can and frequently do interfere with achieving fulfilling and mutually satisfying sexual experiences.

Q: "Is it true that some married people have written contracts which bind them in their marital relationship?"

A: "Yes. A prenuptial agreement is a legal document that is binding on the couple in as many aspects of the relationship as the couple wants specified. Money, property, child-care responsibilities, who gets what if a divorce occurs and other issues can be covered in the document. Agreements like this can also be drawn up for people who live together without being married. Some see this as a mature way of dealing with a potentially difficult situation, especially in the light of recent court cases in which couples who lived together but were not married had to split property, with the women in some cases recently contested in the USA receiving 'palimony.'"

Q: "Is it true that people who have premarital sexual experience have better marriages than those who don't?"

A: "There is no research that is conclusive. My impression is that success and fulfilment in relationships in general, and in sexual interactions in particular, can never be reduced to having or not having experience. Life with another person is complicated, and it is more likely that happiness in any sphere of a relationship is a function of the couple's values, feelings and expectations."

Q: "We are in a long-term relationship, are very happy and although our sex life together is satisfying it's not the single most important thing. Are we unusual or missing out on something?"

A: "No you are not so unusual, and if you and your partner are satisfied and fulfilled in your sex life you aren't missing out on anything. Sex has a variety of meanings within a relationship and each couple needs to work out the proper place of sexual expression within theirs. Many couples try to match their sex life to some arbitrary set of pleasure standards, but this leads to an artificiality of expression which is not in anyone's interest.

"You sound like you are happy and satisfied just the way you are and it's in your interest to remain that way."

The majority of married couples and of unmarried couples in long-term relationships choose monogamy and sexual exclusivity, but there are couples who remain together in their relationship but include others as sexual partners. Swinging, open marriage and affairs are the three most familiar arrangements.

Swinging Swingers are usually married couples who openly exchange partners for sex. The term is more common in the USA than in the UK where "wife swapping" is more commonly used, especially by the popular press who want to titillate their readers with salacious stories of suburban "sex orgies." Although the term "swinging" smacks of 1960s trendiness it at least does not carry the offensive connotation of male ownership where the man can dispose of a woman's sexual favours as and when he likes.

Swinging is fairly highly organized. Swingers make contact through advertisements in newspapers or magazines or they may meet at swingers' clubs. The party may be simply two couples or it may be a large group where coupled and/or group heterosexual or homosexual sex may take place. In America Gilbert Bartell did much of the research on swinging. He estimated that fewer than one percent of the married population was involved in swinging and the figure may be lower today.

Bartell's findings and those of several other researchers indicated that emotional involvement between swinging partners is held to a minimum so that the sexual activity will not harm their marriages. However, most mental health professionals find it difficult to believe that swinging is as emotionally benign as some swinging couples have claimed. Jealousy, guilt and feeling the marriage will ultimately be threatened are some common problems experienced by swingers. Some literature suggests that swingers have had more unhappy childhood experiences and more family difficulties in their youth than nonswingers.

Q: "One night some people we know told us they were into wife swapping. They described it calmly and gave us every detail. We were so turned off by the thought of it. Aren't these people sick?"

A: "It is not possible for me (or for you) to make such a diagnosis. Apparently what you do know is that swinging is not for you and your partner. Your friends, however, seem to be enjoying swinging and they may be emotionally satisfied in their situation at this time. It is possible that their relationship is sound and their swinging is not a sign of a problem. Incidentally, swingers usually do not try to recruit couples who are not interested, so you need not worry about being pressured into participating."

Q: "My wife and I are monogamous and exclusive sexually. All the talk about swingers and swapping makes us feel as though we are in the minority. Is that so?"

A: "No. Most married couples and those in nonmarital long-term relationships consider monogamy and sexual exclusiveness to be more appropriate for them. Young adults not yet married also favour monogamy and sexual exclusivity.

"It is important to appreciate that although various types of alternative marital relationship are widely discussed and may have become more popular, there is no evidence whatever that they have become generally approved or that they are becoming the norm. All the evidence suggests that couples like you and your wife are in the majority and likely to remain so for quite a while."

Open Marriage In 1972 a book by Nena and George O'Neill called *Open Marriage* created quite a stir as it described marital relationships where the couple lived together, loved and cared for each other but were flexible with regard to having relationships with other people. In an open marriage (and there are several variations on the theme) each partner with the consent of the other has the freedom to establish other emotional relationships, which may or may not include sex. These relationships are not intended to interfere with the marital relationship.

Partners in an open marriage want the opportunity to explore friendships, interests and experiences which might not be possible within the context of traditional monogamy. There are no solid statistics on the numbers of couples in open marriages, nor on how they eventually work out. It is certain, however, that open marriages are best handled by mature, resolved and autonomous people in a marital relationship that is solidly established.

Q: "Is an open marriage like a group marriage?"

A: "No. A group marriage is when at least three people (but more usually several couples) live together and maintain a relationship with more than one person in the group. Several reasons are given for entering a group marriage: the desire to relate to more than one person sexually, emotionally, intellectually and socially is one; the opportunity for children to have several parental role models is another; increased feelings of personal security, a strong sense of family bonding and equalization of roles within relationships are yet more.

"There is not much current material on the extent of group marriage, but most informed opinion about marital relationships sees it as a rare occurrence with no real future for influencing the current monogamous marital and family structure. Constantine and Constantine, who wrote a book called *Group Marriage*, provide the most scientific information. They point out that group marriages generally do not last more than a few years; many dissolve after several months. Sexual jealousy, an inability to divide responsibilities equally, financial inequality and sex role stereotyping are some of the causes of failure."

Q: "I know a lovely couple, married for over 20 years, and they have an open marriage. They seem happy together, honest with each other and very relaxed about it all. Can this be as it looks or are they putting on an act?"

A: "I know several couples with the same characteristics. They are confident, trusting and extremely mature, and appear to handle easily the complexity of the several relationships that each has. One couple interviews as a couple any new person who may wish to start a relationship with one of them to see if he or she is the type of person who can handle such a relationship and make it clear that their marriage is the primary relationship. They discuss jealousy, resentment, time sharing and so on to define quite clearly the nature of the relationship.

"I also know a couple who tried an open marriage but were unable to do so because their young children became confused and anxious over the various 'friends' their parents had. Privacy away from home was difficult for the couple to arrange, so they decided to wait until their children got older before pursuing their plan."

Extramarital Affairs There is no evidence to support the widespread belief that almost everyone is having extramarital sex. Indeed, the majority of women and men questioned about their attitude to extramarital sex disapprove of it. In his book *Sexual Behavior in the 1970s*, Hunt concluded that there had been no significant change in the numbers of Americans having extramarital sex since Kinsey did his research. Hunt suggests that the seeming sexual liberation of adults today has made a greater impact on premarital and marital sexual acts rather than encouraging widespread extramarital sexual activity.

In the *Redbook Report*, of 100,000 married American women surveyed fewer than one out of three had had an extramarital sexual affair. Of the exclusively monogamous women in the survey, 62 percent indicated they never had a desire for an extramarital affair. Many of those who were interested in having an affair stated that they had serious problems in their marriages.

Q: "What do the experts say about the effects of extramarital affairs on relationships?"

A: "There is disagreement, but the majority tend to view extramarital sex as threatening a marriage and they suspect it of being evidence of individual personality difficulty. Many experts believe that regular, prolonged or frequent extramarital affairs are unhealthy and that they are an immature, neurotic adaptation to marriage.

"Some experts in the marriage field prefer not to label extramarital sex as neurotic. They suggest that each case must be evaluated individually before a judgment can be made, while others indicate that extramarital sex can have a positive, enriching effect on the primary relationship. It is all too easy for clinicians to use as their case material troubled people in troubled relationships and then make their judgments about the subject on that basis. Nonclinical samples might not show in dividual problems in a relationship as being the cause of extramarital sex, nor might they show out-of-the-ordinary emotional problems among people who have affairs.

"I do not agree with the experts who believe extra-marital sex is the way to adapt to our difficult and complicated present-day culture. Nor do I believe that an affair is always indicative of a problem marriage and/or a problem personality. But if the person who has the affair says it has helped the relationship then the relationship needed help. Loving relationships do not need affairs to make them better. I do believe that extramarital sex, which is a hidden and guilty experience, is evidence of a conflict in the relationship. I do not believe that such an experience can ever strengthen a marriage."

Q: "After about ten years of marriage, I had a brief affair. I guess I wanted to see if I could still attract someone. Anyway, I ended it quickly and I was relieved that it was over. It felt good getting completely back to my relationship."

A: "It is a familiar phenomenon that toward the end of the first decade of a monogamous marriage one of the partners wants to have an affair — the 'seven year itch.' Reaffirming his or her ability to attract a sex partner, wanting to try a new experience and wanting to see if they are missing anything are the reasons usually given. These affairs are usually brief, generally do not cause a major crisis in the primary relationship and some people describe them as experiences that make the marriage closer and stronger.

"This is not to encourage such behaviour because the guilt, anger and humiliation that extramarital affairs commonly produce can easily have a negative effect on a relationship."

Divorce In Britain, Europe and in many other parts of the world, divorce has been on the increase in recent years. The rising number of divorces is not an indication that the institution of marriage is being rejected, as the majority of divorced people remarry (50 percent of first-time divorced people within five years). This has led some authorities to use the term "serial monogamy" to describe a pattern of marriage-divorce-remarriage-divorce-remarriage.

The frequency of divorce today has led some people to observe that the moral fibre of society is deteriorating. They believe that commitments are no longer honoured and worked at; accordingly, at the very first sign of conflict a couple will seek a divorce with all its attendant damage to children and to the parents. It is doubtful that this is an accurate view of the situation. There have always been people who were dissatisfied in their marriages, but the legal barriers, financial burdens and their anxieties about the effects of divorce on the children frequently prevented divorce from taking place. Today, however, legal restrictions have been reduced and there is a real question about the advisability of a couple's remaining together for the sake of the children if they are truly unhappy together. The stigma once attached to divorce has also diminished greatly.

One of the major adjustments divorced women and men must make is in the regularity of their sexual expression with partners. However, divorced men and women resume active sex lives during their divorced period. Men often return to their usual level of activity and in some cases they have sex slightly more frequently than married men of the same age. Women, too, return to an active sex life during their divorced period and in a study by Morton Hunt were found to have orgasm more frequently than when they were married.

Hunt found that both divorced men and women had a high level of satisfaction from their sexual activities and that sex was as creative and sensuous for them as for the young married portion of his sample.

Q: "It's been a while now since my divorce and I am still not comfortable about having sex. The memories of my last relationship still hang heavy on me. Am I being foolish about this?"

A: "No. It is very common for a person in your situation to be apprehensive about entering an intimate relationship with another person. This is especially so if your previous relationship caused you suffering and conflict.

"Some divorced men and women want their feelings to settle before they start up a new relationship. Usually there is a time in a new relationship when you feel it is right to include the sexual dimension, but you should act on these feelings only when you feel ready, and not rush yourself or be forced to act in a way that is not comfortable."

Q: "Right after I got divorced I had sex with just about everyone I went out with. After a while it was just a bore and I began wondering if there was something wrong with me. I'm feeling better now, but was that an unusual situation?"

A: "Some divorced women and men deal with the crisis and self-doubt that a divorce frequently produces by having sex compulsively to prove they are still attractive and sometimes for other complex psychological reasons. This quickly loses its attraction for some people — as for you. Sex with everyone can be like having sex with no-one. Many formerly married people then look for a stable relationship in which sex is a natural part of an overall interaction, not the primary feature of the relationship."

Q: "Is it true that sexual problems are the reason for most divorces?"

A: "No. I don't believe sexual problems are the principal reason for divorce. Problems in a marriage frequently surface in the couple's sex life since this is a couple's most intimate way of relating; general anger, hostility and immaturity can easily emerge here, making it appear that the problem is solely sexual. However, divorces are more frequently caused by subtle combinations of factors that lead to a general incompatibility. Sex may be a problem in itself, but there is a very good chance that sexual difficulties are actually symptoms of problems in one or other personality or in the relationship."

Q: "What does co-parenting mean?"

A: "Co-parenting is another term for joint custody of the children of separating or divorcing parents (in the UK, for example, 60 percent of divorced couples in 1980 had children under 16 years of age). Simply put, it means that after the parents are separated or divorced they will share custody equally. Such an arrangement requires agreement by the children (if able) and a plan that is acceptable to the legal authorities.

"Co-parenting enables parents to participate as a unit in the child-rearing process and enables them to share fully in the growth and development of their children. Although some people are doubtful about the value of co-parenting, more and more parents who are able are choosing this option rather than the sole-custody-plus-visitation-rights agreements of the past.

"The movement toward co-parenting is increasing as men and women question the traditional roles handed out to them: the woman as mother; the man as financial provider. As other traditional roles are revalued (exclusive concern with careers or exclusive concern with home) so a new sense of joint responsibility in children's upbringing is being expressed and undertaken by divorced parents."

7 Mid-life

Between the ages of approximately 40 and 65 most people's concerns are those of dealing with teenage children, family finances, success and failure, planning for the future, and so on. Sexually there are no dramatic changes, but during some part of this period, probably toward the age of 50, both men and women may go through a difficult psychological phase called the climacteric. In addition women experience menopause, which means that they cease to ovulate or menstruate and are no longer fertile. It is helpful to keep the notions of climacteric and menopause separate: menopause is a definable physical change and comes to every woman, whereas the mid-life crisis or climacteric cannot be readily pinpointed and may or may not affect both women and men.

Female climacteric/Menopause Menopause is surrounded by mythology, sexism, fear and misinformation. It is often read as a wholly negative event, as some kind of disease; some people call it the "change of life" to show how marked an event they (wrongly) think it to be. Menopause is as surrounded by ignorance and superstition as menstruation.

This is what happens during menopause. As a natural result of ageing, the quantity of female hormones produced by the ovaries slowly declines. Gradually, ovulation ceases and so does the menstrual flow. Once a woman has stopped ovulating she is infertile. There is no moment at which one can say this has happened. The reduction in hormone production has been gradual over a number of years, but the ovaries will continue to produce some small amounts of oestrogen, and so will the adrenal and other glands. Ovulation and menstruation may become irregular (rather as they are for most girls in puberty) until neither happens at all.

The main physical changes that accompany menopause are hot flushes — also called flashes — and reduced vaginal lubrication. Neither of these need make any difference to sexual desire. In fact some women, freed of the possibility of pregnancy, relax and enjoy a greater level of sexual activity than before. All women retain their capacity to enjoy sex and to have orgasm — menopause should make no difference at all.

The psychological response to menopause varies enormously. Women who have been trained to believe that menopause is a disaster signalling the end of their femininity and of their value as people may react with severe anxiety and depression. They may accordingly seek medical help. Women who, on the other hand, accept menopause as a natural stage of the life-cycle and who are secure in their roles and relationships often find themselves looking forward positively to the next stage in their lives rather than looking back with regret.

The extent of the changes is sufficient to make some women — perhaps 10 to 25 percent — seek medical help. But when they do, the controversy begins. Unfortunately, some physicians are insensitive to the experience of their patients; they prescribe tranquillizers or sleeping pills when an explanation of normal physiology and the meaning of what the patient is feeling could bring greater relief.

The most controversial treatment of menopausal symptoms is

hormone replacement therapy (HRT). Simply stated, there is substantial evidence that women who use replacement oestrogen over a long term have a ten times greater chance of developing endometrial cancer than nonusers. Since many physicians used to believe that HRT was a proper treatment for menopausal symptoms its use was once widespread and in some cases routine. However, since the discovery of the dramatic rise of endometrial cancer rates in postmenopausal women on prolonged HRT this treatment is used much less. HRT is still used to combat extreme hot flush symptoms and severe vaginal wall dryness and thinning (oestrogen creams are used here), but over much shorter periods and in much lower doses. HRT should be viewed as a temporary measure only and patients should be checked every six months; it should never be given if the woman has a history of cardiovascular disease, breast or uterine cancer or blood clots.

Some doctors continue to use HRT but they combine progesterone with the oestrogen. They claim that the combination reduces the chances of endometrial cancer to levels comparable with those of women who are not having any therapy at all. In addition to combating the common menopausal symptoms of hot flushes and vaginal dryness, HRT also helps prevent osteoporosis, a loss of bone density that causes weakening and may lead to bone fractures (especially of the hip). Osteoporosis is not so much a result of menopause as a natural part of ageing. Not all doctors are convinced that osteoporosis is caused by an oestrogen deficit, and therefore many are unwilling to risk oestrogen-related disease on such a shaky basis.

Q: "Why do so many women have serious emotional problems during menopause?"

A: "They don't. Some get depressed for a while, but the impression that large numbers of women have serious emotional problems is a false one.

"The premium placed on youth in our culture is very high, so such an obvious sign of ageing as menopause causes some women distress. On the other hand, most women by the time they reach the age of 50 or so have come to terms with the fact that they are no longer young. The inability to have children in the future worries some women, but on the other hand in reality they would almost certainly have no more children even if they remained fertile. Children are often leaving home at about the time of the menopause and the family seems to be breaking up — that is a reason for distress which, entirely understandable though it is, does not relate specifically to menopause. Then there is the matter of most people's uncertainty about what menopause is and means. The confusion between the physical event of menopause and psychological aspects of the climacteric can result in temporary feelings of depression.

"It is worth noting that women live to an average of 78 years. Menopause, therefore, far from signalling the beginning of the end of active life can indicate the approximate mid-point in a woman's adult life, with as much lying in the future as there was in the past."

Q: "What are hot flushes?"

A: "In response to local variations in hormone levels, blood vessels suddenly expand. More blood comes close to the surface of the skin and the woman appears flushed; this is because the skin is warmer and the body reacts by perspiring. They are entirely unpredictable, may last for seconds or for a minute or so, may recur the same day or not for weeks. Hot flushes can occur anywhere on the body and may be accompanied by sweating. Women who have them feel temporarily hot and tingly but to a very uncomfortable degree.

"Perhaps 50 percent of women experience hot flushes during their menopausal stage. If the flushes are severe a doctor may treat them with oestrogen for a while, but many women tolerate the inconvenience of flushes and wait for them to cease naturally, without medical treatment."

Q: "A friend of mine told me she didn't understand what all the fuss was about menopause and a changing sex life. She said she had no problems and her sex life got better. Can this be so?"

A: "Yes. Some women experience very minor menopausal symptoms and the new freedom from worry about getting pregnant can mean a gain in the spontaneity of their lovemaking. Incidentally, the changes in hormone levels that set off menopause can work to a woman's advantage. The new balance of androgen and oestrogen arrived at during menopause can actually stimulate sexual interest.

"In addition to having few menopausal symptoms, it sounds as though your friend was fortunate in experiencing none of the characteristic problems that may come with the climacteric or mid-life crisis."

Q: "Is it true that during menopause all women have pain during intercourse?"

A: "No. During menopause, especially toward the end of that period, perhaps 25 percent of women experience pain or burning during intercourse. This is due to the thinning of the vaginal wall that comes naturally with age. Vaginal jellies bought without prescription from a chemist may be sufficient to overcome this problem, but in some cases oestrogen cream is prescribed as it helps thicken the vaginal lining. Since the oestrogen is absorbed into the body, this treatment must be carefully monitored."

Q: "When I started to feel signs of menopause, I got confused, angry, and wasn't myself. I handled it after a while, but was what I was feeling abnormal?"

A: "No. What you felt is quite common. After all, as a society we suffer from a terrible lack of understanding about what menopause is and means. Most of the literature on the subject arouses fear; the language used to describe this natural stage of life for all women is enough to cause every woman to react with panic: 'change of life,' 'hormonal imbalance,' 'loss of femininity,' 'drying up,' 'hot flushes,' 'treatment' all suggest something negative and lead us to have confused, inadequate and angry feelings about menopause.

"Many women handle menopause as you did — successfully. But we must all work to change society's negative attitudes that make people view the prospect of menopause with dread and its occurrence with confusion."

Q: "My husband was more worried about menopause than I was. He kept asking how I felt, if it was happening and other questions like that. It happened all right, but it wasn't traumatic."

A: "Like so many of us, your husband has been influenced to see menopause as a disease rather than as a natural stage in the life cycle. Public discussion of menopause has been slanted toward the problem aspects, spending too little time on its naturalness and the ability of women to experience the process without anguish. Literature describing the benefits of oestrogen replacement therapy frequently portrays the husband as a helpless victim of menopause and depicts the wife as irritable, depressed and in pain. For many women (and for many couples) this simply is not true. If they approach menopause and the climacteric positively and with a clear understanding of what is involved physically and what may be involved psychologically, they are much less likely to find it such a traumatic stage in their lives."

Q: "I'm one of those women who had a tough time during menopause. I had these awful hot flushes, headaches, my skin looked old and wrinkled, my breasts started to sag, I started getting heavy. I wondered whether this was real or imaginary and I just felt ugly. I thought everyone was looking at me, and my husband thought I was having a nervous breakdown. I went to several doctors, and although I was taking tranquillizers, sleeping pills, oestrogen pills, and oestrogen creams nothing changed. I really felt I was about to have a nervous breakdown. Believe it or not the thing that really helped me was going to a woman's group with women my age and listening to them talk about something I thought was only my problem and concern. The support and suggestions really helped me understand and accept what was happening."

A: "More and more women are being helped by sensitively run groups of this sort. The bonds of common experience and the opportunity to express feelings and fears honestly and to receive constructive feedback from peers has been a liberating experience. Such groups can give women the chance to appreciate the variability of the menopausal stage, rather than being dependent on existing literature and the (probably brief) advice of their doctors."

Male Climacteric Male climacteric is a much better term than "male menopause" for the kind of emotional/psychological crisis that overtakes some men in mid-life. Since men do not menstruate, "menopause" is an entirely inappropriate term. Some men experience no crisis at all, some experience it mildly. Perhaps 25 percent of men are profoundly affected.

Regardless of whether a man experiences the male climacteric in any obvious way, he will notice certain physical changes at this stage in his life. Just as oestrogen production diminishes in women, so testosterone levels are reduced in men. The physical consequences are: taking longer to achieve an erection, less strongly felt ejaculation and a longer refractory period — the time it takes a man to recover from one erection/ejaculation and be ready for another. On the other side of the equation, ejaculatory control is likely to be increased, desire and pleasure are in no way impaired and the man remains fully able to cause a pregnancy.

Apart then, from a slight slowing down, a man need not suffer any adverse consequences of ageing through the mid-life period, nor need he suffer any anxiety. Some men, however, who are perhaps insecure in their masculinity, react with something near panic. They may question their virility and then seek to prove they are as "good" as they ever were by seeking out the maximum possible number of sexual encounters. It is this group that has given rise to the myth that middle-aged men generally look around for younger women as sex partners. Their behaviour may well be alienating and embarrassing, but fortunately such phases do not usually last long.

Some men have a similar reaction to their gradually declining levels of strength and endurance. Far from accepting that these changes are natural and understandable, a minority of men will rebel and go all out to prove that they are still strong young men — which they simply cannot be. They may associate muscular strength with virility and indulge in all sorts of excessive behaviour to prove that there is no diminishment of their manhood. If a man responds in this way for any length of time, he may be building up problems for himself. If his concept of his masculinity is inseparable from youthful activity levels he may temporarily withdraw from sexual activity, saying that he won't settle for "second best." This in its turn will create problems of private frustration and can only damage his relationships.

When a man does experience the psychological/emotional crisis of the male climacteric, the indicators are likely to be vague and hard to assess. It is something more than the natural reflection of a middle-aged man on the direction his life has taken and on what the future holds, and seems to be more to do with a profound depression for no obvious reason and maybe some personality changes that put a strain on his relationships. The duration of this period is highly variable. It may be concentrated into a few months or it may, on and off, last for several years at any time during a man's 40s, 50s or early 60s.

Q: "I don't know if I had a mid-life crisis or not, but in my early 50s I got very depressed, spent a lot of time thinking about my past and future, and just didn't feel like myself. My wife and children were very understanding and supportive. When I needed to be alone they let me be and at other times they were there to cheer me up. Anyway, it just seemed to disappear. I don't think I did anything unusual, I just started feeling like my old self again. When I look back at that time it was just a weird period."

A: "For some men it is just that — a strange time in their lives. A period of private intensity, of serious reflection and planning, a time when their identity is explored and evaluated, and because of this very serious examination and appraisal, the man's usual demeanour is changed, his moods may swing as he struggles to get a better sense of his identity and what he wants for himself and those around him. This is an intense time for many people and one in which they need support and understanding. Your experience and your reaction to it sound very normal, and your family's response sounds thoroughly sensible because of their sensitivity."

Q: "I read about a 55-year-old man who just got up one day and left his wife and family. He came back after a couple of weeks, was really depressed and had to have psychiatric care. Does that happen frequently during mid-life?"

A: "No. That is obviously an extreme behaviour, so extreme that it may not be related at all to a mid-life crisis. Of the 25 percent or so of men who experience real distress during the male climacteric none would be expected to behave like that. It looks as though this man's crisis was the result of some major personality disorder, though of course its symptoms could have been aggravated by his experiencing a mid-life crisis."

8 Later years

The most likely change in people's sexual expression in later years is some degree of slowing up. All the other changes are conditional upon circumstances: society does not expect older people to have sex and so, in order to conform with what is expected, many individuals will try and avoid it; the older a person is, the greater the likelihood of some significant physical impairment that can adversely affect sexual expression; partners die, and for many reasons new ones are hard to find; lack of privacy can also be a problem for older people who are no longer living independently in their own homes.

Older people need support so that they feel their sexual behaviour is a matter of their choice, not of restrictive societal expectation. These are the important factors that need to be considered:

* sexual interest and sexual pleasure are not related to age
* the changes that occur during menopause and the male climacteric do not signal the end of sexual expression or desire
* reduced frequency of sexual activity is not a sign of a physical or emotional problem in later years, nor does it impair sexual fulfilment
* caressing, fondling and kissing, as well as genital acts, are important expressions of love and affection at every stage of the life-cycle

* masturbation is not a sign of a problem; it is a perfectly legitimate form of sexual expression throughout life
* frequency of sexual activity in later years seems to be related to frequency earlier in life; a person who showed a high level of sexual activity when young is likely to desire sex frequently when old
* continuing interest in sex in later years is certainly not a token of being "sex mad"
* physical disorders may require some modification to the manner of sexual expression, but not an end to it
* barriers to active sexual expression in later years include boredom, overindulgence in food and drink and fatigue due to poor physical condition
* reduced sexual activity in later years is more likely to be due to lack of a partner than to lack of interest.

Q: "What do widows and widowers do for sex?"

A: "Part of the expression of grief when a partner dies is very often a temporary loss of interest in sex, but as the survivor comes to terms with his or her grief, sexual interest usually revives. It is however much more difficult to find a new partner in one's 70s than in one's 20s. Masturbation helps many people, but not if they have spent a lifetime rejecting it as wrong.

"Retirement communities and senior citizen centres provide places for older people to meet and form new relationships. Sometimes these relationships become permanent, as in marriage or living together, or each person may maintain an independent life but have a regular, affectionate relationship in which sexual activity is included.

"Some older people suffer considerable guilt about having sex with a new partner, but with time, patience and understanding such guilt usually passes."

Q: "My mother is 70 and a widow and she still makes sexual references. Is she doing this just to shock or can she really still have sexual desires?"

A: "I can't say for sure, but she certainly could mean it, especially if she enjoyed an active and rewarding sex life in her earlier years. She may also be testing you to see if you disapprove of her sexual interest. Children are frequently horrified that their parents are still sexually active or remain interested in sex: this may be a big test for you — don't fail."

Q: "Is it true that nursing homes are allowing older people to have sexual contacts?"

A: "Yes. Some nursing homes are providing privacy for their residents so they can express their sexuality in an appropriate way. The staff of progressive and sensitive institutions make it easy for people in their care to view sexual acts as proper if they so choose. Privacy can be provided during visits from a spouse or from a friend."

BIRTH CONTROL

This section is divided into four parts:

I   GENERAL ISSUES

FACTS There is a considerable variety of birth control methods, but each one has the same purpose: to make sure that a baby is conceived only when one is desired or planned. That is why birth control is often called "family planning." The chart on the following pages summarizes the different methods, each of which is described in more detail later in the section.

Choosing a proper birth control method is a serious matter and needs to be done with thought and care. It would not be so important if all means of preventing fertilization were absolutely safe, had no side effects or complications, were easy to use, reversible, cost little or nothing, did not require medical involvement, did not interfere with sexual activity, and were universally accepted by religious and cultural belief systems. Since this is not the case, clear, informed thinking must dominate each person's and each couple's decision-making.

There is no one method that is best for everyone. The method you choose must be one that both you and your partner trust absolutely. You must feel comfortable using it and it should not interfere in any way with the spontaneity of your sex life. It should fit comfortably within your religious and cultural beliefs and not provoke guilt or anxiety. The method you choose must have no harmful side effects and it must provide you with the highest possible actual effectiveness in preventing fertilization. Then you have to take into account your age, your available medical care and the frequency with which you have sex; you must also examine your feelings about abortion and what happens if your chosen method fails.

Q: "Is the anti-pregnancy injection available yet?"
A: "No, not yet available, but research programmes are investigating immunity against sperm, and a vaccine which will make the outside of the egg more resistant to penetration by sperm."

CONTRACEPTIVE METHODS SUMMARY

METHOD	FAILURE RATES*		ADVANTAGES	DISADVANTAGES
	THEORETICAL	USER		
Condom	3%	10%	Easy to purchase and carry with you; some protection against STDs	Putting them on means break in lovemaking. Need to withdraw before erection is lost
Diaphragm	4–5%	10%	Not felt in intercourse	Repeat applications of cream before each act of intercourse; periodic checkups necessary
IUD	1–3%	5%	Once properly fitted requires minimal attention for long period	Not appropriate with certain medical conditions; increased menstrual flow
Pills	1–2%	4–10%	Convenient and highly effective; regulate menstrual flow	Not suitable with certain medical conditions
Foam/Cream/ Jelly/Vaginal Pessaries	3–7%	8–39%	Easily available; easy to use	May be messy; especially liable to user error
Condom & Foam/Cream/ Jelly	1%	5%	Easily available; highly effective; shared responsibility	Same as for each method separately, though risk of user error is much reduced
Cap	2–3%	8%	Stays in place for several days	Can be difficult to place; alternative method needed during menstruation; not readily available
Rhythm/ Calendar	Data unreliable; speculation varies from 1–40%		No possible side-effects; acceptable to all religions	Daily attention to calendar/temperature; very high failure rate
Vasectomy/ Tubal Ligation	0%	0%	Totally effective if the operation is performed correctly; freedom from anxiety	Irreversible in most cases at present

*Two failure rates exist because some people fail to follow the directions on using a particular method and/or fail to use it every time they have intercourse.

The theoretical rate applies to those people who use their method on every occasion as directed. The user/failure rate includes both those who use

USED BY	PRESCRIP-TION NEEDED?	EXAMINA-TION NEEDED?	IMMEDIATE PROTEC-TION	COST	COMMENTS
Man	No	No	Yes	Low but steady	Safer if used with foam as well
Woman	Yes	Yes	Yes	Free in Britain on NHS	No side-effects, but care is needed to insert properly
Woman	Supplied by doctor or clinic	Yes	No—backup method needed until function-ing checked	Free in Britain on NHS	Particularly good for regular intercourse
Woman	Yes	Yes	No—backup method needed for first few weeks	Free in Britain on NHS	Good for most younger women; best avoided by over-35s; physicians are recommending a periodic furlough
Woman	No	No	Yes	Free in Britain on NHS	Vital to repeat applications before each occasion of intercourse; timing important
Both	No	No	Yes	Free in Britain on NHS	Much better than foam/cream/jelly/on their own; distinctly better than condoms on their own
Woman	Supplied by doctor or clinic	Yes	Yes	Free in Britain on NHS	Difficulties of availability and use limit an otherwise successful method
Woman	No	No	Yes	Nil	Only for stable couples who accept the high risk of a(nother) pregnancy
Either	Consultation with doctor/clinic; consent forms to be signed	Yes	No—backup method needed until checkup gives all-clear	Free in Britain on NHS	Suitable only for mature, stable people or for people who risk passing on a genetic disorder to a future child

the method properly and those who are careless in following the directions or do not use the method each time they have intercourse. Actual failure   *rates for those who do not use the method as directed each time are accordingly higher than the overall user/failure rate shown here.*

Q: "Are doctors trying to develop more male contraceptives?"
A: "Yes, a great deal of research is being done into the male contraceptive but so far the toxic effects and loss of libido have not been overcome. In addition, the question has to be asked, 'Would a woman trust a man to take it?'"

"Gossypol, a compound derived from the cottonseed plant, prevents sperm production and is widely used by men in China. It is now thought by Western researchers not to be effective; it also has a high rate of irreversible sterility together with changes in appetite, some digestion problems and a general weakness during the first few weeks."

MYTHS Not only are all the following statements untrue, but some of them could, if followed, mean that people who thought they were protected would find themselves without any contraceptive protection at all:

* pulling out ("withdrawal") is an effective birth control method
* it is OK to use a friend's diaphragm
* douching is an effective birth control method
* birth control does not have to be used every single time one has sex
* young girls who have not yet menstruated do not need contraception
* women who use birth control pills go on having periods into their 70s
* condoms come in small, medium and large sizes
* women prefer men not to use condoms
* pregnancy can occur only if the man is on top of the woman
* teenagers need parental permission to buy contraceptives
* birth control is not needed the first few times a woman has sex
* having intercourse standing up is an effective method of birth control
* it is OK to use a friend's birth control pills
* the morning-after pill is a proper routine birth control method
* if a woman doesn't have an orgasm she need not use birth control.

FEELINGS People reject contraception for a number of reasons:

Rationalization and Denial. "I'm not going to have intercourse so I don't need to be prepared."

"This is my safe time, I don't need birth control."

"I just won't get pregnant — it won't happen to me."

"It is more exciting to take a risk."

"Even if you use a contraceptive, you can get pregnant."

"It's not my responsibility, it's her's."

"God loves me so much, He won't allow me to get pregnant."

"By using birth control I'm admitting I'm sexually active."

Love. For many people, love means not worrying about whether you are protected or not. Love is spontaneous, risky and means abandonment — not planning or taking precautions. Getting and using a contraceptive is too calculated and very unromantic.

Wanting and Needing a Baby. Frequently women desperately want someone to love and be loved by. In the absence of a fulfilling relationship with another adult, it is not unknown, for young women especially, to want a baby to meet this need. Pregnancy and a baby can finally bring them the attention they crave and recognition that they too have a role.

Adult women may not use contraception and become pregnant to fill a real emotional need. If they feel emotionally impoverished or rejected, or if they are grieving the loss of a child or a partner, having a baby can be seen as a way to relieve the pain and fill the emptiness.

Availability of Abortion. Abortion is legal, safe and relatively inexpensive. Some people think of it as an easy way out of a pregnancy, so why bother using a contraceptive? Some women want to see if they are really feminine and so they become pregnant just to prove they can. Similarly, some men want to impregnate a woman to make sure their sperm can cause a pregnancy. The availability of abortion makes these risks easier to take. Women and men who permit or cause a pregnancy to prove their fertility are usually struggling with the meaning of their masculinity or femininity. Their self-esteem is marginal and pregnancy is an obvious, if thoughtless, way of gaining reassurance. It is a particularly common urge in early middle age. Sometimes, as a woman moves toward the time when she will no longer be able to bear a child, she may get pregnant as a sign of her continuing femininity. Men, too, may use their ability to cause a pregnancy as a public sign that they are still sexually active and "real men."

Embarrassment and Guilt About Using Contraceptives. The embarrassment of admitting ignorance about what contraceptives are, where to buy them and how to use them keeps some people, and not only young people, from using contraceptives.

Embarrassment about their contraceptive(s) being discovered by family or friends also prevents some young people from taking proper precautions when having intercourse. Sometimes women are embarrassed by the thought of having to speak with a doctor or counsellor or by having to have a pelvic examination.

Many young people are made to feel guilty by disapproving, judgmental doctors, clinic staff or chemists. This guilt may keep them from using contraceptives. Sometimes a doctor's attitude causes anxiety and guilt and prevents a woman or man from getting proper birth control advice and attention and a pregnancy occurs. This is called an iatrogenic cause ("doctor cause") of pregnancy.

Many young people have been raised believing sex is for having babies. Therefore, using a contraceptive means having sex for pleasure, which is wrong or sinful. Not using contraceptives eases their guilt, even if they are risking a pregnancy. Some believe in consequence that getting pregnant is the punishment for the evil they have committed.

Insecurity. Some people have strong feelings of worthlessness and self-hatred. Not using a contraceptive and becoming pregnant may be used to express their hostility about themselves (masochism). Sometimes a woman allows herself to become pregnant as a protest to her husband or family against her feelings of rejection or alienation. Some men cause pregnancies for revenge or to punish a woman because of problems in the relationship, and others will try to cause a pregnancy to prove to themselves they are truly heterosexual.

RELATIONSHIPS The effective use of birth control is an important aspect of every relationship. An unintended pregnancy can create tremendous strain on a relationship, so mature, thoughtful men and women usually discuss their individual responsibilities.

> "Since we started talking about sharing the responsibility for birth control our sexual relationship has become less strained and more enjoyable."

> "I always learn something about a person when they talk about their role regarding birth control use in a relationship."

Sometimes couples are confused about who should do what. Some men still view birth control as the woman's responsibility because it is she, after all, who risks getting pregnant. Some men indicate they would like to take responsibility for birth control in their relationship, but they do not care for condoms and see no alternatives. Other men simply accept the responsibility for ensuring effective birth control in their relationships, feel positive about it, and do not see it as a threat to their role.

Frequently, women feel they have no choice but to assume responsibility for birth control because their partners refuse to use any, they do not want to get pregnant and they do not want to challenge their partners' attitudes and create tension. Very powerful and subtle issues of dominance and submissiveness, proof of masculinity or femininity, proof of true love or independence influence the decision to use birth control.

> "My husband acts like it's a great inconvenience for him to use a condom. When I use something, I get the feeling he thinks he's just won a victory of some sort."

> "I have real questions about the method of birth control I'm using, but my lover won't consider using any. It's a part of our relationship we haven't worked out yet."

> "Sometimes my wife and I are really getting it on sexually, then she has to stop to put her diaphragm in. It's become a turn-off and a real strain."

> "When I had total responsibility for birth control it made me angry. I just could never relax when we had sex. Now we share the responsibility and I feel much better with my wife."

CULTURE AND RELIGION We have records from as far back as 1800 B.C. showing that many different substances have been used in the vagina to prevent conception. They also show that it has always been the woman's responsibility.

In Ancient Egypt Cleopatra apparently used a mixture of sodium carbonate, honey and dried crocodile dung made into a paste and placed in the vagina to block and immobilize sperm; it may have been the very first vaginal jelly. At about that period women also used pieces of cloth soaked with honey, lemon juice or butter.

Aristotle, in fourth-century B.C. Greece, wrote about the use of olive oil and oil of cedar in the vagina as a protection against pregnancy. In eighth-century India, they used rock salt dipped in honey or oil. Twelfth-century Muslims used tamponlike devices with various oils. In Polynesia no birth control methods were known—abortion was the only remedy.

Catholicism. In the Old Testament, parenthood and family were described as virtues, but scripture itself does not provide Roman Catholics with perfectly clear guidance on the morality of contraception. Historically, the official position of the Catholic Church on contraception has come from the Vatican. The strictest interpretation of these teachings prohibits the use of any artificial method of contraception under pain of sin. Recently, Pope John Paul I repeated this traditional position, which had been expressed consistently by Pius XI, Pius XII and by Paul VI in his encyclical *Humanae Vitae*. In this important message, Paul VI stated: "every marriage act must remain open to the transmission of life." Accordingly, abstinence or natural family planning methods are the only means of exercising any choice about parenthood. Some authorities in the Catholic Church would regard the use of these methods for pleasure-seeking only, without any parental responsibility, as immoral.

Although the teaching of the Church on birth control seems clear, a great diversity of opinion and practice exists among Roman Catholics. Serious reflection is leading some Catholic theologians and many ordinary people to form positions of conscience that permit them to use a variety of birth control methods in the interests of prudent family planning.

It appears that the formation of a person's conscience is beginning to replace unquestioning belief in the Church's instructions, blindly followed by so many couples in the past. It is very common today for priests discussing birth control to state the Vatican ruling, but to avoid the implication of sin. The idea that more liberal priests are seeking to convey is that the traditional teaching of the Church — that procreation is central to intercourse — is still entirely valid. But, they suggest, couples who wish to limit the size of their families and space out the arrival of the children in the best interests of the family as a whole are behaving responsibly. Such couples, they imply, are following the spirit, if not the letter, of the Church's teaching.

The decision to use contraceptives is not an easy one for many devout Catholics. It is a matter of conscience, and requires deep reflection to ensure that spiritual health is not sacrificed to medical or economic well-being. More and more people, however, are finding that they can successfully take this responsibility.

Q: "My parish priest told me my wife and I are committing a sin every time we use artificial birth control. A friend's priest told him he and his wife should decide for themselves what they want to do about birth control. What do we do?"

A: "This points up the conflict that exists in the Roman Catholic Church today and the typical confusion that results for people like you and your wife.

"Your priest took the position that contraception is sinful. Your friend's priest places the highest value on the formation of individual conscience. It probably would help you and your wife to talk with your friend's priest and perhaps with other Catholics as you continue to deliberate and search your conscience about what is right for you.

"Your own priest is presenting you with the strictest interpretation of the Church's teaching, but the overwhelming majority of Roman Catholic couples throughout the world believe that it is morally responsible for them to use birth control, provided they have first honestly examined their consciences about the emotional, social, medical, economic and spiritual aspects of their decision. For the majority, love itself is creative, and it is not necessary for every sexual act between them to be open to the creation of a child. Their decision is based on their whole relationship and the nature and meaning of their acts within their marriage."

Judaism. Jewish tradition regards children as a blessing. In the Talmud, the rabbis stated "Four are considered dead: the poor, the blind, the leper and he who has no children." Children were thought of partly as an investment — they could work alongside their parents and then could support and care for them in their old age. Children also guaranteed that the spirit of the parents would live on after they were dead.

Judaism regards having children as a duty required by God, and in light of the Jewish historic experience, it is clear why having many children has been important: the centuries of maltreatment, the numerous persecutions and the Holocaust have meant that a continuing high birth rate was necessary to preserve the race.

However, most Jews other than the strictly Orthodox believers now regard birth control favourably, provided some children are produced and the family established. Modern Judaism, with its new-found security, is concerned with the quality of life of children and the family and respects the right of husbands and wives to make decisions that allow them and their children to live lives that are emotionally, physically, economically and religiously sound.

In the Talmud it is clearly stated several times that a woman may use the absorbent (a piece of cloth placed in the vagina) only if she is a nursing mother, pregnant or a child-wife. The absorbent, an artificial device, is seen by some traditionalists as sanctioning "mechanical" methods of birth control like the diaphragm and condom. Some Orthodox Jews, though, differ with this interpretation. They will not approve any artificial method of birth control, and insist on using natural methods only.

Protestantism. Protestant churches have inherited the same view on the use of sex within marriage for the purpose of having children as the Catholic Church. The difference between most Protestant churches and the Catholic Church in their practice is that Protestants have come to accept officially that birth control methods as family planning are a positive good. In effect, most Protestant churches take publicly the same line that many individual Catholics take privately.

Some fundamentalist Protestant sects do not accept artificial methods of birth control, but their numbers are small. Most Protestant churches believe that family planning is a responsible measure if used for reasons of physical or emotional health, for economic reasons or to promote the quality of life. This does not mean however that most Protestant churches sanction the use of birth control measures outside marriage.

II   ARTIFICIAL METHODS

Condoms

Condoms are rubber sheaths that fit closely over the entire erect penis. They protect against pregnancy by collecting all the semen a man ejaculates and preventing any of it from getting into the vagina. When condoms are used properly their effectiveness is about 97 percent, a rate similar to that of the IUD or diaphragm. When a condom is used together with a contraceptive foam or jelly their combined effectiveness is about 97–98 percent. A condom should not be used twice.

There are no medical risks in using condoms and no medical reasons why they cannot be used. Some people's skin is allergic to latex, but they can change to condoms with anti-allergy additives in the latex. Some women have found that latex condoms irritate the vagina, but the irritation usually disappears when a lubricant like K-Y Jelly is placed in the vagina or on the condom.

Condoms are inexpensive, convenient to use, require no medical examination or prescription, give some protection against sexually transmitted diseases and can be included in lovemaking without interfering much with the flow and feelings of the moment.

How to Use a Condom Correctly. BEFORE intercourse the man, or his partner, places the rolled up condom (they come ready rolled) on the tip of his erect penis and unrolls it down the penis's entire length. Condoms unroll in one direction only. Some condoms have a reservoir tip to receive the semen, preventing the rush of semen at ejaculation from bursting the tip of the condom. When using a condom without a reservoir tip do not roll or stretch the condom tightly against the head of the penis; leave a small amount of space (about half an inch) to allow for semen to be collected. After ejaculation, as you begin to lose your erection hold the back of the condom and withdraw the penis from the vagina. This will prevent the stretched condom from slipping off and allowing semen to enter the vagina. After ejaculation, any thrusting may cause the condom to slip off and allow semen to enter the vagina. Before discarding the condom, check it thoroughly to be certain it did not burst or have any tiny holes.

Condoms must be stored away from heat as high temperatures break down the rubber and cause tearing. Even keeping a condom or two in a wallet, although it may be convenient, is a bad idea — body heat over an extended period is enough to cause the rubber to deteriorate.

Q: "If condoms are so effective and don't cause any medical problems, how is it everyone doesn't use them?"

A: "Because good as they are they can interfere with sexual pleasure. The most common reasons given for discontinuing their use are:

* they reduce the sensation of the penis in the vagina; for a long time men have complained about this and recently some women have begun to do so too
* after ejaculating, the man must stop thrusting and withdraw his penis or risk the condom slipping off and semen contacting the vagina — for both an irritating interruption
* some people report they are always aware of the condom
* both men and women are concerned that the condom may slip off or break if intercourse is vigorous
* some men find putting on a condom difficult, and therefore embarrassing
* using condoms makes lovemaking seem premeditated and not as spontaneous as people would like it to be
* they interrupt the flow of lovemaking
* some men and/or women are allergic either to the latex or to the lubricant on condoms."

How to use a condom properly: the penis should be erect before the condom is put on

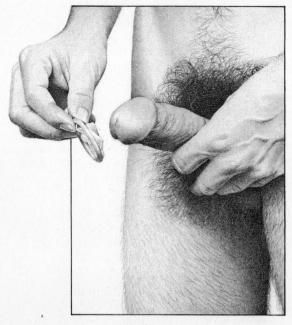
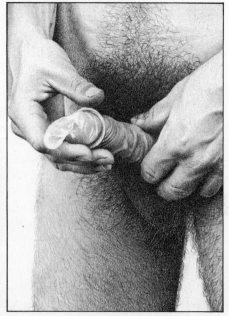

Q: "What are skin condoms?"
A: "Skin condoms are made from sheep's intestines. They look much the same and are used in exactly the same way as rubber ones, though most people use rubber condoms because they cost far less. Some people prefer skin condoms because they say they can feel more during intercourse — this is probably because skin condoms conduct heat better than rubber."

Q: "What about lubricated condoms — are they better than unlubricated ones?"
A: "Yes, they break less often and they cause less irritation to the vagina. Some people, however, are allergic to the lubricant."

Q: "Can you lubricate your own condoms?"
A: "Yes, as long as you use a safe lubricant like K-Y Jelly. Don't use vaseline or cold cream, as they weaken the rubber. (Vaseline also takes the natural lubrication out of the vagina.) Contraceptive foam or jelly used by the woman for added protection also works as a lubricant."

Q: "Is it true that you can't catch VD if you use a condom?"
A: "No, though a condom will help to reduce the risk. If you have sex with someone who has a sexually transmitted disease and doesn't know it, a condom *may* prevent your being infected, but there is no guarantee at all. If you know that you have a sexually transmitted disease or if your partner has, there is only one rule: *no sex at all until the disease is cured.*"

and the penis should be withdrawn from the vagina before the erection is lost.

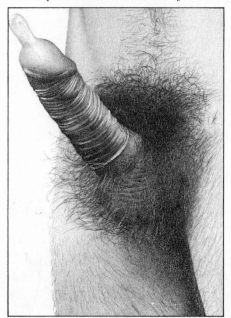
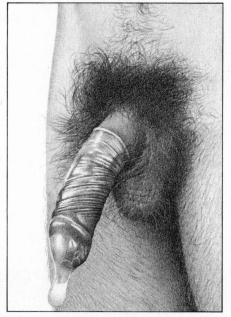

Q: "What should I do if my condom bursts while I am having intercourse?"

A: "The best remedy for a burst condom is to have your partner fill her vagina *immediately* with a contraceptive foam, jelly or cream and leave it in place until it dissolves.

"Don't attempt to carry on without a new condom, however frustrating it may be to stop when you are both excited.

"Your partner must check with her doctor if her next period is at all late. It is most important that she should not douche — that can drive sperm further up.

"The morning-after contraceptive pill is also available as an emergency service (see page 67)."

Q: "Do condoms prevent coming quickly?"

A: "'Quickly' is a matter of opinion. Condoms will not cure premature ejaculation, if that is what you mean. They do, however, sometimes make intercourse last a little longer because they reduce sensitivity and may slow up the approach to ejaculation."

Q: "Do condoms come in various sizes?"

A: "No. All condoms are the same size and are elastic enough to fit any erect penis. In the UK and in most European countries there are government standards which condoms must meet regarding elasticity, strength and leakage before they can be sold to the public. If you are asked what size you prefer when you purchase condoms it means what size pack — three, 12 or more."

Q: "Where can I get condoms?"

A: "You can purchase condoms without a doctor's prescription from a chemist or vending machine, or you can order them by mail as advertised in many magazines. In their original packaging, condoms last about two years before naturally breaking down, so be certain you check its date of manufacture before using a condom, especially if you bought it from a vending machine."

Q: "Are the new textured and ribbed condoms better than the plain ones?"

A: "Yes and no. They are no safer — all condoms must meet the same government quality standards, but some people prefer them because, they feel, the texturing or ribbing increases sensation during intercourse. They are better if you find them so, but not more effective."

Diaphragms

A diaphragm is a dome-shaped rubber device with a flexible rim that is placed in the vagina behind the pubic bone. It fits snugly and seals off the opening to the cervix completely. Properly placed, the diaphragm forms a barrier that helps to prevent sperm from moving into the uterus. Diaphragms should always be used with a spermicidal jelly or cream to kill any sperms that come in contact with the diaphragm.

It is reported that around the year 1750 a primitive diaphragm was devised by Casanova, who cut a lemon in two, scraped out the inside and inserted one half of the lemon skin in the vagina of his lover. Supposedly the barrier provided by the skin and the acid from the lemon combined to make an effective birth control device. The diaphragm used today was designed in the 1880s by a German physician, Dr W. Mensinga.

If a woman wants a diaphragm, she must first be examined by her doctor or a nurse specialist at a family planning clinic. This is to determine which size diaphragm she ought to have — diaphragms come in several sizes and must fit perfectly if they are to work. She will be given a prescription for the precise size of diaphragm to take to a chemist. The

Different diaphragm sizes: it is essential to have precisely the right one if it is to be properly effective.

spermicidal jelly or cream that is always used with the diaphragm can be purchased without a prescription from a chemist.

When a diaphragm fits perfectly and is properly used with a spermicide it usually provides 97 to 98 percent protection against pregnancy. The best diaphragm users are highly motivated, mature women who have interested and responsible partners. When a pregnancy does occur, the cause is usually improper use by the woman. The common mistakes are failure to use spermicidal jelly or cream with the diaphragm, and removing it too soon after intercourse. Diaphragms can develop tiny holes or cracks, and they may also fail if they fit poorly.

How to Use a Diaphragm Correctly. After obtaining the correct size diaphragm, a woman will be instructed by her doctor or nurse specialist on how to use it properly. The spermicidal jelly or cream should be spread all over the diaphragm, including the rim, the outward-facing side and the surface that will be facing the cervix. The diaphragm is then squeezed into an oval shape and placed in the vagina behind the pubic bone so when the woman's hand is removed it springs gently into place and covers the cervix. Each woman usually finds the way that suits her best to insert her diaphragm, but many find standing with one foot on a low stool makes it easy. For those women who have difficulty inserting their diaphragm properly by hand, or who dislike putting their fingers in the vagina, special plastic diaphragm applicators are available from chemists. No prescription

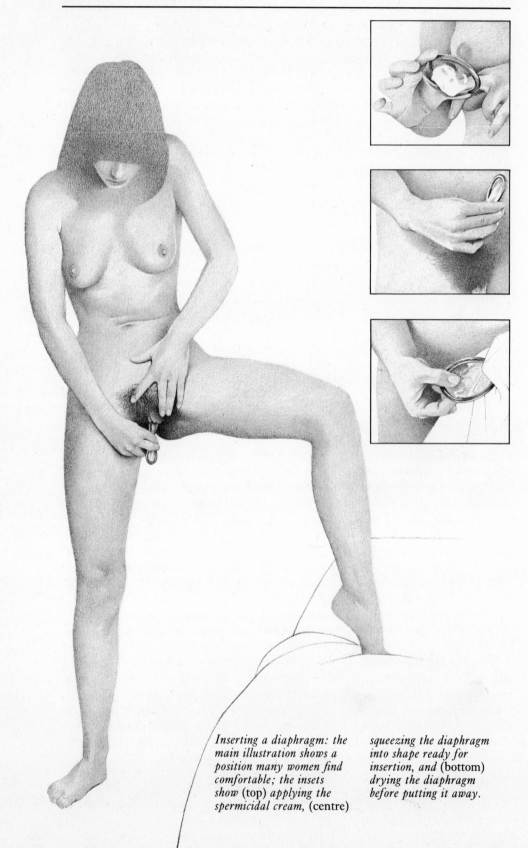

Inserting a diaphragm: the main illustration shows a position many women find comfortable; the insets show (top) applying the spermicidal cream, (centre) squeezing the diaphragm into shape ready for insertion, and (bottom) drying the diaphragm before putting it away.

is needed. In the UK a woman is usually given a practice diaphragm for a week. This must not be relied on as a contraceptive. After a week the woman returns to her clinic or doctor to check whether she is using it correctly and is happy with it.

The diaphragm must be placed in the vagina not more than two hours before intercourse, and left in place six to eight hours after. If it is put in or taken out too early, the jelly or cream will not have its full effect. When intercourse occurs several times in a short period more spermicidal jelly or cream must be placed in the vagina near the diaphragm *each time* and without disturbing the diaphragm. This is easily done with the special applicator that comes with the jelly or cream.

Some men have learned how to insert a diaphragm and have made that a sensual part of lovemaking without interrupting the flow and feelings of the moment.

After the diaphragm has been removed, it should be washed with mild soap in warm water, dried, and returned to its container. When washing the diaphragm, check it for tiny holes or cracks by holding it up to the light. It is always wise to have a spare diaphragm of the proper size in case you discover a hole or crack in your regular one. If a diaphragm is properly cared for, it should last about two years.

Diaphragms have no side effects or medical risks. Once in a while a woman or her partner may complain about a minor skin irritation and blame it on the diaphragm. Frequently this is due to the jelly or cream, so change brands. If changing brands doesn't help, see your doctor.

Unless there is a specific medical problem like an abnormally shaped or prolapsed uterus all women can use a diaphragm if they choose. Men will not feel a diaphragm at all if it is the correct size and has been properly inserted.

Q: "Once you have your diaphragm do you ever have to get measured again?"

A: "Yes. You should always have your diaphragm size checked at your yearly medical exam. It may change if you have gained or lost a significant amount of weight (say 10 lb), if you have had a child, miscarriage or an abortion. If you have done any of these things you may need a new diaphragm. If you are in any doubt — particularly about the effects of weight loss or gain — get checked at once, without waiting for your periodic medical examination."

Q: "My boyfriend says he feels the diaphragm when we have intercourse. What should I do?"

A: "Your diaphragm may be improperly placed in your vagina, or you may be using an incorrect size. These are the two main reasons a penis contacts a diaphragm. Check with your doctor or clinic and take your boyfriend along.

"If you have the right size diaphragm and you've put it in properly, your boyfriend won't normally be able to feel it. Some men, however, once they know a woman is using a diaphragm, *think* they can feel it. What they may be doing is registering a protest against the use of a diaphragm, perhaps because they have a deep-seated reservation about contraception in general, or because they think a diaphragm is too 'mechanical' (the same protest is made against condoms on occasion), or because they want the woman to become pregnant. Get a medical check to be sure that the diaphragm is the correct size and that you are placing it properly, and then discuss the issue openly and honestly with your boyfriend."

Q: "I know someone who used a diaphragm that didn't belong to her and didn't get pregnant."

A: "She was lucky. A diaphragm must be fitted by a trained doctor or nurse to suit you."

Q: "My wife complains that her diaphragm hurts her. Is that all in her mind?"

A: "No. It may be irritating her vaginal wall for some reason, or it may be pressing against a full bladder or a full bowel. Together you should visit your doctor or family planning clinic immediately. Use another method of birth control until you have checked with your doctor."

Q: "Once in place, can my diaphragm move?"

A: "Sometimes even a properly placed diaphragm may shift during intercourse. This is unusual, but it can happen in the woman-on-top position. The thrusting of the penis during intercourse very rarely loosens the diaphragm."

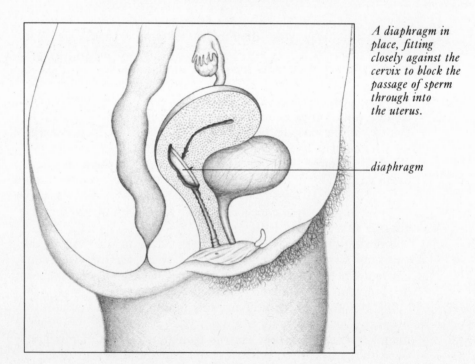

A diaphragm in place, fitting closely against the cervix to block the passage of sperm through into the uterus.

diaphragm

Q: "What should a couple do if they like oral sex, but the taste and smell of the cream or jelly is a turn-off?"

A: "This is a real concern for some couples, but can be overcome if the diaphragm is inserted after having oral sex. Of course, this takes a great deal of motivation and control, as some couples are so involved in what they are feeling that they have trouble slowing down in order to insert a diaphragm.

"There are jellies and creams that some couples have found to have very little odour and no offensive taste or even a pleasant taste and odour. With these, oral sex is fine with the diaphragm in place. If you cannot find a jelly or cream that meets your needs, you will have to consider a new method of birth control."

Q: "Some of my friends use their diaphragms during their periods. What is that all about?"

A: "They are being particularly careful. Although ovulation will not normally occur during menstruation it can happen, so some form of contraception is desirable. Diaphragms are particularly useful during menstruation for couples who dislike the presence of menstrual blood in intercourse. It is perfectly safe to use a diaphragm during menstruation."

Q: "Is it true that some women put their diaphragms in every night before going to bed?"

A: "Yes. If a couple usually have intercourse before going to sleep, routinely inserting the diaphragm each night means they are prepared and don't need to interrupt their lovemaking.

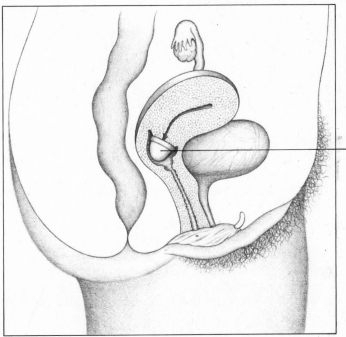

Cervical caps work in a similar way to diaphragms, but are not as widely used, probably because some women find them more difficult to manage successfully.

cervical cap

"Remember though, that the jelly or cream will not be properly effective after a couple of hours. If you have intercourse in the middle of the night or on waking, you will need a new application of spermicide."

Q: "Is a diaphragm another name for a cervical cap?"
A: "No. Cervical caps are small, flexible and thimblelike. They fit over rather than against the cervix. Like diaphragms, they come in several sizes.

"The cervical cap must be used in the same way as a diaphragm if it is to be effective, that is on every occasion of intercourse with the additional protection of a spermicide. It must be left in for at least six hours after intercourse but removed after 24 hours, washed, and if so wished, put back. It must not be left in place from one period to the next without being cleaned.

"Cervical caps have been available for a century and although they seem to suit most women (but not all) they are slightly more difficult to place than the diaphragm and so proper size and fitting instructions are very important. Caps are available in the UK free from your doctor or family planning clinic."

A diaphragm (left) *and a cervical cap for comparison.*

Intrauterine Devices (IUDs)

Intrauterine Devices or IUDs are used by 50 to 60 million women throughout the world. Most women, though not all, can use them, and they are 98 percent effective in preventing pregnancy.

Before a woman is fitted with an IUD she must have a thorough medical examination. There are several types of IUD, and the one chosen will depend upon the results of this examination. IUDs must be fitted by trained, qualified people.

Copper IUDs can be left in place for a year or two, whereas plastic IUDs such as Lippes Loop and Saf-T-Coil can be left in indefinitely (in the absence of any problem). No user should attempt to take one out or reinsert it: that is a job for a trained person. IUDs are easily removed if the woman wants to try and have a child.

Experts are not entirely sure how IUDs work. The more popular theory is that they cause the lining of the womb, the endometrium, to become slightly inflamed; the inflammation prevents a fertilized egg from implanting itself. Some people, though, believe that IUDs cause the Fallopian tubes to contract slightly, speeding the passage of eggs through the tube and thus making it more difficult for sperm to fertilize them.

Advantages of IUDs:

* once properly fitted and checked, they are reliable
* they do not interfere with sexual activity in any way
* they are free in the UK from NHS family planning clinics and GPs who offer a contraceptive service. They are not available from the Family Planning Association
* they do not interfere with the hormonal system
* as long as they are left alone, they are not subject to user error.

Disadvantages of IUDs:

* sometimes the uterus will not accept an IUD; it may be expelled shortly after insertion, or it may come out at the first menstrual flow after it has been fitted; between five and ten percent of women (they tend to be younger ones) expel their IUDs after first insertion
* there is a risk of infection of the uterus, Fallopian tubes and ovaries
* an IUD can migrate through the uterine wall
* there is an increased risk of a Fallopian tube (ectopic) pregnancy

Most women can have IUDs fitted safely and successfully, but there are certain circumstances in which a woman should not have one. If she is already pregnant, fitting an IUD can be very dangerous as it is likely to lead to miscarriage. An IUD should not be fitted if the woman has any uterine or vaginal disease, anaemia or poor blood-clotting. It may be unwise to fit an IUD if she has a tipped or prolapsed uterus. All these are things that doctors normally check for before recommending a particular type of IUD.

Types of IUD Currently there are five types of IUD approved by the FPA and Department of Health and Social Security. They are: Lippes Loop, Saf-T-Coil, Copper 7 (Gravigard), Copper T (both Ortho T and Copper T Kabi) and Multiload Copper 250. The Progestasert IUD is under general review and is not widely available, certainly in the UK.

The Copper 7, Multiload Copper 250 and the Copper T, both of which are made of plastic wound with copper wire, continually release small amounts of copper into the woman's uterus. The effect of the copper is to keep the lining of the uterus inflamed and so make it impossible for the lining to accept a fertilized egg. The amount of copper released is minute — certainly less than you would normally have in your body from the foods you eat. There is no evidence whatsoever that this extremely small addition of copper is in any way harmful; in fact, it doesn't even show up in blood samples. Copper 7s and Copper Ts need replacing about every two years because the copper runs out after that time. Your doctor will advise you about replacement.

The Saf-T-Coil and the Lippes Loop are both made of plastic, the former in a ram's horn shape, the latter in the shape of a backwards S. They

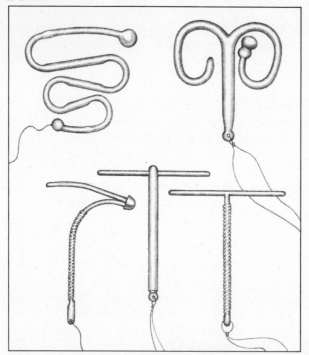

(left) *Five common types of IUD:* (top left) *Lippes Loop;* (top right) *SAF T Coil;* (bottom left) *the Copper 7;* (bottom centre) *Progestasert; and* (bottom right) *the Copper T.*

opposite page:
Inserting an IUD: the IUD, in this case a Lippes Loop, comes in straightened out form inside the inserter tube (left). *The tube is passed through the vagina and cervix until the IUD can be released* (top right). *The Loop is shown in scale with the Fallopian tubes and vagina at bottom right.*

both act in a similar way to the Copper 7 and the Copper T in that they inflame the uterine lining, but both the Saf-T-Coil and the Lippes Loop do it without releasing any substance; their shape and their presence alone are sufficient to cause inflammation. Both these forms of IUD can stay in place indefinitely.

Progestasert is also made of plastic. It releases extremely small quantities of progesterone that affect the lining of the uterus, making it unsuitable for the implantation of a fertilized ovum. Progestaserts need replacing after about a year.

Q: "How do you get an IUD?"
A: "An IUD must be fitted by a doctor or other qualified person like a specialist family planning nurse. After examining you and evaluating your medical history, the doctor will suggest the type of IUD that is right for your uterus size, for your pregnancy history and for your future pregnancy plans. Your possible allergy to copper will be an important aspect of the choice.

"It must be pointed out here that many doctors have their own preferences among the various IUDs available, and so they may urge you to have a particular kind of IUD because they are very familiar with it, having used it successfully on a large number of their other patients."

Q: "How is an IUD put in the uterus? Does it hurt?"
A: "A doctor gently guides a special IUD inserter tube through the vagina and cervix into the uterus. The IUD is in a straightened out position inside the inserter tube. When the tube is in

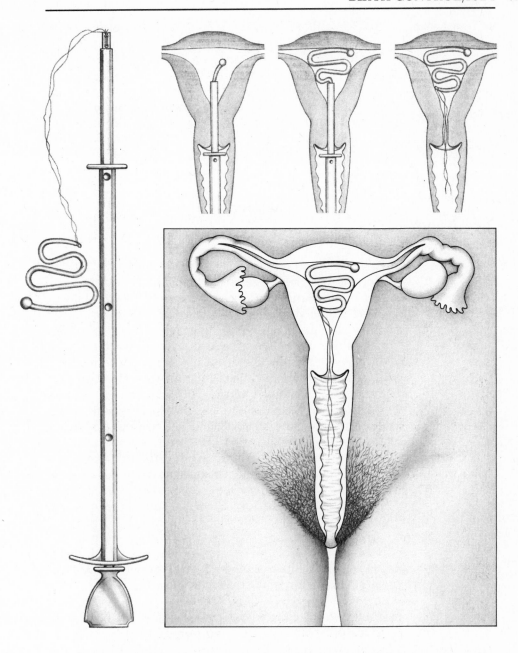

the right position, the doctor releases the IUD, which returns to its original form inside the uterus. The inserter tube is then withdrawn and the thread or threads attached to the end of the IUD are trimmed so they hang through the cervix into the back of the vagina. The threads should be felt regularly to check that the IUD is still there and in its proper position. If the thread cannot be felt or seems to have lengthened or moved forward noticeably, your doctor must be contacted immediately.

"An IUD can be inserted in a few minutes. The insertion should not cause any pain, and the discomfort usually happens when the woman is not relaxed. Good counselling and reassurance greatly help to overcome this tension. You may want to take ordinary pain killers afterwards. Some women have cramping of the uterus and some bleeding for a few days or even a week or two after insertion. If pain is severe and bleeding heavy, you must contact your doctor immediately.

"An IUD can be inserted at any time during the menstrual cycle, but most doctors prefer to insert it during menstruation since the cervix expands at that time making placement easier and less painful; it also excludes pregnancy."

Q: "What happens if you get pregnant with the IUD still in place?"
A: "There is a two percent failure rate and we don't know why it happens. If it does one of the following is likely to take place:

* about half the time a miscarriage will occur within the first few weeks of the pregnancy; strong cramps and bleeding like a heavy period are signs that this has happened; the symptoms are more severe if the pregnancy has continued for a month or two
* pregnancy with an IUD in place leads to strong possibilities of serious infection of the uterus; if an infection does exist, your IUD will be removed by your doctor; a D&C or vacuum procedure will also be performed, which means that the pregnancy will have been terminated
* if the pregnancy is less than 12 weeks and if no infection exists, your doctor may try to remove the IUD without disturbing the pregnancy; although this is difficult to do, some doctors believe it is an important step to prevent the risk of miscarriage and infection later in the pregnancy; if the IUD cannot be removed this way, some doctors may still advise termination of the pregnancy because of the high risk of miscarriage and dangers of infection
* some doctors allow the IUD to remain in place, carefully check the mother and the pregnancy and permit the pregnancy to continue. There have been many births with an IUD in place resulting in no harm to mother or baby.

"If you should get pregnant with an IUD in place, you must consult your doctor immediately and question her or him very closely."

Q: "How soon can you have a baby after the IUD is removed?"
A: "Right away, if you like, though some doctors advise women to wait a month or two before trying to get pregnant. This short period allows the uterine lining (endometrium) to return to its usual thickness and to function again as it did before the insertion of the IUD."

Q: "Can you have an IUD removed at any time?"
A: "Yes. It is simple, safe and painless, BUT DO NOT

remove an IUD yourself or allow anyone except a doctor or specialist nurse to remove it."

The Pill (Oral contraceptives)

Since coming on the market in the UK in 1961 the pill has become the most popular birth control method. Approximately 100 million women throughout the world have used them. Why? Because when taken as prescribed by a doctor, oral contraceptives are 98 to 99 percent effective, they are easy to use, they do not interfere with lovemaking in any way, they are free in the UK, they tend to cause a lighter and more regular menstrual flow and may control menstrual cramps.

This is how the pill works. Various kinds contain synthetic hormones that are carried by the bloodstream throughout the body; they work particularly on the pituitary gland (the master gland), the brain, the ovaries, the uterus and cervix. The hormones that the body produces naturally tell the systems each month that it is time to release a new ovum from an ovary. But when a woman is pregnant the hormone balance in the body changes, and the instruction to release a new egg each month is cancelled. Pills work in the same way. The hormones they contain convince the body's hormone system that the woman is already pregnant, so no new ovum is released. If no ovum is released, the woman cannot get pregnant. However, there will still be a menstrual flow each month because the uterus knows that there is no pregnancy and so it continues to shed its lining.

There are many different kinds of pills. They are of varying hormonal strengths, and have different benefits and drawbacks. Which one is best for each woman has to be decided by her and her doctor after a thorough medical evaluation, including a personal and family history, a cervical smear, STD check, breast and pelvic examination, a complete blood and urine analysis, and a blood pressure and weight check.

This very important examination can show that some women should never use birth control pills. For example, a history of blood clots or heart disease is reason to avoid absolutely the use of oral contraceptives; liver disease, cancer of the breast, uterus or cervix rule out taking the pill. Smoking increases risks, particularly of phlebitis. Equally, if a woman should happen to be pregnant and not know it, such pills can be harmful. There are also other diseases or problems, like fibroids, abnormal vaginal bleeding, gall bladder diseases, glandular fever, diabetes and hypertension, which may warrant the choice of another birth control method. Most doctors will not prescribe pills for women over 35 on the grounds that there is a risk of blood clotting disorders. Healthy adolescent girls and young women show no serious side effects if they take properly prescribed pills, and there is no medical reason for going off the pill. Indeed, the risks of pregnancy are higher during these "rest periods."

Women sometimes derive incidental benefits from using the pills. For example, pills tend to decrease cramps around the time of menstruation, reduce the number of days of the menstrual flow and decrease the amount of blood loss. Premenstrual tension and depression may also be relieved by oral contraceptives, and they can sometimes control acne too.

If you have already been prescribed pills after a medical examination, it is pretty certain that at the time they were prescribed they were right for you. However, anyone's medical condition changes with time. IF YOU ARE TAKING ANY KIND OF CONTRACEPTIVE PILL AND HAVE ANY OF THESE SYMPTOMS, SEE YOUR DOCTOR:

* chest pain
* shortness of breath
* calf or leg pain
* headaches
* vomiting
* dizziness or faintness
* numbness
* vision changes
* breast lumps
* depression
* yellowing of skin
* spotting of blood from the vagina.

Q: "Can you get pregnant if you miss taking one or more pills?"
A: "Yes, it is possible. However, you can take several steps which will avoid the possibility of a pregnancy if you miss a pill on a certain day:

"If you forget one combined pill take it as soon as you remember and carry on normally, taking the next pill when it is due. If your combined pill is more than 12 hours overdue you must not rely on it for contraceptive protection. Complete the course as usual but whatever happens use another effective method of contraception as well as the pill for the next 14 days. This may mean continuing extra precautions during the pill-free week, or even into your next packet. This is the 14-day rule. Women on a progestogen-only pill should take additional precautions for 14 days if they are more than *three hours* late taking their pill.

"It helps to take your pills at the same time each day, so that your body will become accustomed to the regular addition of hormones. If you miss your period contact your clinic or doctor immediately."

Q: "When your start taking pills do you get immediate protection?"
A: "There are various rulings on this now as there are several different types of pill:

"*Combined Oral Contraceptives* can be started on the first day of the period, and no extra precautions (such as sheath or sperm-icide) need be taken; contraceptive protection is immediate. If the pill is started on day five of the period then for 14 days extra precautions should be used before the pill can be relied on as a contraceptive.

"*Every Day (ED) combined pills* (in the UK there are three

brands: Norinyl 1/28, Logynon ED and Minovlar ED). These pills should be started on the first day of the period and 14 days of extra precautions should be used. The reason for this is that these pills contain seven inactive pills to make the number of tablets up to 28; this helps some women remember to take them.

"*Progestogen-only pills (mini-pills)* should be started on the first day of the period and 14 days of extra precautions are necessary before the pill is fully protective."

Q: "What is the mini pill?"

A: "Mini pills are taken every day, contain no oestrogen and only low amounts of progestogen. Progestogen is a manufactured hormone resembling the natural hormone progesterone, which is produced by the ovaries after ovulation.

"The advantage of mini pills is that they contain lower doses of hormone and therefore interfere less with the total system. They have been on the market since 1973, are widely used, mainly by women over 35 who are now advised to consider an alternative method of birth control to the combined pill, by women who cannot tolerate oestrogens and by women who are breast-feeding (the oestrogen in the combined pill reduces the milk flow).

"The mini pill has several different effects. It makes cervical mucus thick and sticky, so that it is more difficult for sperm to pass through to the Fallopian tubes. The progestogen in mini pills also stops the lining of the uterus (the endometrium) developing properly, and some people believe the Fallopian tubes contract more rapidly under the influence of progestogen, thereby interfering with the normal movement of the egg.

"The mini pill has a high (98 percent) actual effectiveness rate, but it must be taken every day without fail. If a pill is missed one day a backup method of birth control *must* be used. Mini pill users seem to have less breast tenderness, but can have irregular periods and spotting; they also have less nausea, headache and leg pain than other oral contraceptive users.

"Complications and risks must be viewed as the same as other pills until research has been completed on mini pills. A complete medical evaluation and prescription must be obtained before using the mini pill."

Q: "Is the mini pill the same as the morning-after pill?"

A: "No. The morning-after pill is an emergency method of preventing pregnancy after having unprotected intercourse (even once) around the time of ovulation. Morning-after contraception tends to be available in the UK only from larger family planning clinics. It can be given in two ways: first, a specific regimen of ethinyl oestradol (an oestrogen) within 72 hours of unprotected intercourse or in the case of a defective sheath etc; second, the insertion of an IUD up to five days after unprotected intercourse.

"There is no substitute for planning. Planning the night before will avoid morning-after problems, and if an oral contraceptive is needed, saying 'No' is the safest and most effective one. Saying no to intercourse does not, of course, rule out other satisfying sexual activities."

Vaginal Spermicides

Vaginal spermicides are sperm-killing products that are placed in the vagina before intercourse.

They come in various forms. All of them are readily available and quite easy to use:

1. Foam
2. Cream
3. Jelly
4. Pessaries

All vaginal spermicides are placed high in the vagina around the cervical area. They are designed to prevent pregnancy in two ways: first, and most important, they contain a safe chemical (spermicide) that kills sperm before it can reach an ovum; second, they spread around the cervical area to create a barrier that prevents sperm from entering the cervix.

Foam, cream and jelly are all placed in the vagina with a special applicator that comes with the product. Spermicidal pessaries are placed in the vagina by hand.

Vaginal spermicides alone are not as effective as oral contraceptive pills, the IUD, diaphragm or condom, but they do provide varying degrees of protection against pregnancy if they are used properly each time of intercourse. The effectiveness of each of the four types of vaginal spermicide will be discussed in the sections that follow.

Vaginal spermicides have no proven health risks or medical side effects. They are available free in the UK from a clinic without a doctor's prescription. They are convenient to use, especially for women who have intercourse infrequently. In addition they offer some protection against some sexually transmitted diseases, including the herpes virus and some vaginal infections, though just how much protection is not yet fully known; certainly if they are · used in conjunction with a condom the protection is improved.

1. CONTRACEPTIVE FOAM

When it is properly placed, high in the vagina, foam works as a contraceptive because it contains spermicide that kills sperm on contact. Also, foam coats the surface of the cervix and acts as a barrier preventing sperm from reaching an ovum and causing a pregnancy.

Contraceptive foam can be purchased without a doctor's prescription in a chemist or family planning clinic and is free in the UK if prescribed. Foam is packaged in aerosol cans and comes with a special applicator. Foam comes in single or multiple dose cans (six, 20 or 34 doses) and can also be purchased in prefilled single dose applicators.

Foam must be stored away from heat. After use, the plastic applicator should be washed with warm water.

The can of foam must be shaken vigorously to mix the chemical and the bubbles. The applicator that comes with the foam is then filled with foam (the instructions show how), the applicator is placed high in the vagina and the foam is released around the cervix. This is done lying down, to prevent the foam from gravitating out of the vagina. Two applications of foam provide added protection. Foam must be placed in the vagina before intercourse, but no longer than 30 minutes before, and must be left in for six to eight hours after. When intercourse occurs several times in any given period, another application of foam *must* be placed in the vagina each time before intercourse.

How effective is foam? By comparison with pessaries, creams and jellies foam is the most effective vaginal spermicide. Some studies show that foam can be 97 percent effective if used with a barrier method, but on average the figure is about 85 percent.

Using foam and a condom together increases the protection against pregnancy to the level of pills, the IUD and the diaphragm.

When foam fails as a contraceptive, it is generally because it has been used improperly. It may fail if the applicator is not inserted deep enough in the vagina, or if more foam is not added *each time* when having sex two or more times within a short period; it may also fail if the foam is applied more than 30 minutes before having intercourse.

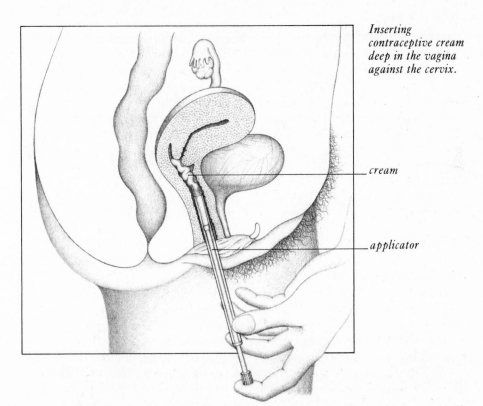

Inserting contraceptive cream deep in the vagina against the cervix.

cream

applicator

Once in a while the foam does not kill the sperm or remain on the cervix as it should. This is a product failure, but it occurs rarely.

Q: "I heard that foam irritates the vagina and penis. Is that true?"
A: "It can be. Sometimes the chemicals in the foam of a particular brand cause irritation.

"Changing brands may be enough to solve the problem. If that doesn't work, and the irritation or discomfort continues, change to another method of birth control. Such irritation is not dangerous and carries no serious medical risk."

Q: "Should I douche after I use the foam?"
A: "No, definitely not. Doctors do not advise douching except for specific medical conditions. If you use a douche, you will probably negate the sperm-killing effect of the foam. *After six to eight hours but not before*, you can wash in and around the vagina if you wish.

"Foam does not drip and is not as messy as contraceptive jelly or cream: there is no actual need to wash after using it — it is a matter of personal preference."

Q: "What about oral sex and foam?"
A: "Couples who enjoy oral sex find that having oral sex first and then inserting the foam prior to intercourse is a satisfactory way of avoiding unpleasant tastes or smells."

Q: "Are the new vaginal sprays and deodorants contraceptive?"
A: "Emphatically, no. They have no contraceptive effect whatsoever, are unnecessary for hygiene and should be avoided as the chemicals in them may cause irritation in your vagina.

"When you buy spermicidal foam at your chemist be sure that the can is marked 'contraceptive' and comes with an applicator. Many chemists place vaginal deodorants and sprays on the same shelves with contraceptive foams and jellies. Never use an ordinary vaginal spray for contraception. It won't work."

2,3. CONTRACEPTIVE CREAM AND CONTRACEPTIVE JELLY

Both contraceptive cream and contraceptive jelly prevent pregnancy in the same way when properly placed high in the vagina *each time* before intercourse: they cover the opening of the cervix, acting as a barrier, and they kill sperm on contact.

Cream or jelly can be purchased without a doctor's prescription at a chemist and is free in the UK with a prescription. It is now statutory in the UK for vaginal spermicide packs to carry a warning indicating that a higher degree of protection against pregnancy will be afforded by using another method of contraception in addition to a spermicide.

Contraceptive cream and contraceptive jelly are packaged in tubes like toothpaste and come with an applicator to ensure proper use each time you have intercourse. The tube of cream or jelly and the applicator have threads so they can be screwed together to ensure that the applicator is filled correctly.

Prior to intercourse, but no sooner than 15 minutes before, the applicator is filled with either cream or jelly is inserted deep in the vagina and the contents released to spread over the cervical area. The woman should be lying down. The cream or jelly will act as a barrier preventing sperm from moving into the cervix, and the spermicide it contains will kill any sperm that come in contact with it.

Two applications of the cream or jelly give added protection. When having intercourse more than once in a short period of time a new application of cream or jelly *must* be added each time *before* intercourse begins. The cream or jelly must be left in place six to eight hours after intercourse.

When the cream or jelly disperses, becomes gooey and starts to drip, only the outside part, the lips of the vagina, can be washed.

How effective are creams and jellies? Contraceptive creams are more effective than contraceptive jellies — studies show contraceptive creams when used with a barrier method to be approximately 93 percent effective and contraceptive jellies to be 77 percent effective. Although these rates are not as high as foam alone, or a diaphragm and cream or jelly, or a condom and foam, using contraceptive cream or jelly alone is certainly better than no method at all.

The markedly high failure rate is partly due to the users. Common mistakes are: not releasing the cream or jelly from the applicator deep enough in the vagina, and walking around immediately after insertion. Not allowing the cream or jelly to remain in place for six to eight hours is another. Applying the cream or jelly too far ahead of intercourse has been known to lead to pregnancy, and not using a new application of cream or jelly before each time of intercourse, however recently the last application was made, has had the same effect.

Q: "My wife doesn't like contraceptive jelly. She says it gets too watery. Is that true?"
A: "Yes. Contraceptive jelly becomes rather watery at body temperature and tends to drip and get a bit messy. For this reason, some women prefer to use a contraceptive cream or foam, both of which drip less."

Q: "Which contraceptive cream or jelly is the best?"
A: "As long as the cream or jelly is spermicidal and can be used alone, the different brands are very much alike and must meet the same government standards. People choose according to cost, odour and the feeling of the foam or jelly in the vagina."

Q: "Can any contraceptive cream or jelly cause an irritation?"
A: "Yes. Some women and some men have found certain brands of cream or jelly to be irritating to the vagina or to the penis. The remedy is usually to change brands, but if the irritation continues you may have to change your method of birth control. Your doctor will advise you."

Q: "I have heard people talk about vaginal contraceptive tablets. What do they do?"

A: "In some countries — the USA in particular — you can buy foaming contraceptive tablets which are placed by hand high up in the vagina five to ten minutes before intercourse. Body heat causes the tablet to foam up, thus creating a spermicidal barrier around the cervix, making it difficult for the sperm to pass into the uterus and fertilize an egg. This sounds fine, but there are problems of reliability. There are no large-scale studies of the effectiveness of contraceptive tablets and failure rates are reported to vary wildly from five to 39 percent, but no one figure has been agreed on by authorities as the average. It was precisely because of the worrying degree of uncertainty and the potentially high failure rate that manufacturers in the UK stopped producing contraceptive tablets in 1978."

4. CONTRACEPTIVE VAGINAL PESSARIES

When a contraceptive pessary is properly placed by hand deep in the vagina, body heat causes it to melt and release a spermicide that kills sperm on contact. The spermicidal action prevents pregnancy but does not harm the tissue of the vagina. The contents of the pessary as they melt also form a physical barrier across the cervix, impeding the passage of sperm.

Pessaries can be purchased without a doctor's prescription at a family planning clinic, chemist, and are free in the UK if prescribed. When buying pessaries in a chemist, be sure they are for birth control and not for hygiene or constipation. They will be marked "Contraceptive Pessaries."

Contraceptive vaginal pessaries come in packages with each pessary in a separate slot for easy removal. Some pessaries are wrapped in a foil which must be completely removed before the device can be inserted properly in the vagina. There are instructions in each package for proper use.

Pessaries are placed by hand deep in the vagina three to 15 minutes *before* intercourse; it takes a few minutes for them to melt completely. It is important to insert a new pessary *each time* before intercourse, and not to wash the vagina for at least six to eight hours after.

Vaginal pessaries are supposed to be in the same effectiveness range as contraceptive foam (85 to 97 percent), but large-scale studies have yet to be completed. Vaginal pessaries offer some protection against sexually transmitted diseases and some types of vaginal infection.

When vaginal pessaries fail to prevent pregnancy, it will be for one of these reasons: insertion of the pessary into the rectum instead of the vagina; not inserting the pessary high enough in the vagina; intercourse before the pessary has melted completely; failing to use another pessary when having sex more than once within a short period; having intercourse too long after the pessary has been inserted.

III   NATURAL METHODS

FACTS Natural family planning is a general term used to describe several methods of birth control that do not depend on using chemicals (as in the pill) or mechanical barriers (condoms, for example). **Rhythm** is the best known natural birth control method, but the **cervical mucus** or ovulation method (also known as the Billings method after its originator, Dr J. Billings) is gaining in popularity.

Natural family planning methods are based on the premise that if a couple understand how the woman's body functions and know what to look for they will know when they can have intercourse with no risk of pregnancy. They will also know when the fertile times are if they wish to have a baby.

A crucial aspect of choosing *any* natural family planning method is to receive advice and instruction from a qualified doctor or clinic on how natural methods work. Natural family planning centres exist in the USA, UK and Commonwealth, and most European countries. In the UK you can get advice from your family doctor or from a family planning clinic where the doctors are specially trained to advise on all methods of birth control. Your local Catholic church may also have a list for your area.

RHYTHM

The rhythm method requires periodic abstinence from intercourse. The goal is to avoid intercourse when ovulation is likely, and to resume intercourse when the woman is not fertile. The two ways that a couple can determine when to abstain and when it is safe to have intercourse are the calendar method and the temperature method (also called the basal body temperature method). They may be used alone or in combination.

The calendar method is the least effective and least scientific natural technique. It requires the woman to keep an accurate record of her menstrual cycles for at least six to 12 months before starting to use it. This record is designed to enable the woman to predict her menstrual cycle each month. Using the beginning of her menstruation as day one and the day before her menstruation as the last day of her cycle, the couple then uses a simple arithmetical formula to determine when they can have intercourse and when they should abstain. Ovulation generally occurs (with slight variation) 14 days before the onset of the next menstrual flow, so if a woman regularly has a 28-day cycle she is likely to ovulate on day 14. Since sperm can remain alive and be active for up to three days and the egg remains viable for a day, abstinence would be in order for several days before and a couple of days after ovulation. Computations for cycles of different lengths can be learned with proper instruction. However, it is often not as straightforward as this in practice because women rarely have such regular cycles: illness, stress, weight loss or gain and environmental changes frequently alter them. In addition, some couples find lovemaking by the calendar too intrusive — they feel it limits their spontaneity; although other sexual acts can be fulfilling, intercourse still remains the most desirable for most couples.

The calendar month can be supplemented by the temperature or *basal body temperature* (bbt) method, or the bbt method can be used alone.

In this approach the woman records her temperature each morning before getting out of bed. A special bbt thermometer available from a chemist or family planning clinic should be used because it is easier to read than ordinary fever thermometers. Temperature can be taken orally, rectally or vaginally but it must be taken the same way for several months each day before getting out of bed. The temperature is recorded on special graph paper which comes with the thermometer. The pattern that appears on the chart is one which usually shows the temperature about the same each day until the time of ovulation, when *there is a slight drop and then a rise in temperature for about three days.* The rise in temperature (due to a surge of luteinising hormone) is small, but a careful reading and marking of the graph will indicate it. The woman is fertile while her temperature is up. Some couples who do not want a child remain abstinent through the first part of the cycle until the temperature has been elevated at least three full days. The temperature falls just before menstruation if conception has not occurred.

It is clear that each woman needs to plot a chart for several months before using the method in order to learn the particular pattern of her body. Some women have a great deal of difficulty in learning the pattern, which anyway can easily be thrown off by a fever or other illness. The reading can be distorted by having to get out of bed quickly and taking the temperature later on. Having to take a reading at the same time each day is a bother for many women. Some couples who wait until after ovulation to have intercourse — *which is the safest application of this method* — complain that they have only 12 to 14 days for intercourse before the next cycle begins.

CERVICAL MUCUS (OVULATION)

(*Billings Method*) This method is based on the fact that from the end of menstruation one month to the first day of the next flow the natural mucus produced by the cervix changes. The presence of a certain kind of mucus indicates ovulation is imminent. Since it is not possible under ordinary circumstances to detect the nature of the cervical mucus during the menstrual flow, those days in this method are considered potentially fertile. Instruction from a trained couple or doctor from a natural planning programme is absolutely necessary to learn how to make this family planning method effective.

The basic principles involved in this approach are: for a few days after menstruation the cervix produces no mucus or very small amounts, making this a relatively safe time for intercourse. When the level of oestrogen rises, the cervix begins to produce a mucus that is clear, stretchy and rather like raw egg-white. This type of mucus is produced for several days and marks a fertile period. It is followed by thicker, sticky, cloudy mucus. The first day of the change to clearer mucus indicates ovulation will occur in a day or two. So these days and three to four days after are fertile, and intercourse should be abstained from if the couple uses natural methods only. In the remaining days of the cycle the thickness and cloudiness of the mucus indicate a safe, infertile period.

Some couples find this is a complicated method as it requires continual monitoring of the mucus (this is done by using toilet tissue several times a day to determine the presence and nature of the discharge), and they also find it unappealing and embarrassing. The method must be practised for a month or two before depending on it. Charting the kind of mucus observed is important to develop a recognizable pattern. Stress may affect ovulation and therefore change usual patterns, and infections, drugs, sprays and even coloured underwear may produce a discharge that interferes with accurate recognition of the state of the mucus. People using the mucus method also have to learn to distinguish semen remaining in the vagina from cervical mucus.

Q: "It appears that using natural family planning methods is a complicated task for a couple. Why use them, with so many other methods available?"

A: "There are several reasons. Many couples who choose natural family planning do so because of their religion. Some religions, notably the Roman Catholic Church and Orthodox Judaism, officially require their believers to use natural methods only. Chemical or mechanical barrier methods are banned.

"Couples may not be able to use the more common family planning methods for medical reasons. Some couples want to learn how to plan a pregnancy using the body's natural clocks and timetable and these methods help them learn. Some couples prefer natural methods because they are 'natural' and that is how they want their sex lives to be. Other couples value natural methods because they are without side effects of any kind. Then, although it is unlikely to be the deciding factor, whoever you are, with natural family planning the price is right!"

Q: "Which is the best natural family planning method?"
A: "From an effectiveness standpoint, the temperature or bbt method with intercourse only after ovulation occurs; it shows success rates in some studies of around 98-99 percent — similar to those of oral contraceptives.

"Effectiveness rates for the calendar method alone have not been widely tested, but are likely to be around 70 percent. Rates reported for the cervical mucus method vary from 70 percent to the high 90s.

"Not enough studies have been done to give us a properly accurate picture of the effectiveness of any of the natural methods. Perhaps because of this — and perhaps because of their political and social motives as well — family planning practitioners are not on the whole enthusiastic about natural methods."

RELATIONSHIPS When a couple master a natural family planning method it seems to be successful not only in controlling pregnancies but in promoting the good of their relationship too:

"Since we started using the ovulation method of family planning I think our relationship is better. We are much more relaxed about the health factors than we were before, and it is exciting to be learning about how wonderfully the body works and to be able to use that to our advantage.

"The fact that this method is in line with our religious teachings is important, and the guilt we once felt in the past is now gone."

"Maybe we are weird but we have learned to be close and sexual without having to have intercourse and that has been exciting to us and has added another dimension to our relationship. I have to bite my tongue because I want to tell our friends about it."

Tell your friends about it! That should be important for other couples too, whether they use natural family planning or not. It sounds like your choice of family planning suits you perfectly, and the harmony you describe in your relationship is an inducement to others of like mind to try such a method.

Q: "We are Catholic and have been trying the various natural methods without much success. We are at a point now where having another baby will hurt us financially and emotionally. What can we do?"

A: "You and your husband can go see your parish priest and explain your situation to him, emphasizing your honest efforts in the past and the results. Indicate that your ability to be loving parents in a stable home environment will be seriously impaired if you have another child.

"Some priests will understand and will support you if you make a decision, based on an honest examination of your consciences, to use another method of birth control. However, it is just as likely that your priest will repeat the Church's traditional position, banning artificial birth control. He might suggest further study of the proper use of natural methods or counselling.

"Changing to an artificial method is not an easy decision to make, for it requires you to reflect thoroughly both on your relationship and on your beliefs. A great many Catholics have come to the view that it is possible to use artificial methods and still be a good Catholic, but that is a private decision for each couple."

IV   STERILIZATION

FACTS Sterilization is a voluntary surgical procedure that prevents permanently either a man fathering a child or a woman conceiving one.

Sterilization for men is called **vasectomy** and is the operation in which a doctor cuts and seals shut the two tubes (the vasa deferentia) that convey sperm from the testicles to the seminal vesicles. After a vasectomy sperm is still produced, but it cannot pass the surgical point and so cannot cause a pregnancy. Vasectomy does not interfere with sexual interest, erection, ejaculation, pleasure or performance.

Sterilization for women is called **tubal ligation**. The procedure is that a doctor cuts, blocks or seals shut the Fallopian tubes, preventing eggs from moving through them and stopping sperm from reaching the eggs, which stay permanently in the other portion of the sealed tube. Tubal ligation does not interfere with sexual interest, pleasure or performance.

Voluntary sterilization has become a very common method of birth control in the United States and Europe. It is estimated that in the UK up to 100,000 men have a vasectomy every year and approximately 50,000 women are sterilized voluntarily. In the USA about 11.5 million adults have been sterilized.

Your Personal Decision About Sterilization. Because sterilization is usually irreversible, no-one should decide to be sterilized without giving it exceptionally careful thought. The issues are emotional, social and physical, and each of them needs to be considered in depth and discussed between partners:

* sterilization should be regarded as permanent; 20–30 percent of cases can be reversed successfully, but you cannot rely on being one
* the decision to be sterilized must be made freely, without pressure from family or friends
* agreeing to a vasectomy or tubal ligation under pressure from your partner frequently causes resentment and bitterness; it can have a serious negative effect on the relationship
* will your current relationship suffer in any way because of the strains sometimes involved in childlessness?
* is it likely that a future relationship will be damaged by childlessness? Marriages are ending in divorce more than ever before, and on remarriage the desire to have a child with a new partner is very common
* what position has your religion taken on sterilization, and will you feel guilty if you go against it?
* will the inability to reproduce affect your concept of being a complete woman or man?
* are you fully aware of the surgical procedure for sterilization? might it be unsafe for you or have undesirable side effects?
* have you talked with your partner about which of you should be sterilized? All things being equal, sterilization is easier for the man.

MYTHS Myths about sterilization, and what it does to women and men are legion. Here are some of them:

* sterilization lowers a person's sex drive
* sterilization affects a person's hormones
* after sterilization, it is common for women and men to become promiscuous
* sterilization will ease marriage problems
* men lose some of their physical strength after being sterilized
* women lose some of their femininity after being sterilized
* you can tell a person is sterilized just by looking at them
* it's the woman's role to be sterilized since she is the one who has the baby
* real men, and real women, do not get sterilized
* sterilization means loss of ovaries for women

* sterilization means loss of testicles for men
* men who have been sterilized have more headaches and backaches because the sperm backs up in their bodies
* a man who is sterilized will ejaculate no semen during intercourse.

FEELINGS Typical responses that men and women have to their sterilizations are:

"At last, peace of mind."

"I could relax while having intercourse."

"I felt like less of a man."

"I'd never have to worry about an abortion."

"A part of me has gone now that I cannot have a baby."

"We decided not to tell anyone about it. I guess we were a bit ashamed, but we had to do it."

As you can see, some are positive, some are negative. Fortunately, most people's response is positive, like the first two quoted. They are the people who took the decision to be sterilized in a positive way, as a means of improving the quality of life of their existing family. They are the people who felt positive about themselves and their relationships, people who felt secure about their own femininity or masculinity.

The negative responses come from people who either should not have been sterilized or who should have waited until they had resolved the issues. They may be people who felt uncertain about or unfulfilled in their masculinity or femininity. Maybe they were using sterilization to cover up a basic flaw in their relationships or maybe they had not resolved religious or social conflicts.

The feelings of people who have been sterilized show up two things: for a great many people it is a life-enhancing experience; for a minority it is a disadvantage. Everyone therefore who is considering sterilization needs to give it the closest possible thought and would be well advised to get and heed professional counselling.

RELATIONSHIPS The overwhelming majority of couples in which one partner has been sterilized report that their general relationship has improved and that their sex lives have shown a particular improvement. Many couples feel more relaxed and spontaneous when the fear of pregnancy has been removed, because the element of anxiety caused by an unwanted pregnancy often interferes with a man's or woman's sexual functioning.

In the certain knowledge that there will be no more children, couples find they can pay fuller attention to their existing family with reduced anxieties about further financial pressures of parenthood.

In a relationship where there are unresolved issues of power, dominance and who controls sex, sterilization will not provide a resolution. In fact, the couple should be counselled to postpone a sterilization until they have worked through their relationship difficulty.

Sterilization can lead to relationship difficulties. If the partner who is sterilized has problems of low self-esteem, he or she may withdraw and/or blame the other partner for pressuring him or her to be sterilized.

It is clear that if a relationship is sound and healthy, sterilization is likely, if anything, to improve it. If the relationship is unsound, sterilization should be avoided until both partners have worked through their problems and resolved them.

RELIGION The official positions of religions on sterilization vary from belief to belief. The Roman Catholic Church and Orthodox Judaism are opposed to sterilization because they oppose any form of birth control except natural methods. The only exception made is when pregnancy and/or the birth of a child is a real threat to the health of the woman. However, there is evidence that Catholics, Jews and others from religious groups with similar views on sterilization do choose it as a way to stabilize family size and avoid the risk of unintended pregnancies and possible abortions. In these cases, the individuals have formed their consciences in a fashion that does not exclude them from continuing their religious practice, even though their judgment about sterilization is contrary to the current official teaching of their belief.

Many of the Protestant churches see sterilization as a responsible act that fulfils, not violates, the will of God regarding family and the quality of life.

Sterilization is a deeply personal issue of great complexity for anyone, but if you belong to a religion that forbids sterilization or frowns on it, your problem is more complex still. It is very important that you should resolve your conscience *before* being sterilized, otherwise there may be conflict and guilt. It can be helpful to discuss your feelings about sterilization with your religious adviser.

Catholicism. The official position of the Roman Catholic Church on voluntary sterilization for a woman or a man is clear — it is prohibited. The only time a Roman Catholic may be sterilized is if a disease is present that can be treated in no other way. Sterilization may not, of course, be used as a contraceptive method.

However, the majority of practising Roman Catholics and many contemporary theologians have opinions that differ from the teaching of the Vatican. Most Catholics believe that sterilization is a matter of individual conscience. As long as the matter has been carefully thought through and the personal and relationship issues have been considered, many Catholics today would accept sterilization as a valid moral act. So if Catholic couples believe that their conjugal love and their parental responsibility would be weakened by another child, for whatever reason — emotional, physical, age, family or social — they may find sterilization proper in the context of their belief.

Sterilization is never to be undertaken lightly, and for Catholics it can never be an easy decision because of the extra religious dimension. It is important, therefore, for Catholic couples to discuss their views with a religious counsellor.

> **Q:** "So, if so many Catholics do it, getting sterilized for a Catholic is really no big thing."
>
> **A:** "That is not true. It is a very serious moral decision that strikes at the centre of real religious beliefs. It is not a simple decision. It is one that requires a couple honestly to search their consciences about why they no longer want children, and why they believe they will never change their minds. In addition, they must feel sure they are acting properly for themselves and for their relationship. This is no snap decision; if it is, the chances are they need to go back and rethink their reasons and intentions."

Judaism. In the Torah, it is stated that it is forbidden to give a man anything to cause sterility. However, references in the Talmud suggest that a woman may be permitted to sterilize herself. The wife of a famous Rabbi, it is said, "drank a cup" so that she would not be able to bear children any longer due to her great suffering in childbearing. Ancient law also permitted women permanently to avoid pregnancy if they had previously borne diseased or delinquent children. This shows the early Jewish consciousness of eugenics and the inadvisability of bearing children if previous ones showed undesirable physical, mental or spiritual traits.

Contemporary Judaism, except for strict Orthodox believers, is very clear in its acknowledgment of voluntary sterilization as a valuable method of permanent birth control once the two people are certain they have completed their family.

Protestantism. Protestant churches up to the early 1930s were opposed to birth control and sterilization. Today, however, many of the major Protestant sects around the world acknowledge that voluntary sterilization is a valuable means of promoting family stability and enhancing the quality of family life. The Church of England, for example, takes the view that if a couple chooses sterilization for themselves it should be done with the full knowledge of the irreversibility of the procedure and with thorough counselling, and the Presbyterians, like the United Methodist Church, find no intrinsic conflict between responsible voluntary sterilization and their religious values.

Tubal Ligation

Sterilization for women is done by cutting, clamping or tying a piece of each Fallopian tube. This prevents the egg from passing from the ovary to the uterus. It is commonly known as "cutting the tubes" or "tying the tubes."

Until recently, abdominal tubal ligation was the chief method used for sterilization of women. Today there are several other ways of cutting or sealing the Fallopian tubes that do not require the serious surgery, hospitalization and prolonged recovery of the abdominal tubal ligation.

These, newer, methods are just as permanent and irreversible, are virtually 100 percent effective, are making sterilization much safer and providing women with more options about which procedure is best for them. It is not advisable to have tubal ligation:

* when you are pregnant or may be pregnant
* when you have a serious medical problem like heart disease
* when you are grossly overweight
* when you have an active infection of the uterus or Fallopian tubes.

All of these issues will be discussed by your doctor when she/he does a medical history and evaluation before recommending any sterilization procedure.

Tubal ligations of any kind are considered permanent. Although microsurgery techniques can make the surgery reversible in some cases, women and couples who choose tubal ligation should be certain they do not wish to have children in the future.

Sexual interest, desire and performance or the ability to give or receive pleasure are not affected by any sterilization method. Female sex hormones are not affected, and tubal ligation of any kind does not interfere with menstruation or cause menopause.

After a tubal ligation many women have reported an increase in their sexual interest and activity due to their ability to relax, be more spontaneous, and not to have to worry about pregnancy.

The following is a brief description of the different female sterilization methods, all of which achieve the same purpose. Your doctor will discuss with you the merits of each method to help you make your decision.

ABDOMINAL TUBAL LIGATION

In this procedure an incision about five inches long is made in the abdomen to expose the uterus and Fallopian tubes. The tubes are then tied and a piece is cut out of each tube.

This is major surgery with all the risks and complications that implies, and requires general anaesthesia, usually five days in hospital and several weeks of recovery time at home. It can be done at any time but is frequently performed after the birth of a child, after a D&C or after an abortion, when a woman decides she does not want to become pregnant again.

LAPARASCOPIC TUBAL LIGATION

In this procedure, a small incision is made just below the navel. In this opening the surgeon inserts a needle through which carbon dioxide or nitrous oxide are released; this causes the abdomen to expand and the organs to shift so that the uterus and Fallopian tubes become more visible. Then through the same small incision the doctor inserts a laparoscope, an instrument that permits outside light to illuminate the internal organs. Inserted along with the laparoscope, or through a second small incision just above the pubic hairline, is a cautery device that will heat-seal (cauterize) each Fallopian tube. Instead of cauterizing the tube some doctors seal them with special bands or spring-loaded clips, and others cut a piece out of the tubes and then heat-seal the free ends. The surgeon then withdraws the instruments, allows the gas to leave the body, closes the incision(s) with a stitch or two and covers them with a surgical plaster.

In the UK this procedure is probably the most popular and is available free through the NHS. It is done under general anaesthetic in hospital although there are a few, mainly private, centres which do the operation as a day-care procedure. Most women go home the same day — a few leave after they have had a day's rest.

Recovery is rapid after a laparoscopic tubal ligation and intercourse can be resumed as soon as the woman is feeling well.

MINI-LAPAROTOMY

In this new tubal ligation method, a small incision, about an inch or two in length, is made just above the pubic hair line. An instrument is inserted in the vagina that elevates the uterus towards the incision. Through the incision the surgeon locates the Fallopian tubes and cuts them off or places bands or rings around each tube to seal them off. The incision is then stitched and covered by a surgical plaster. The "mini-lap" takes less than 30 minutes and is usually performed under local anaesthetic. The woman can return home after several hours.

The mini-laparotomy is quite new, and many doctors have not yet learned the technique. It is not, therefore, widely available.

VAGINAL TUBAL LIGATION (CULDOSCOPIC STERILIZATION)

In this procedure the surgeon makes a small incision in the rear of the vagina, near the cervix, to reach both Fallopian tubes. He or she pulls both of them through the incision at the same time, cuts and ties a piece of each and returns them to their usual place in the abdomen.

General anesthesia is used in this procedure. Some women return home the same day, some need a day or two of rest and observation. Recovery is generally rapid, with all activities being quickly resumed except intercourse, which must be avoided for four weeks to allow for proper healing of the incision.

A major disadvantage of vaginal tubal ligation is the possibility of infection if some of the bacteria that are normally in the vagina, where they are beneficial, get transferred to the tubes, where they are not. Also failure rates are higher for vaginal tubal ligation by comparison with the rates for other methods of female sterilization.

Q: "Is female sterilization very effective?"
A: "Yes. When properly done by a qualified doctor, tubal ligation of any kind is virtually 100 percent effective."

Q: "Must women return to be sure they are sterilized?"
A: "No. If women do go back to their doctor, it usually is to check that the incision is healing properly."

Q: "Is a tubal ligation like a hysterectomy?"

A: "Absolutely not. A hysterectomy is the removal of the uterus and a tubal ligation is only the removal of a section of each of the Fallopian tubes, making it impossible for egg and sperm to meet. After a tubal ligation you will still have your period and you will still ovulate."

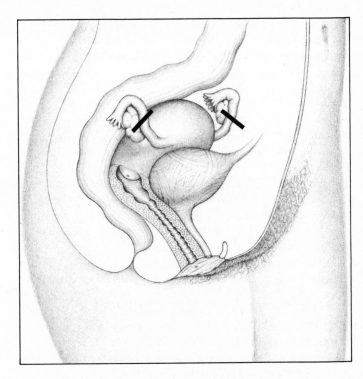

Tubal ligation: no matter which method is used, the effect is always to seal off the Fallopian tubes so that sperm coming up the tubes cannot meet ova on their way down from the ovaries.

Q: "Is it true that tubal ligation is becoming more reversible?"

A: "At present, the odds against reversing a tubal ligation are about five to one, but there are encouraging signs that reversal will be more successful in the near future. Improvements in sterilization procedures will result in less damage to the Fallopian tubes (the spring-loaded clip is a promising advance in this respect), and improved microsurgery techniques should also help to achieve more successful reversals.

   "One potential problem with reversing tubal ligation is that ectopic pregnancies occur ten times more often in women who have had a tubal ligation reversed."

Vasectomy

The standard way in which men are sterilized is by an operation called vasectomy, in which the tubes that convey sperm from the testicles to the penis are cut and sealed off.

   There are two very important points to note: first, it is unlikely that a vasectomy can be reversed — once it has been done, the man will be sterile for life; second, that having a vasectomy will have no adverse effects on your sex life *at all*. You will get erections as before, you will ejaculate as before, you will feel all you felt before. Desire and performance are in no way reduced. The *only* difference is that you cannot cause a pregnancy because your semen no longer contains sperm.

Some men worry that because sperm can no longer get out it will build up in the testicles and cause them to swell. This will not happen: sperm is absorbed just as it is if you do not ejaculate for a while. There will be no discomfort or swelling; you will feel just the same.

Vasectomy is virtually 100 percent effective and almost without physical risk if it is performed correctly. What has to be done is this: the two tubes, the vasa deferentia, that carry sperm from the testicles up toward the penis have to be cut and sealed off so that sperm cannot reach the penis. Vasectomies are normally undertaken in hospital or a clinic.

The doctor first locates the vas on one side of the scrotum and gives the man a small local anaesthetic on that side. The anaesthetic takes effect quickly. The doctor then makes a small incision in the scrotum, lifts the vas through and cuts out between half an inch and an inch of it. The ends are then tied off or cauterized (heat sealed) and replaced in the scrotum. The same procedure is followed on the other side of the scrotum: the other vas is cut through and the ends sealed off. The operation usually takes no more than 30 minutes and generally produces only minor discomfort.

If both vasa have been properly sealed off, they will not open or grow together again; this means that vasectomy is virtually 100 percent certain as a method of sterilization. The skin of the scrotum is so wrinkled that the two small incisions will not be noticeable once they have healed.

There are a few medical situations in which it is unwise to have a vasectomy. A hernia or an undescended testicle may make it undesirable, though sometimes the operation can be performed after such a condition has been corrected. Men who suffer from abnormal blood clotting, very high blood pressure or heart disease will probably be advised that they should not have a vasectomy, as any kind of surgery could be harmful.

Although the rule at the moment is that there is a 20–30 percent reversal of vasectomy there seems a real possibility with the development of microsurgery techniques that reversal rates will be much higher in the future. It must be recognized though that this is speculative. A number of men have already sought reversal after the death of a child, or after marrying when they never thought they would or after their career or financial circumstances have changed so that they felt able to have a child. Some have been lucky and the operation has worked; many have been disappointed.

Q: "But how can you still come after a vasectomy if there is no sperm?"

A: "Sperm makes up a very small part (about one percent) of your ejaculate. The other 99 percent is fluids from the seminal vesicle and prostate gland, which are unaffected by the vasectomy. They keep producing their fluid and that is what continues to leave your penis when you come. Incidentally, only examination of your semen under a microscope would reveal that you had had a vasectomy. The colour, amount and consistency remain as before, so no one could tell."

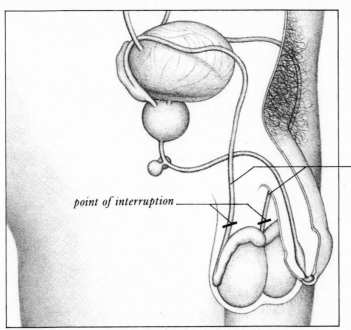

Vasectomy: if each vas deferens is properly sealed off, no new sperm can be ejaculated. The man will not be sterile however until all sperm in the system above the point of interruption have been ejaculated.

_____ *vasa deferentia*

point of interruption _____

Q: "After my vasectomy when can I have intercourse?"

A: "Your doctor will advise you. Usually, doctors suggest that intercourse can begin as soon as it is comfortable for you. Although the surgery was minor, the tissue of the scrotum was cut and bruised and needs to heal, so vigorous intercourse may need to be delayed a bit. Whenever you resume sex, remember: *vasectomy does not provide you with immediate pregnancy protection. Sperm are still alive and present* in the seminal vesicles, prostate and Cowper's glands, all structures beyond the point of the surgery. All of this sperm must be ejaculated before your entire reproductive system is free from sperm. Therefore *you or your partner must use a method of birth control until you no longer ejaculate sperm.* After that time the vasectomy is virtually 100 percent effective."

Q: "How do I know when that happens?"

A: "Your doctor will require you to have two sperm counts about three months after the operation. The sperm count will reveal the presence or absence of sperm in your semen and will indicate whether birth control needs to be continued. It is important to remember that it is not how long you wait after your vasectomy to have unprotected intercourse that is decisive but how many times you have ejaculated to clear your reproductive system of sperm."

Q: "I understand the facts about vasectomy, but I find it very hard to believe that it isn't going to have some effect somehow on my sex life."

A: "You are partly right. If vasectomy has any effect on your sex life, it will be to improve it. Research has shown that some men find that their interest in sex increases and that they have intercourse more often after a vasectomy. This is probably because they can relax entirely and be more spontaneous as there is no chance at all of causing a pregnancy. But only a minority of men are affected in this way, so don't count on it!"

Q: "Can vasectomy make you feel less like a man?"
A: "No. What makes you feel like a man should have little to do with whether your vasa deferentia are closed or open. But if it does make a difference, then vasectomy is not for you! Vasectomy does not change your appearance or your identity, nor does it interfere with your sexual desire, arousal, performance or your ability to enjoy and provide enjoyment for another. Therefore, if you felt like a man before a vasectomy you will feel like one after a vasectomy."

Q: "I heard vasectomy was illegal at one time. Is that true?"
A: "No. As a method of voluntary sterilization it has always been legal. A proper written consent form signed by the patient indicating his full understanding of the procedure and outcomes is not a legal requirement in the UK although most surgeons insist on this as an indication that both partners share the decision. In most situations, thoughtful doctors request that the wife or partner of the man be present for a consultation when the implications for relationships are fully discussed."

Q: "Can I use a sperm bank before a vasectomy?"
A: "Sperm bank facilities are not available on the NHS in the UK for a man seeking a voluntary sterilization. Provision for semen storage is only available on the NHS for a man made involuntarily sterile. As in the USA there are a number of private agencies in the UK which have semen storage facilities in a medical freezing unit if you should wish to have another child after sterilization.

"However, there can be problems. Some of the freezing techniques used have destroyed sperm, and anyway cases have revealed that sperm seem to lose their mobility after being stored for a long period."

Q: "I heard about a pill that can cause sterility in men. Is there one?"
A: "A very qualified yes, since the pill you talk of is in the early experimental stages and is not yet on the market. It is a combination of the drug Danazol with testosterone, and it reduces a man's sperm count so low that he is effectively sterile. Interest in sex and ability to have an erection, ejaculate and have an orgasm are not interfered with. In the very small studies conducted to date the fertility of the men tested returned several months after they stopped using the pill."

BODY IMAGE

FACTS Body image is the concept we have of how our bodies feel and appear to ourselves and of how we believe others see us. It is a very subjective matter. Some people who are by the commonly agreed standards beautiful may have a poor body image and be eternally anxious and uneasy about their appearance. Others who may conventionally rate as unattractive may be entirely at their ease about their bodies.

Confidence and a feeling of security about the "rightness" of one's body, regardless of how it looks, can facilitate a healthy, integrated expression of sexuality. Doubt, self-consciousness and anxiety about one's body image can do the exact reverse, inhibiting fulfilling sexual expression.

Body image is part — an intimate part, but only a part — of our sense of identity. When we think of what we are, we think of our experiences and abilities, our goals and our frustrations, our successes and our failures in the context of our bodies. We may be able to change many things about ourselves, but there is little that we can do to change what we look like stripped naked; at that point all we can do is try to change how we feel about what we see. That is why a person's sense of his or her identity can be altered by body changes resulting from disease or surgery, from putting on weight or losing it and from pregnancy. Many people who have suffered physical changes because of disease or disability have at first reacted negatively before coming to terms with their modified body and regaining a positive body image.

As in so many aspects of sexuality, self-acceptance is the key. What you look like is not nearly as important as how you feel about yourself, and in the end people will respond more to your personality than to your idea of how you look to them.

MYTHS Not one of these statements is true:

* physically attractive men and women are usually self-confident
* all cultures have the same views about body image and physical appearance
* women are more concerned about their body image than men
* generally, the way a person looks is a good indication of how he or she is in bed.

AGE From the moment of birth, adults influence children's body image and thereby their sense of identity. The way a child is held, touched, looked at and spoken to tells it whether it is loved and therefore an adequate person or whether it is disapproved of and therefore deficient. It is at this stage that a child can begin to learn whether its body is regarded as good, a message that will remain with the child throughout its formative years.

This early learning influences to a great extent the attitudes and behaviour of young people as they develop through the natural stages of life. It is my belief that young people who receive positive, affirming messages about their bodies and feel that they are loved and lovable persons are more likely and more able to express love and tenderness as they grow, and less likely to be involved in self-destructive behaviour or exploitive behaviour towards another person.

Although young children are very curious about their own bodies and the bodies of their friends, and although they learn about similarities and differences at a very early age, it is not until puberty that body image tends to emerge as a crucial factor in their developing self-concept. It appears that from that time on there is a continuing interest and sometimes a preoccupation with body image throughout the life cycle.

In western cultures, male and female adolescents alike learn very early that "looks count." Therefore, the natural biological changes they experience during puberty are monitored and interpreted through the culture's contemporary ideals. Physical size, breast and genital development, evidence of pubic hair, skin texture, hair colour and hairstyle, the onset of menstruation and the other typical developmental changes profoundly affect the young person's sense of body image and, for many, their entire sense of identity. Developing a bit later or not developing like everyone else is not seen as an individual difference. It is seen by many people as a sign of inferiority, and can trigger a loss of self-esteem. This is not an overstatement, because at this time in one's life being in step with one's peers is especially important, since it is the peer group that frequently lays down the ideals of how a young person should look. The peer group has its own language, dress code and mores, and if a young person finds it difficult to keep up, this may have a seriously adverse effect upon his or her sense of identity.

Similarly, adults struggle with their body image as they too are affected by changing cultural standards. Society has witnessed all sorts of "looks" that are in and soon out again. The scrambling by many people to keep up-to-date and be "in" is evidence of how looking a certain way and having a certain image of oneself affects identity. In this effort, though, individuality is frequently lost in the service of a collective standard. Many adults subscribe to the notion that self is body rather than self is person who happens to have a body. It is unfortunate that the features of the body have become what some people see as the essence of being a person. Comparisons of self to artificial cosmetic standards are influencing some people toward painful self-consciousness and to devaluing themselves because they do not meet the contemporary requirements of physical beauty. This is not only damaging in itself but has a circular effect too, by influencing young people to perpetuate these anxieties in their own lives.

Q: "My son is really worried about his size. He isn't as tall as his friends and he talks about it all the time. Can I take him to a doctor for treatment that will get things going for him?"

A: "I think you need to indicate to your son that you understand his concern and that you recognize it to be of real significance. It is very common for young boys and girls to want to keep pace with their friends in physical development. Their self-esteem and self-acceptance are usually related to sharing the common experiences of their peers, so you need to be sensitive to his real need.

"I would not advise going to a doctor at this point. Doctors will not interfere with normal growth patterns unless there is evidence of some genuine physical reason which is preventing normal growth. Also, unless your doctor is very sensitive to what is going on emotionally and socially with your son, his or her attitude could lead your son to feel that even a doctor can't help his particular condition.

"Continue to listen to your son, be open and available to him and try to communicate when possible that one rate of development is not better than others. I believe this issue will pass like so many of the other issues you have been faced with as a parent — so bear up and get ready for the next one!"

FEELINGS

"It has always been very important to me to keep pace with every style, every new look. I never thought too much about whether I liked it or not. I just did it. One day I realized I didn't know who I really was."

"Whenever I feel I look good things just seem to go better for me."

"For a long time in my life, I just cared about how I looked. What I thought and what I said were always secondary."

"Every little change in my weight made me feel as if my body had changed. I was obsessively aware of this and rarely thought about other things."

"The biggest change in my life occurred when I accepted how I looked and became concerned with my values and opinions. I had wasted so much time on my body."

Q: "Sometimes I find myself standing in front of the mirror just staring at my whole body — frequently for what seems like a long time. I wonder what I'm looking for?"

A: "Whatever it is, a lot of people do it. Sometimes it is purely physical assessment — trying to check yourself out against an ideal, trying to estimate what your good points are or how best to disguise what you see as your physical defects.

"Often it is more than that, however. Gazing at yourself in a mirror is one way of taking stock of who and what you are. Whatever you mean to do with your life has got to be done in that body — *your* body — so it is quite reasonable for you to spend some time reflecting on that part of your identity."

RELATIONSHIPS Self-acceptance in every way is a principal factor in being able to form intimate relationships and to have the capacity to give and receive tenderness and love. Painful self-consciousness about one's body and never feeling attractive enough are body image issues that interfere with a person's ability to present him- or herself in a confident, enthusiastic manner; they therefore interfere with the ability to sustain relationships or to form new ones.

Q: "When I was pregnant I was really worried that my husband would find me fat and ugly and look around for another woman to have sex with. In fact he found me sexier this way."

A: "I believe it. Some women begin to feel insecure and unattractive when their bodies change during pregnancy and they come to believe that everyone, their husbands especially, shares their view. As you point out, these negative feelings may not be warranted; what is appealing to many partners is not what you see in yourself, but who you are as a whole person.

"It is not unusual for husbands to react to their wives' pregnancies as yours has done. Perhaps you too have experienced the happy situation of your husband's attraction to you allaying your own anxieties."

CULTURE AND RELIGION Body image is enormously influenced by cultural and religious context. Different cultures place greatly different emphases on which body parts make people look good and how. Some cultures place a premium on fatness, whereas our own emphasizes slimness; in some, women's breasts are all-important (our own, for example), yet in some African cultures they are of minimal significance.

Because of the great emphasis on looks in our culture, we have two distinct problems. First, we are inclined to worry about how we present ourselves to other people, and that, on the whole, means how we dress, arrange our hair and use cosmetics. Second, there is what is underneath — how we look when all those image props are taken away and we find ourselves naked with other people. Both are sources of anxiety unless the whole sense of identity is in balance. No matter how they look, people can feel comfortable with their bodies and with the way they present themselves to others if they are secure in their identity.

Whereas appearance has become a major industry, nakedness remains a private anxiety. We have a dual inheritance. The Old Testament story of the Garden of Eden has done much to promote the idea that nakedness is associated with sin, sex and shame. Adam and Eve saw no need to clothe themselves until they had sinned, and churches ever since they were established have tended to imply that the naked human body is something to be ashamed of.

On the other hand, we have a great artistic tradition deriving from the Greeks which says that the naked human body is not only a perfectly normal, natural thing but can be of great beauty too. The Greeks, who tended to remove their clothes for sports, appear to have associated the naked body with fitness, health and self-enhancement.

With these two traditions running in parallel, it is not surprising that we have split minds about our bodies. It is no wonder that people who have inherited the idea that bodies are shameful and disgusting should have difficulty appreciating their own bodies and those of others as sources of pleasure, even though they know that countless people have inherited the alternative idea and found their bodies a source of the greatest pleasure.

DESIRE AND RESPONSE

FACTS We owe our knowledge of how people respond to sexual stimulation to the courageous pioneering research of Dr William Masters and Mrs Virginia Johnson in the US in the 1950s and 1960s. Then, in the 1970s, the work of Dr Helen Singer Kaplan provided some crucial theoretical advances.

Every person responds differently to sexual stimulation, but there is a pattern that applies to most people, most of the time. It probably doesn't apply to any individual all of the time. It is not a measure of what is "normal" — only a description of what usually occurs.

This pattern has three phases: **desire, excitement, orgasm**; there are real physical responses that distinguish them from each other.

Desire. We know more about what happens in the second two phases, excitement and orgasm, than we do about the first. Desire is still something of a mystery.

Desire — also called libido — is what moves us to seek out sexual situations. It is the magnet that draws us towards other people and draws them towards us too. It is difficult to describe scientifically because it is rooted in a brain centre and is therefore subject to hormone levels and the complex circuitry of the brain. As we come to understand the details of brain functioning better, we will have a better appreciation of how desire arises. We do know however that if there is a chemical imbalance, nerve circuit or transmitter problem in the appropriate area of the brain, a disorder — a sexual dysfunction — may result. This disorder may be specifically one of sexual desire or it may show itself as an arousal or orgasm problem too.

The desire phase has been discussed in detail by Dr Helen Singer Kaplan in an important book called *Disorders of Sexual Desire.*

Q: "What about hormone injections for someone who isn't interested in sex?"

A: "Men who show low levels of testosterone are sometimes given injections of that hormone and they appear to help. Sexual desire may be increased and so may the volume of semen. In women, testosterone may also increase sexual desire and may lead to an increase in clitoral size.

"However, lack of interest in sex is not necessarily related to a shortage of hormones. Usually, it is the result of a complex interaction of emotional factors that must be understood by a professional before treatment of any kind is begun."

Q: "I keep hearing about different foods and drinks and drugs that increase desire. Which ones work?"

A: "None of them. There is nothing you can take into your body that will increase the real level of libido. If however you believe that something will have that effect, you may be more active in your responses — or think you are. Desire and response is such a complex interaction of physical and psychological aspects that what you think is happening may be almost as influential on the outcome as the actual physical response to stimulation. That is why drugs such as alcohol are believed to be particularly effective in stimulating desire. In fact they make no difference physiologically (unless taken in large quantities, when they have a sedative effect) but they can reduce inhibitions. Their influence is almost entirely psychological."

Excitement. Several bodily changes happen as desire develops into excitement. The most obvious is that extra blood accumulates rapidly in the genital area in both men and women. This is called vasocongestion.

Vasocongestion in men shows as erection of the penis. As blood flows into the spongy tissue of the penis it swells. How quickly it does so and whether the penis reaches its maximum possible size depend on the nature and intensity of the stimulation and on the man's age (erection usually comes more slowly in older men).

Vasocongestion in women shows as vaginal lubrication: the vagina becomes moist. What happens is that blood flows into the vaginal area and the pressure of it forces natural tissue fluid through the walls of the vagina. Moisture is also secreted from the cervical area. The vagina is then ready to accommodate a penis if intercourse is to follow. Lubrication can take 20 to 30 seconds, but the time depends very much on the nature and intensity of the stimulation.

Touch, smell, sight, fantasy all stimulate both sexes; how quickly people respond depends on how they are feeling and on circumstances as well as on how intense the stimulus is. Another general response that applies to women and men both is an involuntary tensing of the muscles throughout the body. It diminishes after orgasm, which is why people feel relaxed after they have come, and then disappears.

There are several other important bodily changes in this phase, affecting women more than men. Both sexes experience nipple erection, in which the nipples become firmer and stand out more, but it is more common and more obvious in women. The dark area surrounding women's nipples (the areola) becomes darker and their breasts, especially if they have not breastfed a child, increase in size.

As sexual tension mounts, the pulse rate and blood pressure go up in both women and men. At this stage the sex flush is likely to appear in many women. This looks like a rash and usually appears first on the upper portion of the stomach and then spreads to the breast area. It is liable to be patchy and may spread to the back as well. Some men show a sex flush too, though it is likely to be less marked.

A reaction that is wholly female is the sex skin colour change. As the labia swell from vasocongestion, their colour changes. The inner labia of women who have had children change from red to deep wine, and those of women who have not go from pink to bright red. Once the labia have changed colour the woman will have an orgasm if stimulation continues.

Two other important changes happen to women in these last stages of the excitement phase: the vagina lengthens and widens, and the clitoris retracts under its hood. People sometimes get anxious that the clitoris should disappear at this critical moment but they shouldn't. It is natural reaction and it is a good sign, for orgasm is very close.

By the end of the excitement phase both men and women are full of sexual tension and feel that just a very little more stimulation will tip them over the top and they will have an orgasm. Masters and Johnson called this part of the excitement phase the plateau.

Orgasm. Just before orgasm, the pulse rate, blood pressure and breathing rate are at their peaks; many muscles are tensed. What then triggers orgasm is not quite certain. It appears to be a complex interaction of physical, emotional, social and hormonal factors, and there may be others as yet undetermined. Eventually the brain signals spinal cord centres and their reflexes set off orgasm.

When a woman has an orgasm, her uterus and the outer third of her vagina both go into a series of rapid contractions. There may be just a few or as many as 15, and they occur at intervals of less than a second.

The male orgasm divides into two stages. The first is a feeling of inevitability, caused by the semen pooled at the entrance to the urethra. At this point the man knows he cannot help coming. Very quickly thereafter he has a series of contractions of the ejaculatory ducts and the muscles around the penis which causes the semen to be ejaculated. The process takes only a few seconds and the intensity of the contractions decreases after the first few spurts of semen have left the body.

No-one has yet succeeded in describing properly the sensations of orgasm. The pleasure is so intense that it seems there are no words subtle or strong enough to describe it.

The last part of the orgasm phase is called resolution. In women it means a gradual return to normal of pulse, blood pressure and breathing rate; the labia return to their normal colour, the sex flush fades away and the nipples lose their erection. The vagina also returns to its normal size.

In men, resolution means loss of erection and a gradual return of the penis to its normal flaccid state. Any skin flush and nipple erection will also disappear.

Whereas a woman who is in the early part of the resolution stage can have orgasm again if she wants it, a man can not. He has to go through a "refractory period," during which he is unlikely to be able to get an

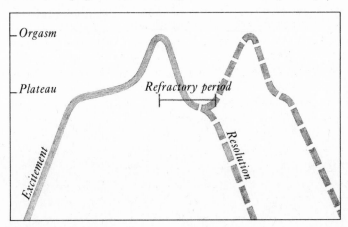

The sexual response cycle of men. A man rises to the plateau phase and then to orgasm, but cannot proceed to a second orgasm until he has gone through the necessary refractory period. The duration of the refractory period depends particularly upon the man's age.

erection, let alone maintain it. The refractory period may be a matter of minutes or of hours, with the general rule that the older a man is, the longer it will take. Women, however, can carry on and with the right stimulation achieve repeated orgasms.

Q: "How did Masters and Johnson study the sex responses of men and women?"

A: "Masters and Johnson studied 382 women and 312 men between the ages of 18 and 89 for more than ten years. During that time, they recorded and analyzed more than 10,000 orgasms achieved by heterosexual intercourse, mutual masturbation and self-masturbation. The subjects were all volunteers and were paid for their participation. During their sexual activity the men and women were monitored and filmed by very sensitive medical equipment. For example, a number of women inserted in their vaginas a clear plastic penis containing a tiny camera so a film could be made of the changes that were going on inside them. Men were filmed as they were being stimulated and getting erections. These and other experiments were repeated thousands of times to give Masters and Johnson adequate data to make generalizations about how men and women respond."

Q: "What does multiple orgasm in women mean? And, if it means what I think it does, can I have them?"

A: "Multiple orgasm means having several orgasms within a short period. Every woman has the physical capacity, though each individual woman may experience multiple orgasm frequently, occasionally or never. It all depends upon appropriate continuing stimulation after the first orgasm. Once you know you can experience multiple orgasm it becomes easier to do so.

"Women who have multiple orgasms are not 'abnormal' or 'nymphomaniacs.'"

Q: "Do men have multiple orgasms too?"

A: "No, not usually. However in 1978 two researchers in California, Dr Mina Robbins and Dr Gordon Jensen, reported on their

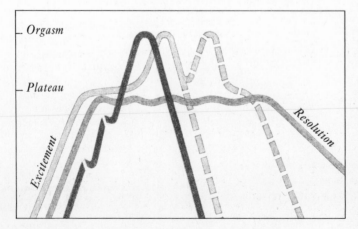

Women's sexual response: the pale line shows a smooth rise to a plateau and then to orgasm, with the possibility of going on to a second orgasm or into resolution; the medium line shows a woman not experiencing orgasm, and the dark line shows an uneven progression directly to orgasm.

work with 13 men who had multiple orgasms. These men reported they had learned how to control ejaculation so they would only ejaculate after having a series of orgasms. Robbins and Jensen believe men can be taught to control ejaculation and experience several orgasms, and further, they suggest that the reason most men don't is that they've grown up with the idea that they can't. Our culture says men can have only one orgasm at a time. More work needs to be done to validate Robbins and Jensen's theory."

Q: "Do women ejaculate like men?"
A: "No, but two American researchers, John Perry and Beverly Whipple, have film evidence that some women in a study they conducted released fluid from the urethra during orgasm. The fluid was analyzed: it was not urine but a substance resembling male semen without sperm.

"They are now carrying out further research on the source of the fluid and the relationship between its presence and certain kinds of orgasmic contraction. If their studies withstand the scrutiny such claims produce, we will hear a great deal more about this interesting phenomenon."

Q: "When I have an orgasm it feels good and I enjoy it, but it certainly doesn't feel anything like those I read about in magazines and books. Should I seek some professional help?"
A: "No. Most literature describing orgasm sets up unrealistic standards and expectations. We get images of unbelievably explosive orgasms, measure our own experiences against them and conclude that ours are nowhere near the 'ideal.'

"The important thing to remember about *your* sex life is that it should be fulfilling for *you* and *your partner*. Your sexual feelings are unique and so are your partner's. The way you respond to each other is unique too. Descriptions of orgasms you read may well be idealized, and even if they are truthful, they are someone else's experience, which can never be the same as your own. Trying to match your feelings with accounts of other people's can only interfere with your enjoyment."

MYTHS There are more false notions current about the way we respond sexually than in most other areas of sexuality. These are some of the common ones:

* mutual orgasm is the ideal for each couple
* lack of multiple orgasms is a sign of a sexual problem
* as men and women age they usually lose their desire for sex
* if a person desires more than one orgasm during a sex act they are probably oversexed
* hormone injections are usually given to people with sexual difficulties
* a few drinks and a relaxing setting will take care of any problems with sexual desire in both men and women

* couples should work at getting their sexual response cycles identical
* orgasm is necessary for sexual satisfaction
* nongenital sexual acts do not produce as much excitement and satisfaction as genital acts
* in general women and men understand their sexual response cycles
* proper orgasms are explosive feelings
* stopping or slowing down during intercourse can lead to serious health problems
* during menopause women do not usually reach orgasm.

AGE The ability to respond sexually continues until death. So does the ability to enjoy sex.

Those two facts are far more important than the effects that aging has on people's sexual responses, but there are effects nonetheless. They vary enormously from person to person, so the number of years a person has lived is a very poor predictor of their sexual responses and behaviour.

For many elderly people the death of a spouse, for example, can mean the end of active sexual expression, but this need not be the case. Health, too, is very important — a number of chronic illnesses are often accompanied by reduced sexual activity, even though the potential for response is still there and functioning. It seems that the most important predictor of how people will behave sexually in their later years is how they behaved when they were younger. If they had an active, fulfilling sex life through their earlier years they are likely to continue it through middle age and after.

But as you would expect, the physical changes of aging affect sexual responses to some degree in most people. These are the ways in which most people change.

Men. A middle-aged or elderly man takes longer to get an erection, and to attain it he probably needs more direct stimulation of his penis. On the other hand, having got an erection he is likely to be able to sustain it longer. Once he loses an erection, after ejaculation or otherwise, it will take him longer to get another.

Aging tends to reduce both the force of ejaculation and the intensity of orgasmic sensation. It seems also that the need to ejaculate with each and every erection also diminishes. The satisfaction and fulfilment that come with orgasm remain just as important however. The volume of semen ejaculated is less, it contains fewer sperm and fewer of those sperm are able to fertilize an ovum. However, a man will still be ejaculating so many sperm, and so many of them will be healthy, that at any age he will still be entirely capable of causing a pregnancy. Male hormone (testosterone) levels do not reduce significantly until a man is into his 60s and 70s. Even then, they are unlikely to fall so low that he loses either his desire or his potency.

The biggest sexual problem that many men experience with aging is that they don't accept natural physical changes. Rather than accept slower erection, slower recovery and reduced ejaculation they sometimes avoid sex altogether, denying themselves and their partners fulfilment. This is pointless and may be psychologically damaging. Sexual satisfaction at any age depends upon your acceptance of your own desires, needs and abilities.

Women. As women approach menopause (see pages 36-39) and their later years their ovaries produce gradually less oestrogen. After menopause, they produce very small amounts indeed, but some comes from the adrenal glands. This reduction in hormone output has several physical effects. However, orgasmic fulfilment remains the same, the capacity for multiple orgasm is unchanged, and the clitoris remains as sensitive as ever.

The physical changes are these: when the woman is stimulated, her vagina takes longer to become lubricated than it used to. Orgasmic contractions are fewer in number and so the duration of each orgasm is reduced. The general muscle tension that goes with being sexually excited, also reduces, and following orgasm the body returns more rapidly to its unstimulated state than formerly. Another effect of the reduced hormone supply is that the labia and vagina thin out — they don't swell up as much as they used to under stimulation — and so intercourse can sometimes be painful. A safe lubricant like K-Y Jelly takes care of this problem though.

The psychological or emotional problems that women may have with sex in their later years tend to concentrate around menopause, when fairly rapid changes occur in sexual responses. Once that sometimes difficult period is passed the responses of most women remain relatively unchanged and the potential for fulfilment and pleasure is as great as ever.

> **Q:** "I know a couple in their 70s who say they still have sex like they always did. Can this be true or is it a bit of wishful thinking?"
>
> **A:** "It can most certainly be true. It is perfectly possible for them to have intercourse as frequently and as pleasurably as they always did. When a partner is available and interested, and when physical and emotional well being are maintained, age makes very little difference to sexual desire and activity.
>
> "Research continually confirms that the best predictor of an active, happy sex life in later years is an active, happy sex life in earlier years."

RELATIONSHIPS The majority of couples do not have simultaneous orgasm, nor is it necessary that they should. However, during the sex act each person has the right to be fulfilled and each has the responsibility to help create a climate in which that can occur. Knowing what is happening in your own body and in your partner's can help you both to express your own feelings and to provide the stimulation your partner requires to ensure a complete response.

Ignorance, fear of inadequacy and selfishness frequently contribute to unsatisfactory sexual experiences. It is not uncommon for men to move rapidly through their excitation phase to orgasm. After orgasm many men reduce the stimulation they are providing, or they sometimes end the experience altogether, leaving the woman in the excitement or plateau phase and sometimes feeling frustrated and angry about what has happened. Recently women have begun to express their dissatisfaction with this situation; they too would like to arrive at a point where they are adequately satisfied. Some men are upset by such expressions of frustration, but ultimately they get the message and become more sensitive partners.

In the past — and for some women even today — sexual acts produce considerable discomfort due to chronic pelvic congestion. This is the result of diminished stimulation or no stimulation at all once the woman is highly excited and moving toward orgasm. The actual physical discomfort combined with the feelings of frustration in this situation sometimes lead women consciously or unconsciously to avoid sex. This results in some cases in the woman's partner accusing her of being "frigid" or of having another sexual partner. Counselling has often been of considerable help in such cases. Information about men's and women's sex response cycles, decisions about one's responsibilities to oneself and to one's partner, and suggestions on ways to change have resulted in many improved sexual relationships. Usually called therapy, much of this assistance is really educational in nature, but the new, enlarged understanding has a therapeutic impact on the couple.

Q: "After several years I finally told my lover that I just wasn't satisfied with our sex life. I'm getting the silent treatment now and I wonder if I did the right thing?"

A: "It is important that you should have an understanding with your partner about your needs. Expressing dissatisfaction with a sexual relationship that has been going on for a long time is especially difficult because it calls into question the quality of the relationship from the beginning. Your lover may find it hard to believe that all the time it has been unsatisfactory.

"Continue the dialogue in a sensitive way. Reach out to your partner, and be sure you discuss the strengths and positive aspects of your sex life. Working at your sexual relationship in a constructive way will eventually overcome the sense of inadequacy and vulnerability your lover probably feels now. It is not easy to do what you did, but since you are taking responsibility for yourself I believe you are acting for the best."

Q: "A couple we know always tell us how wonderful their orgasms are now that they are simultaneous. Is it a good idea to follow their method so we can have simultaneous orgasms too?"

A: "No. Working on some sort of routine to achieve simultaneous orgasm is not a good idea. The point of a sexual act with your partner is to express the feelings you have for each other in a way that is enjoyable and satisfying. Trying to time your efforts in some special way removes the spontaneity and creativity from your experience and can easily make each of you a specatator at your own event.

"If you are happy with your sex life as it is, there is no need to try to pattern it after others. They may be trying to express different things in their relationship and their needs are unlike yours and your partner's."

Q: "Ever since my wife told me that having an orgasm each and every time we had sex was not the most important thing for her our sex life changed drastically. I feel more relaxed now and I don't work as hard so that she will have one when I do. She also taught me something about the real meaning of being intimate with someone."

A: "Frequently men and women work so hard at achieving certain sexual levels during their lovemaking that they forget who they are with and why they are there together. When the performance goals are eliminated from lovemaking and couples cease their efforts to have orgasms that resemble seizures some wonderful, exciting experiences result.

"Women and men have been so orgasm-oriented that all the wonderful feelings and meanings of their acts together before and after orgasm get devalued and trivialized. When couples reeducate themselves to appreciate their sexual acts together as total experiences their orgasms become a delightful aspect of a stimulating and enjoyable total sexual act."

Q: "Sometimes I feel like I'm so quick when I have sex with my wife. She doesn't complain or anything like that, but I'm just not sure if it's OK. Is this a common feeling?"

A: "Yes, and too many men and women keep quiet about it. Talk to your wife about how you feel, tell her your concern. What she says may reassure you or it may be helpful in improving the way you relate during sex.

"Silence about this issue is difficult to overcome, but sensitive discussion can ultimately lead to a more satisfying and trusting sexual relationship."

Q: "My lover just won't talk about his sexual feelings and desires. Is that a sign of a problem in our relationship?"

A: "In general, men have been socialized not to express their feelings. Many men believe that discussing their feelings will make them appear inadequate and vulnerable in an area that they feel they should be comfortable in.

"Many men want and need to discuss their sexual feelings, but they have had so little experience in doing so that it is very difficult for them. If you accept and understand that your lover probably has this problem it may make it easier for him to share his thoughts.

"I believe the inability of many men to talk about their sexual feelings is a powerful sociocultural barrier, not a sign of a relationship problem."

PROBLEMS There are problems both of desire and of response, and they affect both men and women, whatever their sexual orientation and whatever their relationship circumstances. Some people are worried that they simply don't want to have sex for long periods at a time and some people want to have sex but either can't or find it difficult.

Problems with both desire and response can arise for numerous reasons. There may be one cause of a particular condition or there may be a number. Some problems may be rooted within an individual and others may be the individual's response to something that is wrong in his or her relationship. Because of the complexity of this area it is possible here only to illustrate the kinds of problem that exist, not to discuss them in detail.

One caution: because so many factors can influence desire or response, it is always better to seek help from a qualified professional. Self-treatment is not usually appropriate.

Q: "Is it true that most couples have some sexual problems?"

A: "No-one really knows for sure, but Masters and Johnson have speculated that about 50 percent of American couples have some sexual problem.

"Whether or not they have serious problems, it is clear to me that most couples have questions about their sexuality in general and their sexual expression in particular, and I believe answers to these questions would significantly enhance their sexual fulfilment."

Q: "What problems do sex therapists deal with best?"

A: "In general, qualified sex therapists who have a thorough background in psychotherapy can deal with the whole range of sexual problems and personal and relationship difficulties. For this reason it is desirable to seek sex therapy services from individuals with broad psychotherapy training and skills, as well as a proper background and preparation in sex therapy."

Q: "Is it true that the best sex therapists are medical doctors?"

A: "No. There are therapists who are not doctors who have the proper training and can provide sensitive and ethical sex therapy. The two organizations in the UK who are mainly responsible for running sex clinics are the Family Planning Association and the Marriage Guidance Council. The Marriage Guidance Council, who base their therapy programmes on the Masters and Johnson technique, do, in fact, use lay counsellors rather than doctors. Psychosexual clinics are also run by about 40 NHS hospitals.

"By contacting one of the organizations listed on page 448 you will be able to find a therapist with proper training to meet your needs."

Q: "How helpful are those books that instruct you on overcoming sexual problems?"

A: "In general, I am not enthusiastic about the use of books, tapes and films to deal with specific sexual problems. I believe a trained therapist is necessary to help the person or couple work through personal problems, resistances and relationship issues if the difficulty is to be resolved completely. Sexual problems are frequently linked to personality factors that only an objective and professionally prepared person can deal with properly.

"The self-help movement in health care and in sexuality has led to the publication of some books that have educated people and given them permission to learn about their bodies. This has had a therapeutic impact on some people, but books are unlikely to solve specific sexual problems."

Q: "Is it true that some sex therapists have sex with their patients?"

A: "This practice has occurred on occasion and has been uniformly censured by major therapy and sexology organizations.

"There is no theoretical or practical rationale for this practice. It exploits the patient and compromises the therapeutic relationship. The motives of such activities have never been explained in any fashion that demonstrates that the patient really benefits from the sexual interaction. It is interesting to note that the patients who 'needed' to have sex with their therapist as part of the treatment were generally young women. Older women and men are rarely considered to have the same need!"

Q: "Is the use of sex surrogates helpful or is it really just a fancy name for prostitution?"

A: "Some years ago Masters and Johnson used surrogate sexual partners successfully in certain cases, but for legal and other reasons they have discontinued the practice. In the US other therapists have used and are using trained surrogates, and when they are trained and under the supervision of qualified therapists they appear to have a positive effect in helping overcome sexual problems. Surrogates are used most frequently by therapists when the patient has no partner.

"The use of surrogates is usually not advertised or discussed openly, since in law they might be construed as prostitutes — they are, after all, accepting money for having sex, even though it is in a clearly defined therapeutic context. It is therefore impossible to assess the success of surrogate use. All that one can say at this time is that the welfare and rights of the patient or couple must be safeguarded in all treatment programmes."

Q: "I find that I enjoy sex about once a week. It is satisfying and meets my needs. My partner enjoys sex two or three times a week. Things are starting to get strained. Is it a good idea for me to see a therapist to get myself checked out?"

A: "What are you going to get checked out? You enjoy sex once a week and your partner enjoys it more — that does not mean you have a problem and your partner is normal. More does not mean better or healthier; less is not better or healthier. Why not try to work it out yourselves and negotiate this in the same way you do other things in your relationship? If this does not work out satisfactorily a qualified therapist may well be able to help."

Desire. Both men and women suffer from problems with desire and they probably always have. They used to be written off under the heading of "impotence" or "frigidity," which are really response disorders. More recently, therapists have referred to "lack of sexual arousal" and "inhibited sexual interest." Wider interest was stirred in 1979 when Helen Kaplan published in America her classification of desire problems in *Disorders of Sexual Desire*. Kaplan suggested that perhaps 40 percent of people seeking help for a sexual problem have difficulty with desire rather than with response.

The identification and treatment of desire problems is still far from being fully understood. All we can be sure of is that something activates a turn-off mechanism so that the person no longer experiences desire.

The causes of inhibited sexual desire are still the subject of speculation. Anxiety about sex is one possibility; fear of intimacy, anger with a partner and anxieties about relationships are three more. Any of these may interact and there may be other emotional or psychological factors too. It is possible that organic problems may be wholly or partly responsible as well. Certainly anyone with a desire problem (or a response problem, for that matter) would be well advised to have a thorough checkup.

Treatment for inhibited sexual desire is usually multidimensional. Individual and relationship psychosexual therapy is common. Medication to control anxiety or depression may be indicated. Erotic exercises to be performed at home may be proposed by the therapist — touching, nondemanding pleasuring routines, body image exercises and maybe others too, depending on the person and the relationship. The treatment approach is flexible and tends to integrate a variety of psychotherapeutic methods as indicated, but success rates in treating inhibited sexual desire are apparently lower than with other sexual problems.

Response. Problems of response are generally more easily diagnosed than problems with desire. Some can be treated more successfully too. The most common response problems are:

in men:
Premature Ejaculation
Erectile Difficulty, also called Impotence

in women:
Orgasmic Difficulty
Painful Intercourse
Vaginismus

and they are discussed in that order.

Premature Ejaculation. The definition of premature ejaculation is particularly difficult and experts differ. Everyone agrees that a man who ejaculates before his penis enters the vagina is premature, but thereafter? Two minutes? Three to five? Ten to 15?

The most useful definition provided to date has been Helen Kaplan's, as elaborated by Michael Perelman and others. They define a premature ejaculator as a man who is unable to recognize that he is almost ready to come and is unable to act in order to delay his orgasm.

Therapists all agree that premature ejaculation is not only one of the most common male sexual disorders but that it can sometimes lead to other problems — questioning of one's masculinity, relationship conflicts, erectile difficulty and inhibition of desire.

It is unfortunate that for many young men in our society speed in sexual experiences seems desirable. You cannot take your time in the back seat of a car in the same way that you can relax at home. If a young man goes to a prostitute, she is likely to want him to complete the act quickly. A boy who feels guilty about masturbating is likely to do it as fast as he can. It is thought by some therapists that this kind of early experience may contribute to the inability to delay ejaculation.

The causes of premature ejaculation are not certain, but they are unlikely to be organic. Psychological factors such as fear of failure or relationship factors such as anger at the partner seem more likely. Therapists conventionally work through individual and relationship problems when they are treating a man for premature ejaculation.

The treatment for premature ejaculation which has proved most successful is that evolved by Dr J. Semens in 1956 and subsequently modified by others. The idea is to make the man more aware of the sensations that precede orgasm. As the man learns to recognize the stages he learns to modify his movements to delay the ejaculatory reflex. Treatments are highly individual and therefore go beyond the scope of this book, but experienced therapists working with willing individuals or couples achieve high success rates in curing premature ejaculation. A cure may be achieved in a few weeks, but is more likely to take a few months of once-a-week sessions.

Q: "Is premature ejaculation similar to retarded ejaculation?"
A: "No. They are at opposite poles. Premature ejaculation is a too rapid ejaculation, whereas retarded ejaculation (also called 'ejaculatory incompetence') is the inability of a man to ejaculate when he would like to.

"Men who suffer from retarded ejaculation may experience it regularly or on occasion; they are usually able to ejaculate during masturbation and often during oral sex, but rarely during intercourse. It is not a common problem, but men with this condition find it extremely frustrating and often humiliating, and their partners frequently experience it as a powerful rejection and as a sign of their own inadequacy."

Q: "What causes retarded ejaculation?"
A: "We don't really know. Overcontrol of and overconcentration on ejaculation may be one answer, and this might be the result of multiple emotional/relationship factors. Some analysts believe that retarded ejaculation may be connected with symbolic castration or an unwillingness on the part of the man to give."

Q: "Can women come too quickly too?"
A: "Coming too quickly is a problem that doesn't appear to affect women often. A woman who feels that she is not having orgasms of appropriate intensity at appropriate times could however probably be helped by a therapist."

Q: "A friend of mine said that I will last longer during intercourse if I apply a special ointment to the head of my penis."

A: "No. Your friend was talking about an anaesthetic cream which is supposed to reduce sensation and thereby delay ejaculation. This is not a proper way to develop control over ejaculation — becoming aware of the sensations is the important thing. Also, such ointments can rub off on the woman's clitoral area, reduce her sensation and diminish her pleasure."

Q: "I heard that it was wise to think about business or something unpleasant if a man feels he is going to come too quickly. Is that a good idea?"

A: "Absolutely not. If a man comes too quickly it is best for him to try to be more aware of what is happening rather than distract himself as you suggest. Ejaculatory control is the result of recognizing the signals of approaching ejaculation and allowing the ejaculation reflex to function only at an appropriate time.

"Getting into the sensations and experiencing them fully produces ejaculatory control — distraction and thinking unpleasant thoughts does not."

Erectile Difficulty. The term "erectile difficulty" has rather taken over from the older word "impotence" for the reason that impotence suggests unconditional failure rather that failure upon occasion. "Erectile problems," "erectile inhibition" and "erectile failure" are alternatives.

Two kinds of erectile difficulty have been identified. A man who has never been able to achieve an erection for intercourse suffers from primary difficulty. A man who has a history of successful erection for intercourse but during a particular period cannot achieve an erection has secondary difficulty. Secondary difficulty is much more common and can be treated more successfully.

Many men experience single instances of erectile failure at some time or another. Fatigue, anxiety, poor health, medication or alcohol may all be responsible. Erectile difficulty should not be considered a significant problem unless it occurs consistently or long enough to cause real stress to the couple or to the man himself.

Erection is an automatic process, a reflex, and therefore not under the man's control. When a man suffers from erectile difficulty, the extra blood that should flow into the penis and engorge it fails to do so, even though the man is excited and stimulated.

The causes of erectile difficulty can be physical, psychological or both. These are some of the more common causes:

Physical (organic) factors

* injury to the spinal cord
* diseases such as diabetes and multiple sclerosis
* effects of drugs like alcohol, heroin and some prescribed drugs
* surgery, such as a prostate cancer operation
* insufficient male hormone.

Psychological (psychogenic) factors

* anger with a partner or other relationship problems causing conflict
* religious belief that sex is sinful, evil, dirty
* fear of castration if sex is attempted
* boredom with sex
* anxiety about not doing well in sex
* unsuccessful previous sexual experiences
* guilt or conflict arising from homosexual experiences.

In the late 1960s, when sex therapy was beginning to be taken seriously, it was believed that very small percentages of erectile difficulty could be attributed to physical factors. However, research and work with patients suggest that many more men have organic reasons for erectile difficulty than was previously thought, and although psychological factors remain as the likelier causes of impotence, careful medical evaluation must be completed before beginning psychological work with a patient or couple. Research is still under way to determine the full extent of possible physical causes of erectile difficulty.

Masters and Johnson developed a rapid and successful approach to dealing with erectile failure. Subsequently their concept has been varied and elaborated on by others. In outline, Masters and Johnson's approach is to reduce the fear of failure, to direct the couple in therapeutic exercises while at the same time encouraging the development of effective couple communication, and helping reduce any irrational anxiety about sexual expression either of the partners may have.

Masters and Johnson achieve quite high success rates for secondary failure and somewhat less for primary failure. Other therapists report similar success rates. Sometimes success occurs within weeks, but frequently it takes months. Much depends on the willingness of the couple to be open to the therapy, and the extent of complicating personal and relationship issues that must be worked through.

Other therapists have made their own additions and refinements to the basic Masters and Johnson programme. Dr Helen Kaplan, for example, utilizes psychoanalytic concepts, drug therapy and behavioural therapy as well when they are appropriate.

Q: "My husband can't get an erection any more. I know it is just killing him but he won't go for help. What should I do?"

A: "It is natural for men to feel terribly inadequate under these circumstances. The best thing for you to do is to support him and continue to try to get him to go *with you* to see a qualified therapist. In general, erectile failure is seen as a relationship problem even if the man has the most obvious symptom. Perhaps your willingness to play a part in this might at least stimulate him to contact someone for help.

"Sometimes it takes a while before a man will face up to this difficulty. Accumulated frustration may make a man go to a therapist when the simple evidence of the problem is not sufficient to make him do so."

Orgasmic Difficulty. Some women have never had an orgasm, while others used to be orgasmic but no longer are or are so very rarely. Reliable figures are lacking, but it is estimated that about ten percent of adult women have never had an orgasm and about 20 percent have orgasm infrequently. Shere Hite reported in her study of American women that only 30 percent achieve orgasm during intercourse without any additional stimulation.

Failure to achieve orgasm is the most widespread female sexual difficulty. Not only do women thereby lose out on part of the pleasure of sex, but many women experience failure to come as a threat to their self-esteem. They wonder what is "wrong" with them and tense up during intercourse, wondering "Will it happen now?" or "Am I going to come this time?" This tension further inhibits the natural orgasmic release and adds to the problem.

There are numerous possible causes of orgasmic difficulty. Though rare, a physical problem — a neurological, gynaecological or hormonal disorder — may be responsible, but the cause is much more likely to be one (or more than one, in combination) of these common psychological factors:

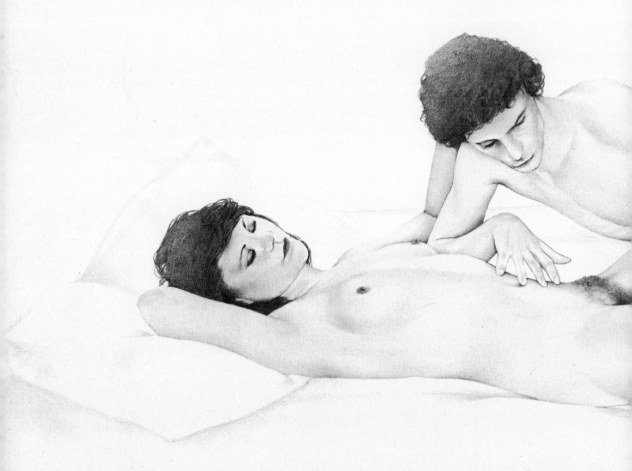

* fear of failure and consequent rejection
* fear of losing control of one's feelings
* fear of the possible intensity of orgasm
* guilt about enjoying sex
* hostility toward the partner
* ignorance of the way the body responds to stimulation
* poor communication with the partner
* being a spectator and waiting for orgasm to happen
* having had a traumatic sexual experience (such as rape)
* early negative conditioning about sex.

It was not until Masters and Johnson's research results were published that comprehensively designed treatment programmes were set up. Until the 1970s, women with orgasmic difficulties frequently sought treatment from psychoanalysts.

The treatment of orgasmic problems in women varies from therapist to therapist and from clinic to clinic. In general the approaches have been: psychotherapy (frequently psychoanalytically oriented); couple therapy (with a sex therapy team or individual therapist); behaviour therapy and various types of masturbation and desensitization exercises; and, more recently, group therapy. More than one of these approaches may be used simultaneously according to the requirements of the case. Women who have never had an orgasm may receive treatment that is quite different

from that undertaken with women who would like to have orgasm during intercourse more frequently but are able to have orgasm during other acts.

Helen Kaplan and her associates in America have developed a very sensible and successful treatment programme for women who do not reach orgasm during intercourse but do so at other times. Throughout, the therapist and couple work on any individual, emotional or relational problems that may exist. At the same time the therapist directs the couple in techniques that are designed to increase general sexual arousal in a nondemanding way.

Q: "I read about women becoming orgasmic through masturbation exercises. Is that accurate?"

A: "Yes. Women can start under guidance to achieve orgasm by masturbation (using a vibrator if required), move on to having their partners masturbate them, and then on to intercourse with additional clitoral stimulation. A programme of this kind set up by LoPiccolo and Lobitz in the US proved quite successful with a small group of women. By the end of the programme the majority were regularly, though not invariably, having orgasm through intercourse."

Q: "What is the story behind these groups where women practise masturbating?"

A: "You are probably referring to a new group treatment started by Lonnie Barbach and Nancy Carlsen in the US in 1972, which has had very high success rates with thousands of women. In this programme, the women do not masturbate in each other's presence — this is done in private by the women alone or with their partners. The exact approach cannot be detailed here but the highlights are as follows:

> * the therapist sees each woman individually and helps design an individual programme of goals
> * sessions are held once a week for ten or 12 weeks with six to eight participants and one therapist
> * women discuss their values and experiences together — sharing, gaining and giving support
> * women learn about their bodies, learn to accept themselves and learn to accept sexual pleasure as a proper expectation
> * myths and misinformation are clarified and cultural beliefs explored
> * the LoPiccolo–Lobitz masturbation programme is assigned to each woman.

Women Discover Orgasm by Lonnie Barbach describes the theory and practice of this important programme."

Q: "I have a terrific relationship with my husband and we enjoy sex. I have orgasm sometimes but I just can't seem to have one during intercourse. I've sought advice, read everything and tried everything but nothing seems to work."

A: "A number of women are unable to have an orgasm during intercourse but can have them at other times with other sorts of stimulation. From your comments about your relationship and your enjoyment of sex, I'd say you are not a failure and you need not be uptight. Your response pattern does not produce orgasm during intercourse, but this is a normal variation in response and should not be devalued. An obsessive concern about orgasm during intercourse is unhelpful to your emotional health and could interfere with what you describe as a terrific relationship."

Q: "I heard that the Kegel exercises can help a woman have an orgasm. Is that true?"

A: "Yes. Kegel exercises (see page 342) help keep the vagina in tone, which in turn improves sensation and can lead to improved orgasmic response."

Painful Intercourse. Painful intercourse, for which the technical name is "dyspareunia," is a problem that does not affect a great number of women. The reasons for it can be either physical or psychological. Physical causes can be such things as: irritations and infections of the vagina, drying of the vaginal tissue, growths in the vagina, structural problems in the pelvic area, and bladder disease. Psychological causes can be equally various: if a woman has been brought up to believe that sex is wrong and will cause pain, she may feel it; painful previous sexual experiences can induce an expectation of pain subsequently; and hidden relationship problems can emerge as pain during intercourse. Any psychological conflict may inhibit or reduce vaginal lubrication, which can result in painful intercourse.

Painful intercourse can usually be treated successfully once the cause has been identified. Organic diseases can usually be dealt with after a thorough gynaecological examination, and psychotherapy and counselling can usually take care of psychological causes.

Vaginismus. Vaginismus is an involuntary spasm of the muscles surrounding the vaginal opening, closing the entrance to the vagina and making intercourse impossible. It is not a very common problem, but it is humiliating and frustrating for women; their partners frequently feel rejected and inadequate.

Vaginismus can be caused by a variety of factors, including strong religious beliefs about sex being sinful, prior physical or emotional trauma related to intercourse, and physical pain during intercourse which produces vaginismus as a secondary response. Some women who suffer from vaginismus are able to enjoy other sexual activities and have orgasm, but become phobic in response to suggestions of intercourse.

The treatment of vaginismus is very often highly successful. The treatment approach is to deal with the emotional factors that are producing the spasm unless there is an organic disorder to which vaginismus is a secondary response. Time is spent demonstrating that the spasm is involuntary and real, but that it is not the partner's fault.

DISABILITY

FACTS Everyone is sexual and has a right to express his or her sexuality. That goes for people who are physically or mentally disabled just as much as for those who have no handicap. For too long people with a physical or mental handicap have been further handicapped by societal attitudes that said they should not expect and could not have a satisfactory sex life. This has applied to people born with a disability as well as to those whose disability occurred later in life.

This attitude has several sources. Health-care personnel have often fostered it and sometimes disabled people themselves have created barriers limiting their own sexual potential. Fortunately, attitudes are changing. While the facts on every type of disabling disease and condition and their effects on sexual functioning are not yet fully researched and understood, it is gratifying to see that disabled people's sexuality and sexual rights are now being recognized. Of great importance here is the recognition that sexual interest is best expressed when the other dimensions of personality are functioning properly. More professional attention is being paid to sexuality within the context of an integrated approach to disabled people's difficulties.

These are some of the advances which we should aim to make in the area of sexual health and the disabled:

* childhood and adolescent sexuality should become a more central concern of parents, teachers, health practitioners, and society in general; body exploration, touching, fondling, masturbation and the whole range of sensual and sexual experiences should be accepted as normal and natural for the disabled young person as well as for those who are not disabled; issues of sexual identity and gender role are important in both general health care and in the socialization of disabled young people
* programmes in sexuality for the visually impaired and deaf should be given more prominence in schools, residential treatment centres and training centres; parents could often be involved in these programmes so they can overcome their own handicapping attitudes and learn to help the deaf and visually impaired to express their sexuality
* the sexuality of mentally handicapped men and women, young and old, has become the subject of an important educational and social initiative; many new publications reflect this important advance; issues like self-understanding, relationships, marriage, parenthood, birth control and abortion are being addressed more thoughtfully and seriously than ever before; the mentally retarded are being recognized as sexual just like everyone else, as maturing physically at the same rate and with the same sexual drive as those who are not retarded; such advances should be emulated
* multiple sclerosis sufferers should be encouraged to explore new ways of achieving sexual satisfaction; men and women with MS and many health-care personnel are working toward reducing the fears and

anxieties that form barriers preventing those with the disease from dealing with their sexual lives and relationships with realism and understanding

* sexual behaviour after a heart attack can be resumed gradually along with other activities unless specific problems lead doctors to order restrictions; unless cardiac disease is severe, the full range of sexual expressions is available to sufferers; even if limits have to be imposed, there are alternative, less stressful sexual activities than intercourse that can be enjoyed
* privacy for the handicapped must be recognized as a right, especially in residential treatment settings
* young people and adults with cerebral palsy should be encouraged by parents, teachers, health-care workers and society to meet, mate and form lasting relationships like others in the community; the problems caused by spasms will be overcome by exploring alternative positions and a variety of sexual activities
* the limits on movement that the pain of arthritis had dictated can be combated by discussion, teaching and a new literature describing positions, techniques and ways of giving and getting pleasure
* a greater understanding of colostomy, ileostomy and urostomy and their effects on sexual functioning has reduced fear and helped many men and women resume their sex lives in fulfilling ways
* as the sexual needs of disabled people are more fully recognized, health-care facilities should be extended to singles and gays; it isn't only in marriage that the sexuality of the disabled is a central issue.

The range of physical and mental disabilities is so great that it would take an entire book to describe them. Even then, the degree to which an individual is affected will modify any general statements, as will the progress of the disease if it is progressive and the readiness and ability of the person to adapt. But to get some idea of how a disability can affect sexual expression and of how its effects can be met by resourcefulness and appropriate care let us look at one fairly common physical disability — spinal cord injury — and then at a fairly common mental disability — retardation.

Spinal Cord Injury. An injury to the spinal cord due to accident, disease or congenital defect can be complete or incomplete. The injury can be high, low or at mid-level on the spine and can interrupt all or some of the continuity of the nerves. Although a thorough evaluation of the injury and its relationship to physical sexual function is important and helpful, the effects of spinal cord injury are unpredictable, vary from case to case, and even change from time to time in the same person.

In men, spinal cord injury may interfere with the ability to have an erection in the usual way. However, a reflex erection caused by direct stimulation of areas around the penis is possible for some paraplegics and quadraplegics. Body movements, positions and room temperature all may be important in determining whether a reflex erection will occur. Practice helps develop the proper technique and some doctors and health-care workers knowledgeable about sexual functioning and disability will discuss this with a man and his partner. Psychogenic erections resulting from sight, sound or smell stimuli, also occur in men with spinal cord injury. The nervous system pathways that make this type of erection possible are not fully understood.

Some men's injuries prevent them from ever getting an erection, but they can have intercourse by the "stuffing" technique. In this method, the man stuffs his penis in his partner's vagina while in the man-on-top position. His partner, using proper hip movement and vaginal muscle control (see KEGEL EXERCISES, page 342) can keep the penis in the vagina and both can achieve pleasure. If the man cannot manoeuvre into an on-top position, stuffing can be achieved with the woman straddling him and getting the penis into the vagina that way. Side-by-side and front-to-back are among the other positions commonly used by disabled men and women. Urine collection apparatus may interfere in some of these positions but that can be overcome by patience and willingness to try new things together. Movements, positions, techniques and the use of the hands and mouth are not classified into right and wrong.

Orgasm is possible and is most frequently reported by men with incomplete lower lesions. Ejaculation is also most common among men with this type of disability. Psychological stimulation (fantasy) has produced orgasm among some disabled men, so direct genital stimulation is not essential.

Having intercourse is a problem for women with spinal cord injuries.The nature of the problem varies from woman to woman, but it is not insurmountable. Sometimes the disability prevents natural vaginal lubrication from occurring but using a lubricant like K-Y Jelly, which can be purchased from a chemist, will overcome that. Keeping the vagina lubricated throughout intercourse prevents irritation of the vaginal tissue (which some women do not feel because of their disability). Various positions can be used, according to movement ability, dealing with apparatus (such as a urine collection device), and how best to reduce the chances of spasm during lovemaking. Water beds are popular with some disabled women and men because they provide easy motion for the couple which makes their lovemaking more pleasurable.

The quality of orgasm in women may vary according to the physical and emotional effects of the disability. Some women believe that the loss of sensation around their genitals prevents them from having an orgasm. This is not true, as it is possible for disabled women to have orgasm not only by physical contact as in intercourse but through breast stimulation, anal stimulation and fantasy. Touching, caressing, cuddling and many other nongenital acts are largely unexplored areas which have enormous potential for producing intensely satisfying erotic and sexual experiences.

Q: "Do spinal cord injured women menstruate?"
A: "Yes. A spinal cord injury usually does not interfere with hormone production so menstruation occurs as usual. Sometimes the menstrual flow is interrupted for several months right after a disabling spinal cord injury occurs, but it will usually resume."

Q: "Is it true that spinal cord injured women can get pregnant and have a baby?"

A: "Absolutely, yes, and they can breastfeed their babies as well. Specially trained doctors help disabled women through the birth process since there are some unusual aspects of this type of birth. Labour pains may not be felt, for example, and bearing down during labour is difficult, if not impossible, for many women with spinal cord injury. Caesarean deliveries are as common among women with spinal cord injury as they are among the rest of the female population.

"It follows then, that spinal cord injured women need birth control, can have abortions and can get and spread sexually transmitted diseases like the rest of the sexually active population."

Q: "Can a man with a spinal cord disability ever have a natural baby?"

A: "Yes. Some men with spinal cord disability have only limited problems with erection, ejaculation, orgasm and sperm production and some can have natural children. Other men with that kind of disability have difficulties with their fertility due to changing temperatures in the scrotum, frequent urinary infections and inflammation of the epididymes, all of which can reduce the sperm-producing powers of the testicles. After a while these factors can lead to sterility. Some men with spinal cord injuries will be sterile for another reason — that they ejaculate backwards, into the bladder rather than out of the penis.

"Efforts by doctors to make semen leave the penis by using electrical stimulation on the genitals have been successful in some cases. The semen is collected in a sterile container and then placed in the wife's uterus by artificial insemination. Normal pregnancy and birth is not unusual if the semen is healthy."

Q: "Can a person in a wheelchair have an orgasm?"

A: "Yes. Some people confined to wheelchairs can have orgasm, especially if their injury does not interfere with the reflex that triggers it.

"However, even people whose injuries prevent their feeling orgasm can recollect the feelings they once had and in the proper circumstances can have intense mental orgasmic experiences.

"It is also important to note that physical orgasm is not necessary for sexual pleasure, as many men and women have discovered whether or not they were disabled."

Q: "So there really is such a thing as mental orgasm?"

A: "Yes. Some disabled men and women have described peak feelings during sexual activity of various kinds, including fantasy. This type of orgasmic experience is probably unlike the orgasm they had before their disability but it is another example of the possibilities for pleasure people have despite the appearance of limited potential."

Q: "But what about those who never had an orgasm before they were injured?"
A: "Reports from some men and women who never had an orgasm before they were disabled indicate they can fantasize what the feelings are like and under the right circumstances can experience them."

Q: "Is it true that some disabled men use a penis stiffener for intercourse?"
A: "Yes. If a man can never get an erection or cannot get one when he wants, a penis stiffener or dildo can be used.

"One type of penis stiffener requires surgery in which a medically safe substance is inserted, making the penis firm enough for intercourse. People who request this kind of implant are usually evaluated psychologically as well as physically before the surgery. Another type of stiffener is a hollow, penislike form into which the disabled man slips his penis. It has a waist belt which holds it in place during intercourse.

"Sometimes a plastic penis called a dildo is inserted into the woman's vagina to provide her with the sensation of a penis."

Q: "Can a person with a colostomy still have sexual intercourse?"
A: "Yes. Men and women with colostomies or urostomies have intercourse. The size and location of the collection point will determine the best position for each couple. Movements during intercourse usually do not adversely affect the attachment.

"People with ostomies naturally pay special attention to cleanliness and emptying the collection pouch when preparing to make love, but otherwise they can continue normally once the couple has understood and accepted the ostomy."

Mental Retardation. Mentally retarded people have sexual needs, feelings and potentials just like everyone else. Their sexuality as such is not related to their mental ability or IQ level, but their sexual expression is often severely limited by what they are taught and what they pick up from their social environment.

Warren Johnson, an American pioneer in sex education for the retarded, has observed that the usual attitude people take toward sexual expression among retarded people is elimination if possible and control if not. This attitude used to manifest itself particularly clearly in the sterilization of mentally retarded people, a practice that used to be widespread. The control element is still active, although it is subject to numerous powerful challenges.

No-one wants to push mentally retarded people into forms of sexual expression that they find inappropriate or unwelcome. On the other hand, we have to bear it in mind that if we stay with the dominant social attitude — that sexual expression and mental retardation don't mix — we will continue to deny disabled people a natural, legitimate source of pleasure and growing self-esteem. The problem, of course, particularly with profoundly retarded people, is to guide their understanding so that their sexual expression is positive and enjoyable rather than negative and humiliating.

Q: "Don't retarded people frequently do things sexually to others and to themselves at very inappropriate times?"

A: "Usually not. Most retarded people can be taught how to express their sexual feelings in ways that are appropriate both for themselves and for others around them. Through patience and understanding retarded men and women can learn to manage their impulses in keeping with what is generally regarded as socially acceptable."

Q: "I heard that retarded people masturbate uncontrollably. Is that true?"

A: "No. There is no evidence that retarded people masturbate more than others. What you heard may come from the written reports of years ago describing residential treatment centres for the retarded where staff observed men and women masturbating. This quickly became seen as a sign of mental illness and helped spread the idea that masturbation led to mental problems. Some were able to get attention drawn to themselves by masturbating. Others found a brief but valued pleasure in their own bodies that was very important to them and brought them back to the activity frequently.

"What has been learned rather convincingly of late is that patients in such treatment centres require recognition of their value as people with a right to pleasure. Of course they will continue to masturbate, but the compelling need to do so can be overcome by acquiring skills in activities and in interacting with other people. As a sense of self-worth is developed, along with it come many other sources of pleasure and self-affirmation."

Q: "Can mentally retarded people be sterilized compulsorily?"

A: "In the UK there is considerable confusion due to unclear legislation. Under the Mental Health Act 1959 there are two classes of patient: voluntary and compulsorily detained. The voluntary or 'informal' patient retains the ordinary citizen's right to refuse any treatment with which he or she disagrees. For the compulsorily detained patient the hospital authorities may assume the right to any treatment they think appropriate. The Mental Health Act does not state whether a compulsorily detained person has the right to withhold consent. However, if a detained patient develops a condition unrelated to a mental disorder then only treatment necessary to preserve life and health should be given without consent. Many civil liberties groups are greatly concerned at the increased risk of abuse because of the legal vagueness surrounding the subject.

"In the US there is similar confusion and until the Supreme Court gives a ruling some states are still free to sterilize patients if they are retarded and wards of the state."

Q: "I heard that homosexuality is very widespread in mental institutions? Is that true?"

A: "Mental institutions do not change a person's sexual orientation and there is no evidence that mentally retarded people are particularly likely to be homosexual. Homosexuality in mental institutions is the same as that occurring in any institution where the sexes are segregated: people's needs for human contact and sexual release are such that they engage in homosexual acts even though they may be fully heterosexual in their orientation."

Q: "Can mentally retarded people get married?"

A: "Yes. Some do and have fulfilling lives together. There are some legal inhibitions on doing so, but the actual effect of these provisions has been very minor.

    "The opinions of the professionals who study mental retardation are shifting toward a more supportive attitude for those mentally retarded people who can carry on a relationship and help themselves by getting married. Retarded people who marry tend to feel more useful, more independent, generally happier, cheerier, and more likely to contribute to society rather than be dependent on it.

    "However, marriage for the mentally retarded cannot be glorified as the answer to the real problems of the retarded. The very special demands of marriage combined with the deficiencies of their disability can make it a very difficult situation and produce disillusionment and problems.

    "One of the reasons the retarded have difficulties in developing and maintaining relationships is that in childhood and adolescence they are frequently protected from involvements with others; they therefore have had little chance to experience communicating with others and learning how to give and share."

Q: "What is the current thinking on a mentally retarded couple having a child?"

A: "This is a complex and highly emotional issue. It is generally agreed that parenthood is an emotionally and financially demanding, time-consuming, and sometimes frustrating experience for anyone. Couple this with the demands of providing a stimulating home environment for the child to live in, the need for parents to be effective in the school and community affairs of their children and the need for them to be able to deal with routine difficulties and emergencies, and the prospects of many mentally retarded people making satisfactory parents are clearly limited. Being realistic, most experts believe that it is unreasonable and improper to encourage a retarded couple to have children. At the same time, experts do not advocate mandatory sterilization but encourage the use of simple contraception. For those who can understand what sterilization means and can consent fully, that procedure is safe and effective."

Q: "Can retarded people use contraceptives properly?"

A: "Yes. Mildly retarded men and women can be taught to use contraceptives effectively. Obviously, their level of intelligence, their motivation and the counsel and support of an interested adult are all important factors in predicting how successful they will be.

   "Some professionals in the field are in favour of using methods which do not require constant attention or know-how. They see methods like long-acting injectable contraceptives (if approved and if all side-effects can be overcome) and other similar advances as the most desirable as these would obviously reduce the need for continuous supervision."

Q: "Can the sterilization of retarded children be regarded as an acceptable practice?"

A: "Opinions on this highly emotive issue are strongly divergent. On the one hand there are groups in the UK (such as Sexual Problems of the Disabled, for example) and the US who consider the idea of such sterilization as a gross violation of the basic human rights of the retarded which, once undertaken, could be applied to other 'unacceptable' minorities within our society. On the other hand, there are those who take what one could call a more 'pragmatic' view. This is however a complex and controversial issue, in which the basic human rights of mentally retarded individuals must be considered first and not automatically made subservient to the convenience of society or family. It is exceedingly difficult to ensure that the right decision is made for each individual."

MYTHS Common false beliefs about sex and disability:

* physical or mental disability usually results in loss of sex drive and sexual feelings
* a disabled man cannot ejaculate
* no disabled man or woman can have an orgasm
* disabled women cannot become pregnant and have normal births and normal babies
* loss of sensation in the genital areas leads to loss of sexual feelings
* men and women confined to wheelchairs cannot have intercourse
* mentally retarded people have unusual sex drives
* after a heart attack, sexual activity must be eliminated
* disabled people turn to homosexuality because they cannot get heterosexual partners
* people who are not disabled are attracted to people who are only because they can't find any other partners.

AGE Disability is a difficulty at any age, but it is probably more difficult for a child than for an adult. It is quite common for disabled young people to be raised feeling they have no sexual identity. Concerns about their education and rehabilitation generally dominate the way their parents and teachers relate to them, so the normal issues of developing sexual needs are not addressed. Even though parents and other adults who relate to non-disabled young people often fail to recognize their sexuality properly, they at least make reference to dating, marriage and raising a family; sex is at least implied, albeit at some time in the future. But the parents, teachers and health-care workers of the disabled young person may overlook his or her natural sexual interests and feelings, and act as if he or she is not sexual and will not become so.

Disabled young people can lose out not just in an obvious failure to recognize their sexuality but in the more subtle social ways that adolescents explore the meaning of sexuality. There are of course going to be limitations on how well they can share in all the activities of their contemporaries, but these are limitations, not reasons for exclusion. A young person's social development — which is the background to relating sexually — can be seriously impaired if he or she does not have the opportunity for learning and sharing with contemporaries.

It is true that the needs of disabled young people are such that managing their day-to-day lives can be an overwhelming task, but to ignore their sexuality is to create a framework of frustration and low self-esteem. The disability tends to overshadow everything else, and when these young people become adults they frequently get angry with themselves and resent others for the restricted situation they find themselves in.

If the handicapping attitudes of parents, families, teachers, health-care professionals and society in general are influenced to help disabled young people understand and accept their sexuality as natural, and if they are encouraged to seek and form relationships of their choice, then the next generation of disabled adults will not be faced with quite such a repressive attitude and will have a better chance of expressing an aspect of themselves that may not be impaired at all.

Q: "What about adults who are disabled?"

A: "If they were disabled as children, their problems as adults will be those they could see developing in adolescence. If when they were young their sexuality was ignored and they were made to feel nonsexual, they are certainly going to have difficulties in adjusting to a fulfilling range of sexual activities later on. Some disabled adults respond by limiting or avoiding sexual opportunities, rejecting themselves and approaches to them.

"If the disability occurred in adulthood, the situation is likely to be even more complicated. Feelings of diminished worth can be overwhelming. Partners may respond supportively or anxiously, making it possible to continue the relationship on a revised footing or making it difficult to continue at all.

"Fortunately, a great many disabled people do make a healthy adjustment, whenever their disability occurred and whatever their previous sexual experience. Self-acceptance is the key, because without that there is a reduced chance of acceptance by others. On the other hand, a better understanding on the part of nondisabled people that the disabled have sexual needs just as they do would make that self-acceptance very much easier to achieve."

FEELINGS A great many people with no disability at all have some problems with their body image, with how their bodies seem to them, and with how they believe other people perceive them. It can be a lot harder for disabled people to get their damaged bodies in positive perspective. The sense of mutilation, the feeling of looking grotesque and the general insecurities many disabled women and men have about their appearance greatly inhibit their ability to be self-accepting and self-respecting. Necessarily they often impede the willingness to reach out to others and form worthwhile sexual relationships.

> "When I see myself in the mirror, I just can't imagine how someone would want to be with me. My body is so different now. I feel so unattractive."

> "When my wife is touching my body, I wonder if she is really thinking about me at that moment."

Some disabled people never work out their body image problems. Their self-esteem is low and they shy away from social situations. This withdrawn attitude, coupled with anger and self-pity, leads to a lack of all-round fulfilment. Many disabled women and men, by contrast, learn to overcome the negative feelings associated with being disabled. They accept what they are and who they are and seek to grow and develop in normal, positive ways. As they continue fulfilling lives, their confidence grows along with their sense of independence. They not only feel competent and desirable but because they feel it, other people see them that way too.

Q: "I'm physically disabled and I want to have a sex life. Where do I start?"

A: "With that attitude you have already started! Wanting to have a sex life and wanting to learn what you can do now is a major step in achieving your goal. Understanding first that each physical disability has some unique aspects that can affect your sexual functioning, you can help yourself even more by answering the following questions:

* what has changed about your body and your sensations?
* what is (about) the same?
* what can you still do and feel?
* what is pleasurable?
* what is unpleasant?
* when is lovemaking a problem?
* does your disability interfere with pleasuring yourself? what are the alternatives?
* does your disability interfere with pleasuring your partner? what are the alternatives?
* are you willing to explore new activities and new areas of sensation to replace familiar ones affected by your disability?
* are you prepared to communicate your feelings, needs and concerns to a partner?

RELATIONSHIPS

"I've just become disabled and I'm so concerned about my relationship. We've been happily married for 15 terrific years. Now, I'm worried she is going to leave me."

It is not unusual for feelings like this to surface after a disability. The dramatic changes disability brings affect every aspect of your life and they can weigh especially heavily on a marriage. Thinking that you are no longer the way you were and therefore have become unattractive and undesirable to your spouse is not an unreasonable reaction. However, many couples in this situation indicate that if they had a well-adjusted, happy marriage prior to the disability they usually find they can continue their relationship happily afterward. Their ability to adjust to the changes produced by a disability depends on how good they were at adjusting before the problem occurred. They go through a period of re-learning and then continue as before.

It has to be recognized, though, that some couples do not survive the occurrence of a major disability. Perhaps they are couples whose relationship was not going to survive anyway, but, to be realistic, the stress that a disability puts on a marriage is the direct cause of some marital breakups, albeit a very small percentage.

Q: "My son is 16 years old and disabled. I think he is flirting with a teenager in our neighbourhood. I'm really worried. It's the first time he has done this."

A: "Hooray for your son! His behaviour with your neighbour is completely natural and means that an important dimension of his personality is flourishing. Although your son is disabled there are more similarities between him and other boys of his age than differences. His flirting behaviour is, I believe, thoroughly healthy and important for his self-esteem and you should support him, not worry about him."

Q: "Now that I'm disabled I wonder if I will be good enough sexually for my husband?"

A: "Chances are that if you and your husband enjoyed each other sexually before your disability, the opportunity is still there.

"Taking as a starting point that you are still whole, still sexual and still capable of giving and getting pleasure, your next step is to take stock of yourself sexually. Determine what has changed or remained the same for you regarding sensation, movements, turn-ons and the like. You may find that your disability interferes with the focus or intensity of previously enjoyable sexual experiences, but this suggests that you should seek to discover new areas of pleasure with your husband and integrate them into your lovemaking. Finding out by experimentation and communication with your partner what is best for both of you will enable you to feel complete in this important area of your relationship. Remember, the possibilities are endless!"

Q: "I still love the man I live with, but ever since he was disabled almost a year ago he's become very withdrawn. We do still have sex occasionally, and it's fine, but it's always my idea. What can I do?"

A: "Two things. You have to help him to realize that his disability extends only in certain directions. Sex apparently isn't one of them. The more you have sex with him, the more he is likely to want it and initiate it.

"The other way you may be able to help him is by encouraging him to go with you for some counselling. The problems you are experiencing are by no means unique; counsellors deal with them every day. Ask your doctor if he can recommend someone to help."

Q: "I've been disabled for several years and my husband had been really good in adjusting and taking care of me. But there are times when I really want sex and he's only concerned with taking care of me. What can I do?"

A: "Nurse and lover are two different roles, and if at any given moment he is in his caring role it may be difficult for him to change immediately. Think of what he is doing and how he's feeling before suggesting sex to him.

"It may be that he is overdoing his function of taking care of you and that he would do well to worry less and make love more. If you really think this is so, tell him very gently and then show him that sex isn't just an occasional need but a positive, building factor in your marriage. Try and encourage him to appreciate once again that the rewards of intimacy are among the most important of all."

DRUGS

A drug is any biologically active substance that affects any organ or tissue. The drugs discussed here are the common ones that may affect sexual responsiveness, arousal, interest, performance, pleasure and frequency of contact.

FACTS The drugs that concern us here fall into four categories, according to whether they are legal, illegal unless prescribed, on or off prescription and whether they have any effect or not.

Legal : alcohol, tobacco (page 124)

Illegal unless prescribed: heroin, marijuana, cocaine, Methadone, barbiturates, amphetamines, Spanish fly, yohimbine, amyl nitrite, hallucinogens (page 127)

On Prescription: drugs to treat high blood pressure, anxiety and psychosis, and depression, as well as hormone injections (page 134)

Aphrodisiacs: there aren't any; alternatively, anything that someone somewhere has consumed in the mistaken belief that it will enhance sexual performance or desire (page 135)

Drugs in the first three categories may all have sexual side effects — indeed, some of them are taken primarily for those side effects; "aphrodisiacs" have no effect, but some people think they do.

Drug use tends to be a private matter, and so does subsequent sexual behaviour. The presence of an observer, or even of recording equipment, could easily distort the user's perception of the effects of a drug and act as a constraint on any ensuing sexual behaviour. Researchers therefore are caught in a trap: do they observe what is happening at the time, aware that their observation is probably distorting the results, or do they rely on people's subjective recollections of what happens to them when they mix drugs and sex? We know that people exaggerate, rationalize and misremember, so neither method is wholly satisfactory.

The relationship between drugs and sex is complicated by a further factor. Because a person used a particular drug and then behaved in a particular way, it does not mean that the drug *caused* that behaviour. There is only an indirect link between drugs and behaviour; there is always a person in between, and we therefore have to consider always each individual person, in context.

These are the variables that need to be allowed for:

The Drug
its chemical makeup
the amount taken

frequency of use
how it is taken (sniffed, drunk, eaten, injected, smoked)
what parts of the body it affects and how

The Person
previous sexual experience
previous experience with drugs
what they expect the drug to do to them
general physical and emotional health
bodily reaction to the chemical

The Setting
what other people expect the drug to do
how appropriate it is to use a drug
how appropriate it is to express sexual feelings
the opportunities available.

With so many variables, it is clearly very difficult to arrive at simple, definitive statements. But research has been done, and we do have a pretty accurate idea about the range of effects of the drugs discussed here.

One more important caution: most of the studies made to date have been of men. As Helen Singer Kaplan explains —

"This is partly due to the fact that the male response is more visible and quantifiable. Erection is certainly more readily studied than lubrication–swelling, and ejaculation is easier to record and measure than the female orgasm."

It is also attributable to the sexual double standard, which has tended to make sexuality the concern of men, not women, and to the fact that there are more reported male drug-users than female. We do not know if the patterns of sex–drug interaction seen in male subjects are true for women as well; we will not know for certain until the experiments are repeated with women.

With more time and more research, the sex–drug relationship will become clearer. But while there are lots more questions than answers, it may be helpful to remember Erich Goode's words:

"Drugs do not act on mindless tissue; their 'effects' are weighed, interpreted, considered, translated, accepted, struggled against, thought about, explained, and woven into certain activities. No drug-taking occurs in a sociocultural vacuum; each of these social processes has an impact on what 'effects' a given drug has, as well as what forms of behaviour follow its ingestion.

"Every drug has a wide range of effects, and each effect touches off a wide range of human reactions. A drug's formal biochemical properties only form a potential. Of the many possible effects that a drug has, or might have, some or one or two may be emphasized by a group or individual taking it. Users may 'attend' to certain effects, while ignoring or discounting others. Users learn to attune their bodies to the specific effects which their social group approves of, and to discount and disregard those that are not 'supposed' to happen. Drug experience is totally dependent on these subcultural and individual conventions."

LEGAL DRUGS:

Alcohol. Alcohol, perhaps better than any other single drug, exemplifies the vast range of possible relationships between chemical use and sexual expression. The effect of alcohol on the central nervous system is that of a depressant. Generally, brain functions are affected first: concentration and judgment are impaired, caution and inhibitions are reduced, self-control is lessened and the senses begin to dull. In greater amounts alcohol is an anaesthetic and reduces sensitivity to pain.

The popular view of alcohol as an aid to seduction is summed up in Ogden Nash's couplet: "Candy is dandy, But liquor is quicker." Indeed, marriage counsellors sometimes recommend the use of small amounts of alcohol to help bring relaxation, to help overcome fear or anxiety and to reduce inhibitions. The emphasis must be on *small*, however. In *Human Sexual Inadequacy*, Masters and Johnson state that the onset of secondary impotence can often be traced to "a specific incident of acute ingestion of alcohol or to a pattern of excessive alcohol intake. . . ." A man who suffers from secondary impotence is one who used to be able to have an erection and sexual intercourse, but has now lost that ability.

The typical case involving alcohol and erection problems begins with a single occurrence of sexual failure after overdrinking. The sedative effect of the drug, possibly coupled with the partner's lack of interest because the man is drunk, results in a failure to achieve erection. The details of sexual interchange may be forgotten by the next morning, but the belief that the man's virility is somehow in question usually remains.

During the next couple of days, the man may mull over the events, and experience a greater than usual preoccupation with his sexual performance. He may well feel a need for reassurance about his virility, and so will probably decide to *prove* to his partner that his one failure was only a fluke — that he is a real man. This time his anxiety gets in the way of his erection and a pattern of erectile failure may begin to be established. The first occasion of impotence came from the effect of the alcohol; thereafter the erection problems come from the anxiety caused by the first failure. Each failure increases the probability that the next occasion will also be a failure.

This is not the only problem that can come from a single incident of overimbibing. Many authorities have noted the increased tendency toward unacceptable sexual acts during intoxication. In *Sex Offenders*, Gebhard *et al.* report on the link between sexual crimes committed in the US and excessive drinking. In addition to those cases in which the offender was drunk, a further three to 15 percent of the cases involved an offender who had been drinking, but not sufficiently to be considered intoxicated.

In contrast, this study revealed that fewer than one percent of the cases of sexual offence involved drugs other than alcohol — 22 out of 2,022 cases. They conclude that ". . . unlike alcohol, [other] drugs are a minor

Offence	Percent with intoxication
Heterosexual aggression	
against children	66.7
against minors	25.0
against women	39.4
Incest	
against children	30.8
against minors	21.2
against adults	20.0
Exhibitionism	30.7
Voyeurism	16.2

factor in the commission of sex offences." A connection between alcohol consumption and sex crimes also comes from several other sources. The Philadelphia Police Department found that alcohol played a role in 217 (34 percent) of the 646 cases of forcible rape they investigated during one year.

Though not documented by specific studies, it is fair to assume consumption of alcohol, especially heavy drinking, may result in unwanted pregnancy and in increased venereal disease. It is charged that under the euphoria of alcohol, judgment is impaired and there may be a decision "to take a chance" without using contraception. The same effect on judgment may make one less selective of a partner or less apt to use prophylactic measures against venereal disease.

The above is all related to sex behaviour influenced by excessive alcohol intake on even a solitary occasion. In addition to the "social drinkers" who are thus at risk, one must consider the alcoholics, of whom there are over $\frac{1}{2}$ million in the UK.

Studies conducted in the UK and abroad all agree on the main theme that alcoholism almost inevitably results in disruption of normal sex life. In a typical report issued in the US, a decided majority of the patients, all of whom were heterosexual alcoholics, showed a diminished interest in heterosexual relationships. Of the 63 men studied, 12 denied all sexual activity and 45 stated that sexual intercourse occurred no more frequently than once every three months. Of 16 women studied, eight denied any heterosexual relations and the rest had frequent sexual intercourse with a variety of partners, but each admitted to an almost complete absence of orgasm. Studies in several New York hospitals suggest that prolonged heavy drinking causes the liver to overproduce an enzyme that destroys the male sex hormone testosterone. This may lead to impotence and perhaps infertility. The trend can be reversed if the subject stops drinking.

Experts estimate that 40 to 60 percent of domestic court cases arise because of excessive drinking by one partner or the other. Alcoholism inevitably has major effects upon the various family members. It can lead to loss of employment too. Recently there has been growing concern about the effects of an alcoholic parent upon children. Exposed to quarrelling when a parent is drunk, their inappropriate or unpredictable behaviour, and possible physical abuse, children of alcoholics may find it more difficult to grow into healthy adults. There may be disturbed development of sex role identity with accompanying difficulty in establishing relationships. In this connection it is estimated that about half of all alcoholics had at least one parent who was alcoholic. It is claimed too that in many instances the wife of an alcoholic is a woman whose father was alcoholic.

While it has long been recognized that alcoholism disrupts all relationships, including sexual ones, too little attention has been paid to the reciprocal effect: that disturbances in sexual relationships contribute to alcoholism (and other drug abuse). Agencies that treat people with sexual problems usually analyze their patients' drinking and drug-use patterns to see if drink or drugs may be affecting their sexual behaviour. By the same token alcoholism rehabilitation centres (and other drug treatment centres) would do well to take a careful sex history of their patients to see if the drug abuse arises in any way from sexual problems. It could well be that in some cases each kind of agency can help the other and treat the cause, rather than the symptom.

As we will see with all other drugs, it is difficult to establish a perfect cause-and-effect relationship between alcohol use and increased or decreased sexual activity. The physiological effects of the drug may directly influence the sexual systems, but there are other factors to be considered. The chronic use of drugs, including alcohol, is frequently associated with poor nutrition, liver disease, and other debilitating conditions, which on their own are sufficient to decrease libido and interfere with sexual functioning.

What all this tells us is that there is no simple, direct relationship between alcohol and sex. A little may have a positive effect; more than a little may have a negative effect; a lot may even be related to committing sexual crimes. We do not know why different amounts affect different people in different ways, but it seems certain that the individual's psychological makeup is an important factor.

Q: "What is foetal alcohol syndrome?"
A: "Foetal alcohol syndrome (FAS) is the name given to a dangerous form of physical and mental disorder affecting babies born to alcoholic women or born to women who are heavy drinkers.

"Mental retardation is probably the chief result of foetal alcohol syndrome, but there are other, less severe, alcohol-related birth defects.

"Of the many problems associated with birth, FAS is one of the few that can be prevented entirely. No pregnant woman should drink heavily on any occasion during her pregnancy."

Tobacco. There is no definitive evidence as yet, but there are strong indicators that heavy smoking is linked to a reduced sperm count; this may lead to infertility. Some men who are heavy smokers also show a reduced sex drive, though it returns to normal if they stop smoking. In both women and men who smoke heavily, nicotine causes blood vessels to constrict and to interfere with the sex response of certain types of erectile tissue.

There is strong evidence that women who smoke heavily while they are pregnant are liable to give birth to babies who are lighter in weight than normal and may suffer the problems of prematurity. Smoking can of course cause all sorts of nonsexual health problems too.

ILLEGAL DRUGS:

Heroin. Heroin is an illegal, powerful narcotic injected into the body. It usually leads to addiction and the use of increasing amounts to obtain pleasure. Heroin is a central nervous system depressant and has a clear effect on sexual interest and desire.

In a retrospective study conducted by the author, Dr G. DeLeon and Dr H. Wexler at a drug treatment centre, 30 male heroin addicts were interviewed individually about their preaddictive and addictive sexual desire and behavioural patterns. The age range of those interviewed was from 17 to 60; the mean was 25. The mean age for first heterosexual intercourse was 14 years, and for the onset of addiction it was 17. These are the results.

In their preaddicted lives 26 (86.6 percent) of the men reported sexual desire as very high or high on a five-point scale (none, low, medium, high, very high), four (13.4 percent) of them reported their sexual desire as being medium. During their addicted lives 24 (80 percent) reported their drive as low, while six (20 percent) reported it to be nonexistent.

After they began to masturbate, the men estimated their average frequency to be twice a week before they were addicted. During their addicted lives 20 (66.7 percent) respondents indicated they did not masturbate at all, while ten (33.3 percent) of the men estimated their masturbatory frequency to be once a month.

All the men indicated that in addition to being noninitiators of intercourse or other sexual activity during their addiction their preference while feeling the effects of the drug was to reduce sensory stimulation, keep interpersonal contacts to the barest minimum and remain as motionless as possible. Every effort was made to protect themselves against anything which would interfere with a total involvement in the experience of the drug. Many of the men reported heroin use protected them against unpleasant, unwanted or difficult-to-handle sexual feelings and they deliberately used it for that purpose.

The findings indicated clearly that during the addiction period the frequency of sexual intercourse and masturbation decreased sharply, sexual drive or desire was for the most part absent, and ejaculation, when intercourse did occur, was almost always delayed. In some cases, ejaculation was not experienced during uninterrupted intercourse for periods in excess of one hour. Some women have reported that they always knew when a lover was using heroin because of his increased holding time during intercourse.

The majority of the information on heroin use and sexual functioning in women concerns menstruation and pregnancy. In general, heroin use in women can cause reproductive problems like cessation of menstruation, cessation of ovulation and sterility. These conditions probably result from heroin's effect on the pituitary and hypothalamus, which control the sex hormones. However, some women do ovulate, and even if they do so irregularly, they can become pregnant, especially since their life-style usually discourages the regular use of contraceptives. Babies born to addicted mothers are addicted themselves and require medical attention.

For women, the effect of heroin use on frequency of intercourse is difficult to determine because prostitution is often used to finance addiction. However, female heroin users do report diminished erotic interest and reduced frequency of orgasm.

Male and female heroin addicts frequently talk about the comparisons between the process of obtaining the drug, its preparation, injection, and experiencing the rush, and the process of foreplay, vaginal penetration, and orgasm. The members of the drug treatment programme with whom interviews were conducted agreed with the analogy, with special emphasis on the relationship between the glamour and drama of making the drug purchase and the process of foreplay.

Marijuana. Opinions about the relationship between marijuana and sexual activity vary more than for any other drug. Opponents accuse marijuana of causing promiscuity, venereal disease, unwanted pregnancy, rape and other sexual crimes. Proponents glorify its ability to enhance all aspects of sex, including frequency of performance, duration of activity, and the quantity and quality of sexual sensations. Dr David Smith writes:

> "With marijuana the time sense is distorted and 'subjective' time seems longer, in which case the pleasure of sexual activity might seem to be prolonged.... If you inquire of couples of whom one is intoxicated and the other is not and get a report separately on the nature of the experience that they have presumably shared, it turns out that they were both present in the same place at the same time, apparently interacting in a fashion that was quite different ... examples are especially those where the male who has been intoxicated with marijuana informs you of how remarkably his prowess was increased. The female, who was not intoxicated, assures you that it was not remarkable at all."

Confusion is generated by researchers who talk about sex and marijuana without specifying the aspect of sexual activity they are discussing.

Erich Goode studied the relationship between marijuana and sexual behaviour. He finds, for example, clear evidence that marijuana users do have intercourse at an earlier age, have it more frequently, and have it with a greater number of partners than nonusers do. However, he rejects the conclusion that marijuana use *causes* this early sexual behaviour. Many marijuana users were having sexual intercourse before they began experimenting with drugs. He believes that it is no more accurate to say that marijuana "causes" sexual behaviour than it is to say that sexual behaviour "causes" drug use. Goode offers evidence that both behaviours are indicators of an individual's involvement in a subculture that is tolerant toward a wide range of nontraditional values and activities.

The physiological effects of casual marijuana consumption are so mild that there is little reason to think that they would dramatically alter sexual responses. However, Dr Robert Kolodny of the Masters and Johnson Institute reported on his study, which demonstrated that men who smoked five marijuana cigarettes a day over a four-week period showed a dramatic drop in the production of the male hormone testosterone. This reduction of normal hormone production led to inability to get an erection (impotence) and could lead to infertility and sterility. These outcomes of marijuana use were temporary, however, and reversed within two weeks of stopping taking the drug. We know too that regular marijuana smoking reduces the numbers of sperm produced and reduces their ability to move normally.

The psychological results of casual marijuana smoking in some people are increased feelings of peace and openness, and decreased feelings of anxiety and inhibition. These feelings may act as indirect sources of sexual stimulation, or they may facilitate the release of existing sexual energies.

This evidence of marijuana's effect is consistent with Andrew Weil's description of it as "an active placebo," a chemical whose apparent influence on behaviour is actually the combined effects of a little relaxation and a lot of expectation. Most individuals smoke marijuana to provide an opportunity or an excuse for experiencing something which is otherwise unavailable to them because of their own attitudes about those experiences. Many people allow themselves to enjoy sex when they are stoned, but not when their heads are clear.

Marijuana does not alter basic personality structure; it does not change a person's biology or emotions. If a person is not interested in forming an intimate relationship, no amount of marijuana use will change that. Equally, the evidence is that marijuana in no way "causes" sexual crimes.

Barbara Lewis interviewed 208 adult, middle-class users. She found that some individuals were turned off sexually when they smoked, others experienced no effect at all, others described a generally beneficial effect on sexual behaviour, including the achievement of orgasm by previously nonorgasmic women. It turned out that respondents' feelings about the person they had been smoking with were much more important in determining sexual responses than the fact that they had been smoking. Sharing marijuana with someone they loved, or with someone they found sexually attractive, resulted in desire. Smoking with someone they disliked resulted in revulsion toward the very idea of sex.

Q: "Does marijuana smoking affect women's systems?"
A: "Tentative studies show that the menstrual cycle can be disrupted in women who regularly use marijuana more than three times a week. Menstrual irregularities have been observed in 40 percent of women who do so. Infertility and perhaps sterility could result from a continuing disruption of this sort. Also, frequent marijuana use may reduce the level of the female hormone oestrogen.

"THC, the active chemical in marijuana, crosses the placenta and reaches the developing baby. While there is no proof at the moment, there is a likelihood that THC may affect the developing gonads of the baby and cause fertility difficulties later on."

Cocaine. Cocaine, also called "coke" or "snow," has become an extraordinarily popular drug with supposed aphrodisiac properties. Cocaine is extracted from the leaves of the South American coca plant. Taken in small amounts it stimulates the central nervous system, producing a mild euphoria. The "rush" or "flash" felt when cocaine is sniffed or injected has been compared to the feeling of orgasm. The effects of cocaine use disappear within minutes, and continued use is required to maintain euphoria. However, such use can quickly lead to psychological dependence, loss of appetite, malnutrition, and sometimes severe damage to the tissue of the nose (holes can occur in the septum, which separates the two nostrils). Trying to stop using cocaine has only minor physical effects, but the depression resulting from trying to quit creates an almost irresistible desire to return to its use.

Cocaine used to be widely used by the medical profession as a local anaesthetic and in presurgical preparation in eye surgery; today, however, it is a highly controlled substance rarely used in medical treatment.

For a time, Sigmund Freud believed strongly in the beneficial effects of cocaine:

> "Woe to you, my princess, when I come. I will kiss you quite red and feed you till you are plump. And if you are forward, you shall see who is the stronger, a gentle little girl who doesn't eat enough or a big wild man who has cocaine in his body."
>
> [from a letter to his fiancée, Martha Bernays]

Sherlock Holmes took it and it is believed that Robert Louis Stevenson completed *Dr Jekyll and Mr Hyde* while using cocaine. Coca-Cola contained small amounts of cocaine in the early 1900s and was promoted as a valuable brain tonic that cured nervous disorders. Subsequently, though, the cocaine content was prohibited by law.

Sexually, certain levels of cocaine appear to affect the brain in such a way as to instil confidence and disinhibit. People can therefore act sexually in ways they had not dared to do before. This reduction of sexual anxiety, combined with the dramatic rush when first using cocaine, has led to its current widespread appeal. Cocaine possession and use also creates a feeling of status for some people, which may help them feel good about themselves and increase their ability to relate sexually. A more dubious advantage is that of some men who apply cocaine to the glans of the penis in an effort to delay ejaculation. This practice has no medical merit.

With cocaine, as with all other drugs, it is important to understand the difference between the *releasing* effect of a drug that allows men and women to do things they wanted but were afraid to do, and the actual chemical properties of drugs *causing* the behaviour in and of themselves.

Methadone. Methadone is a synthetic narcotic that causes both physical and psychological dependence. It is a central nervous system depressant and blocks heroin euphoria when taken daily, which is why it is used by people who were heroin addicts and are trying now to lose the addiction.

Early data suggested that Methadone had a negative effect on the sexual responses of women and men who were maintained on a daily basis. However, recent evidence indicates that Methadone maintenance generally improves sexual functioning in both women and men and does not interfere with normal menstruation, pregnancy and childbearing. Reports from several hospitals in New York where major Methadone programmes are operating show small percentages of sexual difficulty; some men have problems with erection, and some women show low sexual desire and reduced ability to reach orgasm early in the maintenance programme, but these difficulties reduce and then cease once the individual has been in the programme a couple of months. Thereafter sexual patterns return to their preaddicted levels or actually improve, not because of Methadone but because of the establishment of an orderly and productive life in which increased self-esteem fosters the ability to have meaningful relationships.

Barbiturates. Barbiturates, also called "barbs" "yellows," "reds," "downers," are central nervous system depressants which are used medically as sedatives and hypnotics. A long-acting barbiturate is Luminal, intermediate-acting barbiturates are Seconal and Nembutal. Some short-acting barbiturates are used as surgical anaesthetics. Used illegally, they lead first to tolerance and then to physical dependence. Used in combination with alcohol, barbiturates have caused many accidental deaths (they are also commonly used in suicide attempts). Withdrawal from barbiturate addiction is extremely painful and dangerous.

Taken in moderate doses barbiturates affect the body somewhat like alcohol. They depress the central nervous system and secondarily may lead to sexual excitation and stimulation as existing fears and anxieties about self and others recede. But they are not aphrodisiacs. Their disinhibiting effect may allow barriers to be overcome that previously prevented sexual involvement, but they do not endow the user with new powers. As with alcohol, too large a dose will depress the nervous system to the degree that sexual ability is prevented and sleep required. Addiction to barbiturates means that sexual interest and sexual activity diminish sharply and are replaced by a craving for the drug.

Amphetamines. As with other drugs, the effect of amphetamine use on sexual behaviour is the result of a mix of chemical, social, physical and emotional factors. Amphetamines are central nervous system stimulants and are used both legally and illegally. The most common amphetamines are amphetamine, previously marketed as Benzedrine; dexaphetamine, marketed under the name Dexedrine, and methylamphetamine, previously marketed as Methedrine.

Amphetamines are prescribed by doctors to prevent narcolepsy, a disorder which causes a person to go to sleep periodically throughout the day. Amphetamines are also used occasionally to treat hyperkinesis in young people, a condition leading to hyperactivity. Control of appetite by suppressing the hunger centre in the brain is another medical use of amphetamines. Used in proper quantities under medical control, amphetamines do not appear to affect sexual functioning directly.

Misuse of amphetamines is said to be in the billions of doses each year. When used illegally, amphetamines appear to have a dose-related paradoxical effect on sexual behaviour.

Infrequent, short-term use has been reported by some as enhancing sexual response. In men, erections last longer and ejaculation is delayed. In women desire is enhanced and orgasm is achieved more frequently. Mild euphoria is also reported by both men and women.

Higher doses, which usually means intravenous injection, lead to significant sexual problems. Men experience difficulty in achieving and maintaining an erection and in achieving orgasm. Women using high-dose amphetamines have high rates of orgasmic failure. Using amphetamines intravenously can serve as a substitute for orgasm: both men and women have described a powerful chemical "orgasm" caused by the amphetamine acting on the central nervous system. This experience is often called "a total body orgasm" and described as an ineffable pleasure.

However, any seemingly positive effects of infrequent or frequent use of amphetamines are short-lived. They are are physiologically addictive. Continued use rapidly leads to tolerance: a person needs larger and larger doses to maintain the quality of the rush, with the growing desire to experience the rush as frequently as possible. The behaviour patterns necessary to meet this growing obsession are largely incompatible with high levels of sexual expression.

Quaalude. Quaalude, commonly referred to in the US as the "love drug," is a nonbarbiturate sedative hypnotic with methaqualone as its active chemical ingredient. Quaalude is not available in the UK, though a combination of methaqualone and an antihistamine is marketed as a sleeping pill called Mandrax, sometimes called "mandies". Mandrax is only available on prescription and is much less commonly used now than in the past. Methaqualone is likely to cause physical dependence and in high doses can cause heart problems and unusual bleeding tendencies. However, it became known as the "love drug" with powerful "aphrodisiac" qualities and was written about glamorously and widely used by people of all ages.

The truth is that methaqualone, like alcohol and some other depressants, reduces anxiety and fear, allowing sex to occur where barriers once existed. Quaaludes cause a release of inhibitions so that a person can participate sexually when such behaviour is appropriate and anticipated. The drug never creates its own feelings or actions; it only allows those that already exist to be acted on. Unfortunately, using a drug like methaqualone to feel and act in ways you cannot naturally has diminishing returns in the long run, when dependence takes over from pleasure.

Spanish fly. Spanish fly comes from dried beatles (*Cantharis vesicatoria*) found in southern Europe and its active ingredient is cantharidin. It has been used successfully in veterinary medicine to get reluctant bulls to mate, since it produces a urogenital irritation that is temporarily relieved by copulation.

Humans in their never-ending search for "aphrodisiacs" have tried to use cantharidin for the same purpose. In some men, the urogenital irritation may lead indirectly and involuntarily to erection, and in some women vaginal lubrication may occur after a dose of Spanish fly. However, the drug neither produces nor stirs any erotic or sexual interest. In fact, Spanish fly is poisonous. Large doses may lead to stomach pain, disturbances in urinating, damage to the bladder or kidneys, shock, and in extreme cases to death.

Yohimbine. Yohimbine is the bark of a certain type of tree found in Africa and South America which is supposed to have sexually stimulating properties for men. The bark is crushed, mixed with a fluid and drunk. Men who use it claim that they can keep their erections longer.

Medically it is a rarely prescribed drug, available in Potensan and Potensanforte, which was once used as an anti-diuretic and to treat certain nervous disorders.

Amyl Nitrite. Amyl nitrite, or "poppers," comes in liquid or capsule form. Either way it is inhaled. Medically it has been used for relief from angina pectoris attacks. Lately, poppers have become quite popular as an adjunct to sexual activities: saved for the moment of orgasmic inevitability the drug is said to amplify the pleasure of the moment. In addition, it causes a reduction of anxiety and inhibition which may lead to desirable sexual activity, though, paradoxically, the vasodilating effect of the drug may cause loss of erection. Amyl nitrite is a smooth muscle relaxant and is sometimes used when anal intercourse is desired, since the sphincter is made of smooth muscle.

Amyl nitrite speeds up the heart, and so is dangerous to people with unsuspected heart disease. It also causes pressure within the blood vessels of the brain, which can lead to severe headaches.

Q: "I heard about a new type of popper used in the US called 'Rush.' Is it the same as amyl nitrite?"

A: "'Rush' is the commercial name for butyl nitrate, which comes from the same chemical family as amyl nitrite. Butyl nitrate is not available in the UK, but in America it comes in an ampoule, is popped, and the vapours are inhaled. Butyl nitrate produces similar reactions to poppers. Although no physical illnesses have been recorded arising from its use, serious psychological dependence on it as a pleasure enhancer may develop.

"It is worth noting that not everyone who tries poppers of this sort likes or enjoys the effects. While some describe better sexual experiences, including multiple and prolonged orgasms, others describe nausea, terrible headaches and sharp pain behind the eyes.

"Butyl nitrate causes chemical burns if it gets on the skin and it can cause blindness if the liquid touches the eyes. When mixed with alcohol, poppers of any sort can cause rapid grogginess and more severe hangover-like aftereffects."

Hallucinogens. This category includes drugs like LSD (lysergic acid diethylamide), peyote, mescaline, and Psilocybin, whose principal effects are sensory and illusory.

These substances are commonly taken by mouth and are not physically addicting, but they have powerful psychological properties that may lead to their frequent use. When using hallucinogens, people become interested only in themselves. The ability to relate directly to others is inhibited by the action of the drug on the brain, and so sex with another person is unusual though autoerotic behaviour may occur.

The claims about the positive sexual effects of psychedelic drugs like LSD are commonly distortions of reality and are usually individual mind experiences alone. After a "trip" a user may report a wide range of sexual activity, though she or he had been observed to crouch in a corner or to lie immobile during the entire episode.

Q: "I heard using LSD causes chromosome damage to babies. What are the facts?"

A: "There is no evidence that babies born to mothers or fathers who had used LSD suffer from gene damage or other birth defects. However, there is very little data about babies born to mothers who used LSD *during* pregnancy. LSD, like all other drugs, crosses the placenta and could therefore harm the developing baby; it is reasonable to assume that problems can occur if LSD is used during pregnancy."

PRESCRIPTION DRUGS:

Drugs to Treat High Blood Pressure. Some prescribed drugs that are quite effective in treating high blood pressure have a secondary effect of decreasing usual sexual activity. In men the most common secondary results are the inability to achieve erection (impotence), inhibition of orgasm and loss of desire. The loss of desire in these cases is not so much due to the medicine but is more likely the result of having difficulty in achieving an erection, and the anxiety caused by the inability to complete satisfactory sex with a partner. In women, some high blood pressure drugs may interfere with orgasm and may also decrease the desire for sex.

Because there are prescription drugs that can manage high blood pressure successfully without negative sexual side effects, it is important to question your doctor about which drug would be most appropriate.

Drugs to Treat Anxiety and Psychosis. Two of the drugs most widely used to treat anxiety are Valium and Librium. At some dose levels, their sedative effects lead to loss of desire, inability to achieve erection, and delayed orgasm or no orgasm at all. A low dose of Valium can, however, have the reverse effect on some people: reduced anxiety can lead to more successful sex. Some medical sex therapists have claimed positive results by prescribing low-dose valium during treatment for sex dysfunction.

The drugs commonly used to treat the more serious problems (psychosis) are phenothiazines (Largactil, Melleril, Moditen and others). Their use may improve a person's emotional state and lead to a return to their usual sexual functioning, but some people find that the sedative effects of the drugs diminish desire and lead to a significant reduction in sexual activity. These effects are dose-related. In addition, some of the phenothiazines may lead to temporary impotence, and one drug in this class, Melleril, can produce "dry come" (retrograde ejaculation), in which semen is ejaculated into the bladder rather than out of the penis.

Psychosis or severe anxiety must, of course, be treated, and it may well be worth a temporary reduction in normal sexual pleasure to achieve a return to full mental health. But it is important you should understand what is happening to you, so be sure to discuss it with your doctor.

Drugs to Treat Depression. When a person is depressed, sexual desire and activity usually decrease. Treating depression with therapy and/or certain drugs may reduce the depression and allow a return to the person's usual sexual behaviour pattern. However, some drugs used to treat depression can interfere with sexual behaviour or sexual interest.

Two common categories of drug used to treat depression are MAO inhibitors and tricyclic compounds. Drugs from these groups sometimes cause delayed ejaculation or impotence in men, and delayed or difficult orgasm in women. The indirect effects of these drugs can be just as important: if these sexual difficulties do occur and continue for any length of time, the frustration and feelings of inadequacy created may ultimately lead to a loss of sexual desire.

Lithium, which is now emerging as an often prescribed anti-depressant, belongs to neither of the above groups. When it is successful in treating depression, the usual level of sexual interest will probably return. This can be attributed to the person's return to health, not to any alleged "aphrodisiac" qualities of the drug.

Hormones. Testosterone is given to some men whose natural production of this hormone is too low. After treatment they show increased sexual desire, better ability to achieve erection and usually a return to the sexual behaviour pattern prevailing before they suffered a drop in testosterone production. Men with adequate testosterone levels are not prescribed testosterone, and if they take it on their own they do not become hyper-sexual. Women with low libido are sometimes given testosterone to increase their desire for sex — it may incidentally cause a slight increase in clitoris size.

Most men who are given the female hormone oestrogen in the treatment of prostate cancer experience a decrease in sexual desire and sometimes impotence. Oestrogen, which is used in the oral contraceptive, may increase sexual activity in women as the fear of pregnancy is reduced. Some postmenopausal women report increased sexual interest while on oestrogen replacement therapy, but this too may be due to the feeling of freedom from pregnancy or reduced menopausal symptoms and not to the chemical action of the drug.

Lack of interest in sex is not, however, necessarily related to a need for hormones. Usually it is the result of a complex interaction of factors that needs to be understood by a medical professional.

APHRODISIACS Not one of these popular beliefs about the effects of drugs and so-called aphrodisiacs on people's sexual behaviour is true:

  * most women and some men need something to arouse desire

*certain substances — for example eggs, vitamin E and bran — are
sexually stimulating

*if a person is not in a sexy mood, marijuana, cocaine, speed, alcohol
and other such drugs will turn them on sexually.

Q: "Is L-Dopa an aphrodisiac?"
A: "No. L-Dopa is a prescription drug used in the treatment of
Parkinson's Disease. The drug has helped some people return
to a healthy state, with the result that their sexual activity has
also returned to its usual level."

Q: "I went to boarding school and everyone said saltpetre was put
in our food to control our interest in sex. What are the facts?"
A: "Saltpetre in small doses is a mild diuretic. It does not affect you
in any other way. The stories you heard about the use of saltpetre
in schools and in the armed services are myths.
    "Some people, though, will be sufficiently affected by the
reputation of saltpetre and the belief that they are being given it to
reduce their sexual interest and activity. Popular misbelief can be
as powerful in directing sexual behaviour as any chemical."

Q: "Does ginseng have sexual properties?"
A: "No. Although widely used throughout history in the Orient,
and written about frequently today, there is no evidence that
ginseng increases sexual desire or improves performance."

Q: "Are there special vitamins that can help you sexually?"
A: "No. All the nutrition you need to function sexually can be
derived from a normal balanced diet. If for some reason a
vitamin supplement is advised by your doctor, it is for improving
your general health. By so doing your sexual abilities may be
revitalized, but that is due to the improvement in your general
well-being and is not the result of the vitamins' chemical action.
Do not purchase vitamins that claim to improve your sexual
performance. They just do not work. Use your hard-earned
money to eat a proper diet — that is more important than any
nonprescribed vitamin you can buy."

FEELINGS Many people have some half-hidden confusion or guilt about
sex. Inadequacy, vulnerability, even a sense of sin can all, so it seems to
drug users, be pushed to one side with drugs.
    Some people use drugs to anaesthetize the guilt they feel about having
sex or thinking about having it. Effectively they are in the trap of not being
able to have sex without drugs, and the more they conceal the problem the
worse it is likely to get.
    Some people use drugs for the opposite reason. Drugs may weaken
or block desire and ability to have sex. As long as the person has the drugs,
sex is not a problem because there won't be any sexual situations to show
up underlying anxieties. The drugs are an apparently adequate excuse to
avoid sex altogether.

In somewhat similar fashion, there are people who use drugs as a substitute for sex. The euphoria that drugs can bring is, some drug-users say, more desirable than the highs they may get from having sex. It is also — and this is the important point — not associated with another person; there is no possible threat. Some drug-users describe their feelings on drug highs in explicit sexual terms, saying that it is like a "prolonged orgasm" or "an orgasm all over the body."

There is yet another reason for some people to associate sex and drugs. Certain drugs make users feel free, without any feelings about other people. Having sex on that kind of high means that the drug-user has no involvement with sex partners, no need to worry about any relationship.

But relationship is the key to drugs and sex. Whatever happens or is supposed to happen when someone regularly uses drugs in sexual situations, one of the basic reasons for so doing is an impaired ability to establish relationships with others. This may have occurred for all sorts of reasons, but what it is is the inability to express love and to accept it. Low self-esteem is usually at the core. When people plagued by feelings of self-doubt are faced with a possible relationship, their sense of inadequacy and the prospect of failure come to the surface. With drugs, this unacceptable and frightening state can be altered temporarily. The pain of the moment can be avoided, but it tends to return. When it does, the drugs are there to provide protection again.

People can begin to fall into this pattern of behaviour without properly realizing what is happening. It may be only as they find that in more and more situations they hide behind drugs that they come to realize what their actual feelings about themselves and their sexuality are. Some people can face up to it and attempt a relationship without drugs, but if their problem is at all serious it is going to need professional help.

RELATIONSHIPS

"I really feel like I can get it on when I use drugs before sex. I feel so capable."

"I'm a much more creative lover when I am high."

"My concern about how my body looks to my partner disappears when I'm stoned."

"When I use drugs I don't think about right or wrong, sex is just fun."

"I feel so much more relaxed and able to do and say what I am feeling."

"My confidence soars when I use drugs."

When chemicals are routinely needed to achieve greater intimacy, to promote self-confidence, to enhance creativity, or to reduce anxiety and guilt, there is some serious emotional problem that needs recognition and treatment. If someone needs a chemical aid to reach out and give tenderness and love, as well as to receive and accept it, that person is leaning on something which is an enormous barrier to establishing any enduring relationship. Relationships are between people, not between people and drugs.

Of course, this is to be differentiated from men and women who from time to time use chemicals in sexual situations but are not and do not become dependent upon them to feel capable. The problem occurs when a relationship cannot be started or continued without the presence of a drug — when a drug is, so to speak, a third party in the relationship.

Q: "Lately I've noticed that my wife is using pills more and more, especially when we are alone. I think it's affecting our relationship. Do we need to get help?"

A: "If your description is accurate the drug use you describe is a tip-off that your wife is struggling with her feelings and perhaps with the meaning of your relationship. When drugs are necessary to get through the day, or to enable someone to deal with other people, there is a problem that must be examined and resolved. Talk to your wife and tell her about your concern for her and for your relationship and try to find out what the difficulty is, but don't be disappointed if you don't get anywhere. Drug-users are commonly defensive and manipulative, so you may need a doctor or counsellor to help you discover what is at the root of her pill-taking."

Q: "My lover has suggested we use this new drug together when we have sex. He says everyone does it and we will really be turned on by it. I like the way we make love now and I don't like this new idea at all."

A: "Tell him about your feelings and that you will not use the drug he suggests. Then explore with him what is happening in your relationship generally, and during sex particularly, that drugs are now required to have fun and be turned on. Try to find out what is on his mind because not everyone uses drugs when they are having sex. Those who do are trying to find pleasure through chemicals that most people find naturally."

Q: "This guy I know was using drugs and now that we are going together he says he has stopped. Can he be telling the truth?"

A: "Yes. Sometimes entering a rewarding and stable relationship will affect a person's self-esteem in such a way that he or she will discontinue taking drugs. Regular drug-taking is self-destructive in the long run and is a protective shield for some people: indeed, some men and women use drugs in the first place because they do not feel capable of being loved themselves, or giving love to another person. When they find that someone else *can* love them and they can return love too they may well turn from a negative, self-destructive behaviour to the positive, creative activity of building a relationship."

EROTICA

FACTS "Erotica" is a very wide term indeed, covering any object or material that tends to turn people on to sex or that can be used during sex to add a different dimension to the experience.

Essentially, there are two kinds of erotica: 1 written or visual material (photographs, stories, pictures, films and all manner of works of art), which stimulates the sexual feelings and is often called **pornography**; 2 devices made to vary or enhance pleasure during all kinds of sexual activity, commonly known as **sex aids** or toys. Both are named "erotica" after the Greek god of desire, Eros. "Pornography" means "the writings of prostitutes" (*porneia* being the Greek for prostitute). Both pornography and sex aids may be labelled "obscene," which may derive from the Latin *caenum*, meaning "filth." We shall look first at pornography, then at sex aids (page 143).

1. Pornography

FACTS Pornography is usually defined as works whose primary objective is to sexually arouse the observer or reader. However, what arouses one person sexually may not arouse another. Pornography is therefore a relative term, subject to interpretation. It has not been defined legally in a consistent way.

The definition of pornography is extremely difficult — one man's filth is another's art — and legislation in this area is continually under attack. In the UK the Obscene Publications Acts of 1959 and 1964 state that something is obscene if "taken as a whole it is such as to deprave and corrupt persons who are likely, having regard to all the circumstances, to read, see or hear the matter." In 1968 Lord Justice Salmon added his own criteria. Something is obscene if it promotes:

* erotic desires of a heterosexual kind
* homosexuality or "other perversions"
* drug taking
* brutal violence.

Prosecutions are also brought if the material is deemed a "conspiracy to outrage public decency." But the judgment often comes down to a declaration that the definition of pornography is difficult but "I know it when I see it."

Obscene material may also be called *hard core pornography* — the names are effectively interchangeable. The difficulty in distinguishing them only arises when assessing artistic or literary merit. The common understanding of hard core pornography is that it is obviously strictly commercial, with no pretence to artistic merit. Works of art, however, are from time to time claimed to be obscene and perverting despite the defence of artistic value.

Erotica has a history which dates back to the beginnings of civilization, but most of it has been created by men for men. Women creating erotica is essentially a contemporary phenomenon. Erotic works surviving from the Stone Age onward reveal typical male sexual interests and fantasies, as well as representing various interpretations of the idealized woman. It is principally for this reason that traditional material has aroused women only slightly.

But what are the facts? Who uses it? What are its effects on people in general, and specifically on young people? Do men and women respond differently to pornography? What are the attitudes to pornography in other countries?

Who Uses Pornography? The first hard facts came from the historic Kinsey study, which reported that in the sample:

* 48 percent of females and 36 percent of males had some erotic response to sexy films
* 60 percent of females and 59 percent of males had some erotic response while reading erotic literature
* 32 percent of females and 77 percent of males were stimulated by viewing pictures, drawings and other portrayals of sexual activity
* 14 percent of females and 47 percent of males were stimulated by erotic stories told to them.

Sixty percent of the 100,000 married women in the *Redbook* survey had seen a pornographic movie, and 46 percent of these same married women had used pornography in their sexual practices often (four percent) or occasionally (42 percent). In the Spada survey of more than 1,000 homosexual men 51 percent reported using written or visual pornography during sex. The magazine *Psychology Today* asked 20,000 readers whether they had ever used erotic material for arousal; 92 percent of the male respondents and 72 percent of the women reported they had.

In one of the very few scientific interviews of adults in the US regarding pornography, 84 percent of the men and 69 percent of the women indicated they had used such material at some time. These interviews of 2,500 adults were conducted as part of the US Commission on Obscenity and Pornography in 1970.

Although the sampling techniques of these surveys leave something to be desired, it is nonetheless clear that the majority of adults in America use pornography somehow, sometime. Meanwhile, public decency groups are combating pornography in court, claiming that it is damaging to the general population. Without resorting to statistics, the tremendous popularity of magazines like *Playboy*, *Penthouse* and *Hustler* is sufficient testimony to the widespread and continuing use of erotica. Books like *The Joy of Sex*, which has sold more than 7,000,000 copies worldwide, and *More Joy*, which has sold more than 2,000,000 — both of them erotic as well as educational — provide further evidence.

The report of the US Commission on Obscenity and Pornography indicates that about 80 percent of boys and 70 percent of girls have seen erotic material of some sort by the time they reach the age of 18. They also suggest that the majority of such exposure is more than just one or two experiences and that much of it occurred through friends at school or in the community. The young people studied by the Commission rarely purchased pornography. However, as erotica becomes more available it is likely that more young people now are buying it for themselves than when the Commission's report was researched in the late 1960s.

The Effects of Pornography. It is the opinion of many people that exposure to pornography can lead to the commission of more sex crimes, to improper sexual practices, addiction to pornography, reduction of restraints on certain sexual behaviours, obsession with sex, and an increase in sexual activity, especially among the young.

Within the past 20 years several reports have illuminated this area, and have promoted a better understanding of some of the effects, real or supposed, of pornography. For example, data consistently shows that the use of erotica is not related to an increase in sex crimes. The evidence, if anything, points the other way — these studies show that sex offenders in general have had significantly *less* exposure to pornography than non-offenders. A California study confirms this for young people, showing that preadolescents and adolescents who committed sexual offences had less experience with pornography than comparably aged nonoffenders.

The US Commission on Obscenity and Pornography reported that pornography had the following effects on ordinary people:

* people did not change their types of sexual practice after seeing pornography
* people's values about what was acceptable did not change as a result of viewing pornography
* there was no general increase in sexual activity after viewing pornography
* within the 24-hour period after seeing pornography there was a likelihood of increased talk about sex.

In short, the Commission found that the effects are negligible. It is true however, that neither the Commission nor the authors of other studies observed the effects of continuing exposure to pornography over a period of years. This type of investigation may turn up evidence which is not as benign as the data currently available.

Do Men and Women Respond Differently? Kinsey wasn't sure, but he speculated that there could be some neurophysiologic reason for women responding differently from men when exposed to erotic material. As appealing as this notion might be to some people, this issue has been evaluated, and there are no sex-based differences in how men and women respond to pornography.

The main reason for believing there is a difference is historical: most erotica in the past was created by men, and so one would hardly expect women to react to it as strongly. Kinsey, like millions before him and since, was mistaking effect for cause. A West German research team studied the responses of men and women to pornography and found them to be comparable emotionally, physically and behaviourally. Psychologist Julia

Heiman's work also demonstrates that men and women respond similarly to all types of erotica; the similarities between them far outweigh the differences.

Erotica in Other Countries. The most frequently used example about the effects of pornography on a given population is that of Denmark. The sale of pornography was illegal in Denmark until 1967 and the numbers of sex crimes in the country were constant for about 20 years up to that date. In 1967 the sale of pornography was legalized, the numbers of sex crimes dropped dramatically and continued to drop well into the 1970s. Peeping Tom crimes and child molesting crimes, for example, dropped 80 percent and 69 percent respectively. These results only mean that legalizing pornography did not contribute to an increase in sex crimes in Denmark. We cannot be certain that legalizing it was the sole factor causing the drop in crime rates, but the results certainly surprised some people who were expecting the reverse effect.

Sweden, West Germany and Israel also conducted studies similar to that of the US Commission on Obscenity and Pornography. Each country came to the same conclusions — that pornography could not be proven harmful, and proposed that legal restrictions were not appropriate.

Q: "How do researchers know if a person is really getting excited watching a porno film, or reading a porno book?"

A: "In laboratory research on men a penile strain gauge is used to measure the degree of their excitement. A simple piece of tubing filled with mercury is placed around the man's penis. It is attached to a recording device. If he starts to get an erection the tubing is stretched, moving the mercury level. This can be monitored and recorded by the researcher.

"For women, a device called the plethysmograph is used. It is a small, medically safe, transparent tube that is placed in the vagina and records variations in blood flow in the vessels in the walls of the vagina. As sexual stimulation appears and is reduced a photosensitive cell records this information and relays it to the researcher."

MYTHS The following beliefs about pornography are all wrong:

* use of pornography leads to sex crimes
* women are not interested in pornography
* research shows that watching porno films always leads to increased sexual activity
* pornography can be easily identified
* men are more aroused by erotic material than women
* pornography is a recent phenomenon, probably related to the sexual revolution
* sex offenders have a history of reading pornographic material
* pornography and obscenity are problems only in one's own country
* pornographic material is usually harmful to young boys and girls.

CULTURE AND RELIGION Pornography has been with us since the beginning of time. It seems that every civilization has created it, as though it were a fundamental form of human expression.

We know of pornography from ancient Egypt, India, Persia, Babylonia, Greece and Rome; we have Chinese and Japanese pornography, as well as Amerindian and Renaissance European. Some of it was created for religious purposes, some for its own sake (the Indian *Kama Sutra* and the Arabic *Perfumed Garden* are perhaps the two best known nowadays) and some shows an erotic side to a work primarily intended to express something else. Some of it was obviously publicly acceptable when it was created, some was equally obviously frowned upon and for private use only.

Our current situation seems to be neither the one thing nor the other. Erotica is widely produced and widely available, yet it is widely distrusted and widely condemned. We have laws against obscenity but we can't define it. We believe somewhere along the line that pornography is harmful, yet we can find no evidence of harm. Why such a mix of attitudes?

Undoubtedly, many of our antipornography feelings derive from the Puritan–Victorian tradition. The churches have consistently preached that sex is really about conceiving children, and most pornography is plainly about anything but. Many people, therefore, who accept the facts as we now have them that pornography does not harm the social fabric have some underlying feelings that if the moral fabric of individuals is undermined, some important part of the social fabric will be damaged too. They feel that erotica, like sex, is a private matter; just as there are laws against public sex there should also, so the argument goes, be laws against public pornography.

A newer, but very important, strand in our thinking about pornography is the sexist one. As a rule, women are portrayed in pornography as objects, serving men and their apparent need for depersonalized sex. Women are thereby degraded, dehumanized, exploited. Men come off poorly, too, for they are shown as interested only in sex, the more unusual the better, always ready with a penis that is perpetually hard, of enormous length and capable of extraordinary endurance, but they themselves are incapable of sensitivity and tenderness. Women come off far worse, but men have a right to complain too.

So where do we stand? On one hand we are members of a culture that seems unable to satisfy its demand for pornography, on the other hand, many people believe it should be controlled in some way for the general good. As with tobacco, we like it, use it, disapprove of it and make money out of it. It will require a major cultural shift for us to feel comfortable about repealing all legislation against pornography; equally, it would take as large a shift for us to revert to the total legal prohibition of a century ago. The facts are useful, but they have to be interpreted through our most private beliefs before each of us can decide what attitude to take.

2. Sex Aids

FACTS Sex aids are used principally on the genitals or around the genital area, but some can be used on other parts of the body as well. They are sold in special shops or by mail and are sometimes called sex toys. People use them when they are on their own or with partners.

Although the majority of sex aids are sold to people who use them just to enhance their pleasure, certain of them have an additional value. They are commonly used in the treatment of sexual problems. Films, audio tapes and reading materials can be extremely helpful in assisting an individual or a couple to overcome anxiety or lack of information. Sexual devices have been particularly helpful too for some disabled people whose disability inhibits their sexual expression: vibrators, prosthetic penises and similar devices can be very useful to them.

Who Uses Sex Aids? A lot of people and, to judge by the success of sex shops and mail order sex aids businesses, more people each year. In the American *Redbook* survey of 100,000 married women, 39 percent of them used vibrators during sex, 11 percent used penis-shaped objects, and 24 percent used oils and lotions; 97 percent of the women found the use of their sexual aids to be pleasurable. Eleven percent of the women in the Kinsey study used aids such as vibrators and streams of water while masturbating. Thirty-seven percent of the 1,000 gay men in the Spada report on homosexuality used sexual devices during lovemaking.

People who use sex aids do not, on the whole, use them every single time they want sex, nor do they use the same aid(s) on each occasion. People choose to use an aid according to the context and according to the kind of pleasure they are seeking to give and/or receive.

What Sex Aids Are There? The list could be a very long one indeed, limited only by the elaboration of human sexual fantasy. These are some of the common ones:

Ben Wa Balls. This is a device that originated in the Orient. There are two balls in the set. One is solid, and is placed in the vagina near the cervix; the other is partially filled with mercury and is also placed in the vagina, near the first one. Any movement causes the mercury filled ball to hit the deeper one, spreading vibrations through the general area.

Cock Rings. A cock ring is a metal, leather or rubber device shaped like a ring, usually from $1\frac{1}{2}$ inches to 2 inches in diameter. Some leather cock rings have snaps on them to make them adjustable. The testicles and the erect penis are slipped through the ring, which fits tightly, putting pressure on the dorsal vein in the penis. The idea is that the cock ring will stop the blood that has engorged the penis flowing out again. The man will therefore retain his erection longer and, supposedly, be able to prolong his sexual acts. Some men also wear cock rings when they want their genitals to look large under their trousers. The right fit is important if the penis and testicles are not to be bruised.

Erotic Creams, Lotions and Oils. These come in various scents and flavours and are mostly designed to make caressing and massage more sensuous, though some are used as lubricants for intercourse. People enjoy the sensation of them on their skin and may find the scent of them arousing, too. The flavour is important for couples who want to have oral sex or indeed for people who want to kiss their partners' bodies all over.

French Ticklers. French ticklers are a little like condoms in that they fit over the penis. They are different however in several important respects. In the first place, they are *not* birth control devices; in the second, they are pre-shaped, whereas condoms come rolled up; in the third, their surfaces are covered with ridges and little probes to "tickle" the vagina during intercourse and increase sensation; in the fourth, they can be washed and reused.

Leather Garments and Accessories. Leather has a distinctly erotic appeal for some people. It is quite often used in sadomasochistic (S&M) sexual scenes to express dominance. Some people get excited if threatened by someone who is clothed in leather or who is using leather implements. The dominant person in such encounters (the sadist) plainly also derives satisfaction from the proximity of leather. Leather is used too (in the form of harnesses, straps and so on) in bondage and discipline (B&D) experiences, one form of sadomasochistic expression.

Masturbators. There is a device called an Accu Jac, which has a moist sleeve into which a man can place his erect penis. The machine then operates like an electrical cow milker and enables the man to ejaculate and reach orgasm.

Penis Extenders. A penis extender is a hollow penis-shaped device that is placed over the natural penis to make it seem larger. Usually it is held in place by straps or by a harness round the waist.

Vibrators. Vibrators are electrical machines powered by batteries or plugged into the mains. They come in different sizes and shapes but they all vibrate in a steady rhythm in high, low or medium speeds. They are sometimes called massagers.

The most common kinds are: the slip-over-the-hand models, with the vibrating portion on the outside of the hand causing the hand and fingers to vibrate in a steady rhythm; the hand-held vibrator with attachments which can be used on different parts of the body; and the battery powered cylindrical or penis-shaped type. Vibrators must be used gently or sensitive body tissue can be bruised: some people use a towel between the skin and the vibrator to cut down on the intensity of the sensation. They are never to be used in or with water, and battery models may overheat if used for extended periods.

Vibrators are sold mainly through the post, and in special erotica shops.

Vibrators can be used alone or with a partner to expand the range of sexual sensations. The feelings produced by a vibrator can be rapidly felt and intense. Sex therapists sometimes suggest that a woman use a vibrator to get the feeling of orgasm, since a vibrator usually helps produce one quickly. Following that the woman is helped to achieve orgasm manually and then with her partner if that is desired.

Q: "I heard you could get addicted to a vibrator. Is that true?"
A: "Addicted is too strong a term. It is rare that people become truly dependent on the device, and find themselves sexually at a loss unless it is present. Most people who use vibrators learn what gives them particular pleasure and use them or not as they see fit at any given time. Worrying about dependence is probably unnecessary and will only interfere with your pleasure."

MYTHS As a society, we are still in conflict about the rightness of sexual pleasure. Sex aids are designed solely to increase pleasure, so it is not surprising that they are subject to all sorts of popular misunderstanding:

* the use of sexual aids is a sign of being a pervert
* using sexual devices in a relationship is a sign that things aren't going too well
* the sale of sexual devices is illegal
* homosexuals use sex aids more than heterosexuals
* people who use sex aids find it very difficult to give them up.

Not one of these has any truth in it.

FEELINGS Many people feel ambivalent about using sex aids. Using mechanical things during intimate moments is simply contrary to the way they believe feelings should be expressed; it is unnatural, depersonalized, a substitute for the real thing. Other people, by contrast, find aids enriching and enjoyable; they do not feel that a machine is replacing them, nor that it alienates them from their partners.

Some sexual devices sound weird to some people. However the key factor is not whether they sound weird but how they are used and what their use means to an individual or to a couple. If a person uses a sexual device in such a way that it prevents sexual expression with another person, then the use of the device and its significance for that person regularly need to be explored. If the use of sexual aids objectifies or depersonalizes sexual experiences there may be a problem that requires attention. If feelings of inadequacy and inferiority are at the root of the use of any sexual device then it is serving as a crutch, as a defence against emotional stress. Under these circumstances sexual aids can be unhealthy substitutes for more rewarding relationships between people.

RELATIONSHIPS Some people find that sex aids fit comfortably into their relationships, others find they do after some experimenting and some couples prefer to do without them altogether:

"Sometimes I just don't want to expend any effort on sex and a vibrator does it all for us."

"We tried it all, vibrators, oils, lotions and other things, but for us it just didn't work."

"I can take it or leave it – it's just not a big deal either way."

"I didn't think I'd enjoy a mechanical device while I was making love, but after a while it became a pleasant addition."

Using sex aids is not a sign of being liberal, just as rejecting them for personal use is not a sign of being prudish. It is simply a preference expressed within the context of a relationship. It is normal to use them and normal to prefer not to. What counts is how aids are used in relationships. If they are used to add variety to pleasure, well and good. If, however, they are used as substitutes for more meaningful sexual expression, both partners would be advised to consider their own feelings and to seek to discover what the problem is in their relationship.

Q: "I would like to try a vibrator when I am making love with my husband, but he thinks it means something is wrong in our relationship if we do."

A: "Many men feel they are responsible for creating the proper sexual climate with their wives, so he may see your idea of using a vibrator as a sign of failure on his part. He may feel that he is being replaced by a machine. Probably the most useful way to proceed is to see if he can get comfortable with the vibrator by using it on himself — or by having you use it on him. Then move on to both of you using it, and including it in your lovemaking."

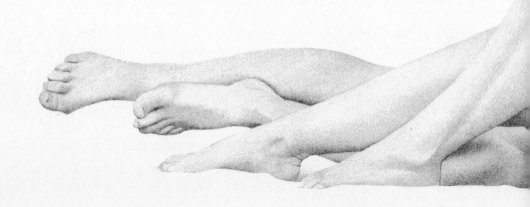

CULTURE AND RELIGION People tend to feel about sex aids rather as they feel about pornography. Both are about sexual pleasure, rather than about procreation, with the result that many of us feel uneasy. We have been taught for so long that sex is a legitimate pleasure as long as it consists of marital intercourse, which, sooner or later, may result in the birth of a child. Seeking sexual pleasure for its own sake is still formally frowned upon by some religious authorities.

Traditional religious teaching, Catholic, Jewish or Protestant, is that sexual acts are proper if directed in the long run toward procreation. Sexual pleasure is incidental to that main purpose, and it is regarded as immoral or sinful to seek pleasure for its own sake. Although most sects have never ruled clearly on sex aids, the understanding is that they are dehumanizing and contrary to the wishes of God.

Reformed or progressive teaching is taking a much more liberal view. Recent Catholic theology and pastoral guidance tends to say that if an act is growth-enhancing, responsible and enriching both to the individuals concerned and to the relationship it is morally right. Reformed Jewish and liberal Protestant groups take a similar view. In this context, sex aids can be legitimate; their use need not be sinful or immoral.

This change of view is not a fundamental change in religious law. Rather, it represents a cautious recognition that not all parts of the law will apply equally to all people in all situations.

FETISHISM

FACTS Fetishism is a fixation on an object or body part and a compulsive need for its use in order to obtain psychosexual gratification. The sexual acts of fetishists are depersonalized and objectified. In general, the sexual release in fetishism is masturbation, and fetishists are usually men.

Objects that commonly serve as sources of excitement for fetishists are shoes and boots, lingerie and leather garments, though the list of objects that fetishists can use for sexual gratification is inexhaustible. Fetishists who have a fixation on body parts tend to be aroused by legs, feet, buttocks or breasts.

People who use a sexual aid or are particularly aroused by certain body parts are not usually true fetishists because they do not depend absolutely upon the aid or the body part to achieve satisfaction. The true fetishist's sexual acts are objectified, whereas those of nonfetishists are part of general sexual arousal and expression with another person.

It may be the case that there is a range of behaviours. At one end is the true, compulsive, fixated fetishist; at other points on the scale are people who at various times and to various degrees use objects or body parts as aids to their experience but do not focus their sexual attention exclusively on them.

Fetishism has many tones and shades and is sometimes combined with other forms of sexual expression. Such acts may not be labelled fetishistic, but some professionals believe that when someone has a compulsive need to objectify the situation in order to gain psychosexual gratification then fetishism is playing a part, however the behaviour is described for diagnostic and treatment purposes.

The causes of fetishism are not clearly established. Some doctors believe it develops from some kind of early childhood experience in which an object was associated with a particularly powerful form of sexual arousal or gratification. Other professionals who use psychoanalytic theory in their work believe the fetishist wishes to be feminine like his mother, has castration fears, and cannot enter into relationships with others for fear of being lost in the relationship.

Research has shown that in general fetishists have poorly developed social skills, are quite isolated in their lives and have a diminished capacity for establishing intimacy.

The treatment of fetishism varies. Psychoanalysis is used at times but there are no large studies to document its success. Behaviour therapy is also used, particularly electrical aversion therapy, in which the patient is conditioned to eliminate the stimulation an object produces by receiving an electric shock when he sees it. Sexual arousal and expression patterns are then reshaped in the treatment programme. There are no definitive studies on the success of this method.

Q: "I have an active and satisfying sex life with my wife. The shape of her legs really turns me on, and I call myself a 'leg man.' Am I a fetishist?"

A: "Probably not. You would be considered a fetishist if the part of the body that excited you, in your case your wife's legs, was your exclusive sexual interest and the sexual experience with your wife as a person was secondary. The fact that you have a satisfying sex life with your wife suggests that you are not focused on her legs to the exclusion of the rest of her or the relationship.

   "It is very common for a man or woman to be excited by a particular feature of a sexual partner or potential partner. For most people that interest is part of the erotic stimulation continuum and is not a sign of a problem."

Q: "I read about a man whose wife always wore garters whenever they had sex. This turned him on and they had great sex. Is that abnormal?"

A: "From what you describe, probably not. Many people enjoy aids of various sorts that excite them during sex without its interfering in their relationship or objectifying the experience or their partner. There is an erotic arousal continuum and we are all on it somewhere. It is those people who can only get arousal and gratification through a compulsive and obsessive focus who have a problem. The tests you need to apply to see if someone has a problem are:

   * does the behaviour cause the person to feel enhanced self-esteem?
   * do the acts depersonalize or objectify the experience or the partner?
   * does the act cut the person off from relating to others?

   If anyone's sexual behaviour contributes to a growth in a relationship and to a greater estimation of both self and partner it is not likely to be fetishistic."

What fetishes are there? People will fixate on just about any body part and on an enormous range of objects. Whatever the fetish (the object) may be, however, there are some common elements in all fetishism. There are also some fairly familiar areas of fetishistic behaviour. We shall look briefly at some of the better known fetishes — exhibitionism, sadomasochism and voyeurism — and then explore one — transvestism — in more detail for the light that it sheds on fetishism in general.

EXHIBITIONISM

Exhibitionism is the compulsive act of inappropriately exposing the genitals to the other sex for the purpose of sexual arousal and gratification. Also known as "indecent exposure" or "flashing," exhibitionism is rarely if ever a female behaviour. Among men it is the most common cause of arrest for sexual reasons. Masturbation may occur during or after the exposure. There is a recognizable pattern in the majority of cases of exhibitionism:

* the men are usually in their 20s or 30s; the majority are married or have been married and have had more than one experience as an exhibitionist
* the act is usually premeditated and the man shows himself to strange women or young girls, rather than to women he knows
* the shock and disgust of the victim's response is what seems to produce erotic satisfaction for the exhibitionist; calm reactions or lack of interest are undesirable from the exhibitionist's point of view
* it is unusual for the exhibitionist to molest or attack his victims, but this should not be taken for granted
* exhibitionistic acts have had a traumatic effect on some women and young girls
* a minority of exhibitionistic acts occur when a man is drunk or mentally incapacitated so as to be unaware of proper social limits.

Some doctors believe that exhibitionists behave the way they do because they are emotionally immature and insecure about their masculinity. Others believe that hostility and anger are at the root of exhibitionism and whenever the man feels inadequate he responds in this inappropriate and hostile fashion.

Psychotherapy is generally used to treat exhibitionists. Helping them feel worthwhile and secure in their maleness, and helping them achieve socially acceptable and appropriate sexual relationships are the principal goals of the treatment. Aversive shock therapy, in which men receive electric shocks whenever they begin to respond sexually to an inappropriate stimulus, has been effective in a small group of patients, but there is no widespread evidence that this method is particularly helpful.

SADOMASOCHISM (S&M)

A sadist is a person who derives sexual gratification from inflicting pain on another person or from theatening to do so. A masochist is a person who derives sexual gratification from being subjected to pain or to the threat of pain. A sadomasochist is a person who is said to be able to derive sexual gratification from either role.

Sexual gratification for either the sadist or the masochist or both does not occur under every circumstance when pain is being inflicted or threatened. It is more usual for the partners to set up some kind of erotic scene in a quite deliberate way, building in elements of inflicted or threatened pain according to their individual preferences and mutual agreement. Roles (the sadistic "master" and the masochistic "slave"), costumes and aids — whips, paddles, hoods, chains, and so on — may all be carefully planned. Sometimes these aids are true fetishes, sometimes they are part of the fetish of pain, dominance or submission.

Sadomasochism is a shadowy area, and we have no reliable way of knowing how many people are involved. From the figures available it seems to be very much a minority activity, but it is unusual among fetishes in that it includes significant numbers of women. Hunt in his American sample found that 4.8 percent of men and 2.1 percent of women had experienced sexual pleasure from inflicting pain and 2.5 percent of men and 4.6 percent of women gained sexual gratification from receiving it. In 1976 a research company supported by *Playboy* magazine did a random sample of college students in the US. The research showed that 2 percent of the 3,700 men and women in the sample liked inflicting or receiving pain during sex. Another 4 percent indicated they would like to try it.

Whereas relatively few people are actually practising sadomasochistic sex, it seems that its potential appeal is much wider. Kinsey found that 24 percent of men and 12 percent of women had at least some erotic response to sadistic and masochistic stories. The causes of sadism and masochism are not fully understood. Some analysts believe they are forms of infantile fixation. Karen Horney believed sadists were acting out a need to demonstrate superiority, while masochists were people who felt insignificant and dependent. Some analysts believe castration fears are lessened and overcome by sadistic and masochistic behaviour. Others believe masochists are punishing themselves for getting pleasure from sex, while sadists relieve their own anxieties about enjoying sex by providing the punishment. Behavioural therapists believe that sadism and masochism originate in early life when sexual arousal and response may be associated with receiving or giving pain.

Literature on the treatment of sadists and masochists is scanty. Those involved do not usually seek help. Psychoanalysis is generally not successful, nor is group therapy or drug therapy. Aversion therapy has its supporters, but there are no long-term studies to suggest that it is effective on a large scale.

Q: "What does B&D mean?"
A: "B&D means Bondage and Discipline and is a kind of sadomasochistic 'scene.' Being bound or restricted and beaten ('disciplined') or being threatened with harm is what some masochists need to achieve sexual gratification. Sadists get off on providing the threat or carrying it out.

    "These 'scenes' are frequently elaborately arranged. Leather apparel and props such as whips, chains, hoods and harnesses are not uncommon."

Q: "My wife and I like to nibble and sometimes gently bite each other during sex. Are we into sadomasochism?"
A: "No. Love bites are usually not designed to cause pain, suffering or humiliation. There is a difference between doing some nibbling and biting in the excitement of a sex act and the deliberate attempt to create a scene where pain or the threat of it produces sexual gratification. Incidentally, in his research Kinsey found that 50 percent of men and 54 percent of women had some erotic response to being bitten."

Q: "Aren't all the people into S&M gay?"
A: "No. In an unpublished doctoral study on sadomasochism Charles Mosher found that 90 percent of his sample of American men and women had a heterosexual orientation. Mosher also found that the majority of those surveyed were neither

exclusively dominant nor exclusively submissive in their sadomasochistic activities, but described themselves as some combination and felt comfortable in either role at various times.

"Most literature on sadism and masochism confirms Mosher's finding that the majority of those who participate have a heterosexual orientation."

Q: "Isn't a taste for S&M due to today's changing sexual values?"
A: "No. Pain and eroticism have been associated for centuries. In the *Kama Sutra*, for example, there are descriptions of this kind of behaviour, although there is no evidence of elaborate 'scenes.' Sadism gets its name from the Marquis de Sade, who was active in the eighteenth century. Masochism gets its name from Leopold von Sacher-Masoch, who wrote about and practised masochism in the mid-nineteenth century.

"There is today though more of a willingness to discuss openly all sorts of sexual behaviour, including sadomasochism, and that may have freed some people who were already interested to find out more about it for themselves. But our current social climate does not make sadomasochists of people; sadism and masochism are the results of deeply rooted personality factors, not of social trends."

VOYEURISM

Voyeurs are almost always men, and they derive sexual satisfaction from watching people undress, seeing them nude, or observing them during sexual acts without their knowledge or consent. Risk and secrecy are important erotic elements in the sexual gratification received through voyeurism, and the voyeur will probably masturbate during or after peeping. "Voyeur" is French for "peeper" — hence "Peeping Tom."

Most of us like to observe other people's bodies, but that does not make us voyeurs. The true voyeur can achieve full gratification only through secretive observation of others.

Voyeurs are usually unmarried men in their 20s and 30s. They usually have a history of feeling insecure and inadequate, and fear rejection in relationships to a marked degree. Their victims are most often strangers, whom they watch through bedroom or bathroom windows, rather than friends or acquaintances. Voyeurs rarely harm their victims, though cases of a voyeur entering the premises and raping a victim have been recorded.

What causes voyeurism we do not know, but it is reasonable to speculate that poor social development resulting in an inability to form relationships must play some part. Both behavioural therapy and psychotherapy are used to treat voyeurs who have either been arrested or who have voluntarily sought help.

TRANSVESTISM

FACTS Transvestism means cross-dressing (Latin *trans*, meaning "cross" or "across," and *vestis*, "clothing") and a transvestite is a person who obtains sexual gratification from wearing or using clothing normally reserved for the other sex.

Almost all transvestites are heterosexual men who feel a need to use women's clothing for an important part of their erotic arousal and satisfaction. Very few transvestites are homosexual and even fewer, if any, are women. Transvestites are frequently married and have children.

We do not know what makes people transvestites, nor, since it is a private behaviour, do we know reliably how many transvestites there are. Dr Wardell Pomeroy, one of Kinsey's original team of researchers, has estimated that there are over a million transvestites in America alone, so although transvestites are a minority, their numbers are significant.

Transvestism is a fetish. A transvestite does not usually achieve full sexual and emotional gratification without using one or more of the other sex's garments. That is why transvestism causes concern. The transvestite needs support in sexual situations from outside himself or from outside his relationship with a partner.

Transvestism is not simply dressing up in the other sex's garments for fun or for temporary effect. The transvestite *needs* to cross-dress to achieve full sexual and emotional release. This is very different from the female impersonator or the drag queen, both of whom are usually playing social roles rather than expressing sexual needs.

Transvestism is regarded as a problem because of its social implications. Women married to transvestites often find it very hard to accept a husband who feels he has to cross-dress: it is against the common expectations of our society. Transvestites and their wives may have very serious questions about their orientation, and a great many people automatically (and wrongly) associate transvestism with homosexuality. Transvestism can easily break up relationships and families.

Q: "You say we don't know what makes people transvestites, but surely doctors have some ideas?"

A: "There are some theories, but remember that they are no more than theories. One is that distant, uninterested fathers and unloving mothers may predispose a boy toward transvestism when he grows up. Another is that transvestism is a sign of some desire, perhaps unconscious, to be a woman. But I repeat, there is no solid evidence."

Q: "Just what kind of clothing do transvestites like to wear or touch?"

A: "Various kinds, though there is overall a preference for undergarments — panties, slips, stockings and bras. They may actually be worn during intercourse or masturbation or any other sexual act, or the transvestite may have them by him to touch."

Q: "How do doctors cure a transvestite?"

A: "Many methods have been tried and the majority of them have had little success. Psychoanalysis has been used by some therapists to try to understand what may be at the root of transvestism. Aversion therapy with electric shock treatment, behaviour modification, desensitization, and certain tranquillizers have also been tried without too much overall success.

"Dr Wardell Pomeroy and Dr Leah Schaefer in the US give the transvestites they treat permission to cross-dress. They also counsel their patients on where and when it may be best to cross-dress. They find that their support and acceptance initially leads to an increase in the patients' transvestite behaviour, but then they find that the patients' compulsion greatly diminishes and in some cases disappears over time.

"Their unusual approach is based on the idea that transvestism is benign, and the sooner the person accepts the problem as social and not psychiatric, the greater his chance of living with it or having it diminish in importance. Neither Pomeroy nor Schaefer tries to psychoanalyse transvestite patients, as their primary concern is not with what may be the root of the problem, but rather to diminish guilt and discomfort."

Q: "Is it true you can get arrested for being a transvestite?"
A: "If you wear clothing normally reserved for the other sex to solicit for sexual purposes, you can be arrested for importuning under the Sex Offences Act 1956. Also, a transvestite can be arrested if his appearance is likely to cause a breach of the peace.

"Usually transvestites keep their cross-dressing private, so they run very little risk of arrest. Female impersonators who walk the streets looking for sex are the ones who get arrested, but generally they are not true transvestites."

Q: "At what age does a person know he is a transvestite?"
A: "Probably not until some time in adulthood. Preadolescents and adolescents sometimes associate other-sex garments with sexual gratification, but this is likely to be a passing experience and not a sign of tranvestism. The label 'transvestite' cannot be used until the need for cross-dressing is fixed. Early tendencies in that direction are likely to pass as development continues."

MYTHS Many people do not understand what transvestites are or what they do. Transvestites are often thought to be homosexuals, but there is no evidence at all in support of that view. Transvestites — people who cross-dress — are often confused with transsexuals (see page 192) — people who have surgery to change their sex. The two situations are very considerably different, and it is incorrect to regard transvestism as a point on the road to transsexualism.

A popular myth is that transvestites dress up to attract attention. This may be true of female impersonators and drag queens, but not of true transvestites. Another false belief is that a man who becomes a transvestite does so because he was brought up in an all-female household. Transvestites have enough problems without this kind of uninformed speculation.

Q: "Are transvestites that way because although they were boys, they were brought up like girls?"

A: "No. Most transvestites whose early history has been recorded were raised as boys, without any confusion on the part of their parents about their biological sex or their sexual orientation."

Q: "Aren't transvestites drag queens?"
A: "No. Drag queens are usually homosexual and are not particularly turned on sexually and emotionally by their clothing.
     "Transvestites are commonly heterosexual, married and have children. They are satisfied with their sexual orientation and usually do not parade publicly in clothing of the other sex."

FEELINGS Few transvestites feel altogether happy with their need to cross-dress to achieve sexual satisfaction. They may find situations in which they can relax, but overall they respond to their problem with anxiety, guilt and secretiveness. This is one typical self-description:

"I've tried everything — therapy, tranquillizers, determination and everything else I thought that would help me stop cross-dressing. Nothing has worked for any length of time. It's just part of me.
"For years I've felt guilty, depressed, unnatural; you name it and I've felt it. I was in constant fear of being discovered by my family. I was afraid of getting involved with a woman because I would be rejected when she found out about my feelings and needs. Anyway my whole life has been terribly affected by my transvestism and what everyone thinks of it.
"Finally, after a long time of turmoil, I've been able to accept myself as I am, and I'm beginning to carry on my life like everyone else. The obsession I've had about 'my problem' is much less now, and although it does bother me occasionally I've been able to manage it better than at any other time."

Q: "Don't transvestites want to be cured?"
A: "Since transvestites know their behaviour is unusual, many feel great anxiety and guilt about it and would prefer to change. Accordingly, many have sought help but without much success.
     "Lately, however, it seems that transvestites are working at accepting their inclinations and needs, and trying to live a life where their dressing will not interfere with their jobs, families and intimate relationships."

Q: "What happens when a woman finds out that her husband is a transvestite?"
A: "The most common single occurrence is divorce. Transvestites will often seek help once their wives and/or families learn about their transvestism, but the strain on the relationship becomes so great that even professional counselling cannot hold it together.
     "The situation is particularly unfortunate if young children are involved, as they have little or no capacity to understand their father's strange behaviour. The mother will normally get custody of the children if the parents divorce."

GENDER AND SEXUAL ORIENTATION

Gender and sexual orientation are two subjects that are very closely linked. This section starts with a discussion of gender (which effectively means the same as "sex") and related issues, and then goes on to describe three orientations — homosexuality (page 163), bisexuality (page 186), and transsexualism (page 192).

I GENDER

FACTS There are a number of sexual terms that we use loosely, particularly those about what we are (male or female) and how we behave. *Sex* or *Gender* is determined at conception: you are female or male. The definition is biological.

Gender Role is the set of rules laid down by society to tell us how to behave according to our sex or gender. Men are supposed to behave in one way, women in another. The rules are made by cultures, not biology, and usually apply from the moment of birth.

Gender Identity is the personal and private conviction each of us has about our femininity or masculinity. It is at the core of how we feel about who we are deep down, and is probably fixed around two years of age when language is being learned; also called sexual identity.

Orientation means whether we share our sexual expression with members of the other sex, with members of our own, or with both. This may be a matter of social rather than biological determination or it may be a combination of the two — we cannot be sure.

Sexism means confusing biology with culture and believing that one sex is superior to the other in particular areas.

An example of how all these definitions hang together: a child is born — a girl, let us say. Because she is of the female sex or gender, she will be taught the female gender role. If she accepts her sex or gender and her role, her gender identity will be clearly feminine — she will accept her culture's rules about how to behave as a woman. It is likely she will have a heterosexual orientation: she will seek sexual expression with men. She will also risk accepting sexism — the idea that women are inferior in some areas and superior in others.

Individual and social tensions arise when people differ from this classic pattern, when they do not accept a necessary link between their sex and the rules laid down for that sex. Because of the immense variety of human behaviours, it is possible to find individuals who contain within themselves every possible mix, even going so far as to have all the outward signs of their biological sex changed surgically to conform with their own idea of who they feel they really are (see page 192).

This last statement points to the root of our problems about sex, gender, gender role and gender identity. Many people believe that boys and girls will follow a natural path toward typically masculine or typically feminine behaviour, as though these patterns of behaviour are biologically determined along with the child's sex.

The idea, simply expressed, is that the genes and hormones that will cause a girl, for example, to have a vulva and to develop breasts will also cause her to be more sensitive and more affectionate than a boy, to be more likely to cry and to be more caring about children. We can be sure that this is well short of the whole truth, since we now know that social learning is crucial in forming a person's sense of how they should behave — that is to say, in forming their gender identity.

So which is more important in determining a person's behaviour: their biological makeup, or social forces? Are people shaped more by an irresistible genetic programme built into them at conception, or by irresistible social forces that tell them how to behave according to the sex they were born?

The best way we have found to date to resolve this controversy is to recognize that the two forces, biological and social, interact. Drs John Money and Anke Erhardt, among others, have shown that the genetic makeup of each individual is expressed within a social climate and that the climate influences the way that an individual's biological potentials emerge. The two cannot sensibly be separated. The biological imprint is enduring and so is the cultural; each expresses itself via the other.

The announcement: "It's a girl," or "It's a boy," starts the gender coding that will continue throughout the child's development. The child is already a she or a he, and will soon be given a typically feminine or typically masculine name.

There is evidence to suggest that boys and girls are held differently and spoken to differently from their first moments in the hospital nursery. Nurses tend to hold baby girls closely, speak softly and coo at them. These same workers hold boys a bit farther away, coo less and address them in a more "manly" way. This is quickly followed by the use of the culturally accepted colours of pink for girls and blue for boys. Soon, the child's clothes, furniture, hairstyle and early playthings will be selected to continue in a very obvious fashion the particular culture's pattern of gender codes.

Some of this is changing and western cultures are providing more options for boys and girls, but on balance traditional, fixed roles are perpetuated by most societies. Boys are still given certain playthings that are supposedly more masculine (trucks, guns, cars, airplanes, sports equipment) and girls are provided with traditionally feminine items (dolls, furniture, cooking sets, skipping ropes, nurses' uniforms, soft animals). The combination of all these messages, subtle as well as overt, about appropriate gender expression results in imprinting at a very early age with the distinctions between males and females, with what they can do, feel and aspire to as young people, and what life will be like when they become older. So by age two — or three at the latest — a young person's gender identity is probably fixed.

Aiding the effects of these gender distinctions is the way parents behave at home as they go about their daily routines. Generally, parents (two or a single) continue the clear separation of roles that the young person has been exposed to from birth. The way that parents behave, whether unwittingly or by design, usually reinforces children's ideas of what women do and feel, and what men do and feel. Here again, there are changes occurring, as some parents try to create a climate at home where their children will see various options to avoid their feeling necessarily locked into culturally assigned roles. These changes initiated by parents are needed and must continue, but they stand a chance of long-term success only if the culture as a whole adopts alternative views of what gender roles can be, and that means in schools, at work and in the media as well as in ordinary social life.

Schools, where young people usually spend more time than they do in direct contact with either parent, continue traditional gender stereotypes and the double standard of attitudes and behaviour. For example, the vast majority of infant and primary school teachers are female, while the majority of the head teachers are male. To the young person, this is a subtle but clear statement about who is supposed to have authority, intelligence and prestige in adult life. It is usually not recognized in precisely those terms, of course, but the repeated image of this through an entire school career is a message about who is capable and expected to do what, not only in school but in life outside school as well. Although change is slowly occurring, the primary messages of the sexuality aspects of the curriculum are either overtly or subtly sexist and sex roles are stereotyped.

Sexism is the conscious or unconscious assumption that there is an inherent superiority of one sex over the other. It shows itself in practice as one sex dominating the other, and having superior access to the development of interests, potentials and skills. Sexism is justified in our minds by our acceptance of stereotypical gender roles. In our elementary schools, young people all too quickly learn who is clever in what subjects, who is strong, who is passive, who is assertive, who can be independent, who takes care of the house, who is successful, and who should show feelings.

Sex stereotypes pervade all materials used in elementary school curricula. For example, my own informal analysis of mathematics books in school libraries reveals that even maths problems are presented in social contexts that reinforce gender role stereotypes. Boys learn to count and add by driving cars, flying planes and other such characteristically male activities. Girls learn to add and count by skipping, measuring cloth and weighing and measuring recipe ingredients. Boys' faces commonly portray confidence while girls' faces reflect bewilderment (until they've been helped by the boys). Sex-typing in social studies and health education books also indicates what is expected in our society. The stereotyped portrayal of scientists, doctors, nurses, explorers, receptionists, assistants and many others continues to imprint young people with clear preconceptions of what is and what is not expected.

This kind of bias, built into the information children are given at an early stage by parents and teachers, is enormously influential. It is constantly reinforced, however, by peer groups — other children of a similar age. The peer group is, especially for the young, a critical source of identity and strength, and constitutes in itself a culture with its own language, philosophy and accepted ways of behaviour. In general, the roles learned early in life are continued and often exaggerated during this period of special group identification.

The media (television, films, newspapers, magazines, and advertising in general) also act as powerful influences in shaping the expectations, behaviours and values of people of all ages. They have been — and to a large extent still are — reinforcers of the familiar gender role stereotypes.

A very serious and compelling result of all this programming coming from family, school, peer groups and the media is the psychological separation of men and women. This results from the idea that what one sex does or feels, the other does not, an attitude which certainly can lead to difficulties in working and living together.

It is clear that during the earliest years of a person's life the culture does little to nurture that person's uniqueness. Rather, people are treated as members of a group with some previously assumed average characteristic. Individuality and self-fulfilment become subordinated to the official culture's line. But it is not important that there be equal numbers of women and men in each role; what is important is that individual differences should be allowed to develop fully, regardless of sex.

The result of all this is that the obvious biological differences between females and males have led cultures throughout the world to assign different tasks, expectations, proper feelings and roles solely on the basis of biological sex; cultures then arbitrarily label those qualities normal and usual. The necessity of conforming to this culturally prepared life map may create confusion, conflict and anger for some people because their identity and self-image is not in keeping with the way society has outlined their prospects. For most, the cultural pressure of what is appropriate forces conformity despite their inner turmoil, but others resist and express themselves in a way that is in keeping with their core identity.

One manifestation of this resistance to cultural pressures is the current interest in androgyny. The word comes from combining the Greek *andros*, which means "man," with *gynaekos*, which means "woman." The idea contained in the word is that people can integrate in one personality characteristics traditionally assigned to the other sex as well as to their own. Some people now believe that androgyny is the ideal social and psychological state, for it requires that women and men go beyond cultural stereotypes and reduce the gap between the sexes.

In its simplest yet most profound form, androgyny challenges the basis of traditional sex role expression in which it is a person's sex that decides who cooks, cleans, cares for children, shops, works, fixes things, plays sports, shows emotion, is tender, dependent or independent. By having the freedom to express their ambitions, their needs, their talents and their desires free of artificial limitations, androgynous people are in a much better position to realize their full potentials than people who abide by traditional sex roles.

MYTHS The following common ideas about gender are false:

* girls who enjoy sports have a tendency toward lesbianism
* boys who enjoy ballet have a tendency toward homosexuality
* girls by their nature are more nurturing and make better parents
* girls who are achievement-orientated make poor mothers
* young boys who play with dolls will have a tendency to be effeminate
* dominant, aggressive women are sexually assertive

* women express tenderness better because of their biological makeup
* men are better suited than women to handle financial matters
* young girls who play with cars and trains will have a tendency to be masculine.

CULTURE Why do we have such definite, deep-seated prejudices about what is "properly" masculine and feminine? The answer is that we have inherited them from every culture that has influenced our own, and along the way we have reinforced them.

One of the earliest cultures to have a great influence on the way we see things now was the Greek, and we can immediately see the origins of many of our attitudes about the sexes in the views that the Greeks established. In ancient Greece, women were thought to be essentially mindless, with limited abilities. Their purposes were to bear children, manage households and provide erotic pleasure for men. If girls received an education it was from their mothers — only boys went to school. Of course, this was not an unbreakable rule and we know there were exceptions; it does not mean either that women were effectively servants — far from it, in some cases. What it does mean, though, is that women then as ever since were thought to be unequal and simply not up to certain tasks.

The Greek attitude was carried loyally on through western civilization, much aided by the Church with its emphasis on a male god with a son, all of whose active supporters were men. ("But I would have you know that the head of every man is Christ; and the head of the woman is man ..." — I Corinthians 11:36.) If not properly subservient to their menfolk, women were liable to be regarded as agents of the devil. In the eighteenth century Rousseau, the French philosopher who proclaimed so many liberties, described women as having no proper knowledge, no love of art and no genius. (Rousseau, incidentally, like several of the other great talents of his age, was happy to accept the patronage and advice of Mme de Staël, a woman of quite formidable intellect and wealth.) Schopenhauer, the German philosopher, in the next century, described women as an undersized, short-legged race with little intellectual capacity, and his words fell on receptive ears.

How could so many intelligent men be so wrong? The short answer is that they were mistaking actuality for potential. Because most women were not nearly as well educated as the men with whom they mixed, their intellectual achievements were likely to be fewer and smaller. That doesn't mean for a moment that their *potential* was in any way inferior. If you exclude women from government, for example, the actuality will be that all politicians are male. The potential, however, is still the same — government could just as well be an entirely female province.

Gradually, as we know, women have come to overcome some of the obstacles placed in their paths. In the course of the last two centuries, but most particularly in the latter half of this one, the idea that women and men are equal has gained general acceptance. What we do not yet accept as a society is that women and men should be *treated* equally, for the old gender roles are still powerfully built into our social experience.

Some people who condemn the negative effects of past and present inequalities of opportunity between men and women nonetheless maintain that the old differences were not entirely without justification. They will tell you that it is a very good thing if a woman can be a physician — as long as she has her children and runs her home well. They will tell you it is a good thing that a man should be a nurse — as long as he will join the army and fight in a time of national crisis. In other words, they are asserting that though there can be a large area of overlap, there are areas of human experience that are instinctively male and others that are instinctively female. What is the evidence from other cultures?

Margaret Mead, the anthropologist, studied several tribes in New Guinea, among them the Tchambuli, the Arapesh and the Mundugumor. Each is different from the other in its gender roles and each is different from our own culture. Margaret Mead described them as follows.

Tchambuli men were artists whose principal concerns were costume- and mask-making and flute-playing. They were insecure, emotional, temperamental and distrustful of each other. Tchambuli women fished, traded, managed money, households and children. They were efficient, thorough and had a real sense of comradeship with other women in the community. Power was in women's hands, and this was symbolized by the statue in each home of a woman with an exaggerated vulva.

A short distance from the Tchambuli lived the Arapesh. Arapesh men and women, Margaret Mead found, were very similar. Both were benign, mild tempered and cooperative. There was no evidence of competition for dominance or authority. Child care was a joint endeavour, with the men as dedicated to nurturing their families as the women were. Arapesh men had no macho image to fill and violence was foreign to their culture.

By contrast, in the Mundugumor culture both men and women were violent and aggressive. Children were taught not to cling to their mothers in fear or for affection. Children's games were violent and competitive, preparing them for adult life within the community.

These three cultures all existed simultaneously in the same country. Whether or not we choose to learn anything from their practices, we have to accept one fact: that our own historical system of superiority and inferiority is not in any way biologically justifiable.

II ORIENTATION

Homosexuality

FACTS Homosexuality is the sexual orientation of some men and women who find their primary emotional and sexual fulfilment with people of the same sex. Homosexuality is not a choice that people make, but is a fundamental fact about their personalities. It may or may not be actively expressed, but a person who is homosexual will usually recognize the emotional and psychological reality of his or her orientation.

The word "homosexual" can be used to describe the orientation of both men and women who prefer same-sex partners. It can not, however, be used to describe the people themselves. The majority of people are heterosexual — they prefer other-sex partners — but we describe them as "people," not as "heterosexuals" unless, that is, we are specifically discussing their sexual orientation. There are heterosexual people and homosexual people just as there are rich, poor, fat, thin, tall, short, black, white, brown and yellow people. The common element is that they are *people*; whatever secondary characteristics they may show are just that — secondary. Identifying people who are homosexual (among other things) by their choice of sex partners reduces the complex dimensions of their humanity to an interest in sex alone.

The term "homosexuality" came into use toward the end of the last century. It derives from the Greek *homo*, meaning "same" plus "sexuality."

Although "homosexual" is now widely used to describe both men and women, there is of course the alternative word "lesbian" for women. This derives from the Greek island of Lesbos, where the seventh-century B.C. poetess Sappho lived and wrote about her passionate love for women.

Q: "What does the word 'gay' really mean?"

A: "It probably started as a kind of code word used by homosexual men and women to communicate safely to each other about their sexual orientation. Secrecy was necessary since society had made it so difficult to be honest about an uncommon sexual orientation. 'Gay' has the happy effect of countering the public image of the depressed, lonely and pathetic homosexual person and means many things to homosexual men and women. It means pride in themselves, it means acceptance of who they are and it conveys the attitude that homosexuality is good and right.

"The word 'gay' is a turn-off to some people (including some homosexual people) as they think it is flaunting a sexual orientation that most people in society have difficulty understanding and accepting. However, the need to develop a gay identity and not to hide and be ashamed is a situation brought about by a heterosexual society trying to get everyone to conform to one sexual orientation. It is understandable that people in a repressed minority may occasionally overstate their case when trying to establish their right to a full identity."

Q: "Why don't some people like to use the words 'homosexual' and 'homosexuality'?"

A: "For many people 'homosexual' and 'homosexuality' imply sexual acts. To describe whole people solely in terms of who they have sex with is prejudicial because it does not recognize their intrinsic personal qualities. Women and men with a homosexual orientation have an equal right to be described in nongenital terms."

In our civilization, homosexuality has at most periods been a condemned, illegal, undercover activity. The extent of homosexual feelings and acts could only be guessed at until Kinsey published his classic studies of male sexual behaviour (1948) and of female sexual behaviour (1953) in the US. Before that time people's guesses had been vague — Havelock Ellis estimated that two to five percent of Englishmen were homosexual and Magnus Hirschfeld put the proportion in Germany at two percent.

Kinsey derived his figures from samples that were not representative of America's men and women, but the report certainly provided an important framework for discussion and further study. The following is a summary of some of the Kinsey team's findings on male and female homosexuality in the United States:

* 37 percent of the 5,300 men studied were involved in at least some homosexual acts to orgasm between adolescence and old age
* 13 percent of the 5,900 women studied were involved in at least some homosexual acts to orgasm between adolescence and old age
* 50 percent of the men studied had either overt or psychological homosexual experience after adolescence

The Kinsey data made quite obvious a fact that many people already knew: that men and women were not always and forever heterosexual, or always and forever homosexual. Also, the studies made it very clear that participating in homosexual acts did not mean a person was necessarily homosexual in orientation, and participating in heterosexual acts did not mean a person was necessarily heterosexual in orientation. In fact, it was shown that there are *degrees* of exclusivity in sexual orientation. Kinsey devised the following sample rating scale to show these degrees.

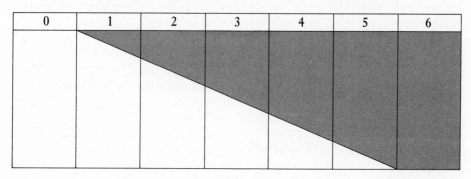

0=entirely heterosexual; 1=largely heterosexual but with an incidental homosexual history; 2=largely heterosexual but with a distinct homosexual history; 3=equally heterosexual and homosexual; 4=largely homosexual but with a distinct heterosexual history; 5=largely homosexual but with an incidental heterosexual history; 6=entirely homosexual

Following Kinsey, further studies on homosexuality have indicated that many men and women do have homosexual experiences at times in their lives, but their major orientation remains heterosexual, while about four percent of men and two percent of women have an exclusive homosexual orientation. Subsequent studies by John Gagnon, William Simon and Morton Hunt in the US and by Michael Schofield in England suggest that Kinsey's data on exclusively homosexual people remains broadly true (about one in 20 adults in the UK, totalling two million).

The Kinsey rating scale made it clear that homosexual and heterosexual orientations were not exclusive and that an individual did not need to be strictly one or the other. The scale also helped do away with the popular notion that there was a certain "homosexual personality" that was evident in that special group called homosexuals.

An important aspect of the data was the clear illustration of how many men and women had several sexual contacts in their lives that were contrary to their primary orientation but which did not alter it. In addition, the classifying system correctly suggested that a person's degree of homosexual orientation or heterosexual orientation can only be evaluated at any given time and will not necessarily remain the same forever.

All Kinsey's work however did not begin to answer another question uppermost in the public mind. What makes people homosexual?

People have theorized about the origins of homosexual orientations for centuries. They have rarely taken the trouble to theorize about what causes a heterosexual orientation, however, and until we can understand what causes an orientation in the first place we are unlikely to understand what causes a homosexual one.

Is it taught? Is it caught? Is it chosen? Is it inborn? These are the questions that numerous people have addressed with speculation and prejudice, and a few with patient, unbiased effort. No-one knows the answer with certainty, but here are some of the more popular theories.

The Genetic Theory. One of the first serious scientific explanations of homosexuality was provided by Kallman in 1952. He claimed that a homosexual orientation was decreed by genes, and that people inherited their homosexuality. Other scientists found themselves unable to supply corroborative evidence and Kallman's theory has been discounted.

The Hormone Theory. A number of people have suggested that an imbalance of hormones in the developing foetus, or even the intrusion of inappropriate hormones, might be responsible for the development of homosexuality. The flaw with this proposal is that we have yet to discover proper physical evidence of such hormonal disturbance in newborn children or indeed in developing or mature people.

The Psychoanalytic Theories. There are a number of these. The problem with all of them is that they have never been tested or verified on the population at large, only on small groups of people in therapy.

Freud believed that a homosexual tendency was a natural stage for people to pass through on their way to maturity. Maturity meant, among other things, a heterosexual orientation. A homosexual adult was therefore someone whose psychosexual development had been arrested. Freud's reasoning behind this argument was that when boys discover that girls have no penises they believe they may lose their own penises if they have contact with women. They feel they will be castrated. Other men have penises, so there is no danger of castration if contact is restricted to them.

Homosexual orientations have also been attributed to distant, hostile relationships with parents. Boys seek out homosexual relationships to provide the male love they never experienced properly from their fathers. Women seek out other women to compensate for the lack of female love they experienced from their mothers. Lesbianism has also been attributed to distant fathers, who made it difficult for girls to learn how to relate to adult men. Male homosexuality, some people argue, is attributable to over-protective mothers who will not release their sons into the competitive male world to fight on equal terms for women.

All the theories about homosexuality and parental relationships seem to break down when tested. The same set of parent–parent and parent–child relationships can produce heterosexual and homosexual children, whether relationships are close or distant.

The last of the really popular psychoanalytic theories is the narcissistic one. Developing children, so the theory goes, sometimes become so involved with their own rightness that they seek sex partners who resemble themselves.

The Peer Influence Theory. Some researchers have suggested that a homosexual orientation is formed by the pressure of a developing person's peers. Up to now it has proved quite impossible to classify young people and their activities with sufficient clarity and meaning to ascertain whether there is anything in this theory. One major difficulty is this: does a young person associate with other young people and they together develop a homosexual orientation, or do young people who may have a homosexual orientation associate with each other because they already have the orientation? This theory, like the others, has got nowhere yet.

So much for why; but something that bothers many heterosexual people is: What do homosexual people do when they are in bed?

The first thing to be clear about is that there are no homosexual acts as such. People make love homosexually much as people make love heterosexually. The one act that is not available to either male or female homosexuals is of course penis–vagina intercourse. Otherwise, the differences are of emphasis only.

Most people, whatever their orientation, include kissing, caressing, hugging in their sexual repertoire. A great many include masturbation and oral sex too. Gay women probably place more emphasis on body rubbing to orgasm (also called "tribadism") than heterosexual couples, and gay men are more likely to practise anal intercourse than their straight counterparts, but neither of these practices is exclusive or obligatory.

The idea of making love to another woman or to another man revolts many heterosexual people. Gay people sometimes say that it is strange at first — gay men are sometimes reluctant to kiss, for example. They go on, however, to argue that gay sex can be very rewarding precisely because the partner is of the same sex. No two women are exactly alike in their responses, but they are more alike than a man and a woman. Women have a head start in knowing how women like to be treated and men have an understanding of what appeals to other men that women can only acquire with experience.

Just as a lot of heterosexual people are confused about what homosexual people do to each other, they are mistaken about how. An automatic assumption many people make is that in homosexual lovemaking there have to be roles, that one person has to be dominant ("the man") and the other submissive ("the woman"). To be fair, it does happen sometimes. There are gay women who will be submissive and play "femme" to the dominant partner's "butch." There are gay men who have thought themselves into a "feminine" role, which can include doing the dishes as well as being penetrated, rather than penetrating, in anal intercourse. But for the great majority of gay people, men and women, regular role-playing of this kind is completely irrelevant. Equality is the keynote, and taking turns the norm.

Q: "Is it true that lesbians normally use dildoes?"
A: "No. Some do, certainly, but by no means all. Lesbians reject the idea that the vagina has to be filled for a sexual act to be satisfying. Using a dildo — or, more commonly, fingers in the vagina — is an option, not a requirement."

Q: "Do all homosexual men have anal intercourse?"
A: "By no means, though it is very popular. Of the American gay men responding in the *Spada Report*, 76 percent said they enjoyed it and 12 percent said they did not. Bell and Weinberg found that gay men ranked anal intercourse second to oral sex as the most favoured sexual activity."

Q: "Surely it's true that when men have anal intercourse the one on the bottom is passive and feminine?"
A: "No, it isn't. Most gay men don't play 'masculine' and 'feminine' roles. They are both masculine and they agree, according to the occasion, what they will do together. In heterosexual intercourse the woman is feminine not because of any position she may adopt but because she's a woman. And she certainly doesn't have to be passive. A man in bed with a woman is still a man whatever they are doing together; he doesn't have to be on top to prove he is male."

Q: "Don't homosexuals have more prostatitis than heterosexuals because of all the anal intercourse they have?"
A: "No, and there is no evidence that anal intercourse results in prostatitis anyway."

Q: "It seems that a lot of gays are into heavy leather and sadomasochism. Is that true?"
A: "A number are, but it is very much a minority activity (remember that some heterosexual people are into S&M too). It seems that there are a lot of them because it gets talked about a lot, but probably the majority of gay men are not interested."

Q: "Are lesbians into S&M too?"
A: "Most lesbians vehemently reject violence of any kind in sex. Indeed, they will often say that one of the reasons they prefer having sex with other women is that women are gentler and more understanding than men.
    "Certainly, you will occasionally see lesbians wearing rather aggressive-looking leather, but the image it projects is usually, it seems, discarded in bed."

Q: "Isn't a man really a homosexual if he has a few homosexual experiences in his life?"

A: "That's hard to answer in a simple way. If his past and current sexual acts and emotional experiences have been focused mainly on the other sex, then he would have a heterosexual orientation — probably a 1 on the Kinsey scale. However, if that man's predominant feelings were about the same sex, while his sex acts were with a person of the other sex, he probably would be classified as homosexual — he might rate a 4 on the Kinsey scale.

"The point is that you have to consider the emotions as well as the acts to evaluate someone's sexual orientation. The acts can be one way, the emotions the other. It is only if both are regularly in line that you can say an individual is wholly heterosexual or wholly homosexual."

Q: "What does 'coming out of the closet' mean, and how do they do it?"

A: " 'Coming out of the closet' describes the events in a homosexual person's life when he or she having accepted his or her sexual identity acknowledges it to family and friends. It means that person's orientation is no longer a secret. 'Coming out' is not a public announcement, but an important ordering of the person's emotional and psychological life, leading to a security that only

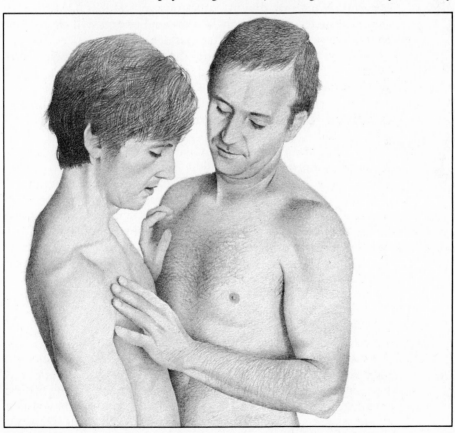

full and lasting self-acceptance can provide.

"A person can come out in many ways, depending on needs and circumstances. Dramatic disclosures are rare — a simple statement to the people who are important to the person coming out is usually sufficient. Introducing a same-sex lover is often all that is needed to make the point."

Q: "How come some homosexuals get married, then years later break up with their families and come out?"

A: "There may be a number of reasons, but two of them are particularly common and important. The first is that if they have been raised conventionally, there will be a lot of social pressure on them to date, marry and have children. They may recognize that they are going to have problems suppressing their true orientation, but they also recognize that they are going to have very real problems if they choose to opt out, come out and try to live in an abused, repressed minority.

"The second very important reason is to have children. Homosexual people are just as likely to want a family life as anyone else, and many of them want it so much that they are prepared to pay the price of repressing their homosexuality and 'acting' a heterosexual role.

"A third reason that some people advance is that a number of people who think they are probably gay feel that if they marry they will be 'cured' of their homosexuality and will succeed in conforming to the heterosexual pattern.

"It is of course tough on the remaining partner if one announces he or she is gay and is leaving the marriage. There are, however, numerous cases of two people, one of whom is gay, marrying, raising children, splitting, and then succeeding in establishing successful relationships with their grown children."

Q: "Isn't it important for a child to live with the mother if the father turns out to be gay?"

A: "No. There is no evidence that a parent's sexual orientation predicts what kind of a father or mother he or she will be. Gay men and gay women have already shown that their ability to be loving, fit parents is not related to their sexual orientation.

"You may be interested to know that more than 95 percent of the children who live with a gay parent have a heterosexual orientation. Also, you must remember that the overwhelming majority of homosexual men and homosexual women were raised by heterosexual parents."

Q: "What does 'latent homosexuality' mean?"

A: "It means the unexpressed, conscious or unconscious desire to have sex with a person of the same sex. If the wish is conscious but controlled the person is repressing the desire. If the wish is unconscious, the person has suppressed it. Freud believed that it was a universal quality, others have believed in its existence in some people. 'Latent homosexuality' is an overworked term. For practical purposes it is not meaningful."

Q: "What does dressing in 'drag' mean?"

A: "It means dressing in the clothing of the other sex, usually in a flamboyant way and usually to amuse. Male homosexuals who dress in drag are often known as 'drag queens.' Dressing in drag is not however limited to homosexuals. Nor does it necessarily indicate transsexualism — the conviction on the part of the person who is cross-dressing that he or she was meant to be a member of the other sex; nor does it necessarily indicate transvestism — the inability to achieve full psychosexual satisfaction without garments normally reserved for the other sex."

Q: "I read that there are ways to change a homosexual to a heterosexual. What is that all about?"

A: "Fortunately the organized medical and psychological efforts to change people's sexual orientations have diminished drastically. It is no longer widely believed by the medical profession that homosexual people must be redirected, albeit against their will, to the 'natural and healthy' orientation of 'everyone else.'

"Trying to change homosexual people into heterosexual people has almost always failed, but great efforts have been made to do so. In the past, doctors and mental health practitioners have tried some barbaric techniques to change the sexual orientation of gay men and women. Hormones, psychoanalysis and aversion therapy, including the use of electrical shocks, have all been tried and all have failed. Other types of behaviour therapy like desensitization, sensitization and conditioning techniques have also come to nothing.

"These failures result from the simple fact that the overwhelming majority of gay men and women do not want to change their orientation. Most people with a homosexual orientation would never consider a change if they weren't made to feel guilty, inferior, sick and humiliated. Remember, changing a person's sexual orientation is not like changing their clothes or hairstyle. Sexual orientation is a bedrock element of a human being's personality and it changes with great difficulty."

Q: "But what about all those effeminate men and tough-looking women who are gay. Don't they really want to be the other sex?"

A: "No. The men and women you see acting that way on the whole do not want to be members of the other sex. They may appear strange to many people because they dress and act in a way that conflicts with our society's rules about permissible roles for men and women, but it does not indicate that they are unhappy with who they are but are merely expressing a preferred social personality.

"Sometimes the media report homosexual (and heterosexual) men and women doing things that are certainly not representative of the way the majority of people live. But we must be careful not to generalize about the majority from the behaviour of the minority; to do so is not only unfair but it distorts the true picture. The great majority of homosexual and heterosexual people share exactly the same values."

Q: "A friend of mine told me there was evidence that gay people come out as psychologically healthy as heterosexuals when tested. Is that so?"

A: "There was an important study in 1957 by Dr Evelyn Hooker in which she compared homosexual males with heterosexual males in a series of psychological tests. None of these men was in therapy and a group of independent psychologists rated the tests without knowing who was homosexual and who was heterosexual. No differences were found between the two groups, and there was no evidence of special emotional problems among the gay men when their results were studied individually.

"In 1967 another psychologist, Dr Mark Freedman, did a similar study comparing lesbian and heterosexual women. There was no evidence that the gay women had any more emotional problems; interestingly the gay women scored higher on independence and self-acceptance measures.

"The results of similar studies show that sexual orientation is not a predictor of emotional disturbance."

Q: "If homosexuals are so healthy, how is it that so many go to psychiatrists?"

A: "I'm tempted to answer: 'If heterosexuals are so healthy how is it that so many of them go to psychiatrists?' The real answer though is that there exists a general impression that all homosexuals are essentially lonely and depressed and therefore

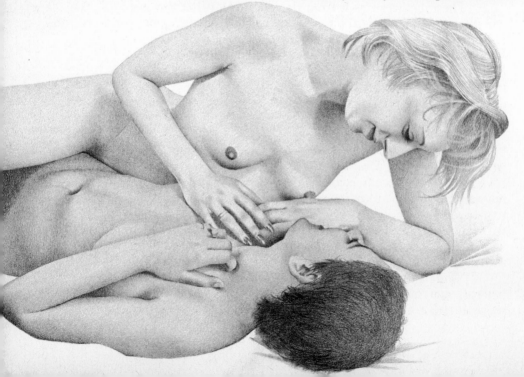

many of them wind up on the psychiatrist's couch. Mental health practitioners themselves are guilty of developing and perpetuating this myth. They have shown a tendency to generalize about all homosexual people from the relatively few they have seen in therapy, a tendency not to know enough about the huge numbers of healthy and happy gay women and men, and a tendency to associate personality disorders with sexual orientation."

Q: "What does 'dyke' mean?"
A: "It's an aggressive put-down used by both men and women to describe women who seem masculine to them in either behaviour or appearance. As with most such terms of abuse, it advertises the user's fear."

Q: 'What does 'homophobia' mean?"
A: "Homophobia is a term used mainly in the US for an unnatural fear of and revulsion toward homosexual people and homosexuality. Homophobia may take many forms: fear that associating with a homosexual will trigger a homosexual response in you is homophobic; fear that associating with homosexuals will imply you are homosexual too is homophobic; fear that associating with a homosexual indicates to them that you are interested in sex with them is homophobic; the belief that homosexuals cannot form lasting relationships and are only interested in random sex is homophobic; physical and emotional violence against homosexuals, and the refusal to give homosexuals jobs, housing and other social rights that all people are entitled to is also homophobic."

Q: "Don't studies show that most homosexuals are promiscuous?"
A: "No. Sexually, gays have the same sort of relationships as non-gays. They may have sex just for fun, out of curiosity, for friendship or for love. As with non-gays they may have random encounters but these cannot be said to exclusively characterize gay sexual relationships. The evidence on both gay men and gay women is that at any one time the majority are in or seeking settled relationships.
        "In all fairness, it must be pointed out that the prevailing attitudes in most Western societies do not encourage open, committed relationships between gay people. The alienation, prejudice and humiliation so many gay people experience encourages them to have clandestine relationships which, because they have to be hidden, are often transient too, though, as with heterosexuals, not all gays are looking for stable relationships and deliberately opt to keep their sex lives separate from their deepest relationships."

Q: "What does 'cruising' mean?"
A: "It means going out looking for someone to have sex with, and

gay people do it just as heterosexual people do. The normal gay cruising places are the streets, pubs, offices, stores, trains — in fact, anywhere that people can meet people."

Q: "What are gay pubs like?
A: "There are not as many gay pubs in the UK as there are gay bars in the United States. Those gay pubs that there are appear on the whole to be perfectly ordinary, except that the customers are predominantly homosexual. Homosexual organizations (such as Gay Switchboard in London) provide information on places of entertainment for gays, including guides to gay pubs and clubs. Gay pubs serve exactly the same functions as straight pubs — meeting places to talk and drink."

Q: "Do lesbians go to gay pubs?"
A: "Yes. Lesbians go to gay pubs to meet other lesbians, to drink, to dance and to listen to poetry and music. Just as in gay men's pubs and straight pubs, an important reason for going is to meet someone to have sex with or to start a relationship with, but it is not the only reason."

Q: "What is a 'cottage'?"
A: "Cottages are public toilets — say in parks or bus and railway stations — that are used as meeting places by men in pursuit of anonymous sex. Interestingly, it appears from research that the majority of men involved in cottage sex are heterosexual in orientation, stopping off for quick impersonal sex and that only a minority of gay men have sex in cottages.

"After a while certain public conveniences become known as safe cottages. Occasionally cubicles will have holes in the wall to allow the penis to be put through for fellatio — these are known as 'glory holes.'

"Sometimes cottages are observed by the police to arrest gays on morals charges. Some are used too by men whose motive is to rob rather than have sex, and sometimes by queer bashers who want to vent their hatred of homosexuals."

MYTHS These are some of the common myths about gay people:

* you can tell which people are gay just by looking at them
* gay men really want to be women
* gay women and men could change if they really wanted to
* gay men and women are more creative than other people
* gay schoolteachers can persuade young people to be gay
* all religions condemn homosexuality
* gay women really want to be men
* gay men are usually hairdressers or artists
* gay women and men usually make poor parents
* when gay people have sex, one plays the part of the woman and the other plays the part of the man

* gay men are frequently child-molesters
* gay people would change if they had good heterosexual sex
* a child who touches the genitals of someone of the same sex is showing homosexual tendencies
* gay people cannot form lasting relationships
* gay men and women generally try to persuade others to be gay
* a person can become gay by associating with gay people
* homosexuality is caused by weak parents
* homosexuality is a choice.

Q: "Isn't it true that gays are really attracted toward children?"

A: "No more than heterosexuals. The notion that homosexual people are particularly attracted to children is an ancient myth that still leads authorities to try and prevent homosexual men and women from holding jobs (such as teaching) where they will come into frequent contact with children. The fact is that over 90 percent of reported child molestations are cases of heterosexual men taking advantage of young girls."

Q: "Okay, but shouldn't known homosexual adults be kept away from children just as a precaution?"

A: "Why? There is no evidence that homosexual adults try to persuade young people to become homosexual, and there is no evidence that one person can change another person's sexual orientation anyway. Even though an individual's orientation can vary a bit at different stages in his or her life, the main direction seems to be developed at a very early stage, regardless of whom the child is in contact with."

Q: "Surely homosexuality is accepted by most people today?"

A: "No. It is discussed more today than it used to be but homosexuals and homosexual acts are not generally accepted. Gay people are still discriminated against in the field of accommodation and the lack of legal protection from job discrimination (gay people have been sacked on the grounds of their homosexuality whether or not they had been previously convicted of a homosexual offence).

"However, the gay movement has made some progress in educating the public. In a Marplan survey conducted in the UK in 1979, 51 percent of those asked agreed that homosexuality between men and between women should be legally and socially acceptable. In a Gallup poll carried out in the same year, 73 percent of those questioned expressed the belief that homosexuals should be entitled to the same job opportunities as heterosexuals. Even so, 23 percent of those questioned still felt that adult male gay sex should be made a criminal offence again. In the UK such pressure groups as Festival of Light and the National Viewers and Listeners Association continually seek to harden popular opinion against the rights of gay people to conduct their lives without oppression."

Q: "Isn't homosexuality on the increase?"
A: "No. What has changed that may make you think it is on the increase is that the subject is more openly discussed now and a lot of previously silent men and women have openly admitted that they are gay. There is no evidence of an increasing proportion of the population becoming gay."

AGE Young boys and girls commonly have genital contact with each other when they play. This makes parents terribly nervous, especially if the contact is with someone of the same sex. Some parents become flooded with fears about their child's future sexual orientation. They discourage genital contact and consult a professional about the meaning of the child's behaviour, but in fact they are getting worked up over a common, developmentally appropriate experience.

In the same way that these acts by young children do not indicate sexual orientation, so the homosexual acts of preteens and teenagers are also generally unrelated to their sexual orientation. The research of Kinsey, Sorenson and others found that same-sex practices are not unusual in young people, especially before the age of 15. Most reports indicate that about 11 percent of boys and six percent of girls have some same-sex experience. If group masturbation, mutual masturbation, fondling and fantasy were also included, the percentage of young people having same-sex experiences would be much higher.

In fact, young people involved in same-sex sexual activity are normally responding to curiosity, peer pressure, genuine enjoyment, the thrill of trying something that is forbidden, and so on. Regardless of the percentage of adolescent activity of this kind, the percentage of the adult population with a homosexual orientation has remained pretty constant since Kinsey began the recording of valid statistics. We should therefore regard the early sexual experiences of boys with each other and of girls with each other as a natural part of their sexual development. It is very possible that such experiences can have no significant effect on a young person's sexual orientation anyway — and many experts feel that it will have been fixed well before.

Between adolescence and middle age gay people suffer society's putdowns and repressions, but the problems they are likely to experience are not all orientation-related. Ours is a youth culture, and older people in it, whatever their orientation, experience some alienation. Young people can be insensitive to the feelings of older people, and young gay people are no exception. These are real problems that everyone may have to face.

The unreal problem of aging gay people is society's stereotype of the elderly, depressed, unattractive, lonely person — the "old dyke" or the "old queen." Of course people of 60 are not going to look as they did when they were 20, but they don't have to be less attractive, less sexually active or less capable of maintaining relationships. Of course some older gay people experience loneliness and depression, but so too do large numbers of heterosexual people. Equally, a great many older homosexual people are well adjusted, settled, comfortable with themselves; they may well be more resilient than their heterosexual peers because of the knocks they have had to take from society along the way. Older gay people are less competitive, more secure in themselves and usually less visible than the young or the disturbed. Precisely because their lives conform so well to the accepted pattern of our society we tend not to notice them.

Q: "We are friendly with a lovely and happy gay couple. Will that be harmful to our kids?"

A: "No. On the contrary, the fact that your children see two gay people happy in their relationship will enable them to be more accepting of gay men and women and make them less affected by society's homosexual stereotypes and stigma. It is also very important for children to see their parents behaving in a civilized way, free from prejudice and fear of homosexual people.
"I don't know what else you had in mind, but remember a homosexual orientation is not taught or caught!"

FEELINGS

"At first I felt 'Why me? What have I done wrong to deserve this?'"

"I used to put myself down because I was gay. Now I've worked it out and I couldn't be happier."

"At first I thought I was peculiar, even sick; but I couldn't go through life like that so I accepted who I was and went on with my life."

"I just never felt it was a problem. Certainly it was difficult at times but I can't say I felt awful and guilty."

"The major feelings I had about my homosexuality have been guilt, anger, self-hate and humiliation. How long can you go on with feelings like that?"

"I felt sorry for who I was for a long time. Then around the time of the movement it happened for me. I don't know if it was all the other people like me who were so supportive or whether I just matured, but I really grew as a person and discarded my negative self-image."

These are only some of the wide range of feelings people with a homosexual orientation have about themselves. They cannot reach the depth of the feelings experienced by gay people in society because words can't adequately describe the continual turmoil, self-hate and humiliation so many gays have felt for so long. Many millions of men and women with a homosexual orientation have been made to pay an enormous price for their sexuality by an unfeeling society, a society whose response to a sexual orientation that is different is to label it inferior and wrong. Being part of a group of human beings so characterized naturally leads to feelings of low self-esteem and self-worth. But some of this is changing. The gay liberation movement, the women's movement and the entire human rights movement have been helpful in providing a climate for gays to develop important support systems and networks to diminish their feelings of alienation and isolation. Support has bred confidence, with the result that many gay people who used to suffer under society's rejection have now achieved far better acceptance of themselves and of their sexual orientation as part of themselves.

The struggle that gay people have had and continue to have with their feelings about themselves doesn't derive from their "condition." It derives from the majority view in our society that says gays are inferior, lack human dignity and therefore deserve neither rights nor respect. When as a society we accept that people are not to be put down for any healthy aspect of any healthy personality, the negative feelings of gay people will have a real chance to dissipate into thin air.

Q: "Don't parents of a gay person feel terrible when they learn about their son or daughter?"

A: "Yes. Most parents do feel guilt and anger when they learn that their child is homosexual. Many parents blame themselves for what they consider to be a terrible condition and they will immediately try to get their child to change to heterosexuality by 'talking some sense into them,' or getting them to go to a doctor. Fortunately, many parents are learning that they are not to blame (as there is nothing wrong) and that their son or daughter is the same person as ever with the same capacity to have loving relationships and to lead a happy, productive life. A very useful book for parents who learn they have a homosexual child is *A Family Matter: A Parents' Guide to Homosexuality*, by Dr Charles Silverstein."

Q: "I'm gay and sometimes I really hate myself. What should I do?"
A: "Some gay people hate themselves and feel guilty because they have been taught that the things their sexual orientation leads them to do are wrong and unnatural. Given the stigma and discrimination gay people live with, it is understandable that these feelings should develop, and that the mix of these feelings can easily lead to a painful daily existence, interfering with the spontaneity and joy that can be a proper part of living. The many gay men and gay women who have overcome self-hate and guilt have done so by a variety of methods. Being with other gay people, sharing problems and learning from them is one. Accepting yourself for who you are and growing with that identity can be achieved with help from a qualified and sensitive counsellor or therapist. Many gay people work through it themselves until after maybe years of personal struggle and self-examination they achieve self-acceptance, feel worthy as people and feel capable of giving love and being loved."

Q: "I saw these two lesbians sitting in the park, holding hands, and I felt very angry. Why do they have to do that and flaunt themselves?"
A: "Did you never hold hands in the park with someone you really cared about? Did you never feel so affectionate toward someone

that you wanted everyone to know about it? Was holding hands 'flaunting' when you did it? You're not really suggesting that genuine gay affection has to be entirely hidden, are you?"

RELATIONSHIPS Gay relationships are complicated and simple, enduring and short, happy and troubled, as varied, indeed, as heterosexual relationships. But there are some problems specific to gay relationships.

When a relationship cannot be legally recognized or sanctioned, when much of society may see it as a threat and when it may have to be conducted with some measure of secrecy, it is bound to suffer some special stress. All relationships go through stressful periods, but if stress is built into the relationship already it is going to be harder for the two people concerned to work through the bad times. One can only pay tribute to the growing numbers of gay people who have developed and sustained stable relationships with members of their own sex despite the hostile social climate.

A real difference between homosexual and heterosexual relationships is that there is no clear precedent for who does what. Even though a great many heterosexual couples have rejected traditional roles, they are still there to fall back on. If the relationship is between two men or two women, who does what has to be decided by discussion and negotiation. In marriages, money earned tends to be pooled — that is the traditional arrangement. But does it apply when both people are pursuing independent careers, as in most gay relationships? Some arrangement has to be arrived at, which will require negotiation.

A traditional heterosexual view of homosexual relationships is that they always show a dominant figure and a submissive one, rather after the stereotype (not the reality) of heterosexual marriage. Certainly there are gay relationships in which this is so, where the roles played are akin to those of father and son, mother and daughter, dominant extrovert and submissive introvert, but they are becoming fewer as more gay people accept themselves as full people.

Some gay women and men argue against traditional relationships and the idea of sexual fidelity. They believe that their personal freedom will be limited if they subscribe by imitation to a cultural system that has oppressed them for centuries. This does not mean that they do not experience and enjoy loving, enduring relationships, but that they reject traditional, dependent relationship patterns.

The future is brighter now for gay people and gay relationships than it has ever been. However, I must quickly add that a quantum leap has to be made before gay people receive from society the treatment they deserve as ordinary human beings. Even so, there is some evidence of scattered social, legal and religious acceptance of homosexual relationships. The emerging self-acceptance of large numbers of gay people is contributing too, as by being positive and rejecting the status quo they develop a gay consciousness that is authentic, just and individually fulfilling.

Q: "How many people get married and then divorced because of their homosexuality?"

A: "About 15 to 20 percent of gay men, and about 25 percent of gay women."

Q: "Would gay relationships last longer if they could be legally recognized?"

A: "Not necessarily. Relationships don't endure or break up according to their legal status. All you need to do is look around at the state of legally recognized heterosexual marriages — legal recognition doesn't make them permanent.

"Relationships that last do so because people care for each other, consider each other's needs and are willing to be flexible."

Q: "When homosexuals live together like a married couple, don't they have special roles like masculine and feminine?"

A: "No. The limited data on this topic makes it emphatically clear that terms like dominant, submissive, active, passive, masculine and feminine are just not relevant. The sharing of responsibilities and the distribution of who does what, when and why is based more on individual interests, ability and a spirit of mutuality than on the role standards set by heterosexual couples."

Q: "Do gay people really get married?"

A: "Although some gays go through some sort of 'marriage', they are not legally married. The gay movement is trying to achieve both legal and religious validation for gay marriage ceremonies. In the UK, for example, there is an organization called the Gay Christian Movement which counts clergymen among its members and which is trying to establish gays' rights to be married in the fullest legal and religious sense.

"There are no large or definitive studies of homosexual 'marriages' yet, but if they do increase in popularity and become easier to study, they certainly won't have to last too long to match the record of heterosexual marriages in the last ten years!"

Q: "What's likely to happen if a person tells his or her children he or she is gay?"

A: "Difficulties, though how severe they will be depends on all sorts of things. How old the children are, how much they understand about homosexuality, what their relationships with that parent are, how the other parent responds, whether the parents are together or apart, how cohesive the family is — all these things can have some bearing. The younger the child, the more likely she/he is to feel confused, abandoned, even guilty.

"Many gay parents feel that they have to face up to the truth about themselves, not just in their own interest but in order that those near to them should be dealt with honestly. The pain and anger that is likely to follow the parent's disclosure is often replaced by acceptance and understanding later on. Some gay parents have very good relationships with their children afterwards, so these situations are not doomed from the outset."

CULTURE There is evidence of homosexuality throughout recorded history. Sometimes homosexual practices appear to have been entirely acceptable, sometimes they were regarded as degrading and dishonour-able. In ancient Egypt, for example, those defeated in battle were forced to submit to homosexual acts as further proof of their victors' superiority. Yet in ancient Greece homosexuality was not only acceptable but proper.

Rome, in its pre-Christian days, also knew homosexuality. Both Nero and Caligula were celebrated for their homosexual activities, Petronius wrote about homosexuality in his *Satyricon* and male prostitutes were common. Things changed in the fourth century A.D., when laws were enacted against homosexuals, making anal intercourse punishable by death. Thereafter in the West, homosexual people were in for a hard time, particularly as Christianity spread.

In the sixth century, the Emperor Justinian called for public penance by homosexuals. By the eleventh century, the *Penitentials* — the guides used by Catholic confessors to assess penalties — were recording very severe punishments, particularly for homosexual priests and monks. In sixteenth-century England laws were passed making homosexuality punishable by confiscation of goods and lands, and even by death.

The first major change of view came with the Code Napoléon, the revised French penal code published in 1804. Under its provisions, homosexual acts became legal between consenting adults. Some other countries followed suit, but England and America maintained their repressive attitudes and reinforced them by laws. Most, though not all, of these laws were directed against male homosexuals; in a number of countries female homosexuality simply was not recognized. When a new bill that had passed through both English Houses of Parliament reached Queen Victoria for her approval and signature, she left in the clauses about male homosexuality but struck out the references to lesbianism, denying that it could exist.

In the past, homosexual men particularly have suffered under the law. In the UK until the 1967 Sex Offences Act, homosexuality between men was illegal in England and Wales. Scotland was only brought into line with England and Wales in 1980. In Northern Ireland, Eire, the Isle of Man, and the Channel Islands all homosexual acts between men are illegal. Lesbianism has never been illegal and lesbians escaped the Act of 1885 which declared male homosexual acts to be "gross indecency" partly because Victorians refused to believe that women could be homosexual. However, the social discrimination against lesbians is probably even more ferocious than that against male gays.

Modern America, despite a large and vociferous gay population, is still more repressive in its legislation against homosexuals than many other countries. Being homosexual is not illegal in America, only performing sexual acts with a member of the same sex or seeking to do so. The laws discriminate and adversely affect the homosexual by outlawing sodomy, loitering to solicit and "lewd behaviour" as well discriminating in the areas of jobs, housing, credit, insurance, divorce and child custody.

Homosexual acts have been decriminalized in France, Scandinavia, the Netherlands, Italy, Spain, Mexico and Brazil. Despite the gradual liberalizing of UK law relating to homosexuals there is still discrimination. The age of consent for gay males is 21 as against 16 for heterosexuals; gays are only allowed to have sex 'in private' which technically means that no-one else other than the two men concerned can be in the same room, house, flat or even hotel; homosexual acts are still illegal for members of the Armed Forces and for merchant seamen at sea.

Q: "With all the problems facing gays, why did they choose to be gay?"

A: "They didn't. They couldn't. No-one can choose to be homosexual or heterosexual. Gay people do not believe that they were born heterosexual and then chose to be homosexual, they believe that their homosexual orientation is a natural part of their personalities just as you believe your heterosexual orientation is a natural part of yours."

Q: "Are the states of the USA in the process of repealing their anti-homosexual laws?"

A: "No. Some states have been successful in repealing their sodomy laws and the laws that discriminated against gays in housing, employment and insurance. However, most communities throughout the US have continued to vote against repealing them in their own states.

"Although things are getting better for homosexual people, American society has a long way to go before they achieve full freedom under the law."

Q: "When did the gay liberation movement begin?"

A: "The movement to achieve and protect full civil rights for gays became most vocal in the US and the New York City Police raid on a gay bar, the Stonewall, June 28, 1969, seemed to trigger a national movement in America. Inevitably the repercussions of this confrontation and the general influence of the gay liberation movement were felt particularly in Britain and Europe. Many people see gay liberation as one part of the overall civil rights movement, which had been gathering pace and effectiveness during the 60s."

Q: "I heard there were some cultures where homosexuality was not considered to be perverted. Is that true?

A: "Yes. In the Swain culture in North Africa, for example, male homosexuality seems to be approved, as it is in Melanesia (although there it seems that an exclusive homosexual orientation is rare).

"The anthropologists Ford and Beach reported that in the majority of the cultures they studied homosexual acts were known and tacitly approved of. Margaret Mead found evidence of male homosexual acts in some tribes in Papua-New Guinea but not in others. Overall it seems that in Papua-New Guinea female homosexuality is rare and not approved."

Q: "Isn't it true that the goal of the gay movement is to separate into their own social group and be apart from everyone else?"

A: "No. The great majority of gays who are active in the gay liberation movement are seeking to live fully and equally in society
without discrimination from the law and without social stigma.
They want ordinary human rights in ordinary society.

"It is true, however, that there are a few political activists
who reject the straight society that has always rejected them.
They are seeking to set up an alternative gay society because they
do not believe they will ever achieve full freedoms under the
present system."

RELIGION Religious teachings have been and still are to a large extent
responsible for the alienation homosexuals have felt and for discrimination
against them. Judeo-Christian teachings on the subject derive from the
Bible and from the pronouncements of scholars and religious leaders. It is
important to point out here that scripture discusses only homosexual acts
and not people with a homosexual orientation. Interestingly, only male
homosexual acts are discussed. Female homosexual acts are mentioned in
the Bible merely in a passing reference.

Catholicism. Catholic tradition and teaching is an extension of the biblical injunction against homosexual acts as sinful and against nature. The
writings of Church authorities such as St Augustine and St Thomas
Aquinas and the contemporary guidelines about acceptable sexual practice
for Catholics have consistently and clearly indicated that homosexual acts
are contrary to the will of God and opposed to fundamental Catholic views
about sex, marriage and procreation. *The Principles to Guide Confessors in
Questions of Homosexuality* indicates that homosexual acts are intrinsically
evil and contrary to the will of God. The 1975 *Vatican Declaration on
Sexual Ethics* describes homosexual acts as intrinsically disordered and
states that they cannot be approved of.

This rigid position has been of little help to the numerous people in the
Church who work with homosexual men and women. Accordingly, some
modern Catholic theologians have no choice but to reject the more conservative teachings of their church and choose instead to accept homosexuality
as a valid life-style and work with homosexual men and women in a just,
Christian fashion free from condemnation and discrimination.

Judaism. Jewish tradition on homosexuality has also been greatly influenced by the biblical record and by scholarly commentaries. Talmudic
literature and the *Responsa* of the great Hebrew scholars regard homosexual acts as abominations because they are unnatural, idolatrous and
hedonistic. According to the Talmud, homosexual acts are grievous and
punishable by stoning to death. Generally, only male homosexual acts were
written about; female homosexual acts were rarely mentioned, but were
also adjudged delinquent and immoral.

Although the basic law of Judaism remains the same today, and
Orthodox believers still view homosexuality as unnatural and wrong, both
the conservative and reformed elements of Judaism are beginning to treat
those with a homosexual orientation with understanding and compassion,
though without accepting homosexual acts as right or normal.

Protestantism. Protestants have generally followed the interpretations of the Old and New Testaments and have condemned homosexual practices. Martin Luther said that homosexual acts were perverse and against nature. Calvin, too, condemned homosexual acts, particularly as they could not lead to procreation.

In America, churches like the United Church of Christ, the Moravian Church of America and the Lutheran Church of America have not only developed formal positions fostering social justice for gay people but they also have made advances in accepting homosexual men and women into the community of God. Britain's Christian communities are also re-evaluating their positions on homosexuality.

In 1979, a sanctioned committee submitted a report to the Methodist Church on human sexuality. Regarding homosexuality they concluded:

> "This involves an acceptance of homosexual activities as not being intrinsically wrong. The quality of any homosexual relationship is to be assessed by the same basic criteria which have been applied to heterosexual relationships. It is the quality of these relationships which matters, not the physical expression which they may take."

The Church of England also received a report, submitted by its Board for Social Responsibility. Although heterosexual marriage is seen as the norm, this Anglican report states:

> "In the light of some of the evidence we have received we do not think it possible to deny that there are circumstances in which individuals may justifiably choose to enter into a homosexual relationship with the hope of enjoying a companionship and physical expression of sexual love similar to that which is found in marriage. Such a relationship could not be regarded as the social or moral equivalent of marriage; it would be bound to have a private and experimental character which marriage cannot and should not have. Nevertheless, fidelity and permanence, although not institutionally required, would undoubtedly do much to sustain and enhance its genuinely personal commitment and aspirations."

Q: "What is the Muslim view on homosexuality?"
A: "Muslims officially condemn homosexual acts. Islam, furthermore, has a special category of forbidden sexual acts for which the punishment is death. Sodomy is one."

Q: "I'm a Christian and lately I've become very confused about what my church believes and what they want us to believe. What is the problem anyway?"
A: "The issue is particularly confusing because of the widespread effort on the part of some Christian communities to rethink their position. For centuries Christianity has had largely unchristian views on homosexuality — punitive, uncaring, denying human dignity and rights. Many churches are still unwilling to rectify their injustices toward homosexuals and are still playing word

games with scripture, interpretation and tradition. Yet it is clear that the Bible is not and was not meant to be a textbook on human sexuality, so trying to ferret out every little passage that may provide us with a hint is just not helpful.

"No human being makes a conscious choice that he or she will be homosexual, and any honest analysis of the scientific data, or knowledge and understanding of the real people who are homosexuals will demonstrate that. So why not accept sexuality and sexual expression as a gift from God, and use the standards of love and fulfilment as the way to make judgments (if we must) about the morality or immorality of a person's acts? Sexual expression that is exploitive, uncaring and insensitive is immoral, while sexual expression that is caring, integrative and growth-producing is complete and moral. Whether the context is a same-sex relationship or an other-sex relationship is only secondary to the meaning of the expression."

Q: "I'm gay and a Christian. Sometimes I feel so alone, is there a group that I can join?"

A: "Over the past decade or so there has been a determined effort by gay Christians, including clergy of many denominations throughout the US, UK, Europe and Commonwealth to achieve recognition as homosexuals with a legitimate position within their respective churches. In the UK, for example, there are gay Catholic, Anglican, Quaker and Unitarian groups contactable through the Gay Christian Movement (BM Box 6914, London WC1N 3XX) and the Metropolitan Community Church (BM Box 6303, London WC1N 3XX)."

Q: "Is there a gay Jewish movement?"

A: "Yes. During the late 1970s a group of American Jewish homosexual people organized a serious religious congregation and were admitted into the Union of American Hebrew Congregations. Although there is no Jewish homosexual synagogue in the UK there is a Jewish homosexual group (BM JGG, London WC1N 3XX) which, along with other Jewish homosexual groups in the West felt the need to have regular religious worship with women and men with whom they felt a true kinship and sense of community. Being with other homosexual people allows gay people to feel a sense of comfort and honesty they were unable to feel in another congregation."

Q: "Is it true that there are clergy and ministers who are gay and still doing their jobs?"

A: "Yes. An Archbishop of Canterbury has admitted that there are many homosexual men in the Anglican clergy, and Baptists, Roman Catholics, Presbyterians and other religious groups have indicated that there are priests and ministers in their religions who have a homosexual orientation. Many of them continue to serve the community without a problem."

Bisexuality

FACTS Bisexuality is the orientation in which a person achieves sexual and emotional satisfaction and fulfilment with members of both sexes. Bisexuality is a lifelong orientation, although relating sexually to both sexes may be limited to a particular period in a bisexual's life. Both men and women can be bisexual.

Many sexologists now accept that bisexuality is as genuine an orientation as heterosexuality or homosexuality. Bisexuals therefore are not people whose orientation is fundamentally homosexual but who have some heterosexual sex on the side, nor are they people whose orientation is fundamentally heterosexual but who enjoy some homosexual sex on the side. Having said that, it is important to recognize that very little scientific study has been done on bisexuality and that there is a considerable element of generalizing guesswork in descriptions of bisexuality. New research could change our opinions.

The Kinsey studies on male and female sexual behaviour showed that sexual orientation was a matter of degree, that people could be found at every point on a scale running from exclusive heterosexuality to exclusive homosexuality. Kinsey also showed that the same person can be at different points on the scale during his or her lifetime.

Kinsey found that 18 percent of white men in his study had at least as much homosexual as heterosexual experience for at least three years between the ages of 16 and 55. Between four and 11 percent of unmarried women and between one and two percent of married women had homosexual experiences as frequently as heterosexual experiences in each of the years between their ages 20 and 35. In the same age range the figures for divorced women were five to seven percent. Clearly, bisexuality is by no means rare.

Why are some people bisexual? We simply don't know, for the same reasons that we do not know what gives some people a heterosexual orientation and others a homosexual one. People have speculated, of course. A bisexual orientation is sometimes attributed to parent–child relationships. Some researchers feel the answer may be found in the effect of certain hormones on the brain centres of a child while it is still in the womb. Others see no need to identify the roots of bisexuality since they deny it exists — they believe that bisexuals are people whose true orientation is homosexual but who are disguising it. Still others believe we are all born with the capacity to relate to both sexes but become socialized into heterosexuality or homosexuality, with a minority remaining bisexual.

Freud was one expert who denied the existence of bisexuality. In his view, people are either heterosexual or homosexual; anyone exhibiting signs of bisexual behaviour is in a transitory phase from one orientation to the other or is suffering a personality disorder. Some psychoanalysts still support that view, though more and more accept that a bisexual orientation does exist and that it is not a sign of a personality problem.

Much of the current information about bisexuality is taken from studies of men and women with a homosexual orientation who have had some heterosexual experiences. It is therefore not representative of

GENDER AND SEXUAL ORIENTATION/Bisexuality 187

bisexuality as an orientation in itself. It has, however, been a starting point, and the work of Blumstein, Schwarz and Klein in America added to it has helped begin the organization of information about bisexuality in an understandable way.

Dr Fred Klein in his book *The Bisexual Option* classifies bisexuality in three ways — transitional, historical and sequential.

Transitional Bisexuality. A transitional bisexual is a person who is moving (probably) from heterosexuality to homosexuality. Moving in the other direction is less common. According to Dr Klein, the movement in either direction may occur within a short period of time, but it can take more than a year to complete. If a person is evaluated during this period the orientation will appear bisexual, but at some time thereafter it will show as homosexual or heterosexual. Dr Klein and the authors of *Barry and Alice: A Portrait of a Bisexual Marriage* have found relatively few people in this stage.

Historical Bisexuality. The historical bisexual is a person who is essentially homosexual or heterosexual, but who, at some point, has had some sexual experience with or fantasy about a person whose sex ran counter to his or her orientation.

Sequential Bisexuality. In this category, the person has a relationship with a person of one sex and following that has a relationship with a person of the other sex. The commitment to the relationship is equal in each case. The number of such relationships will vary, depending on the needs of the person.

The point is that a person with a bisexual orientation does not fit simply into a single mould. There are shades and degrees of behaviour and attitude, all of which must be considered and all of which result in a complexity that is not yet adequately understood.

Q: "Do bisexuals have sex one day with a person of one sex and the next day with someone of the other sex?"

A: "Sometimes a person with a bisexual orientation will have two simultaneous sexual relationships — one with a woman and one with a man — but that is not usual. Generally, the limited data suggest that most people with a bisexual orientation have a relationship with one person and when it ends they are quite likely to seek another relationship but with a partner of the alternative sex. Affairs during a lasting relationship may also be used to express the duality of the orientation."

Q: "Does a person actually have to have sex with people of each sex to be a bisexual?"

A: "Most definitions of a bisexual orientation include having sex with a person of each sex. However, Dr Fred Klein in his book *The Bisexual Option* suggests that nonsexual emotional intimacy with each sex is a dimension of bisexuality."

Q: "Don't bisexuals have sex with people of their own sex and of the other sex on an equal basis?"

A: "Usually not. Most have a tendency toward relationships with one sex more than with the other, but the importance of the relationships appears to be the same to them, regardless of the sex of the other person."

Q: "At what age do people usually discover their bisexuality?"

A: "Usually later than either heterosexuals or homosexuals. The majority of people model the heterosexual orientation and drift easily into that life-style without consciously thinking about it. Most homosexuals begin by trying to fit the heterosexual mould, usually realize by adolescence that it is not satisfying and right for them and so begin to express their homosexuality. Because of the myth that people are either heterosexual or homosexual, bisexuals struggle for a longer time trying to conform to one life-style or the other. It can therefore be well into their 20s or 30s even before bisexual people accept their orientation."

Q: "When men or women in prison have sex with someone of the same sex does that mean they are really bisexual?"

A: "Usually not. Sex with someone of the same sex in a confined situation like a prison is more likely the result of a need for human contact and a release of sexual tension than a real homosexual orientation. Usually, the fantasy lives of such people and their true preferences are directed toward the other sex, but their circumstances dictate same-sex expression or none at all. Although some same-sex expression in prison is genuinely homosexual in orientation, the majority of released prisoners return to their previous heterosexual or bisexual orientation."

Q: "I've noticed that some people in the entertainment business flaunt their bisexuality. Isn't that a bad example for all the teenagers who imitate them?"

A: "No. Sexual orientation is not something that a person can turn off or on depending on the fad at the moment. Sexual orientation is part of the essential fabric of personality and imitating sexual behaviour is just that — imitation. It will not mean anything to teenagers in the long run unless it is truly their orientation."

MYTHS Bisexuality, probably because it has been less noticed and less discussed than, say, homosexuality, has not built up a really widespread network of popular mythology. The myths that are in circulation, however, betray our society's serious ignorance about bisexuality and bisexuals:

* bisexuals are half man and half woman; they are ambiguous
* bisexuals are really homosexuals who protect their identity by having sex with the other sex
* bisexuals develop because of poor parenting
* bisexuals cannot have lasting relationships

* bisexuals are fence sitters trying to get the best of sex from men and women
* a person is either all heterosexual or all homosexual.

FEELINGS Bisexual people's feelings about their orientation are enormously influenced by the social definitions of what is normal, appropriate, right and natural. Under these circumstances it is not unusual for women and men with a bisexual orientation to feel alienated and oppressed, and for them to raise serious questions about their sexual identity.

> "At first I thought I was weird. How could I feel this way about men and women?"

> "I always heard things like a bisexual was a secret gay. That just wasn't me."

> "I had this secret and I just kept it to myself. Finally I've accepted who I am as a sexual person."

> "What will my family and friends think and say about me?"

> "My bisexual identity was late in developing. I always felt it was there but I denied it."

> "I won't explain or justify my feelings about this. It just is."

Constant questioning and self-examination in an effort to understand oneself can be an enormous emotional burden, taxing every moment and effectively preventing a rich and fulfilling life. Living and growing with who you are is difficult and a challenge for everyone, but for the bisexual minority, as for the homosexual minority, the historical, social and personal barriers make it doubly so. Clearly, the problems can be resolved and the growing support of understanding people may be particularly helpful, but surely the first step must be squarely to face the issue of one's identity. Once one's outside and inside are together, it is then necessary to work with the same resolve on the important family and social connections that need to be dealt with. Sometimes a qualified and sensitive counsellor or therapist can help, but in the end the answer must lie within each person. Hostile though the majority of society's attitudes are, it is possible to turn what at first seems a set of unfair obstacles into an enriching, creative life-style.

RELATIONSHIPS It is not only bisexuals who may have relationship problems but, even more, the nonbisexual people with whom they get involved:

> "I think I'm bisexual, but I'm sure my relationship would break up if I acted on it."

> "Although I really don't like the fact that my husband is bisexual, our relationship is OK. I just don't think about him with another person."

"I wouldn't get involved with a bisexual — they just don't know what they want or who they are."

"Bisexuals are fence sitters. I keep away from them until they find out who they are."

"I said 'yes' to a bisexual relationship, but I said 'no' to having children."

"My lover knows I'm bisexual. It's just a part of me like everything else in my personality. It doesn't get in the way at all."

Of these six comments from and on bisexuals, only one claims that bisexuality causes no relationship problems. Bisexuals have particular difficulties in relationships — they are both different and often misunderstood. Being different usually means some degree of rejection, making it harder to form relationships. Being misunderstood has the same effect: people who do not have a bisexual orientation themselves often find it hard to understand that their relationship with a bisexual person can be properly valid and rewarding. Bisexual people can therefore, through no fault of their own, not only find it harder to start relationships than people whose orientation is heterosexual or homosexual but can also find it harder to keep them going.

Jealousy, which can be a problem in any relationship, is particularly likely in a relationship in which one partner is bisexual. If both partners are bisexual the possibilities are theoretically vast. The real sense of competition that can arise may be threatening and will create stress. Some authorities on bisexuality believe the chances of these problems arising are greatly diminished if a bisexual person is fully resolved in his or her orientation. People who are bisexual and fully self-accepting in fact claim positive benefits from their orientation, saying that it offers them enormous possibilities for personal growth.

Bisexual people have similar problems to those that homosexual people have in "coming out" and making their orientation known to family, friends and children. How much is it fair to tell whom? Is it better to face them with the whole truth or to protect them by disguising it? Even the most sensitive handling of these circumstances creates stress for the couple and therefore in the relationship.

As bisexuality comes to be studied we will no doubt learn more about the rewards and problems of relationships in which bisexual people are involved. At the moment, all we can be reasonably sure of is that many people in relationships with bisexuals find their partners' orientation confusing and on occasion difficult to handle.

Q: "I read about some married couples that are bisexual. They have their marriage and they also have lovers of their own sex. This sounds weird to me; does it really happen?"

A: "Yes it does, but it is not very common. There are reports of couples who have accepted their bisexuality, remained married, had children and had same-sex relationships while their marriages continued, apparently successfully. In the book *Barry and Alice: A Portrait of a Bisexual Marriage*, the authors describe exactly this experience and suggest that there are more couples like themselves who are involved in this kind of relationship.

"In a society so accustomed to male–female marriages, children and grandchildren, understanding a nontraditional relationship structure is quite difficult; accepting it as a valid life-style is an even more troublesome task. Nevertheless, people are unique, and have continually resisted classification into set models. Throughout history people have learned that there is value and merit in respecting differences."

CULTURE Numbers of the most famous people in history appear to have been bisexual. Alexander the Great, conqueror of the known world, was twice married and certainly had sexual relationships with men too. His fellow Greeks Socrates and Plutarch were following the proper Greek pattern in marrying and having children as well as having sexual relationships with boys. Julius Caesar had a reputation for having sex with whomever was available — man or woman, young or old — despite three marriages (one to Cleopatra).

Leonardo da Vinci and Michelangelo may both have been bisexual. Nearer our own time, Oscar Wilde, commonly regarded as one of the most celebrated homosexuals of history, had a wife and children with whom he lived and to whom he was devoted. André Gide and Somerset Maugham also related to both sexes, despite their popular reputations.

This list could go on for a very long time, and we would never be able to say with certainty that anyone on it was a genuine bisexual. Social pressures can condition the appearance of sexual orientations out of all recognition, making it impossible for us to judge retrospectively what really motivated the behaviour of an individual. What we can be sure of is that a great many people throughout history have exercised their capacities to relate to both sexes.

Why is this all about men? Because women have at most times and in most places been decreed into an inferior position, which made their activities "not worth recording." Quite often it has been thought that women were either uninterested in sex or incapable of relating sexually to other women. No wonder that, until now, there has been an almost complete lack of information about who has a bisexual orientation and how it is expressed.

RELIGION The traditional teaching of the Roman Catholic Church and Orthodox Judaism on bisexuality is to reject it, following their general principles that heterosexuality, marriage and procreation are the ideal; likewise the fundamentalist Protestant groups. Even the Protestant, Roman Catholic and Jewish groups whose beliefs about sexuality are more progressive have not yet developed public positions on bisexuality. Although there is a likelihood that these groups would be sympathetic toward people with a bisexual orientation, their attention to issues of orientation is limited to homosexuality for the time being. It is possible that a resolution of their positions on homosexuality may lead on to a greater recognition of bisexual behaviour, but that is unlikely to occur for quite a while yet.

Transsexualism

FACTS A transsexual is a person born biologically male or female but who passionately believes he or she should have been born a member of the other sex. Transsexuals believe that a biological mistake has been made and they were born with the wrong body for their feelings and desires. Therefore, many of them seek medical help to change their physical identity to match their internal, emotional identity. The term "transsexual" is generally used to describe people with these feelings whether they have sex-change surgery or not.

Since a male transsexual believes he is really a woman he desires a relationship with a heterosexual male. Accordingly, the male transsexual has erotic, romantic and emotional responses to men and fantasies about them. Likewise, a female transsexual believes she is really a man and therefore desires a relationship with a heterosexual female. Accordingly, she has erotic, romantic and emotional responses to women and fantasies about them.

These situations are difficult to handle, but they are *not* homosexual and transsexuals involved in such situations do not think of themselves or their relationships as homosexual. Conversely, most homosexuals are not transsexuals.

The dilemma of transsexuals did not receive worldwide publicity until the famous Christine Jorgensen case in 1952. Christine Jorgensen was formerly George Jorgensen, but received a sex-change operation in Denmark. At around that same time, Dr Harry Benjamin used the term "transsexualism" at a New York Academy of Medicine meeting, and from that time on, with Benjamin providing the initial leadership, transsexuals and transsexualism became a medical subject. In 1967, the Johns Hopkins Gender Identity Clinic in Baltimore, Maryland, began to study this problem. Soon they began to perform sex-change surgery, making it a legitimate and accepted part of medical practice. Gender clinics are now attached to a number of hospitals in Europe and America.

Since Christine Jorgensen there have been several other transsexuals who have received international publicity. There are though no accurate reports available on the exact numbers of transsexuals who have had surgery. In the US estimates are that there are several thousand who have had surgery and eight to ten thousand who have not, but who still identify themselves as transsexuals. Some people believe that since the medical standards in the US for sex-change surgery are very strict, many transsexuals go to Europe for the operations as requirements there are apparently less rigid.

Who are transsexuals and how do they get that way? We have no way of identifying people as prospective transsexuals. There are no physical, genetic or hormonal characteristics that can certainly identify them.

Some sexology researchers have begun work with boys and girls who show a variety of behaviours and feelings inappropriate for their sex at a very young age. For example, Dr Richard Green reports that adult men and women who were transsexuals recall that their toy preference, friend preference and clothing preference as children was usually the opposite of what was expected of their biological sex. This preference was not a phase similar to the natural variation of interest that all young people experience; it was a constant, fixed need despite their parents' efforts to change them to more "appropriate" behaviour. As yet, though, this work is still only speculation and any evidence requires rigorous testing with many more subjects before it can be taken as a serious sign.

Other researchers, such as Stoller and Guze, theorize about the roles of transsexuals' mothers and fathers. Very seductive mothers, weak, passive or absent fathers, castration anxiety and other combinations of parental feelings and behaviours toward their children may, Stoller and Guze believe, have some real influence. But this too is still speculative.

There is also a hormonal theory, which is held by most significant researchers in the field. It is thought that perhaps during a very sensitive period of foetal development certain hormone levels may predispose the child toward transsexualism. This theory, too, requires further examination and documentation.

We know nothing for sure about the causes of transsexualism. All we know with certainty is that some men and women feel a compelling need to change their bodies to match their emotional and psychological identities. No amount of psychotherapy or any other kind of counselling can influence the desire to change. If the present suspicions of some researchers that there is a biological determinant are confirmed, we shall presumably as a society accept the fact of transsexualism and no longer seek to persuade transsexuals that their feelings are unreal.

Before Surgery. Sex-change surgery is the final and irreversible step of a long and difficult process. Today, the surgery is usually performed 18 months to two years after the person has been accepted in a gender identity programme at a hospital where the surgery can be carried out. The following things have to be done before surgery can be attempted:

* medical tests are carried out to be certain the person is healthy, can take hormones and withstand surgery and hospitalization over a period of time
* psychological tests are conducted to be certain the person is not suffering from a character disorder or other serious mental health problem that would confuse transsexualism with some other conflict that would need to be resolved before treatment could begin
* personal interviews are conducted to get a full picture of the person's family, social and employment situation and history; the information is checked with alternative sources
* living the life of the intended sex is required before surgery for transsexuals; even if they have been living the life of their intended sex before getting involved in the programme, they must continue to do so in order that their behaviour be monitored and evaluated. During this period both sexes begin the hormone treatment, which they must continue throughout their lives. Male-to-female trans-

sexuals are put on oestrogen therapy (by tablet or injection), which develops breast tissue, reduces testicle size, softens skin, causes erectile loss and reduces muscular strength. This therapy is monitored carefully to be certain illness or disease does not result. Sometimes, surgery to reduce the size of the Adam's apple is also performed during this period, and some male-to-female transsexuals take lessons to raise their voice pitch. Electrolysis is used to remove facial hair and inappropriate body hair. Female-to-male transsexuals are placed on androgen therapy. This reduces menstruation and ovulation, increases facial and body hair, deepens the voice and enlarges the clitoris. Androgen sometimes increases libido, and may lead to the development of acne; hysterectomy and breast reduction or mastectomy are completed during this period

* extensive counselling is necessary to help the transsexual prepare for surgery and its consequences; issues of employment and family relationships, problems and concerns with sexual activity and physical appearance, are continually discussed both before and after sex-change surgery

* legal issues: there are many areas that create difficulty in the lives of those who seek to change their sex and the legal obstacles are among the most thorny. The problems begin prior to surgery when the transsexual is already dressing in the other sex's clothing and therefore may be arrested for insulting or indecent behaviour likely to cause a breach of the peace or for importuning. Transsexuals do suffer from this harassment and the anxiety that they may be questioned and arrested for what appears to others to be inappropriate and contradictory dress and behaviour. This embarrassment occurs even though preoperative transsexuals carry medical certificates that they are in treatment prior to surgery. After the surgery there are all sorts of barriers to overcome. Legally changing one's name and sex and getting it on a new birth certificate is difficult, time consuming and costly, as the authorities often resist doing this unless medical and legal issues have been absolutely clarified. Obtaining a new driver's licence, social security, mortgages and medical and life insurance coverage can be very difficult too, though not impossible. It does appear that the legal obstacles are lessening as transsexual surgery becomes more acceptable both as medical practice and as a feature of our society.

Q: "What happens if a man or woman changes their mind about the whole thing and they decide to act and live how they were born. Can they do that after hormones and all that?"

A: "Yes, as long as they haven't gone as far as surgery.

"They stop taking hormones and their biological characteristics return. Males regain their erectile ability, beard growth and their usual strength. Their breasts, however, may remain a bit puffy. Women resume ovulation, menstruation and their previous appearance, with the exception that they may have more body hair than usual. Androgen therapy also thickens the vocal chords, so their voices may remain a bit deeper."

Q: "I heard constructing a penis is a problem, so why do so many transsexuals have it done?"

A: "Many female-to-male transsexuals don't feel complete in their new identity until they have all the body parts of a man. Also, some transsexuals fear that they may be discovered and will have problems if they don't go all the way with their change. Public toilets or having to change or strip in front of other people can be so embarrassing without a penis that many transsexuals choose the multiple hospitalizations and surgery necessary to achieve the complete change."

Q: "I saw a transsexual woman with really big breasts. How did that happen?"

A: "Oestrogen, the female hormone, helps breast tissue develop, but some transsexuals also have surgical enlargement with silicone implants."

Q: "Why are there more male-to-female transsexuals than female-to-male transsexuals?"

A: "Although the disparity between male-to-female and female-to-male sex-change operations is decreasing the position is still as you state it. The fact that the surgery is more difficult and has a greater chance of complications is offered as one reason for the difference. Some researchers believe that transsexualism is a hormone-related problem and that men are more likely to suffer from it. Some believe sex-change surgery is a male invention to serve male needs; they believe that just as many women need the operations, but because they are (at that stage) women their needs are not acknowledged.

"Current data suggest that men and women are interested in sex-change surgery in more equal numbers than ever before."

Q: "Isn't it a bit much to allow these sex-change operations to continue? A male is a male, and a female is a female. Tampering with nature just isn't right. What are they going to do next?"

A: "It is very reasonable that you have difficulty understanding and accepting sex-change surgery. It is a very confusing issue for most people. However, highly trained, qualified doctors believe that it can be the best thing for those very few people who were born with a mixed identity. For them, sex-change surgery is almost a life saver because it gives them a chance to have a complete and happy existence.

"Transsexuals who have the sex-change operation go through a very difficult time. They feel it is worth it to have a chance of leading the kind of life that all people are entitled to. Difficult as it is for the rest of us to understand what they have gone through and to comprehend their motivation, we owe it to them to try and accept how they are. They have been a lot less fortunate than most of us who have no difficulty accepting our sexual identities."

Q: "How is it known for sure that transsexuals enjoy sex and have orgasm?"

A: "The reports from both transsexuals and their sex partners consistently indicate that sex is pleasurable, fulfilling and orgasmic. No-one has studied or watched them to be certain they are telling the truth so we accept their reports at face value — just as we have accepted the reports of nontranssexuals about their sexual experiences.

"The transsexuals I have spoken with described their sexual experiences in a very believable way without boasting at all. They discussed their feelings about themselves as sexual beings, their partners, the stimulation they prefer and the variety of their responses, including orgasm, in a natural and convincing manner."

MYTHS The following are some common myths about transsexuals and transsexualism:

* you can spot a transsexual a mile away
* transsexuals can't enjoy sex
* transsexualism is caused by wearing sissy clothing early in life
* transsexuals are usually sorry they had the operation
* transsexuals are really homosexuals looking for more sex
* male transsexuals are weak looking
* female transsexuals are flat chested and have broad shoulders.

Q: "Aren't transsexuals really gay since they have sex with someone of their own sex?"

A: "No. Though a man who really believes himself to be a woman usually chooses a man for sex and a woman who really believes herself to be a man usually chooses a woman for sex, they do not see it or feel it as a homosexual act. They are more likely to see having sex with someone of the other sex as homosexual since both people's sense of their sexual identity would then be the same. It is important to understand that true transsexuals in a way reject their bodies in order to stand by their convictions about their real sexual selves."

AGE Transsexuals tend to know they are different early in life. Most reports from transsexuals indicate that they just didn't feel right very early in childhood. Some recalled inappropriate behaviour for their biological sex even though they looked and were treated like ordinary girls and boys. Some transsexuals recall vague feelings of uneasiness about themselves and remember them becoming more fully formed in adolescence and early adulthood.

Because of the difficulties of being a transsexual, many adult transsexuals try and set limits to the extent of their transsexual behaviour in order to conform in part at least to the common standards of sexual behaviour. This may mean that the decision to enter treatment is put off until the person's late 20s or 30s, when they realize there is no alternative for them.

FEELINGS Words cannot fully capture the range and depth of the feelings transsexuals experience when their odyssey is complete. Their years of dreaming, confusion and depression come to an end when they have their long-awaited surgery.

Some of the same feelings of exhilaration are present for those who choose to have all the treatment except surgery.

"I cannot describe the feelings of total joy and fulfilment I had after my surgery. The suffering and pain was worth it."

"Some people think I'm weird. Let them. After all that I've been through I truly don't care about what others think or say. I'm finally happy."

"Since my surgery I finally feel together, complete."

"Sometimes I really grieve the loss of my family and friends, but I was so unhappy I just had to go through with it."

"Although there are problems now, and life does get difficult, it's better now than it's ever been for me."

"The happiest day for me was the very first time I went out into the street dressed and made up as I had always wanted to be. That was a terrific feeling!"

RELATIONSHIPS If someone decides to have sex-change surgery it usually has a major impact on those close to him or her. Transsexuals who are married usually get divorced, either on their own initiative or on the advice of counsellors. Remaining married is unlikely to work. Transsexuals' families too usually require counselling and support. Parents need to know "it's not their fault" — that the issue is medical, not psychological.

The support of families can be very valuable to a transsexual undergoing sex-change surgery, but, being realistic, few transsexuals can expect it. Most people have such difficulty accepting the idea of someone close to them changing sex that they are to some degree lost in their own confusion. A breakdown of communication followed by separation is unfortunately very common.

Wives or husbands are particularly hard hit, and are likely to be in need of supportive counselling and maybe therapy to deal with their anger, guilt or humiliation. Since some transsexual parents will leave their children's lives permanently once they have made their decision to have surgery, the remaining parent has a particularly difficult problem at a particularly difficult time. Explaining what a sex change means to a young child is a staggering task, and trying to work out some meaningful future relationship can be very difficult. But it has been done. For safety's sake, psychological monitoring and support for the children seems a good idea, though we have no long-term research to show what the consequences are for the children of sex-change transsexuals.

Q: "I heard these transsexuals date, and even get married. How do they do it and what kind of people do they have a relationship with anyway?"

A: "Dr Richard Green and others report that the boyfriends, girl-friends and spouses of postoperative transsexuals are very heterosexual in their orientation, so their relationships with the transsexuals are clearly heterosexual. This is a very important condition of a relationship for the transsexual, since she or he is erotically aroused, romantically inclined and responsive in a heterosexual way and always has been. Postoperative trans-sexuals tend to be very conventionally masculine or feminine in the way they dress and present themselves, and they tend to choose partners with whom they will represent a model heterosexual couple.

"Reports on the quality of the relationships up to now are impressively on the positive side. Female-to-male transsexuals marry and frequently adopt the children of the wife's previous marriage. Also, female-to-male transsexuals are so keen to have children that they often seek artificial insemination by donor.

"The people who date and/or marry postoperative trans-sexuals are not distinguishable in any negative way. Sometimes they are aware of their partner's situation and sometimes not. In marriage of course there is a more open and honest disclosure, but up to now there is no evidence to show that problems will inevitably arise."

Q: "Just what do transsexuals do when they have sex?"

A: "Male-to-female transsexuals find that their vaginas are fine for intercourse and they report having orgasm regularly — sometimes multiple orgasm. Since they experienced orgasm as males they know the feeling, and they usually describe it as similar but more intense. They cannot get pregnant because they have no internal organs of reproduction (uterus, ovaries, Fal-lopian tubes), but they practice and enjoy the usual range of sexual acts.

"Some female-to-male transsexuals who have had surgery can use their surgically constructed penis for intercourse if they use a special penis firmer. They do not ejaculate since they do not have semen-producing organs, but they report having fulfill-ing orgasm. Since the clitoral tissue remains they can and do experience a lot of pleasure.

"Transsexuals' partners seem to have no special problems in enjoying sex and achieving fulfilment.

"In fairness, though, sex in the lives of transsexuals cannot be described as perfect. They, like all people, struggle at times and have problems in their sexual relationships. Their unusual past, their surgery and appearance frequently present difficul-ties that are sometimes insurmountable, but for many it is worth the struggle in order to have a physical identity that finally matches their emotional identity."

INCEST

FACTS Incest means sexual activity between members of the same family and may include oral sex, masturbation, caressing and fondling as well as intercourse. Definitions of what constitutes a family in this context vary, but on the whole they include not only parents and siblings but grandparents, uncles, aunts, nieces, nephews and step kin; cousins may be included too. Penalties vary as widely as definitions, from fines to 50 years' imprisonment.

Incest is an under-studied subject. There is strong circumstantial evidence that it occurs far more frequently than is reported, but it is so closely surrounded by emotion and controversy that it is difficult for dispassionate observation to discover the true facts. Some speculations however seem to be consistently supported by such facts as we have:

* sibling incest is probably the most common form and is the least likely to be reported
* father–daughter incest is the second most common type and is the most frequently reported
* mother–son incest is the least commonly reported type, but appears to be more prevalent than reports suggest; it also appears to be highly damaging to the sons
* both father–son and mother–daughter incestuous relationships exist; they are the least studied of all forms of incest, but appear to be particularly damaging
* emotional and psychological coercion is more commonly used to establish incestuous relationships than physical force
* estimates are that five to ten percent of the population have been involved in incestuous acts
* in almost all cultures incest is unacceptable
* although there are some reports of individual cases of parent–child incest not resulting in psychological damage the majority of known cases appear to have been harmful to the child
* incestuous acts usually occur over a period of time and not just on a single occasion
* more than half of adolescent prostitutes of both sexes and of adolescent female drug addicts in the US have a history of incest
* incestuous relationships are more likely to be initiated by parents than by children
* incestuous relationships appear to occur in all socioeconomic classes.

Why incest should be subject to a near universal taboo we do not know. It has been suggested that the taboo is one way to protect the family unit from disorganization and conflict. Another speculation is that the management of sexual impulses within the family allows for the full emotional development of children, who can then form stable relationships outside the family and thereby improve and expand the social order. The idea, mistaken though it is in part, that children born of an incestuous sexual act would be mentally deficient must have influenced people strongly to avoid such relationships. Whatever the real reasons for avoiding incest are, they have to be more cultural than biological.

What are the causes of incest? Incest is a symptom of personal and/or family conflict. One of the recurring characteristics of incestuous situations is general family disorganization and improper and confused role development. Incest, especially father–daughter incest, frequently occurs at peak points of marital stress. Sometimes fathers turn to their children for the warmth and validation they need; through their children they are kept from facing their fears and failures. Disturbed relationships between mother and daughter are also evident in some father–daughter incest.

Alcoholism and overcrowding are secondary factors which, coexisting with other, more powerful, forces lead to some incestuous behaviour. In cases of sibling incest, social inhibition, isolation and poor personality development are factors; so are poor family structure and passive, ineffectual parents. Sometimes sibling intercourse results after periods of preadolescent genital exploration that have been continued beyond the appropriate period.

Although there are some conflicting reports about the results of incest, the overwhelming available evidence is that incest is emotionally damaging to both parties. The damage may be short lived or it may last throughout life.

The effects on the child and on the adult are not the same in every case. Much depends on the family, the participants and whether the relationship ends by mutual consent or is discovered. Girls who were involved in incestuous relationships frequently have a diminished self-image, and feel guilt and anger toward their families for not protecting them and taking proper care of them. Frequently they feel dirty and worthless, suffer depression and may have long-term difficulty in establishing affectionate, mutually satisfying sexual relationships with men. They may have orgasmic problems and desire problems, and a string of casual, distrustful relationships.

Fathers involved in incest face criminal action, humiliation in the family and community and risks of marital and family separation. Guilt over their acts remains with some fathers throughout their lives. Boys involved in mother–son incest have a difficult time developing full emotional lives. They may also suffer guilt, anxiety and depression for many years after.

Many services are required for the successful treatment of incest. In-depth evaluation of the family and a thorough psychological assessment both of those involved in the incestuous acts and of other significant family members is one aspect. Medical examination is also required. Individual psychotherapy, group psychotherapy and family therapy are used and self-help groups for adolescents have been found valuable. Residential treatment programmes may be desirable if the young person cannot or will not remain at home.

Q: "Isn't it true that children born from an incestuous relationship are retarded or have physical problems?"

A: "No. Although there is data showing that some children born of incestuous relationships are mentally deficient, there is other data that shows some children born as a result of incest are physically healthy and mentally superior."

Q: "Just what type of man would have incest with his daughter?"
A: "Only loose generalizations can be made about this as many of the studies have been conducted on disturbed men imprisoned for incest. Other clinical data rounds out the picture but there is no surety about the profile. Many of these men cannot deal in a mature fashion with other adults, especially with adult women. Frequently they are passive and dependent, lacking in self-esteem and self-confidence. Some are fundamental religious believers. Many of them had deprived economic and emotional lives as children and many have a history of problems with alcohol and/or other drugs."

Q: "Is it true that some experts are now saying that incest is OK?"
A: "My understanding is that they believe the area requires more thorough and systematic research in order to understand better the causes, effects and treatment of incest. The sanctions against incest are so strong, and reactions to the subject so emotionally loaded that careful study and analysis has not occurred until very recently. Words like 'victim,' 'trauma,' and 'child molestation' are routinely used when discussing incest and they tend to distort a proper examination and understanding of the subject.
    "It is true that some expert opinion is now saying that some cases of incest may not have been as damaging as was once generally thought. Some adults have been discovered whose history of incest in childhood does not appear to have been particularly harmful, but it would be wrong to generalize from the fortunate few when we know of so many people who have suffered so much definite harm."

Q: "I heard about a man who said that his children were his responsibility and if he chose to have intercourse with his young daughter in order to teach her properly that was his right. Is that a common explanation?"
A: "No, it is not, but it has been used by some men. It is important to help children learn about sex and sexuality, but having intercourse with them is not the way to do it. To me that is an unacceptable behaviour, irrespective of the reasons offered."

Q: "Can a young girl decide for herself that she wants to have sex with her father?"
A: "She may indicate that she can decide for herself what she wants to do, but I do not believe a preteen or early teen (these are the most common ages for incest) can do this responsibly and thoughtfully. And any father who thinks his daughter has made that decision for herself and then participates voluntarily in incestuous acts is just kidding himself. He is more likely satis-

fying his own needs than anything else, and he is behaving irresponsibly and criminally. Developmentally, young people have a very difficult time making decisions about relationships and feelings, and the additional complexities of sex with a parent make it a situation impossible for them to evaluate."

Q: "But surely it is true that sometimes a child will be very seductive toward a parent and act like they want to have sex?"
A: "Yes. On occasion children do act in a flirtatious and seductive way towards the parent of the other sex. This may happen when a young girl is beginning to develop physically, recognizes that she has an attractive quality and begins to test it. However, a father needs to be a mature adult in this situation and not respond sexually in return.

        "It is unacceptable for a father to use this situation to satisfy his own needs."

Q: "Does incest occur at one particular age more than another?"
A: "Father–daughter incest, the most frequently reported type, is liable to occur when the daughter reaches puberty or soon afterward. Sex with older teenage daughters is also reported, but less frequently, as older daughters tend to have a greater capacity to reject the sexual advances of the father."

FEELINGS Young people who have been involved in an incestuous relationship commonly feel confused, at fault and very vulnerable:

"Even though I know I didn't start it, I still feel so ashamed. People ask why didn't I tell them or report it, but I knew if I did our whole family life would end and I would be put away."

Such a situation is a major challenge for a therapist. If the young person is not to be haunted by this early experience, the therapist has to rebuild her or his self-esteem. If that is not done, the young person's guilt and confusion may live on to impede the formation of satisfactory adult relationships. Sometimes the guilt and confusion will pass of its own accord, but we know of many cases in which this has not happened.

RELATIONSHIPS One of the compelling consequences of incest is its negative effect on family relationships: husband–wife, parent–child and sibling relationships all can be enormously influenced, both during the time the incestuous acts are taking place, and after their discovery.

While an incestuous relationship is going on, role confusions are common. In father–daughter incest, the daughter may see herself as her father's lover in competition with or superior to her mother. Other daughters and sons may be treated less favourably by the father. The wife may be jealous, angry or covertly in alliance with the whole thing. Needless to say, the tone of the household is dramatically altered by this unhealthy distortion of relationships, and the alteration may have consequences that last way beyond the period during which the relationship occurs.

INFERTILITY

FACTS The temporary inability to have a natural child is called infertility; if the condition is permanent then the person is sterile. At any given time, ten to 15 percent of all couples are infertile; 40 percent of the time infertility is due to problems with the man, 40 percent of the time infertility is due to problems with the woman, 10 percent of the time to a combination of reasons too difficult to separate according to sex and 10 percent to unknown causes. Regardless of the source of the problem, infertility is a couple concern, one which must be shared and worked through together. The pressure a couple feels from family, friends and society to have a baby may place a tremendous strain on their relationship, and more than anything else they need support and understanding during this period, not pity.

> **Q:** "Isn't it true that infertility is mostly psychological?"
> **A:** "No. Eight or nine times out of ten there is a clear physical cause. The reasons in the other cases are sometimes psychological, sometimes unknown."

Probable Causes of Infertility
In the man:

Problems with Sperm. A man may be infertile if: his sperm does not move on its own once it is in the vagina; it is not properly formed or is immaturely developed; it is being produced in insufficient numbers.

Diseases and Disorders. Contracting mumps as an adult can lead to tissue damage in the testicles. A varicose vein in the scrotum (called a varicocele) increases heat and can lead to reduced sperm production if untreated. Having undescended testicles after puberty causes damage to the sperm-producing tissue and leads to infertility and then, usually, to sterility. A high body temperature for a long period, as with a prolonged fever, can also produce temporary infertility. Radiation therapy in the genital area can damage the sperm-producing ability of the testicles. Gonorrhoea can cause scarring of the vasa deferentia and other structures, preventing the natural movement of sperm. Prostate surgery, severe diabetes and certain types of nerve damage may cause semen to be propelled backward into the bladder instead of through the penis. Many cases of male infertility are the results of infection, such as prostatitis.

Psychological Factors. Emotional stress may prevent a man from having an erection. Stress can also lead to a rise in the use of drugs like alcohol, tranquillizers or barbiturates, which can negatively affect sexual desire and lead to a decrease in sexual intercourse.

In the woman:

Infections. Scars from infections may form in the ovaries, Fallopian tubes and uterus, preventing the free passage of egg and sperm. Gonorrhoea and pelvic inflammatory disease can lead to this type of scarring.

Endometriosis. The endometrium may abnormally move into areas like the tubes and ovaries, interfering with ovulation or obstructing the egg's passage.

Cervical Problems. The cervix may be infected and prevent sperm from passing through into the uterus and Fallopian tubes. The mucus secretion of the cervix may be hostile to the sperm.

Ovulation Difficulties. Hormone imbalance or cysts covering the ovaries may prevent ovulation from taking place at all. A number of drugs, including heroin and morphine, also prevent ovulation.

Uterus Shape and Position. The uterus may be misshapen, out of position or contain a tumour, all of which could well prevent conception.

Psychological Factors. Emotional stress is presented as a theory why some women are infertile, although there is little evidence to support this. Stress can affect hormone levels and cause organs to function improperly. Stress can also lead women to avoid having sex.

> Q: "What are some of the shared causes of infertility?"
> A: "Not knowing sexual facts is a major reason for infertility when there are no physical causes. For example, some couples do not know that intercourse near ovulation is more likely to result in fertilization than having intercourse at other times in the woman's monthly cycle. Two weeks before your next period (days 13–14–15–16) is the best time to have intercourse if you are trying to get pregnant. Some couples use an improper lubricant to help them when having intercourse: vaseline and some other jellies and creams have a sperm-killing effect so they must be avoided. Douching, because it washes the sperm out of the vagina, should also be avoided — it is rarely a good idea anyway. Disorders of the pituitary, thyroid or adrenal glands can also cause infertility, in either the man or the woman.
> "Couples trying for pregnancy should have intercourse with the woman on her back, knees up, with the man between her knees being sure to make deep penetration at ejaculation. If the woman can keep her knees up after ejaculation for 20 to 30 minutes, sperm will have the best chance to move from the vagina towards the Fallopian tubes and the waiting egg. Placing a pillow under the woman's hips enables sperm to remain in the best area for movement towards the egg."

> Q: "What is the treatment for infertility?"
> A: "There is no one treatment that takes care of all kinds of infertility. The first step is for both the woman and man to have a complete evaluation of their medical history and a series of tests.

Although everyone is anxious for an answer right away, the evaluation and tests will take time, so they need to be patient.

"Once the problem has been identified, the clinic or doctor will devise a treatment plan and discuss it with the couple. The medical treatment for infertility may include corrective surgery on some part of the uterus or Fallopian pathways, or the prescription of certain drugs or hormones to bring about regular ovulation. A programme of sex education may be suggested to advise about the most fertile times to have intercourse and the intercourse positions that facilitate deep penetration and allow sperm to remain deep in the vagina. Counselling may be advised if emotional problems underlie the infertility."

Q: "What is the success rate in curing infertility?"
A: "Exact figures are not available, but it appears that 60 to 70 percent of couples have a baby once they begin seeing a doctor for infertility. However, the treatment period can be extensive."

Q: "What about those fertility drugs I hear about?"
A: "Clomid is a drug commonly used if a woman does not ovulate regularly. This drug causes ovulation in women who have not been ovulating and has been quite successful in treating infertility stemming from that cause; it has no dangerous side effects. Pergonal is another drug used to treat infertility and was responsible for the multiple births you read about — the result of several eggs being released from the ovary at the same time. Pergonal is now commonly used and rarely results in multiple births, except twins, as doctors now have ways of establishing the precise dosage."

Q: "What is a sperm count test?"
A: "A sperm count is a medical test where a complete ejaculation is examined under a microscope to discover if a proper number of sperm is present. It will also determine the maturity of the sperm and how well they are able to move. It is one of the standard tests when a couple is being examined to discover the reason for their infertility."

Q: "Well, how do they do the test?"
A: "Semen is collected by masturbating into a clean container, kept at room temperature, and delivered to a laboratory within an hour or two. Sperm may need to be examined a few times over several months to see if the count ever changes. Prostate massage or interrupting intercourse to collect semen are unacceptable, since all the semen from a full ejaculation must be examined. Use of condoms to collect semen is unhelpful since many condoms contain sperm-killing chemicals.

"Some men have problems going ahead with this test because their religion forbids masturbation. But remember, this is not masturbation for pleasure or release; it is a medical test of a body fluid, just like an examination of a blood specimen. Most religious advisers understand perfectly well why the test has to be conducted, so if you find it hard to reconcile this particular act of masturbation with your creed's prohibition of it, go and talk to your adviser."

Q: "What is artificial insemination, and do they use it when you are infertile?"

A: "Artificial insemination is the placing of living sperm on the cervix in order to achieve fertilization, and yes, it is one of the methods used to overcome infertility.

"Artificial insemination using the husband's semen (AIH) is done when, in a stable relationship, the husband's sperm is fertile but pregnancy cannot occur naturally for any of these reasons: a marginally low sperm count, hostile cervical mucus in the wife or physical or psychological problems with ejaculation. The ejaculate is collected in a sterile container and taken to the doctor, who then places the semen on the cervix. In some cases couples are instructed by their doctor on how to place the semen in the proper place by themselves.

"A more common form of artificial insemination is using the semen of a donor (AID), who closely resembles the husband physically and ethnically. AID is used when the husband is sterile, but it must be done *only* with the husband's full understanding, consent and support or he may feel anger and humiliation, which can lead to serious marital difficulties. Donors and recipients are unknown to each other for legal and emotional reasons. When possible, a donor's semen and the husband's semen are used together to build in the chance that the husband will be the natural father, although this can decrease the chances of conception as the poor sperm can chemically influence the donor's better sperm. Doctors keep the artificial insemination procedure very confidential and usually advise couples who are successfully inseminated not to discuss the procedure with others, in order to safeguard their legality as parents.

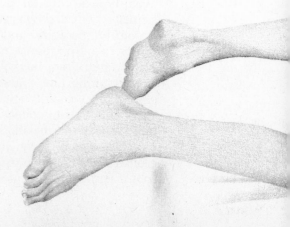

"Artificial insemination is a sensitive and emotional matter and sometimes leads to real stress in a relationship. Continued affection and understanding are essential in order to overcome the natural tensions that are created when a couple is infertile, especially when they are trying to work out a solution to their problem."

Q: "If my wife and I want to have a baby, how many times a week should we have intercourse?"

A: "Doctors generally advise that two or three times a week should give you a good chance. Remember, too, that intercourse before and during the time ovulation usually occurs will maximize the chances of pregnancy and this is the most important thing if you are really trying hard."

Q: "Just when are you considered infertile?"

A: "If a couple has regular intercourse without contraception for at least one year without a pregnancy, they are considered infertile."

Q: "Don't women frequently get pregnant right after they adopt a baby?"

A: "That is not always the case. Only about five percent of women who adopt become pregnant after they adopt. But five percent of women who are infertile and do not adopt also become pregnant without any treatment at all.

"To blame a couple's infertility on emotional factors is unfair and inaccurate. Probably the worst thing you can say to a couple struggling with infertility is 'take it easy and relax and you will become pregnant before you know it.' This does nothing to remove the likely physical reason for their problem and will usually make them more nervous."

Q: "What is a test-tube baby?"

A: "It is a baby born after a man's sperm has fertilized a woman's ovum outside her body. The fertilized ovum is then placed in the woman's uterus to grow in the normal way.

"The technique was developed by an English doctor, Patrick Steptoe, and the first test-tube baby, Louise Brown, was born in 1978. Steptoe removed an ovum from one of the mother's ovaries and added the father's sperm to it (in a dish, actually, not a test tube). When a sperm had fertilized the ovum he placed it in the womb, ready to grow into a normal foetus in the normal way.

"Dr Steptoe's success caused considerable excitement and was hailed by some as the solution to many fertility problems. In fact, there is no way of guaranteeing success with the technique every time and it is far from universally available."

MYTHS The following statements are false:

* eating seafood will help you get pregnant
* if you had sex frequently before marriage, your chances of conceiving are reduced
* penis size or breast size are predictors of a person's fertility — the bigger they are the more fertile you are
* if you can just relax while having intercourse, you will get pregnant
* usually the woman is at fault when a couple can't have a baby
* if a man or woman is infertile, their spouse inevitably looks for sex outside the marriage
* masturbation causes infertility
* most infertility is psychological
* if you are infertile, you cannot enjoy intercourse as much as when you can have a child
* after an infertile couple adopts a baby, she inevitably gets pregnant.

RELATIONSHIPS

"Why me, why me, why me? Knowing I am the one responsible for us not having a baby hurts me deeply and makes me feel like less of a man. It is always on my mind, and I wonder if people know it is my fault we don't have any kids. I even had trouble telling my own father and mother. Even though we are going to a doctor, I still feel humiliated, and it is beginning to affect my relationship with my wife. I always feel she is about to bring it up and use it against me. She hasn't yet, but it's always on my mind. I'm a mess and I think my marriage is breaking up."

This is the real reaction of a man with an infertility problem. The pain he is feeling is obvious, and his diminishing self-esteem is working against his relationship. A woman who is infertile suffers in much the same way; our culture defines her role as a woman by her bearing a child and being a mother. Being unable to fulfil this expected role produces in many women deep feelings of inadequacy, anger or depression, and may create stress in their existing relationships.

Even when medical help has been sought, the endless tests, high costs, various treatments and interference from family and friends can sap a couple's emotional stamina and produce friction in their relationship.

Having intercourse on a specific schedule takes the spontaneity out of loving acts and can make them a chore. Marking dates and times of intercourse on a chart is not very erotic and may place an unusual strain on the relationship. All this is occurring against a background of alternating self-doubt and hope on the one hand and outsiders' comments — "Isn't it time you two had a baby?" — on the other.

Q: "Can our relationship make it if we are infertile?"

A: "Yes. Your relationship can withstand the special stress of infertility if you are continually open, honest about your fears and hopes, and at the same time supportive and understanding to your partner. Leaning on each other and trusting each other with your feelings can also help to keep your relationship healthy. Some people have found discussion groups with other couples going through the same thing to be helpful; they don't feel so cut off when they realize that their stress is something other couples are coming to terms with. Of course, having a supportive and sensitive doctor is very important to this process, so be certain you get medical help from someone who understands the special stresses on you as individuals and on your relationship."

Q: "Is it true that marriages can be annulled because of infertility?"

A: "In general, no. The exception may be when one of the parties knew before the marriage took place that he or she was infertile and concealed the fact. The Roman Catholic Church, for example, will in principle agree to annul a marriage on those grounds. Prior knowledge can be very difficult to prove, however, and the comparatively few cases of annulment that you hear about may well be complicated by other factors."

LOVE

FACTS Of all the subjects in this book, love is the most difficult to define. To define it would be to make it finite, whereas love is infinite — no matter how much you love or give love, it is still there in you. I love and I feel loved and yet I can only begin to describe, not define, what love is.

What I am certain about is that at every stage in the life cycle we need to love and to be loved. From the moment of birth a baby begins to learn what love is as it is held and nurtured by its parent(s); the emotional bond between a baby and its parents, the child's first experience of love, is the foundation for the child's abilities to give and receive love for the rest of its life. Without this elementary education, the child's life will lack a crucial ingredient.

We learn more of love as we develop. Not only do we receive love from our parents and give love to them, but we learn more of what love means from the ways that parents, siblings, more distant family members and other adults interact. We learn gradually to accept ourselves as people capable of giving love and worthy of receiving it. We learn to love ourselves, and we learn that without being able to love ourselves we are unable to express love properly for others. Love is learned.

Views of love are almost as numerous as the people who have sought to define it. Plato, for example, taught that the god Zeus cut people in half and gave each half the desire to find the other; matching the two halves meant completion and love. St Paul's description of love is justly famous:

> "Love is patient and kind; love is not jealous, or conceited or proud; love is not ill mannered, or selfish or irritable: love does not keep a record of wrong: love is not happy with evil, but is happy with the truth. Love never gives up. Love is eternal. ... There are faith, hope and love, these three; but the greatest of these is love."

Sociologist Robert Winch believes that love is the result of two people with complementary needs getting together — the weaknesses of one are balanced by the strengths of the other. Erich Fromm sees love as the way out of the isolation we all feel, while another psychologist, Harry Stack Sullivan, believed that love was caring for another as one cared for oneself. Dr John Money, the sexologist, takes a fairly original view when he speculates that there are pathways in the brain that are particularly concerned with love; when we understand the circuitry of the brain we will understand more about what makes us love. It seems that whatever love is, it contains elements of an inbuilt urge to express care and nurturing, support and affection. When we love, we express some profound and intrinsic parts of ourselves. But what of the relationship between love and sex?

Q: "Can sex be separate from love?"
A: "Yes. Although there seems to be a growing tendency toward making true affection a precondition of sexual activity, many people have had pleasurable and nonexploitive sex without being in love. Psychologist Albert Ellis, among others, believes sex without love should be socially acceptable as long as no harm is done to either partner, and that such an attitude would remove the guilt from many sexual relationships.

"For me, however, sex and love are connected. I believe that sex is one of the ways in which love is expressed: sex is the

language of intimacy, mutuality and friendship. It is dignified and it embodies commitment to oneself and to one's partner. It is in this context that sex can be truly fun and playful — within a loving relationship, playfulness in sexual acts does not reduce the dignity of the communication, rather, it is an additional, valuable dimension.

"When someone has once experienced sex and love together I believe it is the combination he or she will seek thereafter."

Q: "Why do people sometimes talk about romantic love as something maybe different from ordinary love?"

A: "The concept of love changes a little from society to society and from age to age; the word 'love' is always there, but slightly different meanings attach to it. 'Romantic love' was the name given to a modified view of love that came into fashion about 200 years ago. It was intended to convey the highest, purest, most passionate form of love, defying all laws and conventions and superior to all other emotions.

"The ideas contained in romantic love were not new, but they were more dramatic and insistent than what was around at the time. We have a strong legacy of romantic love in our popular view of what we call 'love,' but we tend now to mix it with more practical considerations of making relationships work."

Q: "Can there be love without sex?"
A: "Absolutely. People who choose for whatever personal or
religious reasons not to express their sexuality in a genital way
can and do love. Parents love their children, but their love is not
genital; platonic love is described as a friendship, chaste in expression and characterized by love and respect, but without sex.

"Men and women have always had same and other sex
friendships that were deep, enduring and loving, but in which
no genital acts took place. The Greeks defined two such types
of love: *philia*, friendship or brotherly love, and *agape*, an idealis-
tic love that is for the welfare of others. (The Greeks described
love that included sex as *eros*.)"

AGE There are no age limits on loving or the need to be loved. From the
moment of birth to the moment of death, men and women alike need to
be loved and can express love. The ways in which love is felt and expressed
vary from stage to stage in life but the central need and ability remain.
Loving during infancy is different in its expression from love during
adolescence. In adulthood, loving relationships have their basis in what
was learned during earlier years and the expression will probably change
again as adulthood proceeds. One of the enduring myths about age is that
older people cease to love and at best let their love dwindle to a serene
affection. Their capacity for loving is undiminished, as is their need to
receive love.

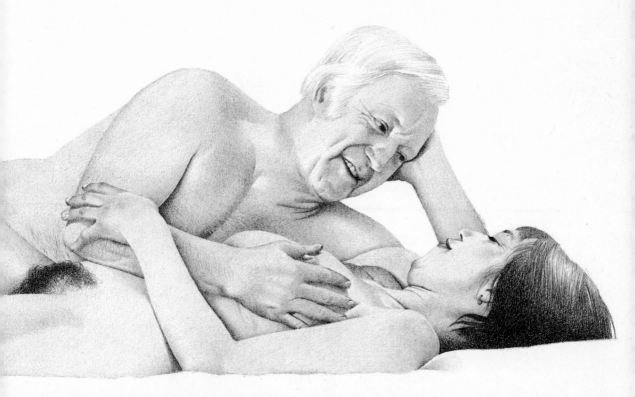

Q: "We have been together for many years, and I still have strong feelings of love for my wife. Sometimes my friends tell me I'm an old romantic. Is romantic love out nowadays?"

A: "No. Romantic love is in like it has been in one fashion or another for centuries. Keep giving your good example!"

Q: "During my adolescent years, I remember having crushes on several people. Could they have been love?"

A: "Yes, why not? They may not have been the same as your feelings of love now but at that time those feelings had the ingredients of love. That kind of love may not be an adequate foundation for an enduring relationship, but the feelings are nevertheless very real."

RELATIONSHIPS When people appreciate themselves and recognize their value and worth, it could be said that they love themselves — not in a narcissistic, unhealthy sense, but in a mature, respectful one. When a person has achieved a true sense of him- or herself in this way, he or she has the capacity to enter a relationship and love another person. Love is infinite and will not run out when shared, but to love fully people have to have learned how to love. Part of learning to love is appreciating the worth of other people, and part of appreciating their worth is coming to an understanding of one's own.

Q: "At first I thought we were truly in love. We were inseparable and it felt so good. I just thought that the sexual thing was part of what love meant and even though we had sex frequently it was

OK. Then we were in situations where we couldn't have sex so easily, and I noticed a change. At first I thought it was my imagination, but soon I began to realize that we couldn't really be alone without sex being involved. Then when I began to resist having sex from time to time we didn't talk about it or anything. Our relationship just seemed to end. I felt used. What we had can't have been love, can it?"

A: "Physical attraction and sex are powerful forces and keep many relationships going, some for short periods, and some for longer. Physical attraction alone is not however the proper foundation for an enduring relationship. Knowing this and having experienced it can be very helpful in preparing for future loving relationships. The important thing to remember is that there is a future."

Q: "Do you think a person can love more than one person at a time?"

A: "Yes. Love is not a commodity that must be rationed out for fear of losing it all. Most people love more than one person at a time: a spouse, friends, children and parents all can be loved simultaneously. The sexual acts which are the special language and communication of one kind of love may be expressed in one relationship only, but the loving relationships with the other people are still valid.

"The situation that presents more difficulty is when someone feels love for more than one person and wants sex too. If you believe in sexual exclusivity in relationships, then you have a fundamental decision to make about how to carry on. No-one can prescribe an answer here, it must come from within. The experience of others – good or bad – is unfortunately no better guide than their advice."

Q: "Once I really loved a person and was hurt deeply when I was rejected. Now I am very frightened about getting hurt again, so I find myself shying away from relationships."

A: "This is very common and very natural. Loving someone means among other things allowing yourself to be vulnerable, and when the relationship does not develop as you expected you not only get hurt but you can also lose trust in the potential of other loving relationships.

"If you anticipate being hurt again and guard against it by not opening up and giving love, you may never love fully again. From your previous experience you know how much love can mean, so why rule it out for ever? Opening yourself up to someone else can be very scary once you've been hurt, but if you didn't care about the value of loving relationships, you probably wouldn't have made your comment in the first place."

MEN'S SEXUAL SYSTEMS

Men's sexual systems consist of I the external genitals — **1** the **penis**, and **2** the **scrotum** — and II the internal genitals (testicles, prostate, and so on). Penises can swell up in the process known as **erection** (page 220); failure to achieve erection is known as **impotence** (page 224). The foreskin of a penis may be removed by **circumcision** (page 225).

The penis, together with erection, impotence and circumcision, is discussed in the pages immediately following, then the scrotum. The internal male genitals are described on pages 228–245.

I EXTERNAL GENITALS

1 Penis

FACTS The penis consists of a head, called the glans, and the shaft or body. At the very tip of the glans is the urethral opening through which urine and semen leave the body.

The glans is covered by a fold of skin called the prepuce or **foreskin**. The foreskin is like a hood and can be rolled back to expose the head of the penis, except in newborn boys. Shortly after birth some boys have this skin removed by a procedure called circumcision.

The glans is smooth and contains many nerve endings, making it very sensitive. Surrounding the back part of the glans or head of the penis is a rim called the corona. On the bottom or underside of the penis where the head and body of the penis meet is a sensitive area called the frenulum.

The body or shaft of the penis is made up of soft tissue very much like a sponge. This spongy tissue is served by numerous blood vessels that are filled full of blood and swell up during sexual excitement. The ring of muscle tissue inside the base of the shaft contracts forcing blood through these vessels and thus causing the penis to harden and increase in size. This growth from a soft (flaccid) penis to a harder, stiffer penis is called erection. There are no bones or cartilages in the penis to cause erection. The penis returns to a softer state after ejaculation or after stimulation stops.

Penis Size. Penis growth is most rapid during puberty and is complete at the end of the pubertal stage — around the age of 16 or 17. Many adolescent boys, however, are very concerned that their penises are not big enough, that they will be inadequate for lovemaking. Almost all boys have doubts about their penis size at some time, but experience generally shows that their anxiety was uncalled for. As they start to have sexual experience they discover that the penis functions adequately and falls in the normal size range.

When a penis is soft, it usually hangs loosely away from the body and averages about $3\frac{1}{2}$ to $4\frac{1}{2}$ inches in length and one inch in diameter, though every one differs — some are smaller and some larger. The problem with stating an average soft penis size is that the same penis can vary even when soft. For example, cold air, cold water, fear or anxiety generally cause the

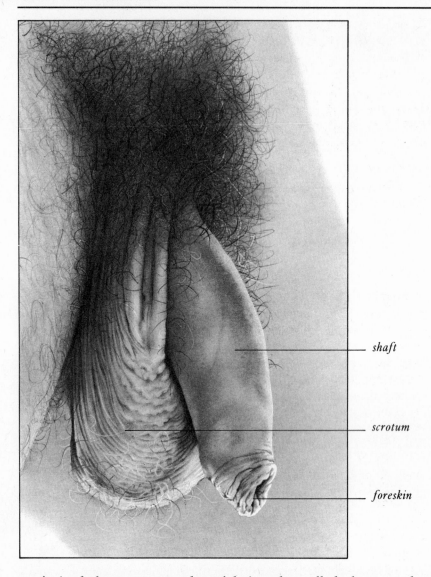

shaft

scrotum

foreskin

penis (and the scrotum and testicles) to be pulled closer to the body, thereby shortening its length. A soft penis can actually lengthen in warm water or when the man is completely relaxed.

A man's weight, build and height bear no relation to the size of his penis in either the soft or erect state.

MYTHS The penis is said to shrink in size if not used enough — "Use it or lose it." But a penis cannot shrink unless there is a disease of the tissue fibres in the penis, and this occurs very rarely.

Some men fear their penis will be trapped in the vagina (they are called "penis captives"). There is no medical evidence that this has ever happened. This anxiety may come from misinformation, but it may be used as an excuse not to get involved intimately with a woman. Fear of the penis being trapped in the vagina may really mean a fear of involvement with a woman or perhaps worry about being dominated by a woman.

Penis size is not related to body size, body build or race, so it cannot be predicted by nose size, thumb size, foot size or any other feature.

The *Kama Sutra*, the famous love guide from India, describes men as hares, bulls or horses depending on their penis size and shape. The implication is that penis size is related to the ability for and quality of lovemaking, but that has no foundation. A man's penis size is simply not a factor in achieving a fulfilling sexual relationship with another person.

FEELINGS The terms castration anxiety and castration complex were developed by Sigmund Freud and are used today by psychoanalysts who subscribe to Freud's theories to describe the concerns young boys and girls have about their genitals.

In Freud's castration theory, a young girl may believe she does not have a penis either as a punishment, because she is not sufficiently loved by her mother, or because she was injured and had to have her penis removed. She may then develop an envy of a boy's penis. Blaming her mother for her not having a penis, the young girl turns to her father in an affectionate and erotic way, beginning the "Oedipal phase" of development. Some psychoanalysts believe that when girls finally realize they do not have a penis like a boy, they begin to feel inferior to boys and may carry those feelings of inferiority throughout their adult lives.

Young boys value their penises and are greatly concerned lest the penis should be lost or harmed. They may indeed become preoccupied with protecting this vital organ. When a boy enters his Oedipal phase he has rather strong affectionate and erotic feelings toward his mother. He sees his father as a rival and may fear that his father will cause harm to his penis in retaliation for this competition for his mother's attention and love. These feelings are a form of castration anxiety.

Castration anxieties in girls and boys can also be produced, according to the theory, by guilt over masturbation, wet dreams and other sexual experiences which may be interpreted as leading to harm to the genitals.

As development continues and when relationships with parents stabilize and are appropriate, both girls and boys move on through other developmental phases toward adulthood. Castration anxiety, so the theory runs, recedes as young people get farther away from childhood.

PROBLEMS Occasionally, penises have to be amputated, either because they have been irreparably damaged in an accident, or because of disease. Cancer of the penis occurs in one–two percent of all men. Men whose penises have been amputated can still be stimulated physically and psychologically to orgasmic peaks; their desire can continue unchanged. The difficulty for them, of course, is to satisfy a partner, though it is entirely possible to do so without their having intercourse.

A penis can be created surgically — the operation is called phalloplasty. The new penis is made from tissue taken from the genital area but it is not erectile tissue, so though it can allow urine flow it will not erect in the normal way. Instead, the surgeon makes it firm enough for penetration during intercourse, without making it so firm that the man would be embarrassed by a permanent full erection. Ejaculation is not a problem if no other organs were diseased or damaged, and the man may still feel orgasm if his emotional health and self-esteem are not seriously affected (as they may well be) by the loss of his penis.

Artificial penises are also provided for women undergoing sex-change operations (transsexuals). They serve for intercourse and orgasm is possible, but ejaculation is not, as the semen-producing systems are not there. Urine may leave through the new penis or the urinary system may be left as it was.

Traumatic though the loss of the penis must be, the effects of amputation can, with difficulty, be overcome in many cases. Some men, however, feel that their masculinity is so much reduced by the loss of their penis that they are unwilling to try and continue a fulfilling sex life. They see the penis as *the* centre of pleasure, even though there are many other erotic and sensual areas throughout the male body that can provide pleasure and even orgasm. Losing the penis is so shocking, such a blow to self-esteem, that some people prefer to renounce sexual activity altogether rather than compromise and adapt.

Q: "My friend has to have an operation because the hole at the tip of his penis is in the wrong place. What's that all about?"

A: "Your friend has a condition called hypospadias, which means that the urinary opening is not at the tip of the penis where it usually is, but is somewhere else on the head of the penis or along the shaft. Hypospadias is a congenital abnormality and appears about once in every 600 male births. If the urethral opening is on the head or glans of the penis but not at the tip where it should be, urination as well as sexual activity may not be too great a problem. However, if the opening is along the shaft of the penis, corrective surgery is usual, since urination and sexual activity will be very difficult and quite embarrassing. Infertility may result from some cases of hypospadias since semen has difficulty leaving the misplaced passageway."

ERECTION

FACTS Erection can take as little as several seconds or it can occur gradually over a longer period of time. Whether it happens rapidly or slowly does not affect a man's ability to enjoy sex or to function effectively.

Erection depends on the blood supply and nerve connections to the penis working properly. Spongy spaces, the *corpora cavernosa* and the *corpora spongiosa*, fill with blood in response to physical stimulation, psychological stimulation, or both.

An erect penis is usually between five and seven inches long with a diameter of $1\frac{1}{4}$ to $1\frac{1}{2}$ inches. Of course, there are normal variations in this range which allow for some smaller and some larger penises. The size of a man's erection is not related to his ability to please a partner or to enjoy sex himself. Continually thinking about penis size and its adequacy can in fact get in the way of giving and receiving pleasure.

People sometimes think that a penis which appears to be fairly small when it is flaccid will be relatively small when it is erect. It is also a common belief that a larger than average flaccid penis will become a larger

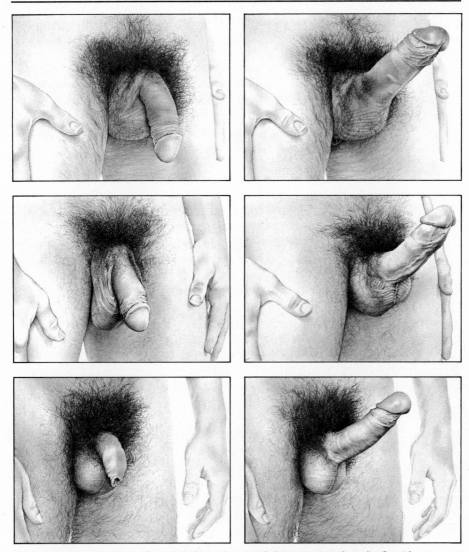

Three penises, each shown flaccid (left) *and erect* (right), *proving that the flaccid appearance is no predictor of the size when erect.*

than average erection. Both these ideas can be true, but most of the time they are not. A "small" flaccid penis can show a remarkable change in size as it erects and a "large" flaccid penis sometimes changes very little in length or thickness as it becomes erect. There appears to be no obvious relationship between the size of a penis when it is flaccid and its size when it is erect.

Q: "My penis curves a bit when it is erect. Is that normal?"

A: "Yes, it is. Many erect penises are slightly curved. The degree of curve varies from man to man, but it should cause no discomfort, nor should it interfere with sexual activity of any kind.

"A few men though have a very pronounced curve, which makes erection painful and sex difficult to enjoy. This condition is called Peyronie's Disease, and is caused by the development of hard, fibrous, inflamed tissue in the shaft of the penis. It is normally curable."

Q: "Why can't a man have an erection and pee at the same time?"
A: "When a man has a full erection, the neck of the bladder closes, so that urine cannot get out of the bladder into the urethra, along which semen will pass if the man ejaculates. This is automatic. The body prevents urine and semen from mixing, since the acid content of the urine would weaken the sperm."

Q: "I read about a man with an erection that wouldn't go away for days. Is that possible?"
A: "Yes. The condition you read about is called priapism and is usually caused by nonsexual factors like spinal cord disease, leukaemia or sickle cell disease; sometimes it happens for no known reason. In cases of priapism, the increased blood flow that causes erection is unable to leave the penis in its usual way because the release mechanism has been broken down by the disease."

Q: "Why do I sometimes wake up with an erection?"
A: "This happens to all men at some time. It used to be thought that morning erections were due to the pressure of a full bladder, but it seems now that they are related to the refreshing qualities of deep sleep."

Q: "I have a strong genital odour. What can I do about it?"
A: "Genital odours are common and vary in strength from person

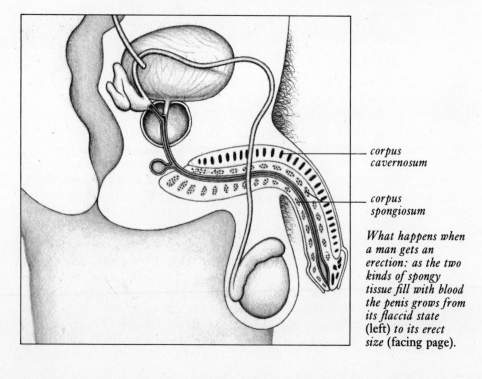

corpus
cavernosum

corpus
spongiosum

What happens when a man gets an erection: as the two kinds of spongy tissue fill with blood the penis grows from its flaccid state (left) *to its erect size* (facing page).

to person. In uncircumcized males they may be caused by smegma under the foreskin. Washing with mild soap should be enough to take care of this. Genital odours can also be caused by urine drops remaining in your undergarments. Pressing the last few drops of urine from the penis after urinating should eliminate this problem. If every day you change your undergarments and wash your penis, scrotum and rectal area, you should have no trouble with unpleasant odour.

"Genital odours can arise for other reasons as well: they can be entirely natural and not related to poor hygiene, and can be sexually attractive. They can also arise because of an infection. The gonorrhoea discharge, sores and lesions in the genital area caused by other sexually transmitted diseases (e.g. chancroid, granuloma inguinale), and discharges from infections of the urethra may all lead to strong odours. They will disappear once treatment has begun."

AGE Erection usually occurs quite quickly (in a matter of seconds) throughout the major part of a man's life. In their later years however, beginning in their 50s and increasingly in the 60s and 70s, men generally take longer to achieve an erection even with sufficient stimulation. At this stage in a man's life, erection may occur in seconds or it may take several minutes. This is a normal result of aging, but causes some men distress as they equate the ability to achieve a quick erection with their maleness or with their ability to please a partner. These painful feelings of inadequacy are often erased as men realize that they are able to last just as long in intercourse before ejaculating as when they were young, and quite often longer than younger men.

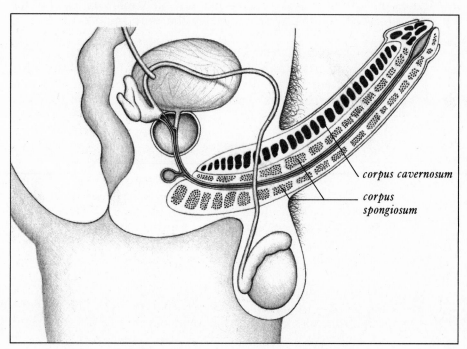

corpus cavernosum

corpus spongiosum

IMPOTENCE

Impotence is the inability to get or maintain an erection sufficient for intercourse. If a man has never been able to achieve an erection for intercourse, he has primary impotence. If a man has had a history of successful erection and intercourse, but during some particular period cannot achieve an erection, he has secondary impotence. Secondary impotence is much more common than primary impotence.

Impotence, or erectile failure, may be the result of a physical malfunction or it may have a psychological cause. Physical malfunctions include the results of drug abuse as well as the effects of certain diseases, and psychological causes include anxiety and conflict in the relationship. For a fuller description of the problem see pages 104–5.

It must be pointed out here that if a man does not get an erection occasionally, it is not proper to call his condition secondary impotence. He may be fatigued or distracted at that time and the next day he may be able to have an erection without difficulty. Accordingly, Masters and Johnson believe as a result of their research that a diagnosis of secondary impotence is called for if a man cannot achieve an erection 25 percent of the times he would like one. Not having an erection is usually very distressing for a man and/or his partner regardless of its frequency, but the label impotence should be used only when erectile problems actually interfere with a relationship, causing difficulty, stress, or an unacceptable situation for a couple.

Impotence can occur in men of any age, social class and race. Although nobody really knows for certain, it is estimated that many men have had at least one occasion when they couldn't get an erection when desired.

The word impotence is being used less by sexologists and other professionals because it has a negative connotation and tends to label the whole man in an unfair way. Terms like erectile problems, erectile inhibition and erectile difficulty are replacing the word impotence.

Q: "Does impotence mean you can't get an erection at all?"
A: "No. Some men can get an erection during masturbation, oral sex and other forms of lovemaking, but lose their erection as soon as intercourse is expected. This is a form of impotence."

Q: "I'm 68 and it's taking me an awful long time to get it up. I remember when I could get it up in seconds. Am I getting impotent?"
A: "No, you are getting older. One of the natural results of aging is that it takes men longer to get an erection. It is quite normal, and if you relax and accept it your pleasure, enjoyment and ability to please your partner should be the same as always. Some men of your age indicate that once they get an erection they last longer during intercourse than they did before."

Q: "If a man is impotent, can he still ejaculate?"
A: "Yes. The ejaculation reflex is separate from the erection mechanism, so a man can come without an erection, as long as he is sufficiently stimulated."

CIRCUMCISION

FACTS Circumcision means the removal of the foreskin, the fold of skin that surrounds the glans of the penis. A great many men in a great many societies have been circumcized, either because their religion or culture requires it or because circumcision is thought to be more hygienic.

The operation is a very simple one which, if it is properly done, causes little discomfort. It can be performed at any age; in some cultures it is delayed until adolescence and performed as a puberty rite, but in western societies it is usually done shortly after birth.

Circumcision makes no difference whatsoever to a man's sexual behaviour.

Q: "Surely circumcision must affect your sex life in some way?"
A: "No. It makes no difference to sexual excitement, erection, the

A circumcized penis.

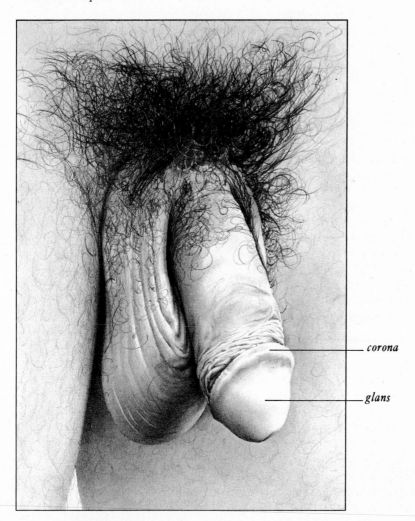

corona

glans

ability to reach orgasm or the ability to have a pleasing and complete sex life with a partner. People sometimes think that a circumcized glans is less sensitive, because it is always exposed, than an uncircumcized glans. There is absolutely no evidence for this at all."

Q: "Just why is circumcision done on all males?"
A: "It isn't. A circumcision is performed only on those boys whose parents request it. It is a rather common practice in the United States, Canada and in some other countries, but most people in Europe, for example, are not circumcized. The primary reasons for circumcision are religious and cultural. Thus Jews, Muslims and others have their male children ceremonially circumcized to comply with religious and cultural beliefs that have been handed down for centuries.

"The secondary reason for circumcision is supposedly cleanliness, in order to prevent the accumulation of a white, cheesy secretion, which gathers under the foreskin and can possibly lead to irritation, infection or offensive odour. This substance, called smegma, is a natural secretion from glands in the corona area, but its accumulation can be avoided simply by moving the foreskin back and washing the area daily. Circumcision, although not dangerous, is seen by more and more people as an extreme step to remedy the occurrence of smegma."

Q: "What about the high rate of cancer in women who have intercourse with uncircumcized men?"
A: "There has been speculation that women who have intercourse primarily with uncircumcized men contract cervical cancer (cancer of the neck of the womb) more frequently than women who have sex mostly with circumcized men. It has been suggested that smegma (the secretion that collects under the foreskin) may be responsible for transferring a virus that may encourage cervical cancer. These claims have not been proved."

Q: "My friend is 16 and his doctor says he has to have a circumcision now. Can this be true?"
A: "Yes. Although circumcision is often performed when the boy is very young, it may be left until about the age of puberty and can in fact be done at any age without harmful results.

"Circumcision may be necessary for your friend because he has phimosis. This is a condition in which the skin covering the head of the penis is too tight to roll back painlessly when required during urination, masturbation or intercourse. The discomfort that results from this tightness of the foreskin is easily corrected by circumcision."

FEELINGS Some psychiatrists believe that circumcision — the removal of the foreskin — is symbolic castration — the removal of the penis or testicles. The idea is that the powerful father is expressing his dominance over his infant son. This early act is said to remain in the unconscious mind of the boy and to have an enduring effect on his relationship with his father.

In contrast to this powerful symbolism, it appears that many men today have rather neutral feelings about their own circumcision. It is something that happened to them when they were infants and they really do not recall the event or attach any significance to it. They accept it because the religious aspect may be important to them, and/or they may believe that there are positive hygiene benefits.

There is, apparently, no medical advantage to circumcision. The back-to-nature movement, which says things are best left as they naturally are unless they are defective, is reinforcing the medical research, and many parents are now preferring not to have their sons circumcized.

Cosmetically, some men feel their uncircumcized penis is not as attractive looking with its wrinkled skin around the glans. Others, however, like not being circumcized as the foreskin makes the penis look longer.

Men are also concerned about how women feel about circumcized and uncircumcized penises. Generally, women are more interested in a person than in his foreskin — or lack of it. Of course, Jewish women who want to be true to their religious beliefs will choose a Jewish man who is circumcized. But they're choosing a Jewish *man*, not a circumcision, a person rather than an operation.

CULTURE AND RELIGION Circumcision is a word from the Latin meaning "cutting round." It later acquired the sense of "cleansing" or "purifying."

Historically, it appears that the practice of circumcision originated among the Egyptians and was then adopted by the Hebrews. In Genesis 17: 10–13, circumcision was established as a covenant between God and Abraham. Abraham was over 90 years of age at that time and he circumcized himself after the covenant was established.

Other than the religious meaning, the origin and significance of circumcision is still unclear. Some have called it a tribal mark used to distinguish and separate Jews from other people. This may have been true in earlier times, but today circumcision is quite a common procedure throughout the world.

In many parts of the world where circumcision has a special cultural or religious significance there are established rituals attending the operation.

In Australia the Aborigines called the circumcision ceremony the *dhapi*, and performed it when a boy was ten or 11 years old. The men of the community would take the boy off and perform the ceremony away from the women. In the ceremony, a man lay on his back with the boy on top of him facing upward. The man held the boy in position and the foreskin was removed by a sharp stone, sometimes jagged quartz. Bleeding was stopped with hot coals and wet leaves. This ceremony was part of the boy's training in stoicism and suffering, preparing him for battle.

In Polynesia, circumcision is called superincision, occurs at puberty and is a religious consecration. The foreskin is stretched over a stick, slit with a sharp stone and removed. Herbs and hot stones are used to promote healing. The stick is saved as a symbol of the boy's entrance into manhood and as a token of good luck. While the boy is healing, he is secluded and tended to by an older woman. It is said that the boy has ritual intercourse with this woman when his penis is healed. Once healed, he returns to the community and displays his penis.

2 Scrotum

The scrotum or scrotal sac is a thin-walled, soft, muscular pouch, containing two compartments to hold the testicles. Each testicle is connected to a cord (spermatic cord) that consists of blood vessels, tubes and nerve and muscle fibres. The spermatic cord can be felt on each side of the scrotum. Under certain conditions — cold, in particular — the muscle fibres in the scrotum cause the entire sac to contract or wrinkle up, drawing the testicles closer to the body in order to keep them warmer. Under other conditions — like heat or complete relaxation — the scrotum becomes very loose and soft, with a smooth surface. The testicles then hang farther from the body in order to keep cooler.

These actions point out the primary function of the scrotum as a natural climate control centre for the testicles. The temperature in the scrotum is a degree or two lower than the usual body temperature of 98.6°F or 37°C. The job of the testicles is to produce sperm, and they cannot do this at body temperature; they need to be cooler. If the testicles are kept at body temperature or higher for a prolonged period, infertility or sterility can result. The scrotum continually monitors the environment and responds automatically in the way that is best for healthy sperm production.

II INTERNAL GENITALS

Men's internal sexual and reproductive organs consist of 1 the **testicles**, which produce **sperm** (page 234) and **hormones** (page 237); the testicles occasionally have to be removed in the operation called **castration** (page 237); 2 the **epididymes**; 3 the **vasa deferentia**; 4 the **seminal vesicles**; 5 the **prostate gland**; 6 the **ejaculatory ducts**; 7 Cowper's **glands**; 8 the **urethra**.

The external genitals, the penis (including erection, impotence and circumcision) and the scrotum, are discussed on pages 217–228.

1 Testicles

FACTS The testicles are the two small balls (their common name) that hang in the scrotum below the penis. They are also known as testes and they produce sperm and hormones.

The testicles are oval in shape, about $1\frac{1}{2}$ inches long, 1 inch wide and $1\frac{1}{4}$ inches across. An adult's testicles weigh about an ounce each, although the left testicle may be a bit heavier and larger and hang a little lower than the right. The reason why this should be so is not known, but it may be to stop the testicles from striking each other in a painful and perhaps harmful way as the man walks.

The testicles have two functions: to produce sperm (short for sper-matozoa) from puberty until death, and to produce male sex hormones called androgens, of which testosterone is the most important. Hormone production from the testicles is evident at birth, but increases enormously around puberty and maintains a high level throughout adulthood until it shows a decrease during the later years of life. Sperm production does not begin until puberty, though it follows the pattern of hormone production in falling off in old age.

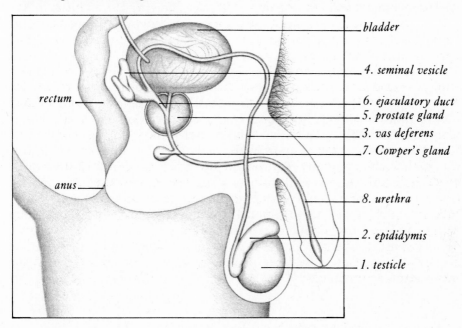

bladder

4. seminal vesicle

6. ejaculatory duct
5. prostate gland

3. vas deferens
7. Cowper's gland

8. urethra

2. epididymis

1. testicle

rectum

anus

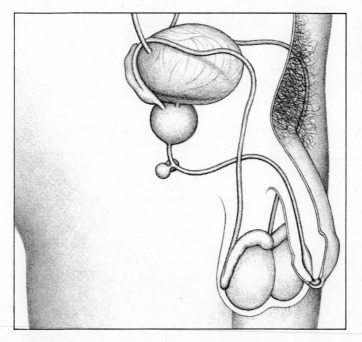

A man's internal genitals seen (above) *from the side and* (left) *in three-quarter view.*

Sperm are produced in each testicle in special structures called seminiferous tubules. These tubes are in the centre of each testicle and connect with a series of passageways that convey the sperm to other important organs, and ultimately out of the penis if required.

Near the seminiferous tubules in each testicle there are numerous cells called interstitial or Leydig's cells. These are responsible for producing the male sex hormone (testosterone), which is secreted directly into nearby blood vessels. At puberty, the majority of the changes in a boy are due to the increased amount of testosterone flowing through his body.

During sexual excitement, the testicles increase in size. Blood fills the vessels in the testicles, causing them to become larger. After ejaculation they return to their usual size.

The testicles are drawn closer to the body just prior to ejaculation. After ejaculation the testicles move back to their usual position in the scrotum. This same drawing-up of the testicles close to the body occurs during times of intense fear, anger or when the man feels cold. Thus, naturally, the body protects this delicate and vulnerable mechanism.

The testicles hang away from the body in order to keep them at the slightly lower temperature required for sperm production. In hot weather or a warm bath they hang lower — farther away from the body and its warmth; conversely in cold weather they move up closer to the body's heat to maintain optimum temperature. If they are kept at body temperature, testicles fail to produce sperm and so the man is sterile. When a man's muscles tense — as when he prepares for flight or aggression, or just before ejaculation — a set of muscles in the scrotum automatically pulls the testicles up.

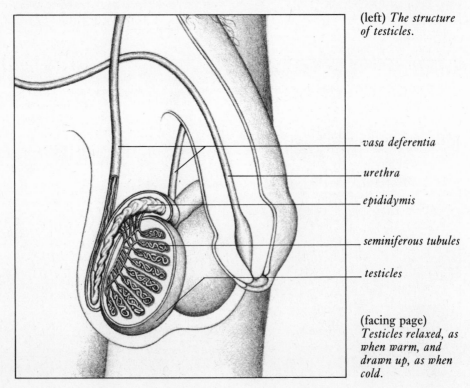

(left) *The structure of testicles.*

vasa deferentia

urethra

epididymis

seminiferous tubules

testicles

(facing page) *Testicles relaxed, as when warm, and drawn up, as when cold.*

Q: "Why does it sometimes feel uncomfortable if I don't ejaculate after getting an erection?"

A: "When a man becomes sexually excited, blood fills the vessels in the genital area, causing erection of the penis and enlargement of the testicles (this process is called 'vasocongestion'). If he does not ejaculate, he may feel a general discomfort and perhaps some tenderness in the testicles due to this engorgement of the blood vessels.

"The condition usually does not last long and the real pain associated with not ejaculating can be exaggerated. Psychologically, men have been socialized to ejaculate when they get an erection during sexual activity, and failure to ejaculate and to feel orgasm often adds frustration and disappointment to the reality of the physical condition. Some men find masturbation to be a sucessful remedy.

"Fortunately, men are beginning to learn that ejaculation is not a requirement in every sexual situation, and that pleasure and meaning can exist without reaching ejaculation and orgasm."

MYTHS It has been widely believed — and in some places it still is believed — that eating human or animal testicles is a way of increasing potency. This is not true. Neither the sperm nor the male hormones secreted by an animal's testicles can be added to your own; you are eating meat, not magic.

AGE Testicle growth is prompted in the early months of pregnancy·by the presence in the foetus of hormones which have masculinizing properties. The testicles usually drop into the scrotum around the seventh month of pregnancy.

Through childhood, testosterone is produced by the testicles in small amounts. Signals from the brain cause the testicles to produce substantially

more testosterone during puberty, and this leads to the distinct physical changes seen during adolescence. The testosterone level generally remains constant from adolescence through to the 60s and 70s, when it falls off somewhat.

Testicles grow more in puberty than at any other period in a man's life, achieving full size at around the age of 16 to 18. The size and weight of the testicles then remain constant until after the age of 60, when they usually become smaller and softer.

After about age 50, the testicles do not move completely next to the pelvis before ejaculation. Elevation does occur, but the testicles are not drawn in quite so close to the body as before.

Very early in life, babies discover their testicles and spend varying amounts of time touching and tugging the scrotum. It is clear from observation that children derive pleasure from this, and it is an entirely appropriate form of sensuous exploration at this stage.

Attention to the testicles and the scrotum continues in varying amounts throughout adolescence and adulthood. Fondling the testicles by preadolescents, adolescents and adults is as much erotic as sensuous in nature. It is a significant part of autoerotic pleasure, leading to general sexual satisfaction. Learning the kinds of touch on the testicles that bring pleasure is helpful because it enables you to inform sex partners about what you like.

CULTURE AND RELIGION The word "testicle" possibly derives from the Latin *testis*, meaning "witness," "testimony," or "testament" (to a man's virility). Certainly some cultures have apparently taken this to be the meaning: in Arab and some other Eastern cultures, men still swear to tell the truth not by placing a hand on the heart, but on the testicles, the centre of their manliness. Both Genesis and I Chronicles describe this practice.

Testicles have become a symbol of virility to such an extent that it is common for men to be accused of "having no balls" if they do not act in the way that society has decreed to be manly. Apparent weakness or indecisiveness are equated with effeminacy: they are meant to be attributes of women, who have no testicles.

Because of this equation of testicles and virile roles, women who speak and act in an aggressive way toward men have commonly been called "ball breakers," or said to have "real balls." The idea here is that when a man is dominated by a woman, or is in a position where the woman is in control of his situation, the man has lost his balls, the core of his maleness. This is part of sexism, and is based in the belief that men are superior to women, and that their testicles are visible symbols of their natural superiority.

Perhaps it is because we place such enormous symbolic significance on testicles that we in the West have invented a garment that is not known in many parts of the world. It is common for men in Western societies to wear a protective strap to hold the testicles in place when they engage in strenuous physical activity — particularly sport. However, in many cultures around the world this is not found to be necessary: the men hunt, fight and play sports with no special protection for the testicles. This may mean that in the West we are overly concerned about our testicles and possible damage to them; they have become the symbolic focal points of virility which may signify a fundamental lack of confidence or understanding of what maleness really is.

PROBLEMS A small percentage of boys are born with either one or both testicles still in the body and not in their natural place in the scrotum. This condition is called undescended testicles. In many of these cases the testicle or testicles drop into the scrotum on their own while the child is still an infant. In other cases, a special hormone is necessary to help the testicle drop, while in yet others, surgery is required. The large majority are cured by the time they reach adulthood, although just a few remain incurable. When it is impossible to make the testicles descend the condition is known as "cryptorchidism."

Undescended testicles require medical supervision because, one way or another, the testicles must reach the scrotum prior to puberty or their sperm-producing ability will be permanently destroyed. The hormone-producing ability of the testicles is not normally damaged if they remain undescended for such a period of time.

Q: "A young friend of mine had surgery to drop one of his testicles. They had to remove it because it was diseased. What will happen to him?"

A: "One testicle is sufficient to produce enough sperm and male sex hormone. Your friend will grow and develop as a normal man. His sexual desire, capacity for erection and ability to have an orgasm will not have been affected, so his sexual life will be unchanged. If your friend chooses, he can cause a pregnancy and have a child.

"In your friend's situation, an undescended testicle may show early signs of tissue disease, so rather than wait for problems to occur later on, the decision was made to remove the damaged testicle.

"After the removal of a testicle it is possible to insert a safe silicone testicle, the same size, shape and weight as a natural one. This allows the man to relax and not worry about feeling or appearing unusual."

Q: "But what if you lose both balls?"

A: "If both testicles are removed due to disease or accident, the man cannot produce sperm and is sterile. Also, his major source of male sex hormone, testosterone, is no longer present, and this will affect him to a great extent if he has not yet reached puberty, and to a lesser but still serious extent if he has. If he has not yet reached puberty, the loss of male hormone will prevent his pubic and facial hair from growing completely, his voice will not deepen, his penis and scrotum will not grow to adult size and his general muscle size and strength will not reach the normal range. Although the adrenal glands produce some male hormone, and hormone therapy may be helpful, sexual activity and ejaculation is not usual, even though it may be possible.

"Emotional problems — loss of self-esteem and feelings of terrible inadequacy — are quite common in cases like this, leading to difficulty in forming sexual relationships. Even if the man has the ability to function sexually, his emotional and social problems make it difficult, if not impossible, to develop a relationship. This may in turn lead to the loss of the physical ability to function.

"If a man loses his testicles in adulthood, there is evidence that his general muscle size decreases, his metabolism and respiration are lowered, his body fat diminishes, and he has a less typically male shape. All these are due to the loss of the main source of testosterone. Carefully regulated doses of male hormone may enable him to continue to function sexually, but he may feel the emotional stress associated with the loss of his testicles so strongly that it prevents him from engaging in sexual activity, even though he has the physical ability to do so."

Q: "My brother is 21 and has had to have his testicles removed because of a disease. Will he be able to get an erection and have sex?"

A: "Knowledge about the effects of castration on sexual desire and performance is incomplete. In some cases of castration of adults there is evidence that the men involved have been able to continue having erections and orgasm. Their desire and the frequency of their sexual activity have not been interfered with. In other cases there is evidence that desire and sexual activity in general diminish after castration. This may be a result of the surgery itself or it may be due to depression and feelings of inferiority and inadequacy following on from the surgery. It may also very well be a combination of the two."

Q: "My older brother got mumps and everyone was worried he would be sterile. Could that happen?"

A: "Yes. It is possible that the virus that causes mumps could infect the testicles, causing permanent damage to the seminiferous tubules that produce sperm cells. This permanent damage results in sterility, and is already one of the leading causes of sterility in men. Boys who contract mumps before puberty usually do not have this problem, since the sperm-producing areas in the testicles are not yet developed and are therefore not damaged by the virus."

SPERM

FACTS From puberty on, sperm are made in each testicle. It takes approximately ten weeks for an individual sperm to develop. Billions of sperm are produced each month, with some decrease in the later years. If sperm are not ejaculated they simply break down and are absorbed by the tissue in the testicles. No damage or pain results from this natural process. You cannot see an individual sperm without a microscope. In fact, sperm are so small that all the sperm that created every person who ever lived would fit in a thimble.

Sperm have three parts: a head, a neck and a tail. The head contains 23 pairs of chromosomes, which carry the man's contribution to the heredity of the child. The other half is contributed by the female egg or ovum, which also contains 23 chromosomes. The neck and body of the sperm contain material that can be converted into energy so that the sperm can move on its own once it has been ejaculated by the man. The tail of the sperm whips back and forth, rather like a tadpole's, to enable the sperm to move in the vagina, uterus and Fallopian tubes. Sperm move about five to seven inches per hour.

Sperm was first identified in the seventeenth century by the Dutch scientist Leeuwenhoek, the man who invented the microscope. From puberty until death sperm are constantly being manufactured in a man's testicles. Although it is hard to believe, a healthy man produces about 50,000 sperm a minute, or 72,000,000 a day. They are so tiny, however, that even this enormous number amounts to less than a speck of sand.

The process of sperm production is called spermatogenesis, and it generally takes 60 to 72 days for a mature sperm to develop. This process occurs in stages: first the spermatogonium appears which develops into a spermatocyte, then into a spermatid and finally into a spermatozoa or sperm.

Sperm can be stored for a while in a sperm bank. Sperm banking (or cryobanking) is a form of fertility insurance. Cattle breeders first used this technique to insure that they could continue to breed cattle by artificial insemination if natural breeding did not work. A complete ejaculate of semen is collected and stored at an extremely low temperature. Although it is said that semen, properly frozen, remains capable of fertilizing an egg, it appears that after four or five years sperm begin to lose their mobility. Their capacity to fertilize an ovum may thus be impaired.

Men who use sperm banks are usually those who are about to undergo a vasectomy or who are about to have radiation treatment. The sperm bank provides them with a chance of having a natural child by artificial insemination at a later date.

Q: "Can you ever run out of sperm?"
A: "No. Sperm production is a continuous process from puberty throughout life as long as the man is healthy. Even if a male ejaculates frequently sperm will still be present in his semen, although the number of them and the total amount of semen is likely to decrease after successive ejaculations over a short period of time."

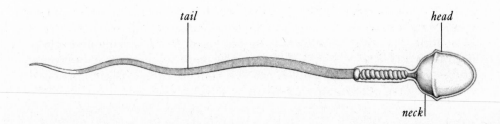

tail   *head*

neck

Q: "Are there any special foods or vitamins that help you produce more sperm?"

A: "No. There are no foods, beverages, vitamins or special substances that will help you produce more or healthier sperm than you already produce as long as your body is working normally. A diet that enables you to do the things that you need to do each day is sufficient to continue the healthy production and development of sperm. The so-called special potency and virility recipes and traditions that have existed for hundreds of years about the sperm-producing qualities of certain foods, drinks and substances are all untrue."

MYTHS An influential myth that has been around for centuries is that ejaculation of sperm causes a man to lose his strength and energy. In the long run, the myth says, he will become feeble if he ejaculates frequently. Years ago, people believed that sperm was in some way part of the blood system, so vital fluid was lost at each ejaculation; hence the dreadful effect. This is entirely false.

An extreme case of the conservation of sperm is the Indian Tantric practice of training men not to ejaculate in intercourse. Tantrics regard semen as the vital force and spirit of a man, and intercourse as a spiritual experience. Orgasm is achieved by Tantrics, but as a state of mental bliss.

Athletes have been warned for generations that ejaculation prior to a sports event will weaken them and reduce their performance. As a result many men, including large numbers of married men, have avoided sexual contact for periods of sometimes weeks and even months before competing. There is no justification at all for such unnatural behaviour. Provided a man doesn't ejaculate just moments before his event, his performance will not be adversely affected by ejaculation even on the day of his competition.

A related myth is that men completely lose their ability to produce sperm, or they run out of sperm, once they reach their 50s or 60s. Sperm production, however, continues at a steady, uninterrupted rate into the 70s, when there may be a slight drop in the quantity of sperm produced, but it is not sufficient to interfere with the ability to father a child.

It is also widely and wrongly believed that "too many" ejaculations in a short period of time cause a man to run out of sperm. This is a myth for many reasons. First off, "too many" is a phrase that is meaningless. What is too many — two, five or ten ejaculations? Second, although semen volume and sperm count do, in fact, reduce after several ejaculations over a short period, his body provides a man with all the semen and sperm he can need. Usually the body will signal through fatigue that it is time to rest.

The idea that semen ejaculated into the mouth and swallowed can do harm is equally wrong — as long as the man who ejaculates does not have a venereal disease like syphilis, gonorrhoea or herpes. If he has, the person swallowing the semen may contract the disease. Swallowing semen is something that some people enjoy as part of their lovemaking and others prefer to avoid. Liking it or disliking it is certainly no measure of how open or free you are or how much you care for your partner: it is merely one of the many ways people choose to express themselves.

CULTURE AND RELIGION In the Book of Genesis, Onan did not want to impregnate the wife of his dead brother so he withdrew his penis and allowed his semen to spill on the ground. In so doing he broke a Hebrew tradition that a man should fertilize his brother's widow; as a punishment he was struck dead. Over the centuries, this story has been enormously misinterpreted to mean that masturbation, a form of "spilling one's seed," is an evil and sinful act, to be punished as Onan was. Masturbation, therefore, has wrongly been called onanism and uninformed medical opinion has portrayed masturbation as dangerous self-abuse, forbidden by the Bible. Fortunately, many sects and most doctors have recognized the error of this interpretation and now accept that masturbation is physically harmless and can be thoroughly beneficial.

HORMONES

Testosterone is the chief male hormone of a group collectively called androgens. They are produced mainly in the testicles, with very small amounts also being produced in the adrenal glands. Men's testes and adrenal glands also produce small amounts of oestrogen, the female sex hormone.

Testosterone production in the testes is stimulated and influenced by a very complex signal system with the pituitary gland and the hypothalamus. The growth and development of the penis, scrotum and testes, and the development of pubic hair, beard growth and the other secondary sex characteristics are the results of greatly increased levels of testosterone released at puberty and thereafter. Testosterone also influences sexual drive and sexual interest, so a low testosterone level causes the libido or sex drive to decrease.

CASTRATION

FACTS The process of removing the testicles is called castration. It has been practised on men and animals in many societies for various reasons. Because the testicles are the source of testosterone, the male hormone, their removal before puberty means that the male will not achieve all the sexual characteristics of a male with testicles. If the male, human or animal, is castrated after puberty, the adult sexual characteristics already acquired will tend to soften and diminish, producing what some erroneously consider to be a more female-seeming person.

Aristotle, in the third century B.C., kept notes on the effect of castration in both animals and men. He observed that when the testicles of a young rooster were removed, the bird grew larger, the meat was more tender and the comb and wattles failed to form. This operation is still practised — we call the resulting bird a capon. Aristotle also noted that when a boy's testicles were removed, he did not acquire secondary sex characteristics — he did not grow body hair and his voice did not deepen.

Castration can also mean the removal of the penis as well. For psychoanalytic theories about castration anxiety and castration complex, meaning principally the removal of the penis, see pages 17 and 219.

CULTURE AND RELIGION During the Renaissance in Europe, outstanding boy sopranos were castrated in order to retain and develop their high voices for church choirs; they were known as *castrati*. It was felt to be necessary at the time to do this, as women were not allowed to participate in church services except as members of the congregation. The choir of the Sistine Chapel in Rome, for example, regularly contained castrati.

The practice lasted until the nineteenth century, and as music developed outside the church, castrati became the leading singers of their day, as wealthy and celebrated as the great operatic stars of today. Their voice range was approximately that which we know today as *falsetto*, and they grew tall, with long limbs, narrow shoulders and broad hips. Because they had no testicles, they could not produce sperm and were therefore sterile; but, according to reports, not all were impotent. Some could still get erections and were alleged to be very active sexually.

The other name, apart from castrati, for boys or men who had their testicles removed, is "eunuch." In the Middle East, eunuchs were commonly used to guard harems — the name "eunuch" comes from the Greek, meaning "guardian of the bed." The position of eunuch was one of considerable trust and honour, guarding as he did some of the most treasured possessions of a prince and being indirectly responsible for the purity of the royal blood line.

Castration has also been used as a punishment for sexual offences in a number of countries. It was common, during the colonial period and after, for American blacks to be castrated if they made sexual advances towards a white woman. Most countries have officially prohibited castration as a punishment, since it is clearly inconsistent with contemporary views on human rights.

Apart from being used as a punishment, castration has on occasion been applied as a tool for regulating the quality of the population. Sometimes the mentally deficient used to be castrated to prevent their becoming parents, both on the grounds that they might make inadequate parents and to prevent them from passing on their deficiency (even though no-one knew whether the deficiency was hereditary or not). Sterilization is sometimes used today to achieve this same end.

2 Epididymes

On the upper portion of each testicle you can feel a slight ridge. This is an epididymis. It is a tightly coiled tube, which adheres to the surface of each testicle and acts as a maturation and storage chamber for newly developed sperms as they move out of the seminiferous tubules. Sperm stay in the epididymes until they break down and are absorbed by the surrounding tissue or until they are ejaculated.

3 Vasa Deferentia

Attached to the epididymis on each testicle is a narrow tube called a vas deferens. Each vas is approximately 16 to 18 inches long, and sperm move up them from the epididymes into other organs. Once they have moved up a vas, sperm mix with fluids from the seminal vesicles and prostate gland, forming a new substance, semen. This is what a man ejaculates.

Since the vasa deferentia carry sperm and are easily found in the scrotum, they are ideal places for the simple male sterilization procedure called vasectomy (pages 83–86). To perform a vasectomy, a surgeon cuts both vasa, one on each side of the scrotum, and ties them, or a piece of tube is removed preventing sperm from travelling beyond that point. Sperm are still produced in the testicles and move through the epididymes, but they cannot get beyond the point of surgery and therefore they cannot leave the body to create a pregnancy. They break down and are absorbed just like all the other sperm that are not ejaculated.

After a vasectomy the fluids from the seminal vesicles and prostate continue to be produced, and they leave the body during intercourse, masturbation or wet dreams; orgasm feels exactly the same. The absence of sperm in the semen is impossible to detect except under a microscope.

4 Seminal Vesicles

Located just above and on each side of the prostate gland, are two seminal vesicles. They are pouches about three inches long that secrete a sugar-like fluid (fructose). This seminal fluid joins sperm (which has now moved from the testicles through the epididymes and vasa deferentia) and fluid from the prostate gland in the ejaculatory ducts, from where the semen (as it now is) is passed through the urethra and out of the penis.

The seminal vesicle fluid provides nutrition for the sperm, and enables them to move more effectively. It is suggested that the fructose in an ordinary ejaculation of semen provides it with a nutritional value of approximately 6 calories!

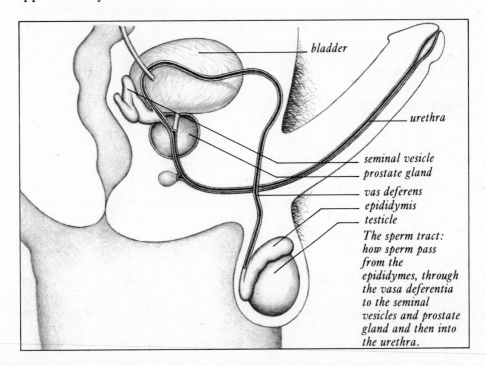

bladder

urethra

seminal vesicle
prostate gland
vas deferens
epididymis
testicle

The sperm tract: how sperm pass from the epididymes, through the vasa deferentia to the seminal vesicles and prostate gland and then into the urethra.

5 Prostate Gland

FACTS The prostate gland is located below the bladder and rests against its neck. The prostate is the size of a large chestnut, and consists of a number of sections called lobes. The urethra, the tube which allows urine to pass from the bladder, where it is stored, runs through the prostate gland and into the penis. If the prostate gland swells, it can press on and shut off the neck of the bladder or the urethra itself. In these cases, medical attention is required immediately.

From puberty on, the prostate secretes a substance which, like the fluid from the seminal vesicle, aids in the nutrition of the sperm and contributes to the sperm's ability to move on its own. The fluid from the prostate makes up approximately 39 percent of the semen, fluid from the seminal vesicle contributes about 60 percent; only about one percent of semen is sperm. Prostate fluid is secreted through the gland's many passageways to the urethra, where it joins with the sperm and seminal fluid coming from the ejaculatory duct. The semen is now complete and ready to be ejaculated.

Most men know they have a prostate gland, but they take no notice of it. It is small, hidden and it functions. But when a problem occurs the prostate can become very important indeed and can cause a radical upset in a man's life.

If surgery is required to correct a prostate difficulty, there are two risks to the man's sexual functioning: he may become impotent, or he may become sterile.

As a society, we have traditionally placed enormous importance on the penis as the centre of male sexuality. The penis, for us, is the symbol of manhood. It is what gives a man the right to claim he is a man. It is seen as the centre of gratification, both for himself and for any partners he may have. If the penis no longer works, if the man becomes impotent and cannot get an erection, the traditional view is that he is only half — or less than half — a man.

This traditional view ignores the greater part of what we know now about male sexuality; nevertheless, we all feel its pressure. Few men, however relaxed and understanding they may be about their sexuality, are immune to the feeling that if they become impotent their maleness has been reduced.

As a society, we also place great importance not so much on fatherhood as on the ability to father a child. Because we have traditionally seen that ability as a proper, natural, normal part of being masculine, sterility — the inability to father a child — has come to imply that a sterile man, though not so reduced as an impotent man, is still not a complete man.

It is true that both men and women come to appreciate that intimacy and loving can be expressed without an erect penis ejaculating healthy sperms. Nonetheless, many men who undergo prostate surgery have very real difficulty in facing up to their new state. A sympathetic partner and professional counselling are both helpful and important, but the man is still likely to feel both depressed and humiliated; his self-esteem is likely to be seriously damaged for a while, until he adjusts positively.

If a prostate operation has the effect of making a man impotent, not only does he have to deal with the consequences for his ability to relate sexually but he also has to deal with the blow to his self-esteem. His partner, however, has to deal not only with both those things, but will have to help discover new ways that the couple can express their sexuality if things go well, and deal with anger, resentment, depression and withdrawal if they don't.

Partner   "After he came home from the hospital, I thought sex would be fine once he was fully recovered. The first few times he didn't get an erection I thought he was just nervous and worried about hurting himself. Then he started avoiding closeness and sex completely. I tried not to make too much of it, but we can't go on like this. I wonder, maybe I don't turn him on anymore."

Patient   "When I had my prostate removed I really didn't think too much about whether my sex life would be changed. I was just glad they got to the problem before it got really serious. Was I surprised when I couldn't get an erection! It was on my mind all the time, and the harder I tried the worse it got. So I started avoiding sex if I could. Things really got confused in my relationship. I know my partner felt rejected and angry, but I just couldn't talk about it. Finally, I went to my doctor and was told that the surgery was responsible for my problem. My doctor said we discussed the possibility of this happening but I suppose I didn't want to hear it. Anyway, the problem hasn't changed. What kind of a man am I now? How can I have sex without an erection?"

It is clear that more medical information about the possible sexual consequences of a prostate operation needs to be provided, both to the patient and to his partner, before the operation is performed. If the patient is adversely affected by the operation, it is appropriate for his medical adviser to help the couple explore alternative ways of expressing intimacy — the genitals are not the only way of giving and receiving, as many couples have found.

It is, however, difficult for many people who have always thought of their genitals as the principal — indeed the essential — way to express their sexuality to come to terms with nongenital sexual expression. They need reeducation. They also need willingness to communicate openly and to experiment in their search for a new pattern of fulfilment. It can be done, but many many people fall into the trap of silence, defensiveness, resentment and withdrawal. This only worsens the situation, for it strains the relationship more and more as each partner withdraws into sexual solitude and frustration, rather than reaching out to each other for shared fulfilment.

Prostatitis — inflammation of the prostate — can cause difficulty on a single occasion or for a short period (acute prostatitis) or it may be long term (chronic prostatitis).

Prostatitis occurs for different reasons. Sometimes bacteria will cause the infection, and antibiotics may be prescribed. Nonbacterial prostatitis, for which irregular patterns of ejaculation may be responsible, may be treated by prostate massage. To massage the prostate, a doctor inserts a finger in the rectum and massages the gland to cause any accumulated fluid to be passed out of the urethra. This is uncomfortable, but men who resent the discomfort should be grateful that they are not living in ancient Egypt. There the treatment for prostatitis was to push a thin reed up the urethra to ease the blockage: a distinctly more painful process than massage.

Cancer of the prostate is a common form of cancer in men, and has been increasing over the past ten years. It is most likely to occur in men aged over 60. Surgical removal of the entire prostate or a part of it can have an effect on a man's sexual activity, and the physician must present this possibility to the patient and to the patient's partner.

Q: "What is a prostate operation?"

A: "Surgery to remove the prostate gland or part of the prostate gland is called prostatectomy. A prostatectomy is performed when the prostate is diseased (e.g. cancerous) or enlarged, causing pain and interfering with urination or sexual activity. The cause of prostate cancer is unknown, but we do know that it is *not* related to too little or too much sexual interest or activity.

"It is very important that no-one should have a prostate operation on the basis of one diagnosis only — a second opinion should always be sought."

Q: "How do they get the prostate out?"

A: "There are two main ways of performing this operation: the prostate can be removed through a small opening in the abdomen between the navel and the pubic bone (the retropubic method); alternatively a diseased portion can be taken out

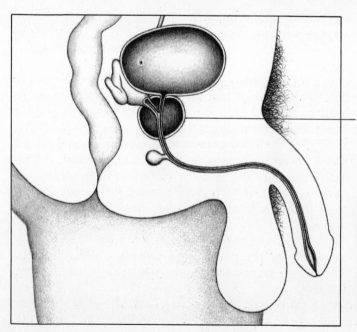

——— *healthy prostate*

Prostate problems: the illustration on this page shows a healthy prostate for comparison with the swollen prostate on the facing page. It is easy to see how the urethra can be constricted by the swelling.

through the urinary opening (the transurethral method). The procedure used depends on the extent of the problem and how best to get at the diseased prostate. The decision to perform surgery is made after several tests, including an X-ray in conjunction with a dye."

Q: "Can you still get an erection after a prostate operation?"
A: "That depends on the type of surgery that is used and the extent of the disease. If the surgeon has to remove the entire prostate gland and the capsule that surrounds it, important nerves and muscles may be cut or damaged with the result that the patient may be unable either to achieve an erection or to ejaculate. It is possible that the seminal vesicles will also have to be removed or that they are so severely damaged during the operation that they no longer function. Although in this case the impotence will be due to physical and not emotional problems, most men find impotence, regardless of its cause, an extremely threatening and humiliating condition, even though they have previously been informed by their doctor, as they must be, that impotence is a probability."

Q: "Are there any other problems with sex after a prostate operation?"
A: "Frequently after a prostatectomy, semen will be ejaculated backward into the bladder and not out of the penis. This backward movement of semen is called a 'dry come' or retrograde ejaculation, and is the result of the sphincters in that area working improperly after the surgery. Sexual excitement, erection and orgasm remain the same as before surgery even if retrograde

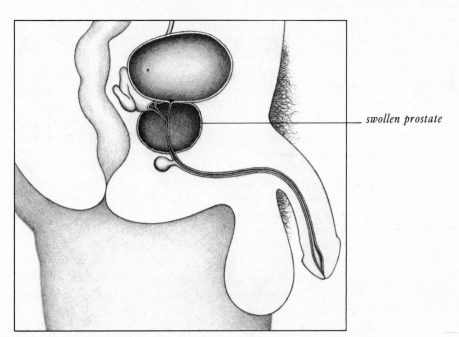

swollen prostate

ejaculation occurs. Retrograde ejaculation causes sterility since the semen doesn't come out of the penis."

Q: "Can you pass prostatitis on to your sex partner?"
A: "If the prostatitis is caused by bacteria, a woman may contract an inflammation or irritation of the vagina (vaginitis), or an inflammation of the urinary opening, the urethra (urethritis). However, use of a condom will allow sexual activity to continue and will help to avoid the possibility of infection. There is no evidence of oral or anal infection being caused through contact with a man who has prostatitis unless he has some other infection, such as gonorrhoea."

Q: "Is surgery the only treatment for a cancerous prostate?"
A: "No. Oestrogen (female hormone) therapy is often used and so are X-ray and cobalt radiation therapy. It is the case though that these methods are likely to be used in conjunction with surgery; they are not usually adequate on their own."

MYTHS Perhaps because the prostate is hidden away and yet is very important to men's sexual activity, falsehoods have grown up:

* once you have a prostate problem your sex life is over
* prostate problems are caused by too much masturbation
* wearing an athletic support too long causes prostate problems
* taking hot baths will cause prostate disease.

Not one of them has any truth in it.

AGE The prostate of a young boy is very small and inactive. At puberty, under the influence of greatly increased secretions of testosterone, it increases in size and begins its production of fluid.

Thereafter, the prostate is unlikely to cause any difficulty until middle age. The prostate thickens gradually as a man gets older, especially after the age of 55 or so. This is quite natural, and probably results from the drop in testosterone levels which is a standard feature of this age. Enlargement of the prostate may follow, however, particularly after age 60. This is known as prostatomegaly, a symptom of which is frequent urination, particularly at night. It does not affect desire or sexual ability, but if urination stops completely, or if pain occurs when urinating, a doctor, usually a urologist, should be contacted immediately.

It is very important for men over 40 to have their prostate examined by a doctor each year. This examination is done by the doctor inserting a finger in the rectum and feeling (palpating) the surface of the prostate for lumps or other unusual surfaces.

Q: "Can young men have prostate problems?"
A: "Yes. Prostate problems generally affect men aged 50 and over, but occasionally a teenager or a man in his 20s or 30s can have a prostate problem. Usually it will have arisen from an infection

of the prostate, sometimes due to gonorrhoea or non-specific urethritis."

6 Ejaculatory Ducts

Within the prostate gland, the ends of the vasa deferentia join the seminal vesicles to form the ejaculatory ducts. The ducts are about an inch long and lead to the urethra. During sexual intercourse, semen collects in this area and when excitation reaches its peak, a spinal reflex causes rhythmic contractions in the general area and propels the semen out of the urethra in spurts. This process is called ejaculation, and once a man reaches a certain point of excitation he can no longer resist coming. There are generally between three and eight spurts within a few seconds.

Linked with ejaculation, but separate from it, is the subjective feeling of orgasm. Orgasm is that intensely personal, pleasurable kind of explosion or release flooding through the body. Orgasm is in fact the release of neuromuscular tensions that have been built up during sexual stimulation.

7 Cowper's Glands

On each side of the urethra, just below the prostate, are Cowper's glands. During sexual arousal, but before ejaculation, these tiny glands secrete a small amount of fluid into the urethra which comes through the urinary opening and appears on and around the top of the penis. This small amount of fluid from Cowper's glands contains enough sperm which has leaked out of the ejaculatory ducts to cause a pregnancy, even though no ejaculation has occurred. Therefore, pulling the penis out of the vagina before ejaculation is not a method of birth control, since the fluid from Cowper's glands is present from sexual arousal on. Cowper's gland fluid is alkaline; this may help neutralize the acid climate of the urethra and enable the sperm to live longer once they have been ejaculated.

8 Urethra

The male urethra is about eight inches long and runs from the bottom or neck of the bladder, through the prostate, and through the length of the penis. The urethra has two functions: to allow urine to flow from the bladder out of the penis and to allow semen to be ejaculated.

Q: "Sometimes after I come, I urinate in a double stream. Do I have a disease?"

A: "No. Some men urinate in a double stream immediately after intercourse because some semen has remained in the urethra."

NORMALITY

FACTS Sexuality raises many questions in many people's minds, but perhaps the biggest, most taxing question of all is: "Am I normal?" Almost all of us ask the question at some point in our lives, in relation to our sexual development, to our sexual practices or to our feelings and desires.

The trouble is that the proper answer is usually: "It depends." There is no simple standard by which we can tell if something is normal. We all know, for example, that in our society it is normal to be a married parent. Does that mean that childless couples and unmarried people are by definition "abnormal?" Or does it mean that they are entirely normal but in a minority?

The popular idea of normality is a kind of compound of these other ideas: healthy, good, right, acceptable, typical, average, proper, common, permissible, appropriate. This does not, however, give much guidance to someone worried about her or his sexuality. Extramarital affairs, for example, are certainly typical and common. People having extramarital affairs may find them healthy, good and appropriate, and yet there is an overall community standard by which extramarital sex cannot be labelled proper, permissible and right.

So how do we assess normality? Wardell Pomeroy, one of the original Kinsey researchers, faced up to this problem and recorded his view that we have multiple standards: statistical, religious/moral, psychological/sociological.

Statistical Normality. If the majority of people do it, it is normal. This sounds straightforward and helpful, but in fact it is less so than it sounds. Take masturbation as an example. Research tells us that masturbation is a very common behaviour indeed — most people do it at some time or other. And yet in some societies it is not seen as normal, and in our own it is condemned by several major religions. Masturbation is therefore statistically normal but does not accord easily with some of our important principles.

Religious/Moral Normality. If a behaviour is frowned upon by a significant religious grouping or is at odds with the general moral code of a society, it does not qualify as normal. This also sounds straightforward, but it isn't. We know, for example, that a great many Catholics use contraceptives — it may well be statistically normal; and yet those same people are defying a teaching of their Church, which regards their behaviour as immoral and abnormal.

Psychological/Sociological Normality. This is a standard that is fairly independent of both statistical and religious/moral norms. It says that if acts lead to diminished self-esteem, or if they are angry, hostile or vengeful, they can be described as abnormal. The same applies if such acts harm other people or society in general. This, too, is an obviously helpful standard. It would, however, be more helpful if it were truly independent of other norms. Who is to decide what constitutes harm to another person or to society? That judgment has to depend in part on moral attitudes.

There are two more standards in current use:

Legal Normality. If it violates the law, it is abnormal. There are two problems with this standard. First, we make laws to reflect social values, so the legal standard must necessarily be intimately bound up with our moral and religious norms. Second, legal restrictions on sexual behaviour vary according to time and place in such a way that an individual, without changing his or her behaviour, could be subject to prosecution for "abnormality" one day and decreed perfectly "normal" the next.

Phylogenetic Normality. This is an attempt to get down to biological basics. Simply put, this standard says that if mammals do it, it's okay. The value of this standard is that we can observe mammal behaviour unencumbered by moral values. We may see a group of mammals that plainly accepts both incest and homosexuality without apparently harming the group or individuals. So far, so good, but you cannot make a direct transfer to humans unless you discount the whole of human culture and religion, and this we know to be a set of powerful forces affecting our behaviour.

Perhaps this set of standards is insufficient, but it shows us several things. No one standard is properly sufficient on its own. Sexual behaviour is culturally and religiously relative. Standards of sexual behaviour vary with time and place. Scientific research, by giving us a clearer view of what actually happens, can alter our views.

Q: "A friend of mine told me that my young daughter's behaviour was abnormal. I'm really worried now and I'm considering taking her to a doctor."

A: "I don't know what your child was doing but it could be just that she was doing something your friend's daughter doesn't do. The first rule is: don't let a friend tell you what is normal or abnormal, especially about *your* youngster. You be the judge of your own child's behaviour; be sure to remember that all children are different and it is their differences that make them unique and special, which is certainly not the same thing as abnormal.

"Talk with your wife, talk with other parents, read about child development and form your own impressions before you consult a doctor. There may indeed be something in your child's development that requires attention, but the chances are very much against it."

FEELINGS Anxiety about being normal is rife. This is one of the most common questions sex experts get asked:

Q: "How can I tell if what I am doing is normal?"

A: "If you can't, I can't. I don't know what your values and beliefs are, I don't know what your past experience has told you and I don't know your goals. If, however, 'normal' to you means what is good and right *for you*, answering these questions may help:

* is what you do hurtful, physically or emotionally, to yourself or your partner?
* do your feelings and behaviour cause you to feel valuable, worthwhile and increase your self-esteem, or do your thoughts and acts make you feel worthless, valueless and lessen your self-esteem?
* are your acts with another person responsible, open, mutual, consensual, enjoyable, or are they irresponsible, coercive, anxiety-filled, guilt-producing and joyless?
* do your acts further your contact with others and continue your development as a whole person, or do your acts depersonalize, cut you off from others and limit your chances of personal growth and becoming a full person?

"There is no scorecard to be filled in, no magic tally of points which means your are certified 'normal.' The questions are designed only to help you look closely at your sexual behaviour and see if it is genuinely positive and life-enhancing."

Q: "I'm doing things sexually that really make me feel abnormal, but I don't want to lose my partner."

A: "Treat yourself like a first-class person and talk to your partner about your feelings. Partners usually like each other to be happy and fulfilled. Your silence about your feelings is probably being taken for consent, so if you don't like what is happening, say so. Your partner can never know about your feelings until you express yourself. Feeling you may lose your partner as a result is a common anxiety that frequently turns out to be unfounded."

Q: "What can I do to convince my sex partner that trying new things is normal?"

A: "Who says it's normal? Even if I thought there was an answer to that question, I don't think I'd tell you. I don't know what 'new things' you are talking about; I don't know what they mean to you or your partner; I don't know what your relationship is like or what your goals are as a couple.

"I think you need to do some thinking about these things. I think you also need to be aware that the line between convincing and coercing is a fine one, and coercion is unhealthy. Reflect on what seems right for you as a couple before trying to change what you are doing now."

Q: "My wife says oral sex is abnormal, how can I convince her it isn't?"

A: "You can't. You can talk with her about her feelings, you can learn about her concerns and you can try to discuss the issue in a loving and nonaccusing way. Perhaps she is worried that oral sex has medical risks. Perhaps she is worried about genital odour.

Perhaps she has no specific argument against oral sex but simply prefers not to do it. Maybe reading some of the literature on oral sex will help, but you will in the end have to accept her choice on the matter.

"And what is your part in this? What does oral sex mean to you? Are you as enthusiastic about cunnilingus as you want her to be about fellatio? Are you putting her under too much pressure to satisfy your own needs? And how good do you think that pressure is for the general good of your relationship?"

CULTURE AND RELIGION Culture, in the widest sense, means a system of shared beliefs, values, customs and agreed actions, all determined by a group of people for themselves. What is culturally "normal" varies from society to society according to the rules that each has evolved. A large and complex society may in addition consist of several subgroups, with identifiable cultural differences. What is more, societies change their cultural rules according to time and need.

There are, therefore, no universal cultural absolutes, and each society makes its own judgments about what is sexually normal. For example, we allow ourselves one marital partner at a time when much of the world says that more than one wife is normal. It is normal for us to discourage extramarital sex, but not for some other cultures. As a culture, we disapprove of and even punish homosexuality; yet there are cultures in which homosexuality is not an issue at all and others still in which homosexual acts are permitted as entirely normal.

We can also see how things change, even within our own culture. Though polygamy is not a way of life for the mass of the people, the Mormons have been practising it consistently. We say that extramarital sex is "wrong," yet enormous numbers of people have premarital sex and a great number have extramarital affairs; they obviously don't feel it is "wrong" or "abnormal" and as a society we don't, on the whole, punish it. Some countries sharing the general Western ethos have done a complete about-turn on homosexuality, making something which was highly illegal quite acceptable by the rules.

Religious authorities have sought to influence and regulate sexual behaviour for many centuries. They have set up ideal sexual behaviours and punishments for deviations from that ideal. They have also to some extent been flexible, changing the sexual precepts of a religion according to their appropriateness in a given time and place.

It is worth making some simple comparisons to see how much religion affects our views on sexual expression. The Judaeo-Christian tradition for example is monogamous — one man, one woman. Parts of the tradition maintain this rigidly (almost no divorce in the Catholic Church) and other parts have become flexible, so that divorce is accepted and serial monogamy (a series of one man–one woman relationships) has become religiously acceptable. Islam, by contrast, traditionally favours polygamy, though it too is changing in practice toward monogamy. Buddhism advocates celibacy in order to attain the highest spirituality. Your sense of normality is going to be conditioned by the way that the demands of religion have been integrated into the daily life of your culture.

PREGNANCY

There are several important and distinct stages in the nine-month-long process of having a child:

I   FERTILIZATION AND CONCEPTION (page 251)
    this includes pregnancy tests and whether the baby will be a boy or girl
II THE STAGES OF PREGNANCY (page 257)
    the three trimesters and what happens in each, together with complications, antenatal preparation and choice of childbirth method
III LABOUR AND DELIVERY (page 272)
    what normally happens, together with a review of the standard birth complications.

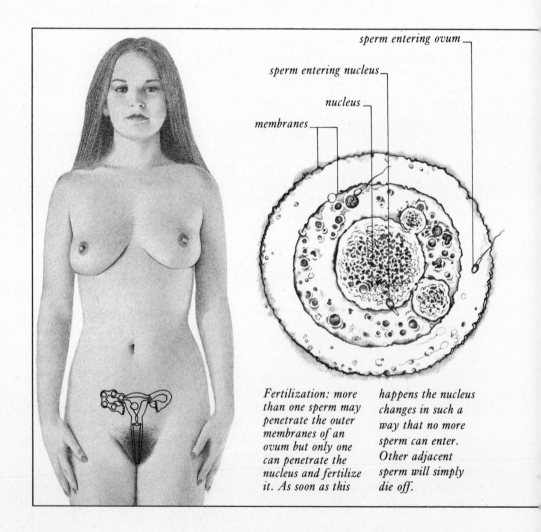

sperm entering ovum

sperm entering nucleus

nucleus

membranes

Fertilization: more than one sperm may penetrate the outer membranes of an ovum but only one can penetrate the nucleus and fertilize it. As soon as this *happens the nucleus changes in such a way that no more sperm can enter. Other adjacent sperm will simply die off.*

I FERTILIZATION AND CONCEPTION

FACTS Fertilization means a sperm penetrating an egg. The head of the sperm has to bore or wriggle its way through the outer layer of the ovum, and move toward the centre. After that point no other sperm can penetrate that particular ovum. Fertilization occurs in a Fallopian tube usually within 24 hours of ovulation, so there is only a limited time in each woman's monthly cycle when she can become pregnant. Sperm remain alive in the vagina, uterus and Fallopian tubes for several days, and can penetrate an egg during that time, but an egg loses its ability to become fertilized after 24 to 36 hours. Therefore, knowing when ovulation occurs is very important for planning or avoiding pregnancy, especially when you are using a birth control method that depends entirely on the natural cycles of the body (see pages 73–6).

Once a sperm has penetrated an egg fertilization has taken place and a single cell exists (called a "zygote"). Soon, usually after a few hours, that cell begins to divide and multiply; it splits first into two cells, then into four, then into eight, doubling each time as it continues its four-to-five-

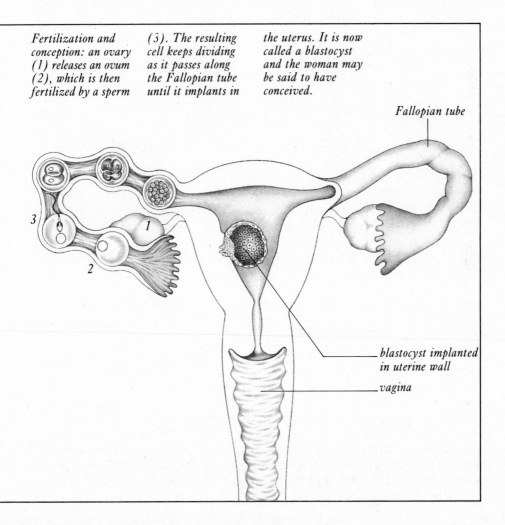

Fertilization and conception: an ovary (1) releases an ovum (2), which is then fertilized by a sperm (3). The resulting cell keeps dividing as it passes along the Fallopian tube until it implants in the uterus. It is now called a blastocyst and the woman may be said to have conceived.

Fallopian tube

blastocyst implanted in uterine wall

vagina

day journey down the Fallopian tube to the uterus. Once in the uterus, this minute cluster of cells, now called a "blastocyst," with its various parts already destined to become specific body structures, is ready to burrow its way into the lining of the uterus, the endometrium. The endometrium is ready and prepared to receive this fertilized egg, and will provide it with a natural nesting place and immediate nutrition. The implantation of the egg in the endometrium usually takes place a few days after the egg has been fertilized in a tube, and it is at this time that you can say the woman has conceived and a pregnancy has occurred. Since all of this activity — fertilization, the movement of the fertilized egg down the Fallopian tube, and implantation — occurs within seven to ten days, the woman has still not missed her period, so she isn't aware of her pregnancy.

Signs of Pregnancy. Some women just know when they are pregnant. Medical tests only confirm what their bodies have already told them. Many women, however, don't have that feeling of sureness. Here are some possible signs of pregnancy:

* a missed period
* breast fullness and tenderness with veins becoming more visible under the skin
* increased vaginal discharge
* the nipples enlarge and the skin around the nipples darkens
* more frequent urination than usual
* nausea and vomiting (morning sickness)
* general fatigue and loss of energy.

Any of these symptoms should be checked with a doctor.

> Q: "Is the drug used to control morning sickness dangerous?"
> A: "Ancoloxan, which is prescribed by some doctors to help women overcome morning sickness, was suspected of causing serious birth defects, but no association has been formed after significant testing. Remember, morning sickness is a good sign of excellent hormone support for your pregnancy and will disappear after ten to 12 weeks."

PREGNANCY TESTS Soon after a missed period most sexually active women are anxious to know if they are pregnant. The desire to know for sure is quite natural, but the earliest that a definite pregnancy diagnosis can be made is ten days after a period is missed. Some doctors believe that both a positive pelvic examination and a positive laboratory pregnancy test are required to confirm early pregnancy with certainty.

Pelvic Examination After three to four weeks of presumed pregnancy, an experienced doctor can sometimes tell if the woman really is pregnant by pressing gently on the area between the cervix and the uterus (Hegar's sign). One hand is placed on the abdomen and two fingers are placed in the vagina on an area near the cervix and uterus. A certain softness and change of shape are indications of pregnancy.

Laboratory Pregnancy Tests

Urine Test. The earliest time this test can be made is ten days after a missed period. Early morning urine in pregnant women contains HCG (human chorionic gonadotrophin), a hormone made by the developing placenta. The presence of HCG can be detected within two minutes. This test is 95 to 98 percent accurate but can be false if performed too early and there is not a sufficient amount of the hormone in the urine. Although it is fairly simple to carry out this test, reading the result, especially in the early stages of pregnancy, can be more difficult. It is therefore best if the test is done by someone with experience. A woman can either take a specimen of urine to her doctor who will usually arrange for the local hospital laboratory to perform the test, or she can use one of the many reputable chemists who offer a pregnancy testing service, as do the various pregnancy advisory services. The last two will charge a fee for doing the test. Family planning clinics will also do the test.

Home Pregnancy Test Kits. This new test, which is quite safe, can be taken at home by mixing early morning urine with a special chemical included in the kit. After two hours, if a certain colour and shape appear in the solution, the woman is pregnant. The printed instructions in the kit are easy to follow and show what to look for. After a positive result, you should get the diagnosis confirmed by your doctor. Be sure that the home kit you purchase from your chemist is not out of date (there will be a code stamped on the package which tells you the date by which the test must be used).

Blood Test. There now exists a very sensitive pregnancy test which is performed on a sample of the woman's blood. It must be ordered by a doctor and can confirm a pregnancy within a few days of a missed period, but is usually applied in conjunction with other tests to be sure of a completely reliable result. This test is not used very often.

Q: "I got a false positive pregnancy test result. What does that mean?"

A: "A false positive is a test result that indicates you are pregnant when in fact you are not. This does not occur very often. A false positive result may be due to the presence of an unusual chemical in the blood or urine, to an improper reading of the test or to an incorrect application of the test.

"Sometimes a woman may have a false negative result, which indicates she is not pregnant when she actually has conceived. This may be due to the test being improperly given, taken too early in the pregnancy or read incorrectly. In this case the woman will not get her period, so it will become clear that another test is necessary."

Q: "I heard about hormone pills that can tell if you are pregnant. What about them?"

A: "In the past, if a pregnancy was suspected, some doctors gave women the hormone progesterone for several days in succession.

If the woman was pregnant no bleeding occurred, but if she was not pregnant, her period would begin. This test should be avoided because if the woman is pregnant the extra hormones may damage the baby at a critical stage of its development."

GIRL OR BOY?

Every cell in every person contains 46 chromosomes arranged in 23 pairs, except sperm cells, which have only 23 chromosomes, and egg cells, which have 23. When egg and sperm cells unite at fertilization, each one contributes its 23 chromosomes to make one complete cell with 46 chromosomes. Chromosomes are mostly DNA (deoxyribonucleic acid) groupings called genes, which are responsible for passing the heritable characteristics of the mother and father to their child. These blueprints or codes are a person's biological inheritance from his or her parents and are fixed at the moment of fertilization.

Among the 23 chromosomes in each sperm or ovum, there is a special one called a sex chromosome. There are two kinds, known as X and Y. Each sperm cell contains either an X sex chromosome, or a Y, and it appears that men produce as many X-type sperms as Ys. Each egg cell contains only one kind of sex chromosome, an X. If an egg is fertilized by a sperm containing an X chromosome, the combination will be XX and the child will be a girl. If an egg is fertilized by a sperm containing a Y chromosome, the combination will be XY and the child will be a boy. Chance determines whether it is an X or a Y type that fertilizes an egg.

Q: "Is it true you can choose the sex of your child?"
A: "No. It is all down to chance. However, according to some experts, there are methods which may improve your chances of having whichever you would prefer. For example, Dr Elizabeth

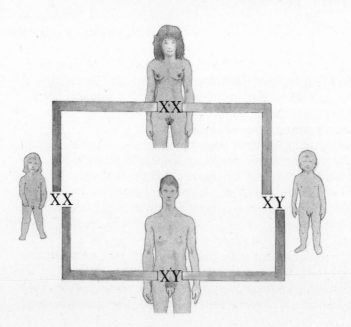

Sex chromosomes and how they combine: all ova are Xs but sperm may be X or Y. If a sperm with an X sex chromosome fertilizes an ovum the combination will be XX and the baby a girl. If the sperm has a Y chromosome the combination will be XY and the baby will be a boy.

Whelan, in her book *Boy or Girl?*, reports on work which suggested that timing of intercourse is the key factor in determining the sex of the child. Intercourse five days or more before expected ovulation increased the chances of having a boy, and intercourse close to ovulation increased the chances of having a girl. This method can only have a chance of working if the couple know the time ovulation occurs precisely.

"A less convincing theory of sex selection relates to douching before intercourse with either an acid or an alkali. An acid douche — vinegar, for example — is supposed to increase the chances of conceiving a girl; an alkaline douche, such as baking soda, is meant to increase the chances of conceiving a boy. The douche method has no evidence to support it."

Q: "Is it true that if the woman has an orgasm on the occasion she conceives the child will be a boy?"

A: "No, this is a popular myth, but there is no truth in it that anyone has been able to prove."

Q: "What is that test they use to tell if a pregnant woman will have a boy or girl?"

A: "Amniocentesis. A small amount of amniotic fluid is taken from the pregnant woman by a doctor who inserts a needle through the abdomen into the uterus. The tissue cells floating in the fluid are examined and can give information on the sex of the baby, its development and, as some diseases are sex related, the presence of abnormalities such as spina bifida, hydrocephalus and Down's Syndrome (mongolism). The procedure is painless, is done after 15 weeks of pregnancy and presents only a slight risk if performed by a qualified doctor."

AGE A woman's fertile years are usually from her early teens to her mid-40s, but there may be complications if she has her first child at either end of this span. If she has her first baby very young, she may not be socially or emotionally mature enough, and the environment may not be an appropriate one for raising a child. If she has her first child very late, there may be physical complications that have harmful repercussions on the baby. It is for these reasons that doctors on the whole believe it better that a woman should have her first child in her 20s or early 30s.

In 1964, Michael Schofield carried out a study in the UK of the sexual behaviour of a group of 15- to 19-year-olds in which he found that 16 percent of the sample had had sexual intercourse. Ten years later, a similar study of 16- to 19-year-olds revealed that 51 percent of those interviewed had had sexual experience, and that nearly half of these had had their first experience before they were 16, the legal age of consent. Although some of the teenagers were using some form of birth control, it was usually the least reliable methods and often irregularly. Some were using no protection at all. The result is more than 5,000 girls under 16 become pregnant every year. Three out of five of these pregnancies end in abortion. In 1979, over 55,000 births were to girls under 19 years of age.

In the US there were approximately 1,000,000 pregnancies among 15 to 19-year-olds in 1977, of which 600,000 unwed teenagers gave birth, and over 90 percent of them kept their babies. The remaining 400,000 pregnancies not resulting in live births were accounted for by abortion, stillbirth and miscarriage, most of them by abortion.

Early childbearing can have serious personal, relationship, health and economic consequences:

* pregnant teenagers are less likely to obtain necessary antenatal care compared to pregnant women age 20 or more
* some studies suggest that pregnant teenagers have more pregnancy problems (toxaemia, anaemia) and more labour complications (prolonged labour, unusual bleeding, abnormal position of baby and/or placenta) than women in their 20s
* younger teenage mothers are more likely to have more complicated deliveries — forceps, breech, Caesarean — than mothers in their 20s
* the maternal mortality rate for teenagers is ten to 15 percent higher than for women in their 20s
* teenage parents (sometimes including the father) tend to drop out of school, thus affecting their future educational opportunities; without schooling, teenage parents do poorly in the workplace and frequently need welfare support; these factors are likely to undermine the self-esteem of the young person and result in depression, anger and frustration — proper child care and satisfying social experiences can hardly take place in such an environment
* teenage parents tend to be involved in cases of child abuse in their homes more than other age groups
* lack of income frequently leads to poor nutrition for both the baby and the mother
* lack of proper emotional support frequently leads to depression and isolation and may be one of the reasons for a higher than average suicide rate for teenage parents when they reach their 20s
* between 50 and 60 percent of teenage parents do not get married, which makes their lives difficult; sometimes the baby's care is taken over by others and this frequently leads to anger and frustration
* the divorce and separation rate for teenagers who do marry is noticeably higher than for people who marry later
* death rates for babies born to teenagers are estimated at twice those for children born to women in their 20s
* low birth-weight babies are more frequently born to women in their teens than to women in their 20s
* the economic and emotional cost of providing care for the teenager and her baby sometimes disrupts the life of the family with whom she is living
* teenagers who have one baby tend to have at least one more before reaching age 20 and their babies are more closely spaced than those of women who have their first baby in their 20s; this situation can have serious physical and emotional health implications for the mothers and for the babies.

At the other end of the scale, the problems tend to have been exaggerated. A great many women have proved that it is entirely possible to have a normal, healthy first pregnancy in their late 30s and even in their early 40s. The risks of harm to the baby do increase however as the woman gets nearer to menopause, so careful monitoring of the pregnancy is highly desirable; but if the mother is healthy and the monitoring good, the chances of a successful pregnancy and birth are high.

Q: "Isn't it true that teenagers get pregnant because they want and need a baby to love and want someone to love them?"

A: "In general, the answer is no. Some pregnant teenagers and some teenage parents have indicated they wanted a baby for the reasons you mention, but usually that answer comes from teens who are already pregnant or who already have children. Their responses under these circumstances could hardly be viewed as totally objective.

"The teenagers I've worked with from every socioeconomic group have rarely indicated they wanted or needed a baby to love or to love them. Most teenagers are able to feel sufficiently good about themselves without having to have a baby to foster self-esteem."

Q: "If you are over 35 and pregnant can you find out if your baby will have a problem?"

A: "Yes. After 15 weeks of pregnancy fluid taken from the amniotic sac in a procedure called amniocentesis is studied to detect defects in the foetus."

Q: "Just what are the reasons for not having a baby after 40?"

A: "There are several. Mongolism or Down's Syndrome is one. For some reason women past 40 are more likely to have mongol children, which are the result of an extra chromosome causing abnormal foetal development. The risks of spina bifida and hydrocephalus are also increased.

"In a woman's 40s she is more likely to have problems with her uterus. These can show in premature birth, labour problems or postnatal haemorrhaging. Women in their 40s also have more underweight babies and more stillbirths than women in their 20s and 30s.

"Remember that amniocentesis can help tell if a foetus is developing problems and that a number of women have their first baby after the age of 40 with no complications."

II THE STAGES OF PREGNANCY

FACTS Babies are born after the ninth month of pregnancy, around the 266th day after the last period was due. Pregnancy (also known as "gestation") is divided into three-month periods, called trimesters. The first trimester is the first, second and third months of pregnancy, the second trimester is the fourth, fifth and sixth months, and the third and last trimester is the seventh, eighth and ninth months.

A few days after the fertilized egg reaches the uterus, it sinks into the endometrium, which becomes the developing baby's primary source of nourishment for the moment. Also at this time the **placenta**, a very important exchange and filtering system, begins to develop between mother and baby. Oxygen and nourishment from the mother's blood are filtered through the placenta to the baby, and waste products from the child are returned through the placenta to the mother for disposal. The baby and the placenta are connected by the **umbilical cord**.

This exchange between mother and baby continues throughout the pregnancy. After the baby is born the placenta is also passed out of the body through the vagina (the "afterbirth").

Throughout pregnancy the placenta produces hormones — HCG, HPL, oestrogen, progesterone and others — all of which are necessary to maintain a healthy pregnancy. HCG is what is looked for when a woman has a pregnancy test, since she starts to produce it only after conception.

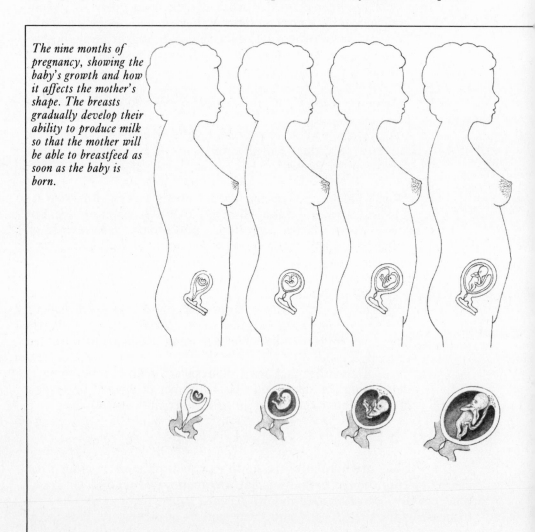

The nine months of pregnancy, showing the baby's growth and how it affects the mother's shape. The breasts gradually develop their ability to produce milk so that the mother will be able to breastfeed as soon as the baby is born.

After the first few days of implantation, a transparent sheath called the **amniotic sac** begins to grow around the baby. The amniotic sac fills with a special fluid, but since the baby receives its oxygen directly into the bloodstream from the mother, it cannot drown in the fluid in which it is completely surrounded. Each day the fluid from the sac is exchanged for new fluid in a continual replacement system. The fluid in the amniotic sac acts as a cushion to keep the developing baby safe from outside bounces and shocks. Frequently just before delivery, the sac breaks (the "breaking of the waters"), releasing maybe a quart of fluid through the vagina.

The names given to the developing baby, from the moment of fertilization up to the moment of birth are:

* at fertilization — zygote
* after one week — blastocyst
* after three weeks — embryo
* from twelve weeks onward — foetus.

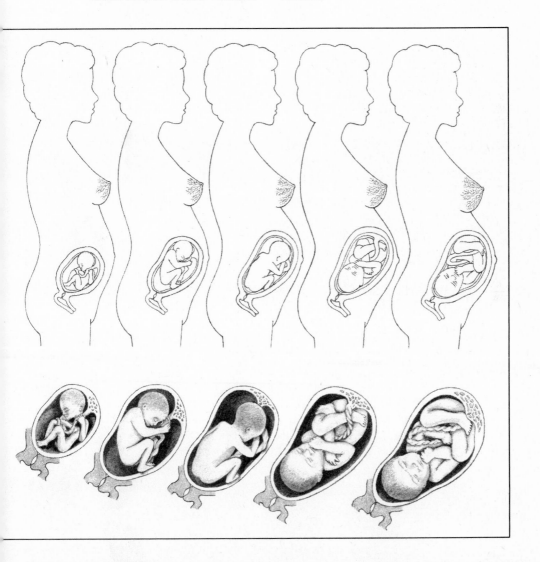

First Trimester By the end of the first month the developing embryo is about one-tenth of an inch long, has a heart that beats strongly, has the beginnings of a head, spinal cord, nervous system, lungs and the buds of arms and legs. Even as this incredible growth is occurring, the woman's period is still only two weeks late and she may not know she is pregnant.

During the second and third months the embryo continues to develop such features as bone cells, nose, eyes, ears, fingers, feet and toes. This refinement of body parts also includes teeth sockets and the beginnings of finger nails. The budding of the clitoris, and the budding of the penis and scrotum also take place at this time, but are not refined enough to be distinguishable as female or male until sometime in the third month. This extraordinary development is very rapid during the first trimester; the foetus is still only two to four inches long and weighs less than one ounce, but it is already looking unmistakably human.

Second Trimester During the second trimester, the body systems and organs of the foetus are still being refined and some finishing touches are

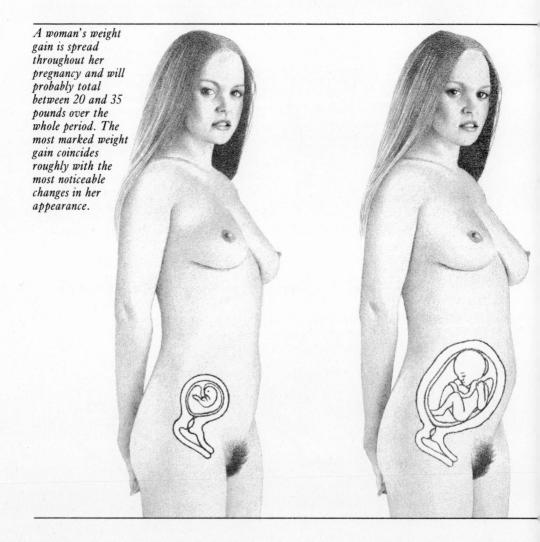

A woman's weight gain is spread throughout her pregnancy and will probably total between 20 and 35 pounds over the whole period. The most marked weight gain coincides roughly with the most noticeable changes in her appearance.

now made to the already existing basic structures. Hair (lanugo) begins to grow not only on the baby's head but all over its body too. This fine covering of hair is usually shed just before birth. Eyebrows and eyelashes begin to appear and the eyelids of the foetus begin to open and close. The foetus's skin is very thin and transparent, making the blood vessels appear to be on the outside of the body. The muscles of the foetus have developed enough to allow it to move its arms and legs; for the first time the mother can feel the definite presence of life in her. This first motion is called "quickening" and it marks a new, joyful stage in the pregnancy, for the presence of a new life becomes much more real to the parents. During the second trimester, the heartbeat of the foetus can be heard with a stethoscope, and the foetus will grow enormously, reaching approximately two pounds in weight and 14 inches in length.

Third Trimester During the third trimester it is usual for the foetus to toss and kick quite a bit, making its presence very obvious. In the seventh month and the first part of the eighth the foetus gains weight and grows

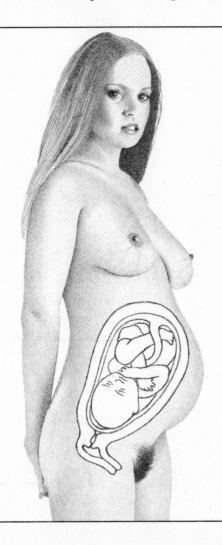

tremendously, tripling its weight and increasing its length to nearly 20 inches. In the eighth and ninth months the baby's organs and structures are developed enough to function on their own. During the final few weeks of pregnancy the baby, which has been in an upright position, gradually turns completely over until its head is pointing downward. It is then ready to be born, as soon as the muscles of the uterus start to contract and begin the baby's passage out of the uterus, through the vagina and into the waiting world.

Do's and Don'ts When You Are Pregnant

Diet
DO   eat a well-balanced, high protein diet
DON'T   skip meals

Sleep
DO   sleep as much as you feel like
DON'T   fight sleep — you need more now, but don't be alarmed if the baby disturbs your normal pattern

Exercise
DO   keep fit; both your pregnancy and delivery will be easier
DON'T   let yourself run to seed

Sex
DO   continue your usual practice
DON'T   think that your pregnancy means you mustn't have sex

Drugs
DO   consult your doctor before taking any drugs; that includes alcohol, aspirin, and sleeping pills
DON'T   smoke anything

Travel
DO   behave normally, without overtiring yourself
DON'T   fly after the seventh month; labour can start any time then

Work
DO   work normally as long as you comfortably can (up to 28 weeks)
DON'T   involve yourself in heavy physical or emotional stress.

Q: "Is it OK to have a chest X-ray when I am pregnant?"
A: "Nonessential X-rays should be avoided as they may harm the developing baby. However it is quite safe to have necessary X-rays under proper supervision and with proper precautions."

Q: "Why are German measles dangerous during pregnancy?"
A: "German measles (rubella) is a virus that passes through the placenta and destroys the sensitive tissue of the foetus. Rubella is especially dangerous if contracted during the first trimester,

but after that period the chance of serious damage to the foetus is sharply reduced. A vaccine protecting women against rubella is now available, so the problem is not as widespread as it was.

"Women who have had rubella in childhood are immune to the disease as adults. A simple blood test will indicate if you are immune. If not, you can arrange with your doctor or clinic for an immunization injection. Your immunization must not be given if you are already pregnant, since the vaccine itself can harm the foetus. Also, after the immunization it is essential to wait two to three months before trying to get pregnant.

"Ordinary measles will not harm a foetus, whether the mother contracts the disease in pregnancy or has previously suffered from it."

Q: "What does Rh mean?"
A: "The Rh factor is a genetically determined part of everyone's blood. Everyone is either Rh negative or Rh positive.

"If both parents have the same Rh factor (positive or negative) the baby will be the same as them. If one parent is positive and the other negative, the baby will usually be positive.

"Complications arise when the father is Rh positive and the mother Rh negative. The baby will probably be Rh positive, but its birth, miscarriage or abortion may cause antibodies to develop in the mother's bloodstream that could damage a future foetus. In this situation the mother is given an injection of anti-D gamma globulin, which, administered after birth, prevents the antibodies from developing.

"If the mother is Rh positive and the father Rh negative, the baby will probably be Rh positive. Both mother and baby then have the same Rh factor and complications will not normally arise.

"Blood tests are usually made on the mother as soon as pregnancy is confirmed, so that if there is going to be a problem, the doctor is alerted. If there is a problem one injection of anti-D gamma globulin after birth is all that is normally required; it has no unpleasant side effects and is entirely safe."

Q: "Surely some drugs must be OK during pregnancy?"
A: "Any drug you take, including aspirin, passes through the placenta and reaches your baby, and during the first three months of pregnancy especially, the drug may damage the baby's sensitive developing organs and systems. Drug use during the second and third trimesters is also dangerous, but not as hazardous as during the first. If your doctor advises you to use a certain drug be certain to discuss its possible side effects on you and your baby."

Q: "Does that go for smoking too?"
A: "Yes. Tobacco contains chemicals that pass through the placenta to the baby, and there is medical evidence that regular

smoking during pregnancy may lead to slightly low-weight babies who may be more susceptible to problems during their development after birth. Heavy smoking may also increase the chances of having a premature baby. A premature baby is one that is born earlier than expected, is low in weight (less than 5lb 8oz) and is liable to greater health problems than babies born at full term."

Q: "Is it OK to smoke pot during pregnancy?"

A: "No. Marijuana contains a very active chemical (THC) which passes through the placenta and into the baby. THC may be stored in the testes or ovaries of the developing foetus and this can lead to fertility problems later on. Marijuana affects the brain, perception and sensation, so ordinary good sense as well as medical advice suggests marijuana smoking should be avoided during pregnancy."

Q: "I've heard there are problems about sex in pregnancy. What can you do about it?"

A: "There are no absolute rules. However, it is important to understand and accept the fact that no harm can come to the baby or mother if you have intercourse or any other kind of sex during pregnancy unless your doctor has advised you not to. Another very important guideline is to be aware of any distance or barriers that may be developing in your relationship. Talk it out, share your anxieties with each other and you will have taken a major step towards avoiding a painful situation. Admitting your anxieties and being sensitive to the concerns and fears of your partner take the loneliness and worry out of these difficult but temporary problems and allow you to function naturally during pregnancy."

Q: "What about weight gain during pregnancy? How much is OK?"

A: "Weight gain is a natural and normal part of pregnancy, so you don't need to worry or feel guilty about it. Your doctor will advise you how much you can or should expect to gain during your pregnancy — 20 to 35 pounds is the normal range. The weight gained is spread throughout the pregnancy, but the major part of it is likely to be later on.

"Being thin in pregnancy may be an attractive idea, and in keeping with the high value currently placed on thinness. However, not eating properly during pregnancy can lead to malnutrition of the mother and to the birth of a low-weight baby. Low-weight babies ($5\frac{1}{2}$ lb or less) are susceptible to more medical complications. Excessive weight gain, say over four stones, can also cause serious problems."

Q: "What about drinking alcohol during pregnancy?"

A: "Alcohol is a drug and when taken in large amounts during pregnancy can harm the brain cells of your baby or lead to abnormalities of the heart or limbs — this is called the foetal alcohol syndrome. Having an alcoholic drink from time to time during pregnancy will not harm the mother or child, but regular or heavy drinking must be avoided."

Q: "I'm on a vegetarian diet. Will I have to change once I'm pregnant?"
A: "You might. A carefully planned vegetarian diet can provide you with the daily nutrients necessary to maintain both your personal health and your pregnancy, but be sure to discuss your usual diet with your doctor to be certain you are providing yourself and your developing baby with adequate nutrition."

Q: "I'm almost about to give birth and I am urinating even more now than before. Is there something wrong?"
A: "No. Late in pregnancy your baby shifts position and this causes more pressure on the bladder and increases your urge to urinate. This is all perfectly normal."

Q: "Can a pregnant woman pass syphilis on to her baby?"
A: "Yes. Once the placenta is formed, syphilis can be passed from the mother to the unborn. This can have three different results: the mother may miscarry at any stage in the pregnancy; the baby may be born alive but with a serious medical problem: or the baby may be born apparently healthy but later in life develop a disease caused by syphilis. All pregnant women's blood is tested for syphilis at their first antenatal visit."

Q: "Can anything be done to help the baby and the mother?"
A: "Yes. Medical treatment (usually penicillin) can cure the disease rather quickly, even late in the pregnancy, and lead to the birth of a healthy baby."

MYTHS The following statements are false:

"You can't get pregnant if you have intercourse standing up."
"You can have twins if you have intercourse twice in a short period of time."
"You can't get pregnant if the man withdraws before coming."
"You can get pregnant if you eat certain foods, like seafood."
"I can't get pregnant because it's the first time I am having intercourse."
"If you have intercourse during pregnancy, the baby is born with a tell-tale mark on his or her body."

FEELINGS How did you feel when you found out you were pregnant?

"I hope this doesn't change my relationship with my husband. I'm worried he might be turned off by my pregnancy."

"Proud."

"I thought of my husband."

"Worried."

"On top of the world."

"I couldn't wait to tell someone."

"Can I really be a parent?"

"Can we afford this?"

"I really feel now that I'm a woman."

"I hope I don't get too fat."

The changes that pregnancy brings are not only physical but deeply emotional. From the moment a woman learns she is pregnant, her sense of her identity, her feelings and her attitude toward her partner change. Occasionally, pregnancy creates feelings of confusion, denial and anger; usually, however, pregnancy leads to emotional growth, maturity and a special feeling of completeness, despite the periods of moodiness and feeling low that accompany most pregnancies.

It is not uncommon for pregnant women to feel unhappy about the way their bodies change as pregnancy progresses. Weight gain and an increasing belly cause many women to feel they are somehow less attractive, less desirable. They wonder if they have become unattractive to their husbands or lost their sex appeal. These feelings occur in many pregnancies, but they usually pass and leave no residue of major problems about self or marriage.

Occasionally a man gets jealous during a wife's pregnancy. The wife receives a great amount of attention and interest, and husbands sometimes feel neglected and resentful. But this, like a pregnant woman's doubts about her attractiveness, usually passes. Lately, husbands have become very involved with their wives' pregnancies, accompanying them to the doctor, attending childbirth education classes and being present during the delivery of the child. This new attitude of sharing and obvious support reduces the negative feelings that can otherwise intrude and prepares the couple for a shared parenthood. Additionally, it is becoming clear that fathers are becoming more and more active and helpful and filling roles that used to be filled exclusively by women. Most people see this new involvement as a positive force in parenthood.

Q: "I heard a man could develop symptoms like cramps and food cravings when his wife is pregnant. Is that true?"

A: "Yes. This situation is called 'couvade' from the French word *couver* which means 'to hatch.' In some societies, couvade is a ritual. In ancient Greece, parts of India and Africa the husband of a wife about to give birth actually went to bed and simulated the birth process. However, there is also a couvade syndrome, which is not a pretence but involves physical symptoms like nausea and stomach pain which parallel what is happening to the woman. Sometimes psychological reactions like anxiety and depression accompany the physical responses."

RELATIONSHIPS Pregnancy creates powerful feelings in women and men which may result in a change in their relationship. For some, this change is an unhappy one, if an unplanned pregnancy affects finances, living space, employment and roles. In these situations, the stress may be felt by one partner or by both, and may be resolved as the pregnancy progresses by continuing communication, honesty and working at adjusting together.

In some cases pregnancy brings a couple closer than they ever were before. The excitement of beginning a family together, the anticipation of being a mother or a father, may create a different sense of responsibility toward each other and a level of love and warmth not experienced before.

Some Pregnancy Complications

1 Ectopic Pregnancy. An ectopic pregnancy is the growth of a fertilized egg outside the uterus, where it properly belongs.

Ectopic pregnancies occur in a Fallopian tube — they are sometimes called "tubal pregnancies" — the majority of the time, but on rare occasions a fertilized egg can implant and begin to grow in the abdominal area, in an ovary or even in the cervix. Ectopic pregnancies result in the death of the foetus and can be fatal to the mother too: they may cause sudden bursting of the Fallopian tube, massive internal bleeding, sharp pain and weakness resulting from the loss of blood. These problems occur late in the first trimester, usually between the eighth and 12th weeks.

Whereas tubal pregnancies cannot be allowed to continue, abdominal pregnancies sometimes result in a successful birth. The foetus survives because the placenta draws blood from the mother's blood supply in that area. Once the baby grows to full term it is delivered by Caesarean.

An ectopic pregnancy may lead to a positive pregnancy test result and a doctor may not see any early signs of difficulty when examining the woman. Typical signs of ectopic pregnancy are: pain and cramping on the lower right or left side of the stomach; bleeding through the vagina; weakness, fainting or dizziness (signs of internal bleeding); a regular period even after pregnancy has been detected.

There are about four ectopic pregnancies for every 1,000 normal ones.

Q: "What is the treatment for a tubal pregnancy?"
A: "Surgical removal of the burst Fallopian tube, salpingectomy, is the usual treatment, though sometimes the tube can be repaired. After such surgery a woman can still become pregnant, and her chances are not reduced by the absence of one tube. Also, a woman's chances of having another ectopic pregnancy increase after having one such pregnancy."

Q: "Can a doctor tell if my wife has a tubal pregnancy before the bursting and bleeding?"

A: "Yes. If her doctor suspects your wife has an ectopic pregnancy following a vaginal examination, an ultra-sound examination will show whether the foetus is growing in the uterus or in a Fallopian tube."

Q: "Then what?"

A: "Surgery is usually performed as soon as the condition is diagnosed. Quick action avoids the possible bursting and heavy bleeding so common in ectopic pregnancies and reduces the probability of serious harm to the mother. It also gives the surgeon time to make an unhurried decision about whether to repair or remove the tube. Even if the tube is removed, it is still perfectly possible for the woman to get pregnant again and carry the child successfully to term. One tube is all that is actually necessary."

2 Miscarriage. Miscarriage is the spontaneous separation and discharge through the vagina of a developing foetus before it is ready to be born. Miscarriage seems to be the natural way the body terminates a pregnancy that is not developing properly. Most miscarriages take place early in the first trimester and occur in about 20 percent of all pregnancies.

Early miscarriages are usually not painful. The chief signs are cramping and bleeding, rather like a heavy menstrual flow. Medical care is required for a miscarriage as all the foetal tissue must pass out of the body. If some tissue remains infection will occur, so a doctor must gently remove the remaining unnecessary tissue from the uterus by D&C.

Seventy-five percent of all miscarriages occur during the first three months (first trimester) of pregnancy. The remainder occur in the second three months of pregnancy (second trimester). Signs of second trimester miscarriages are severe, labour-like cramps, and heavy bleeding followed by the discharge of the developing foetus. Medical attention is required to be certain all foetal tissue has passed out of the body.

Any foetus passed out of the body after the 28th week is called a premature birth rather than a miscarriage.

Q: "Can you tell if you are going to have a miscarriage?"

A: "Sometimes you can tell a miscarriage is threatening when you have slight bleeding or spotting and slight cramping early in your pregnancy. Your doctor may advise you to stay in bed and wait to see what develops. If the signs of miscarriage disappear the pregnancy will continue to develop normally, and you can return to your usual routine.

"It does happen, though, that the bleeding and cramping may increase and some tissue and blood clots will pass out of your vagina, indicating a miscarriage has occurred. Your doctor may ask you to collect this tissue if possible, since there are tests now that can be done on it to determine the cause of your miscarriage. This information is important for future pregnancy planning and will probably show you and your partner that the miscarriage was a chance event and was not the result of a major problem."

Q: "What causes a miscarriage?"
A: "Generally, miscarriages are caused by an egg and sperm dividing or implanting improperly. Sometimes a woman's hormonal level is lower than it should be, causing the lining of the uterus to weaken so much that it is unable to hold a fertilized egg. Problems with the shape of the uterus or cervix are rare but possible causes of miscarriage."

Q: "After my wife had a miscarriage, we were very depressed. Is that normal?"
A: "Yes. It is very common for a couple to be depressed after a miscarriage. Most couples are delighted when they know that the woman is pregnant and they quickly start planning for themselves and their child. When she has a miscarriage their joy and hope often turn into feelings of blame, guilt and grief.
       "Some couples then descend into silence and brooding, when what they should be doing is talking, supporting each other and paving the way for a new pregnancy."

Q: "Can you have a baby after a miscarriage?"
A: "Yes. After a miscarriage, you can start having intercourse again once the cervix has closed and returned to its normal shape — this will take about four weeks. Most doctors advise a wait of a month or two before trying for another pregnancy, however, to give the lining of the uterus time to repair itself."

3 Toxaemia. Toxaemia is a disorder that begins in some women usually during the final trimester of pregnancy. The exact cause of toxaemia (pre-eclampsia) is unknown, but many doctors believe poor nutrition is partly to blame.
   Signs are weight gain and rising blood pressure, swelling of the hands and ankles (due to water retention), and if left untreated the disorder causes abdominal pain, headache and poor vision. Toxaemia affects the baby because the placenta does not do its job properly and the baby is more likely to be small, premature or delivered by Caesarean. The management of toxaemia is rest, a properly balanced diet and avoiding excess salt in your diet. Toxaemia must be treated, as in extreme cases untreated toxaemia can lead to the death of the foetus and even of the mother.

Q: "How do you prevent toxaemia?"
A: "The best way to prevent toxaemia is to ensure that you get good antenatal care from the earliest stages of your pregnancy. It is also very important to rest and to eat a balanced diet."

Q: "Don't they give water reducing pills to women who have toxaemia?"
A: "Not any longer. Water pills or diuretics remove fluid from the

body, but during pregnancy that is only treating the symptom, not the cause of the fluid build-up. Also, fluid removal by repeated use of diuretics causes the loss of important nutrients from your body. Avoid the routine use of diuretics during pregnancy."

Q: "What if you have VD when you are pregnant?"
A: "If a woman contracts syphilis during pregnancy and it remains untreated, the disease can pass through the placenta to the foetus and cause severe tissue damage or even death. If the syphilis is treated early in the pregnancy (before the 18th week), the disease will not damage the foetus. Women are tested for syphilis on their first antenatal visit.

"A woman may pass gonorrhoea to her baby as it is delivered through the birth canal. This can make the baby blind, but it very rarely happens today as the eyes of the newborn can be treated to prevent damage."

Antenatal Preparation: Childbirth Classes

Childbirth education classes have grown in popularity and have been enormously helpful to women and their husbands in preparing them for what to expect during labour and delivery and how to reduce pain and discomfort during the birth process. In addition, since couples are encouraged to attend childbirth education classes together the experience is an important one to their relationship and to the way they will regard and care for their child.

Childbirth classes are an important part of good antenatal care. Broadly speaking, such classes fall into two main categories in the UK: those run by hospitals or local authorities at the antenatal clinics which are provided free on the NHS, and those run by the National Childbirth Trust (NCT). As a charitable organization existing on voluntary support, the NCT has to charge fees for its classes.

The classes begin two to three months before the expected date of delivery and provide a mixture of teaching, group discussion and physical preparation for the birth. The classes are led by trained teachers, usually midwives or physiotherapists.

The first classes usually help the couple understand the changes going on in the woman's body, and the changes that will occur in the rest of the pregnancy and during labour and delivery. Subsequent early sessions are devoted to learning relaxation and muscle toning exercises to prepare the body for labour and delivery. These exercises are taught to the couple, and they practise them with the husband acting as coach, a role he may play during labour and childbirth.

After these early sessions the emphasis is on learning proper breathing techniques for use during early labour. The partner's coaching role is discussed and rehearsed, and sessions at home are also outlined. Subsequent training deals with breathing and mental preparation when strong contractions occur, and how to deal with pain. Recognizing when true labour is occurring and then what the woman and her partner need to do during the actual delivery is discussed and practised during the final sessions of most classes. What will happen in the early moments after delivery is also discussed.

Studies show that women who attend antenatal classes tend to have shorter, less anxious labour and less painful delivery than women who choose not to go. They also tend to use drugs less.

Alternative Childbirth Methods

Homebirth For a growing number of people having a baby at home is a fulfilling and rewarding experience. Homebirth is usually the result of a couple's conviction that it is best for all concerned for the baby to be born in what will be its natural home, rather than in an alien hospital or clinic.

A great controversy exists over whether homebirths are safe. The medical community generally believes that homebirths are dangerous to the mother and baby and that both run serious health risks. However, women who have complete antenatal care, who have reason to expect a straightforward birth and who have proper emergency back-up personnel and equipment available if necessary can have a homebirth in relative safety. It is the way most people were born before this century after all.

But there are some situations in which homebirth would be dangerous: breech positioning of the baby; problems with previous pregnancy, labour or delivery; a larger than usual baby's head; malnutrition; hypertension; diabetes; suspected multiple pregnancy.

Those who favour homebirth suggest that the principal reason doctors are opposed to it is because of the "economic" necessity of keeping hospital beds occupied and because it reduces their control over the labour and delivery procedure. Doctors respond by maintaining that this is not the case, but the health and safety of the mother and baby is the crucial consideration.

The Lamaze method Fernand Lamaze, a French doctor, developed this labour-and-delivery method which he called "psychoprophylaxis" to teach women to become active in labour and delivery by changing their breathing pattern and their body position as labour progresses. The idea is that with proper preparation, labour and delivery will be virtually free of pain. Expectant mothers are taught the proper breathing pattern from the sixth month onward.

Dr Lamaze and Dr Grantly Dick-Read, an Englishman who taught concentration and relaxation during labour and delivery, are principally responsible for the widespread childbirth education classes now available throughout the UK, the US and Europe.

The Leboyer method Frederick Leboyer is the French doctor who developed a unique theory and method of delivering a baby. Principally, Leboyer believes that being born is a terrifying shock, and so the newborn baby should meet life outside the womb with a minimum of noise and dimmed lights, it should be touched gently and held by both parents, and immersed in a warm bath to bring back the liquid weightlessness it felt for so many months in the womb. Dr Leboyer believes the screaming and crying of the newborn is in response to the panic felt at being outside the uterus and being separated from the mother. He believes this imprints the baby in a way that makes later independent development difficult, and so the more that can be done to make the baby's passage into the world an easy one, the more easily the child will develop later. The violent context of childbirth must be replaced by gentleness.

The Leboyer method requires the usual delivery room environment and procedures to be changed. It also requires a retraining of staff. For these reasons, the Leboyer method is used infrequently in most countries. In addition, there still is no evidence that the claims of Dr Leboyer are scientifically valid, although the philosophy and delivery methods sound loving and kind.

III LABOUR AND DELIVERY

FACTS Labour is the last short phase of pregnancy in which the muscles of the womb move the baby from the uterus through the cervix, through the vagina, and out into the world.

We still don't know exactly what causes labour to start. We do know that the quantity of the hormone progesterone in a woman's body decreases sharply in the last stages of her pregnancy; this may have some

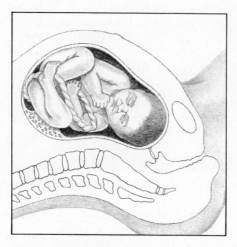

Labour and delivery. In the last month or so of pregnancy the baby rotates so that its head is next to the cervix (left). *When labour starts the cervix dilates* (below, left) *and the baby starts to move through the birth canal until its head shows. This is called crowning* (below). *The baby will then be eased gently out of the birth canal* (below, right). *The last part of delivery is the removal of the placenta once the umbilical cord has been tied off.*

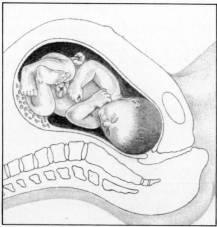

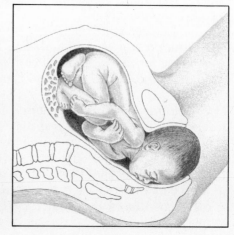

influence. The level of oestrogen increases at the onset of labour and the hormone oxytocin appears which helps to maintain the contractions necessary to squeeze the baby out of the womb. The hormone prostaglandin, which pregnant women naturally secrete, helps cause contractions. But we still don't know exactly how the labour stage is triggered off.

The details of what happens during labour are different for every woman and for each pregnancy. Generally, though, there are three stages.

Stage 1. Labour starts with uterine muscle contractions, called labour pains. These contractions last 30 to 60 seconds each, and occur every 15 to 20 minutes. They can last 12 to 15 hours, particularly if it is the woman's first baby. Women who have already had a child do not experience these contractions for as long. These first-stage contractions begin to open and thin out the cervix or mouth of the uterus.

During this first stage, it is likely that the mucus which has plugged the opening of the cervix throughout the pregnancy will be loosened and released. Many women notice this "show" as it is called in their undergarments, or in the toilet after urination. Sometimes the "show" is released some days before true labour begins.

Late in the first stage of labour the contractions last longer, are more intense and come closer together. When contractions are occurring regularly every five to six minutes the time has come for the woman to go to her hospital. It is now a matter of only a few hours before the baby should be born.

As the contractions push the baby toward the cervix the amniotic sac filled with fluid bursts, releasing from a pint to a quart of fluid.

At the hospital, a woman usually has her pubic area shaved (totally or partially) in preparation for delivery. An enema may be given to the woman and she is encouraged to urinate each hour.

Throughout the contractions phase, the cervix is continuing to open up (dilate) and thin out (efface). Dilation is measured in centimetres or fingers. When a woman's cervix is dilated 8–10 centimetres (4–5 fingers), she is ready for the birth.

During this late first stage of labour many women feel pain in the lower back, but it seems to be severe in only a minority of cases.

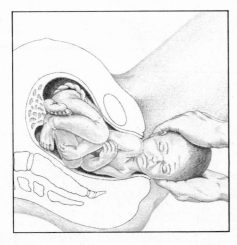
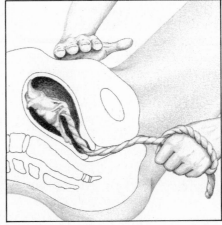

Stage 2. The baby is pushed through the now fully opened cervix, through the vagina (now referred to as "the birth canal") and into the outside world. This stage usually lasts an hour or two for women having their first baby, and between 20 minutes and an hour for women who have already had a child. The difference is because the latter group's birth canals have already been stretched.

As the baby moves through the opened cervix into the vagina its head becomes visible pressing against the vaginal opening. This is called crowning. When crowning occurs, it might be necessary to make a small incision, called an episiotomy, between the bottom of the vagina and the anus. The episiotomy is performed to prevent the possibility of the mother's skin tearing as the head is passing through the vagina. Usually an anaesthetic is used to prevent pain, but if the episiotomy is done just at the right time, when the head is really stretching the vaginal opening, no painkiller is required; there is a natural anaesthetic action. The episiotomy is stitched after the delivery and it heals quickly, with only some soreness and itching.

Early in the second stage of labour, an anaesthetic may be given to ease any pain during delivery. Various forms of regional anaesthetic affecting the spinal column such as the epidural are popular as they allow the mother to experience fully the birth of her baby while limiting her pain and discomfort. A general anaesthetic where the mother is put to sleep is undesirable, as it affects the baby too and slows down the entire labour and delivery process. With a general anaesthetic the mother is unable to witness the birth of her child, and for many women this is sufficient reason to use another type — if one is needed at all.

Within minutes of the birth of the baby, several things are done rather quickly. The mucus and any remaining amniotic fluid are suctioned out of the baby's mouth to make natural breathing easy. The umbilical cord, which is attached to the placenta at one end and to the baby at the other, is clamped or tied and then cut. A very dilute solution of silver nitrate may be applied to the eyes of the baby if there is any risk of eye disease caused by gonorrhoea, and the vernix, a white substance that clings to the baby's skin in the womb, is cleaned off. During all of this, the medical team checks the baby's heart rate, respiration, muscle tone, reflexes and skin colour to be certain they are within normal medical limits. Even while all this important checking is happening just moments after birth, the mother and father usually have a chance to see and hold their baby, to begin the important bonding process between themselves and their child.

Stage 3. The third stage of labour is the separation of the placenta from the uterine wall and the passing of it out of the body as the "afterbirth." Although the afterbirth usually leaves the body in 20 to 30 minutes following the birth of the baby, it can take up to an hour to be passed. Once out, it is examined to be certain no piece still remains in the uterus. A remaining piece of placenta can cause infection and haemorrhage later on, so all of it must be removed.

Q: "I've read about women having a great deal of pain, and screaming and thrashing around during childbirth. Is that very common and should it be expected?"

A: "It does not happen today nearly as much as it used to before the marvellous advances of medical science and the important contributions of childbirth classes. Some pain is inevitable in the majority of births: it is a natural result of the baby being forced out of the uterus through a rather narrow passage. But now painkillers can be administered to help some women deal with excruciating pain. Even then, drugs will be given only after labour has been under way for some time. Childbirth classes

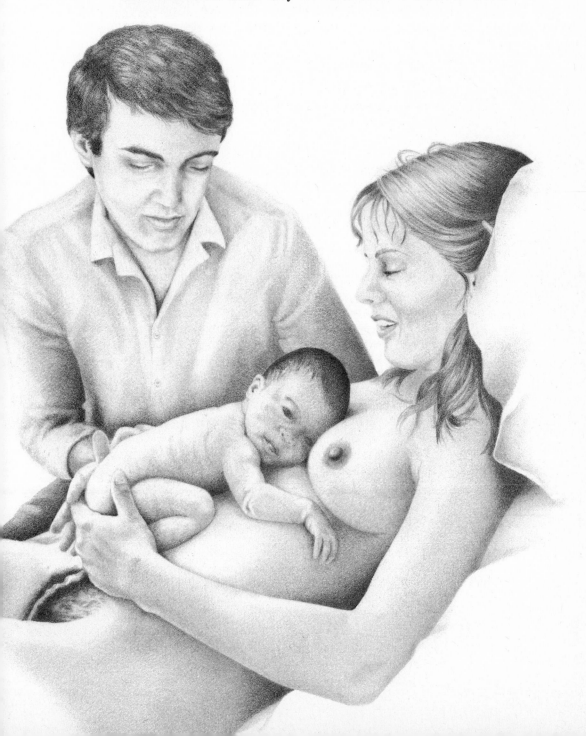

help reduce fear and anxiety — it is the woman who has extreme fear who tends to feel pain more than women who are prepared. Pain may however be a sign of a real physical problem so it must always be taken seriously, even if the woman has attended childbirth classes."

Q: "What are false labour pains?"

A: "False labour pains are irregular contractions of the uterus that do not increase the opening of the cervix or prepare the woman for labour and delivery. False labour pains are common in women who are having their first baby and may cause them to dash off to their doctor or hospital only to be told it is a false alarm. The pain is real enough, but these are not the contractions that will dilate the cervix and push the baby out, and they are not a cause for anxiety. However, real labour will soon start."

Q: "Some women have painless contractions before they start proper labour, don't they?"

A: "Yes. Doctors call them Braxton-Hicks contractions and they're quite normal. It seems that the uterus is having a rehearsal for the real labour that is about to begin. If a woman has Braxton-Hicks contractions (and not all women do) she can practise her childbirth breathing and get used to what real labour contractions are going to feel like."

Q: "A friend of ours told us not to get any painkillers at all when my wife is in labour. Are painkillers really that bad?"

A: "Your friend is rightly concerned about the medical effects of anaesthetics on the baby and the fact that some anaesthetics may interfere with your wife's ability to enjoy fully the birth of her baby. Painkillers — especially general anaesthetics — cross the placenta quickly and affect both baby and mother in a negative way. Regional anaesthetics like caudal, epidural, spinal blocks, paracervical blocks and pudendal blocks, diminish the discomfort of labour but allow the mother to experience the moment of birth.

"Remember, though, that labour is not an endurance contest. Some women find they give birth fairly easily without much pain, while others find that they want painkillers."

Q: "My husband and I are keen to have a baby, but he hates hospitals and says he won't come with me when I go into labour. Will that be bad for the baby if he doesn't see it until I come out of hospital?"

A: "Although it is preferable for the father to be present during labour and delivery, it is unlikely that his absence will be detrimental to the baby's future development or to their relationship. After all, men have only recently been able to be present during labour; before then they had little chance even to hold the infant until mother and baby arrived home. Our present system is more desirable, but the old one worked pretty well. Another point to consider is that if your husband is so ill at ease in hospitals, his anxiety or tension could be passed on to you, so it may be better for all of you including the baby if his contact is in the relaxed environment of your home."

Q: "I heard about a delivery using acupuncture instead of drugs. Can that be true?"
A: "Yes. Acupuncture has been used without problems in a few births in the UK as well as in the US, France and Italy, for both vaginal and Caesarean delivery. In China, where the science of acupuncture has a long and respected history, this technique is widely used for deliveries."

Q: "What is induced labour?"
A: "Induced labour is the term used to describe labour started artificially. The normal method is that a hormone, such as Pitocin, is dripped intravenously, causing the uterus to contract and so beginning labour. Induced labour must be carefully monitored by the medical team.
    "Labour is induced if the medical opinion is that waiting for natural labour to begin constitutes a health risk to the baby or the mother. Induction should never be used to satisfy the convenience of the doctor or the mother."

Q: "Are prostaglandins used to help in the birth process?"
A: "Yes. Prostaglandins are hormones produced by the endometrium in women, the seminal vesicle and the prostate gland in men. They are sometimes used to stimulate the smooth muscle of the uterus, causing it to contract and to begin the labour process or to help labour that has already begun. Whether or not to use prostaglandins is a medical judgment to be made by the doctor who is handling the delivery."

Q: "A friend of mine had a baby recently and is having a tough time enjoying sex. Is there a physical reason?"
A: "Physical changes due to childbirth rarely interfere with sexual interest and enjoyment. Once she has recovered a woman and her partner should be able to return to their previous level of sexual pleasure, though it may take a couple of months or so. When there is a change for the worse the reason is probably emotional, but the woman should be checked by a doctor. Women sometimes feel fear, anger or depression about being a mother or about being a mother again. If this situation persists, your friend ought to seek help from a trained counsellor."

Q: "How soon after childbirth can I have sex?"
A: "You can resume sexual contact immediately after having your baby, but most couples wait until after the post-natal examination before resuming intercourse. Some doctors will advise you

about this but some won't, so your best bet is to wait until you feel physically comfortable again.

"Remember to use a contraceptive, unless you're prepared to risk getting pregnant again immediately. You may not be ovulating right away after the birth, but you could be."

Q: "I've heard of women bleeding a bit for some days after they've had a child. Is that normal?"

A: "Yes. It's quite normal, lasts about three weeks and is called lochia. Lochia consists of blood and mucus and is, in fact, the final cleaning out of the uterus. The colour will change gradually from red to clear. If the lochia smells unpleasant, the woman should contact her doctor; part of the placenta may have remained in the uterus, and this can be dangerous."

FEELINGS The pain of going into labour can be considerable, but so for many women is the sense that they are bringing to a head one of the most important experiences a woman can have. Within a few hours — even minutes — nine months of anticipation will bear fruit and a dream will come true:

"God, I hope I can do it right."

"I wish these people would stop telling me what to do."

"I heard this was going to be hard work but I didn't think it would be this hard."

"This is not going the way we learned in childbirth class."

"I feel so close to my husband."

"Will this ever end?"

"I am so happy he is here to watch and help me."

"I hope I don't spoil things now after waiting nine months."

"The pain is very intense."

"I wish I could do more to help my wife."

Wanting to please, to do it right, is also very important. The members of the medical team are there to help, but many women feel that they must perform well not to let the team down. Husbands have rarely seen their wives in such tense circumstances: they too are there to give support, but wives often feel that they themselves must perform well in return.

And there is the anxious anticipation. Will the baby be strong and healthy? Will it come out right? What will it really feel like to hold my own baby for the first time? What will it be like to see it, feel it, fondle it?

Some women want to get through labour and delivery any way they can, take the baby and go home. Others try and suppress the discomfort and the anxiety by focusing on the moment when they will hold the baby.

The luckiest of them all are those women who are genuinely exhilarated by the experience, who feel a new level of intimacy with their partners and a pride in their achievement; the moment of delivery marks them indelibly.

RELATIONSHIPS The current trend of encouraging husbands to be present and to help during labour and delivery can have an enormous positive impact on a relationship. The birth of a baby is still one of the most marvellous events in a couple's life, and to experience it together can strengthen the bonds of the relationship. Being together during labour and delivery and seeing the baby enter the world has helped some couples to a different, more intimate phase in their relationship.

After nine months of watching and worrying, many men are delighted at last to have the opportunity to do something active, for now they can help with proper breathing, concentration and reassurance. This is the first time they can feel really involved in a process of caring and sharing that will last for years to come.

The traditional labour and delivery procedure, with husband and wife separated and with the husband waiting outside for the news about his baby, may be an alienating experience for both parents. It is not that a relationship necessarily suffers because of this separation during labour and delivery, rather that an opportunity is missed to build on a good relationship by sharing the rare experience of birth.

Some Birth Complications

Every birth is different, just as every baby is different, but there are some standard variations that require special procedures. Late in the pregnancy, many doctors and clinics will routinely check for possible delivery complications, and all will if they suspect that anything may be amiss.

If a foetus is developing abnormally or is improperly positioned, or if the placenta is poorly located for birth, special action will have to be taken. At the very least, the doctor needs to know about it so that he or she can be alert to the first signs of trouble during labour or delivery.

There are two common tests to discover complications: ultra-sound (sonography) uses high-frequency sound waves that are bounced off the foetus to produce a picture of it. It's the same principle as underwater sonar and is entirely safe. Amniocentesis is the procedure in which a needle is inserted through the abdominal wall into the amniotic sac so that the doctor can check if the amniotic fluid is clear. Occasionally the fluid is greenish, indicating that meconium, material from the foetus's large intestine, has been released. If this has happened, the foetus is in trouble and must be delivered quickly. The common forms of complication with delivery are:

* Caesarean, in which the baby has to be lifted out through a cut made by the surgeon in the lower part of the abdomen
* breech birth, in which the baby is the wrong way up

* premature birth, in which the baby is born before the full 36 weeks of development in the womb
* forceps delivery, in which the baby gets stuck and has to be pulled out of the vagina.

Caesarean. A Caesarean, sometimes referred to as a "section," is an operation in which an incision is made through the abdominal wall into the uterus, so that the baby can be lifted out. A Caesarean is performed: if the placenta begins to precede the baby (*placenta previa*); if the baby starts to come through the cervix buttocks first or sideways and the risks are too great to continue the birth that way; or if the baby or mother shows signs of distress that require the delivery to be completed quickly. Caesareans are also performed if the baby just cannot get through the cervix, either because the baby is too large or because the mother's birth canal is too small, and for several other reasons besides. If a woman has already had a baby delivered by Caesarean her subsequent deliveries will probably also have to be by the same process, although she can have a natural vaginal birth if her doctor feels that is proper for her.

Having a Caesarean means running the risks of surgery, but it is usually safer than continuing a vaginal birth if significant problems are occurring. A general anaesthetic is usually given before a Caesarean, but sometimes it may be a regional type because they affect the baby less and allow the mother to see and touch her baby once it is lifted from her uterus. Recovery time varies but usually a week is sufficient for the stitches to heal and for the mother to regain her strength.

In some cases, the decision to perform a Caesarean is made rather rapidly and long conversations between the doctor, the woman and her husband are not possible. Whenever possible, though, the problem and the solutions available should be discussed before permission is granted to go ahead with the surgery.

Caesareans are done in about eight percent of births in the UK; in the US the figure is ten to fifteen percent. Both these figures are increasing.

Q: "Where does the doctor make the incision for a Caesarean?"
A: "There are two ways of making the skin incision. The classical way is a vertical cut in the abdomen. This method is favoured when speed is the most important thing. The other way is the transverse or bikini cut, in which a horizontal incision is made near the pubic hair line. The resulting scar is less obvious, and won't show if the woman wears a bikini. It is easy to repair but it does require a little more time to perform.

"Once the surgeon has opened the skin he or she will probably make a low, transverse incision in the uterus. For surgical reasons this is preferable to making a vertical incision in the uterus."

Q: "Is it true that many Caesareans are not really required?"
A: "It does seem the case that the number of Caesareans performed each year is increasing and it is hoped that this number could be reduced in favour of normal deliveries. It is hoped that advances

The two kinds of skin incision a surgeon can make when performing a Caesarean section: the classical vertical and the transverse or bikini. Whichever kind is used to open the skin, the incision in the wall of the uterus will probably be transverse.

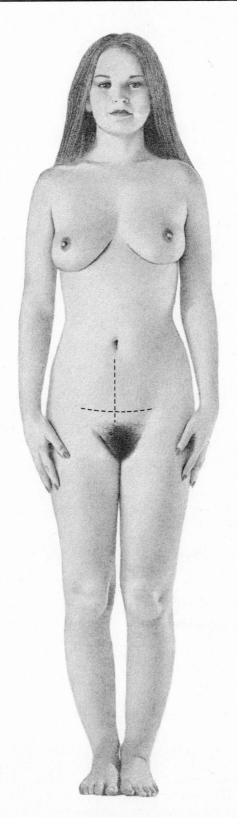

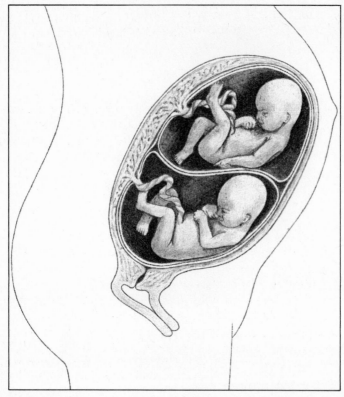

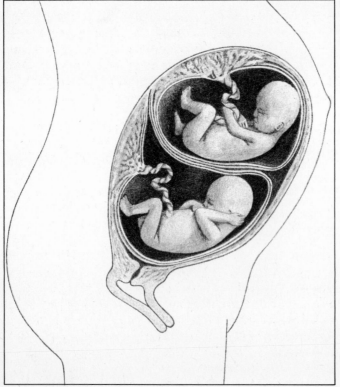

Twins and how they develop in the uterus. There are two kinds of twin — identical (left) and fraternal (below). Identical twins result from the spontaneous division of one fertilized egg. Each grows in its own amniotic sac, but the surrounding outer membrane is common to both and they share a placenta. Identical twins are of the same sex. Fraternal twins are the result of two ova being released and fertilized at the same time. Each has its own placenta and a separate outer membrane surrounds each amniotic sac. Fraternal twins are not necessarily of the same sex. Triplets, quadruplets and more are fraternal rather than identical, developing from the release of three, four or more ova at once.

in foetal monitoring and a willingness on the part of doctors to carry on with difficult vaginal deliveries of normal babies would make such a reduction possible."

Q: "I had a Caesarean and now I would like a regular birth. Is that possible?"

A: "Yes. If the reason for your first Caesarean no longer exists, and if the incision made in your uterus was of the low transverse kind, there is a good chance you can have a vaginal delivery. However, if your first uterine incision was the classical vertical type there is a real chance your uterus may rupture and endanger you during labour and delivery. Your doctor will review the possibilities with you."

Premature Birth. A baby is described as premature if it is born at least three weeks before the expected time. The baby is smaller than if the pregnancy had continued to term and runs increased health risks for missing those last few weeks of development in the womb.

Prematurity can be caused by toxaemia or severe infection in the mother, by a multiple pregnancy, or by early separation of the placenta; sometimes it appears to happen for no specific reason. When true premature labour begins some doctors try to halt it by using drugs and ordering complete bed rest. Sometimes, these efforts work, and as long as the amniotic sac does not burst the pregnancy can continue normally.

A baby arriving prematurely has a powerful psychological effect on its parents. The suddenness and unexpectedness of the birth, coupled with anxiety about the baby's future and the possible guilt felt by both parents, but by the mother in particular, make coping with a premature birth difficult. Close involvement on the part of both parents with the baby and with the early medical care process helps to overcome some of these difficulties. Talking about any frustration or guilt is also important, as passivity and blame-taking only complicate an already tense situation.

Breech Birth. When instead of the baby's head coming out first its buttocks or feet attempt to do so, it is called a breech birth. Although a vaginal delivery is sometimes possible, most doctors will not risk it and will deliver the baby by Caesarean.

Sometimes a doctor will discover the baby's unusual position during an examination in the last month or two of pregnancy and may be able to turn the baby into the proper position by appropriate pressure on the mother's abdomen.

Some of the common causes of breech birth are: a large baby unable to turn fully into the proper head-down birth position; the baby not having its legs bent; excess amniotic fluid which allows the baby to float around and not become engaged in the birth position; and tumours in the uterus interfering with proper positioning. Breech births are also common in twins: one baby is often delivered head first and the second in a breech position. Breech births account for about three percent of all deliveries.

Forceps Delivery. Sometimes a baby will get into the birth canal, then cease to make progress. It needs helping out. Sometimes in the course of a normal vaginal delivery the baby will show a faint or irregular heart-beat and need to be delivered in a hurry. Equally, the placenta may begin to detach before the baby is clear of the birth canal, making it imperative that the baby have a quick exit. In all these circumstances, and whenever it becomes urgent to get the baby out of the birth canal quickly, forceps are used if conditions permit.

Forceps are two pieces of metal joined near the handle — rather like salad tongs. There are different kinds of forceps: which one is used will depend upon how far through the vagina the baby has got. If needed, they are inserted gently into the vagina to grip either side of the baby's head. The baby can then be carefully eased out.

Forceps usually leave marks on the side of the baby's head or on its cheeks, but they soon disappear.

Ventouse (vacuum) delivery. This is an alternative to forceps delivery. A small metal suction cap, attached to a pump, is applied to the baby's head. By drawing the suction cap gently downwards, the baby's head can be delivered through the entrance to the vagina and the delivery completed normally.

Q: "What is a stillbirth?"
A: "A stillbirth is when the baby is born dead. This kind of tragedy occurs less often today because of the overall quality of health care during pregnancy.

"A stillbirth can have a profound impact on the parents. The grief and the emotional pain are very difficult to deal with. Guilt, denial and anger are common responses, but it doesn't help to bottle them up; they should be allowed free expression. After a stillbirth, the husband and wife need each other's support more than ever, and they also need the understanding of family and friends."

THE POST-NATAL PERIOD

Once a baby is born, particularly if it is the first, there are numerous adaptations to be made by the parent(s) and new skills to be learned. Such practical matters as holding and bathing a baby, breastfeeding, dealing with nappies and coping with new sleep routines require information and practice; psychological adjustments may be necessary too, particularly if the mother experiences postnatal depression. These special considerations of nurturing and living with a newborn baby are beyond the scope of this book, but there are many sources of help. Family and friends may well be of assistance, family doctors can offer good advice and there are many baby-care books that give practical information. Most prospective parents start to make preparations and begin to inform themselves well before the baby is due to be born and find that the better they have equipped themselves with knowledge of what to expect, the more they can enjoy the first few months after birth.

PREGNANCY TERMINATION

FACTS Pregnancy termination, commonly known as abortion, means removing an immature foetus from the womb or deliberately causing a miscarriage (the Latin *abortio* means "miscarriage").

Abortion is *not* a method of birth control. It is a last resort, to be used when carrying on with the pregnancy would be more harmful to the woman than terminating it. It is also ethically a highly controversial issue, and one which is surrounded by powerful religious constraints. It is therefore essential that a woman contemplating having a pregnancy terminated should reflect thoroughly on what it will mean to her. If the father of the child can be party to this reflection, so much the better. It is equally important that the decision be taken quite quickly, as the longer the delay, the greater the risk of medical complications. Abortions should be completed within the first 12 weeks and must not be done after 28.

In the UK the 1967 Abortion Act states that the termination of a pregnancy is legal under certain conditions. This law, however, does not apply in Northern Ireland, where abortion is still illegal, as it is in Eire. According to the law an abortion is not illegal if two registered medical practitioners give an opinion in good faith that a) to continue with the pregnancy would involve risk to the life of the pregnant woman or injury to the mental or physical health of the pregnant woman or any existing children of her family, greater than the risk of terminating the pregnancy; or b) there is a substantial risk that if the child were born it would suffer from such physical or mental abnormalities as to be seriously handicapped. Legalizing abortion in certain circumstances has had the effect of making it safer — the numbers of deaths resulting from termination procedures dropped significantly in the UK after the passing of the 1967 law. This is because the procedures are now performed by trained doctors who take due account of the circumstances and can provide adequate follow-up care. As an example of how common termination is, about 157,500 pregnancies were legally terminated in the UK in 1979.

Terminating a pregnancy is a very serious matter which, as has been said, demands measured reflection. On the other hand, the great majority of abortions are easily and safely performed, and most women who have an abortion do not suffer any long-term physical or emotional damage. Provided that the termination is correctly performed, the woman's future sexual interest and pleasure will be in no way impaired. A few women suffer long periods of guilt and depression, but most experience no significant long-term emotional or psychological problems.

Before a woman (or a couple) decides to have an abortion there are three important issues that need to be thought through: the practical, the ethical and the emotional.

The practical issue is whether it would be possible to raise the child properly if the pregnancy were allowed to continue to term. In what circumstances would the child grow up? Would it have proper emotional and financial security? What would the effects be on the mother's career and expectations? What would be the effects on her relationship with the father? If the woman already has children how will another child affect their well being?

The ethical issue is whether that particular woman or couple can feel entirely sure that termination is morally legitimate. If they are convinced that the future child's right to life is more important than their right to control their lives then termination would clearly be against their personal standards. It is a matter of conscience.

The emotional issue is perhaps the most complex of the three. Even if a woman can say, after due reflection, that she is sure it is more practical to terminate the pregnancy and that she is clear in her own mind that it is ethical to do so, how is she going to feel afterwards? Will she always feel regret or guilt? How would she feel about having the child and then offering it for adoption? The emotional aspect of the matter may confuse logical decision-making.

Counselling may well be of help here: an informed, objective person can often see not only more of what is involved but more of how it will affect that woman also. Most women seeking an abortion will receive counselling both before and after. These help the woman to be sure that her decision was the right one for her and inform her on the procedures and choices. Counselling after the termination has been performed should include a discussion of appropriate birth control methods to lessen the chance of the woman having to seek another abortion later.

If the woman and her doctor agree that abortion is the right course of action, the doctor will refer the woman to a gynaecologist at a hospital. Some doctors don't approve of abortion on ethical grounds and will refuse to do the operation, in which case the woman will have to find another doctor. If the specialist agrees that a termination should be carried out, the operation will be performed in hospital on the NHS. There are also a number of private or charitable agencies who will advise on abortion. Two doctors will examine the woman and if they recommend a termination, the agency will arrange for the operation to be performed at a specially licensed clinic or nursing home.

Methods of Termination. The methods vary according to how many weeks pregnant the woman is. The most common method used is vacuum aspiration which can be used to terminate pregnancies of up to 12 weeks. The operation is quick (it takes about 20 minutes) and safe. A flexible tube (a cannula) is passed up the vagina, through the cervix and into the uterus. The other end of the tube is attached to a vacuum pump which gently draws out the contents of the uterus. The operation is usually done under general anaesthetic (though some clinics use local anaesthetics). The woman may stay overnight or, if all is well, she may be allowed to leave after a few hours.

Dilation and Curettage (D&C) is used for terminations between 12 weeks (and sometimes before) and about 16 weeks. This is almost always done under general anaesthetic. The cervix is stretched (dilated) and the contents of the uterus removed by suction as in vacuum aspiration. The doctor then scrapes the uterine lining with a curette, a metal loop on the end of a long handle, to ensure that the uterus is thoroughly evacuated. The procedure usually involves an overnight stay in the hospital or clinic.

For terminations between 15 or 16 weeks and 28 weeks the method is normally to induce a miscarriage. Until recently, this was done by means of injections of saline solution but most doctors now use prostaglandin, which is a substance that appears naturally in a woman's body at the time of a full-term labour. The introduction of prostaglandin either orally or as vaginal pessaries, or directly into the uterus, outside the amniotic sac, causes the uterus to contract and expel the foetus and placenta. Although a general anaesthetic is not used, the woman is usually sedated during the process.

Q: "Can menstrual extraction be used to terminate a pregnancy?"
A: "Yes. No-one can be sure that they are pregnant until their period is two weeks late, but menstrual extraction, sometimes called pre-emptive abortion, can be used to evacuate the contents of the uterus within the first 14 days after unprotected intercourse. The technique is not yet widely used in the UK."

Q: "What is a hysterotomy?"
A: "A hysterotomy is a surgical method of abortion involving a Caesarean section under general anaesthesia. It is not common, but it is used when for medical reasons the ordinary methods of terminating a pregnancy are ruled out."

Q: "What do most psychiatrists feel about abortion?"
A: "In general they favour it if a woman is clear about her choice. They believe not being able to have an abortion when desired interferes with a woman's concept of being in control of her own life, and may impair her future ability to fulfil herself."

Q: "Are most religious believers opposed to abortion?"
A: "Polls show that the majority favour a woman's right to choose."

Q: "What about the anti-abortion movement?"
A: "As soon as the abortion law was passed, various groups started campaigning against it. In general the movement seeks to change the law to make abortion illegal. The two major organizations are the Society for the Protection of the Unborn Child (SPUC) and 'Life'. Members of such organizations base their anti-abortion argument on the belief that the foetus is a person from the very moment of conception and that abortion is therefore murder. There are anti-abortion groups in every country where abortion is legal. In America, the Right to Life Group have developed proposals for amending the Constitution and thus changing current legislation.

"This attitude is opposed by organizations such as the National Abortion Campaign and 'A Woman's Right To Choose Campaign' who seek to sustain the legality of abortion and support women in making informed, noncoercive decisions about their own reproductive health. Pro-abortion supporters are very active politically, campaigning to prevent legislation being passed that would restrict abortion choice any further and pressing for complete legalization of abortion so that the women themselves, and not the doctors, are given the right to choose."

Q: "Hasn't abortion become such a big business that many doctors, clinics and so on want to keep it legal for economic reasons?"

A: "No, I don't believe that is the case. Most professionals in the sexology field would like to see the need for abortion removed. We should ideally be so successful at education and prevention that no woman would ever have to face the decision to have an abortion.

"Professionals in the reproductive health field care about people and the quality of their lives, and they are in general agreement that abortion is a necessary solution in some instances, but that we should all work toward preventing its necessity. To do this, effective and sensitive sex education must be developed in families, schools, communities and religious institutions. Communicating the meaning of responsible sexual behaviour and a concern for mutual wellbeing is the principal way to eliminate the need for abortion."

MYTHS There is no truth in any of these statements:

* only poor people have abortions
* an abortion puts an end to a woman's interest in sex
* you can't have a normal pregnancy once you've had a termination
* all religious groups oppose abortion
* abortion is illegal in most countries
* if a woman has one abortion she will probably have several more
* pregnancy termination is medically a very risky business
* women who have abortions usually have long-term psychological problems
* most adults believe that abortion should be made illegal
* abortion is a modern issue, and results from a recent decline in moral standards.

FEELINGS It is by no means only those women who have strong religious affiliations who find decisions about pregnancy termination very stressful. These are some typical comments from women and couples in an urban community:

"I felt so desperate I didn't know what to do."

"I wanted it but I was ambivalent. I had an uncertain feeling for several months afterward."

"I felt so relieved after I had my abortion."

"Afterwards I felt more mature and independent."

"I felt guilty, like I had done something wrong."

"I didn't want to go with her but I did. After all I'm involved too."

"I didn't tell anyone about it for years."

"I was just so glad he came with me."

"I felt lucky to be able to have one, and I was never going to get myself in a situation like that again."

"After seeing what she went through and what I was feeling I promised myself that this would never happen again."

"I was happy it was over and I was happy I was feeling good."

"At first I think I grieved, then it was OK."

"I couldn't go near a guy for a long time after my abortion. Some people thought I was antisocial, others thought I was gay. It took a while to get over it."

Fortunately, these women and their partners had reflected on the situation before making the decision to have an abortion. In addition, they had taken preabortion counselling sessions very seriously. Carrying to term, having the baby and motherhood had been explored fully, along with the abortion alternative. It was their feeling that having an unplanned baby promised to be a greater trauma than having an abortion. Although the feelings of these women who had had abortions were complex and often included guilt, on balance the most prominent feeling afterward was relief.

RELATIONSHIPS The decision to terminate a pregnancy affects relationships differently, according to the responses of the partners, their respective views on abortion in general and on their situation in particular:

"I just found that after my abortion my husband was much more concerned about birth control. It certainly took long enough!"

"My husband didn't touch me for months afterward. He thought he would hurt me I guess. Either that or he felt guilt because of our unplanned pregnancy."

"It was her choice, but I was so angry that she did it. I know I acted strange toward her for a while."

"After we went for some counselling, things got better in our relationship. For a while, it was very rough on us."

"My parents and friends were all against it, so it put a real strain on our relationships with them."

Relationships can be severely tested when a woman plans a pregnancy termination and her husband or boyfriend does not agree. After discussion many women exercise their rights over their own bodies and have an abortion despite the opposition. The likely consequent strain in the relationship may not be resolved unless the couple genuinely works at it, and they may find they need some professional counselling as well.

A close and supportive relationship both before a termination and after is enormously helpful. Being able to express fears and ambivalence knowing that feelings will be accepted and respected makes the decision to have an abortion less alienating.

RELIGION Pregnancy termination is even more controversial from the religious point of view than birth control. Birth control, which is a serious enough issue for many religious people, has to do with preventing the start of a new life; abortion has to do with a life that has already in some sense begun. The question for some believers is this: is abortion murder?

Catholicism. Although Catholic teaching on abortion has shifted through the centuries, the current position is clear: abortion is murder. This position has been fixed since 1869, when Pope Pius IX reinstituted the doctrine that the soul enters the body at the moment of conception; from that moment on, the foetus is therefore a person. Furthermore, because the foetus has a soul it must be baptized in order to remove original sin. Catholics therefore believe that not only is abortion murder, but it also condemns the unborn person to limbo.

Judaism. Through the centuries, Judaic scholars have agreed that therapeutic abortions — those performed to save the life of the mother — are permissible. However, when abortion is requested for other (including emotional) reasons, the opinions of rabbinical scholars have varied over the centuries. Some teachings in the Responsa have been quite strict, others quite liberal.

Currently, the majority of liberal Jewish believers follow the law adopted by the Israeli Knesset in 1977. Abortion is permitted in Israel if, with the woman's consent, it is carried out in a properly recognized hospital to ensure the physical or emotional health of the woman, to prevent the birth of a physically or mentally handicapped child, if the pregnancy resulted from incest, rape, or adultery, or if the woman is under 16 or over 40.

Protestantism. Because there are so many separate Protestant churches, there is no one clear ruling on abortion that applies to all Protestant believers. The Church of England upholds the belief that the unborn child must be protected. However, the Church recognizes that in those cases where a pregnancy threatens the wellbeing of the woman or her family, abortion is a legitimate choice. Different churches propose slightly different restrictions and considerations, but on the whole they agree that the rights of the living outweigh those of the unborn.

PROSTITUTION

FACTS Prostitution (from the Latin *prostituere*) is the exchange of sexual services for money. The majority of prostitutes are women who sell their services to men. There are also some men who sell their services to women or to other men, and there is a very small minority of women who sell their services to other women. Acts of prostitution are voluntary, usually anonymous and affectionless.

Prostitution is legal in some countries, illegal in others. In Britain, it is not illegal but there are so many offences relating to prostitution that it might as well be. In several countries there are vigorous movements, often led by prostitutes themselves, to make prostitution legal. The prostitutes say that they themselves would benefit by being able to carry on their business openly and without harassment. The community would benefit by having prostitution confined to certain locations and by the application of proper health standards and the state would benefit by collecting taxes on prostitutes' earnings. The arguments against such movements are that the state would be seen to be acquiring earnings from immoral activities and that the community would be giving its blessing to prostitution in defiance of the expressed wishes of many of its members.

Prostitutes between them represent just about every kind of social, educational and religious background. A high proportion of those whose histories have been recorded come from unstable families. Reports of early sexual activity and of early sexual abuse are common. Some become prostitutes for the money and some as a rebellion against their families and against society. There are working prostitutes who have husbands and sometimes children too — they regard their occupation as a regular job in much the same way as any other working wife or mother. Women do not become prostitutes because they are oversexed.

There are several different kinds of prostitute. The most obvious, and those charging the lowest prices on the whole, are the streetwalkers. They solicit their customers (whom they call "tricks," or "Johns") in an obvious way and provide their services in a nearby rooming house, for which the client pays. They may also have sex with the client in his car. Then there are prostitutes who work in some massage parlours, offering sex in addition to the massage, steambaths and so on that the parlours are supposed to provide.

Brothels are probably less popular now than they were 100 years ago. Also known as "whorehouses" and "cathouses," brothels are run by madams who organize the business, help entertain customers and take a cut from the women's earnings.

The most elegant professionals among prostitutes are call girls; they are also the most expensive and the most selective. They work from stylish apartments or houses, making their appointments by phone. Call girls may serve some of the emotional and social needs of their clients as well as selling them sex.

Many prostitutes, especially those on the streets, work for a pimp. He protects his women (his "stable") from legal interference and from violent customers. On the other hand, he is likely to be ruthlessly violent with the women working for him, recruiting and keeping them against their will and taking the lion's share of their earnings. A pimp will sometimes require sexual services from his stable for himself, and may take a particularly good worker as his "wife," even though she continues as a full-time prostitute.

Prostitution is commonly called "the life." Prostitutes are also known as "hookers," "whores," "harlots," "tarts," and "pros."

Q: "What kind of man goes to a prostitute?"
A: "All kinds. Kinsey found that about 69 percent of American men in his study had had at least one experience with a prostitute. Some men who go to a prostitute are married and away from home, other married men use a prostitute to perform acts they would not perform with their wives. Some men want more sex than they get at home so they use prostitutes to satisfy their needs. Single men who are inhibited about dating or forming relationships also use prostitutes, as do some young men seekings initiation or sexual experience. Some men use prostitutes because they want sex but are concerned to avoid emotional attachments."

Q: "What is a gigolo?"
A: "Gigolos are men who sell their sexual services to women. They are usually young, attractive men who prey on the vanity and affectional needs of older, lonely women. They escort these women to social functions as well as having sex with them. In exchange they receive money and gifts."

Q: "Are gigolos like male hustlers?"
A: "No. Male hustlers are usually men or boys who sell sex to other men. Some are gay and offer sexual services of any type while others indicate they have a heterosexual orientation and usually only allow themselves to be fellated."

Q: "Do prostitutes earn a great deal of money?"
A: "In general, no. Call girls probably have the best income and the best life, and they can make quite a lot of money. Streetwalkers, massage parlour and brothel workers do not earn as much and they usually have to share their earnings with their pimp, madam or parlour owner."

Q: "Do prostitutes get involved in relationships with their customers?"
A: "It is unlikely. Prostitution is a business and prostitutes are interested in fees for service. Getting emotionally involved with a customer is just not good for business.

      "Men sometimes idealize a prostitute because with her they feel understood and accepted, but that is part of the service and efforts to develop a relationship beyond that of paying customer are unacceptable. Call girls are more likely to form relationships of sorts with some of their customers, acting as social companions on vacations, business trips and the like, but these are not seen as permanent.

"Occasionally a prostitute retiring from 'the life' will marry a past or current client, but that is a minority situation."

Q: "Do prostitutes enjoy sex with their customers?"
A: "It seems that prostitutes on the whole regard sexual acts with customers as business transactions. It is not uncommon for prostitutes to say that what is happening during a sex act is happening not to them as feeling people but to their bodies as separate entities. Also, they have to be constantly aware of the client's needs and desires, performing as he wishes rather than as they might desire.

"Some prostitutes find their working life as a whole rewarding in that it makes them feel needed, and some like the feeling of being in control. A number resent their situation, feeling angry that they have to do such work, which they tolerate only as long as it is necessary."

Q: "Do prostitutes have orgasm?"
A: "Yes. Paul Gebhard and his associates at the Kinsey Institute in America indicate that prostitutes have orgasm 20 to 30 percent of the time. Other interviews suggest the figure may be lower. It is certain that the customer can't really tell because prostitutes frequently fake excitement and orgasm."

Q: "Aren't most prostitutes lesbians?"
A: "No. Studies show that a large majority of prostitutes were heterosexual before they became prostitutes and remain so."

Q: "Why is prostitution called a victimless crime?"
A: "Some people call it that because it is a crime by legal definition only. No-one gets hurt or robbed — it is, in theory, a simple business transaction, though of a kind the law rejects.

"The argument is, however, more complicated than that. The prostitute is seen as an object, and acts with prostitutes can therefore be seen as a kind of sexual abuse; certainly they abuse the concept of dignified sexuality for all people.

"Then there is the matter of the cost to society of arresting and prosecuting prostitutes, on which large sums are spent annually. Some would argue that this money could be better spent and that society is therefore the victim of the crime of prostitution, though it is a weak argument when one considers that it is society that decides to spend the money in the first place."

Q: "What do most men ask for from prostitutes?"
A: "Customers ask for every possible act and then some, though oral sex seems particularly popular."

Q: "Do prostitutes spread venereal disease?"

A: "Yes, inevitably. Being known to have a disease is very bad for business, so prostitutes tend to take good care of themselves, but from time to time they contract infections from some clients and pass them on to others in between regular medical checks."

AGE Some prostitutes are in their early teens — particularly if they are runaways. Many male hustlers are quite young. The majority of prostitutes are generally in their 20s or 30s, but it is not uncommon to find women in their 40s and 50s who are still working. Gigolos are usually in their 20s and 30s. Some prostitutes who have grown too old to earn well become maids to younger prostitutes, and a very very few who are successful run brothels as they get older. The middle and later years of some prostitutes may be difficult, but quite a lot marry and lead normal lives.

CULTURE AND RELIGION Prostitution has an ancient history — it is still referred to as "the world's oldest profession." In countless societies there have been women and men selling sex. Sometimes it has been a legitimate, overt occupation, at other times it has been covert and furtive.

In many parts of the ancient world there was a close association between prostitution and religion. In ancient Babylonia, Mesopotamia and Greece, for example, temple prostitution was a recognized institution. Temple prostitution was part of the service of many gods and was an act or an occupation of honour, in which women were either resident or occasional prostitutes available to worshippers.

Christianity has on the whole taken the view that prostitution is immoral. Many religious authorities however — St Augustine and St Thomas Aquinas among them — accepted prostitution as a necessary evil. On the one hand, churches have condemned sexual acts outside marriage, but they have also had to remember that Christ forgave Mary Magdalene, a prostitute, and told a group of moneylenders and Pharisees that harlots would go to heaven before them.

Organized attempts by moralists and civic groups to suppress prostitution appear to have had very little effect. They have from time to time succeeded in driving prostitution underground, but never in banishing it other than in limited areas for limited periods.

Some people do not see prostitution as a problem at all. They say that if it is acknowledged, legalized and regulated, everyone will be better off. This, however, overlooks the fact that we live in a society in which depersonalized, nonintegrative sexual contacts flourish. It is therefore a society in which many people's sexuality is not receiving its most rewarding expression. Perhaps prostitution is the symptom of a malaise rather than the malaise itself.

RAPE

FACTS Rape is an act of violence, a sexual assault that includes the following elements: Force or threat of force to have vaginal, oral or anal intercourse, or to have specifically sexual manual contact; rape also includes achieving sexual contact through fraud, the use of drugs, or taking advantage of someone who is mentally incompetent.

The rape victim is usually a woman. Although it has not yet been proved in court, a woman may be raped by her husband. Some men are raped by other men, and infrequently men are raped by women.

This is a wider description of rape than is commonly allowed in law. Though the current definition varies from country to country, it is usually defined as an act of sexual intercourse with a female who is not the wife of the assailant and against her will.

Regardless of the definition of rape you accept, it must be a concern for everyone. It is a violent invasion that profoundly affects self-esteem, self-worth, and relationships with others. It does violence to our natures, it breeds mistrust and suspicion between women and men, and it reveals the darkest side of our personalities. It must be stopped.

The word rape comes from the Latin *rapere*, which means to seize or carry off. Our use of the word reflects earlier cultural situations when men carried off women and forced them to live with them as their wives and their property. In some societies this was regarded as a male right, and to this day some men's attitudes have not changed much.

There are no accurate figures for the numbers of rapes that occur each year since it seems that the majority of rapes and attempted rapes are unreported. Some authorities estimate that at best only 25 percent of rapes are reported. The number of *reported* rapes in the UK has increased from 869 in 1969 to 1,170 in 1979.

Rapes go unreported partly because of the victim's shock, humiliation and fear and partly because of the commonly insensitive behaviour of many legal authorities, which frequently seek to suggest to the victim that she is an accomplice to the crime.

Although there is no typical victim and no typical circumstance, rape facts have been loosely classified using information from reported rapes. For example, most records indicate that the age group most at risk is 13 to 25. Single women are raped more frequently than married women (that fact follows the age data). Married women are raped at one quarter the rate of single women. Predictably widows are raped ten times less frequently than single women (age must have some effect here too). Rape victims are of all social classes. The situations in which rape most often occurs are when the victim is going to or from school or work, or in her home, either as a result of forcible entry for the purpose of rape, or on impulse while the home is being robbed. Women are rarely accused of raping men and even more rarely are they convicted.

There is some doubt as to what is evidence of rape, what is admissible at a trial, and what punishment may be administered. Women's organizations are prominent among groups trying to develop a uniform and just

system for rape cases. It is believed that a normalization of penalties —
especially if they are in line with penalties for assaults generally — would
lead to more convictions for rape. This does not happen at the moment,
as rape sentences can be prison terms of up to life or unlimited fines.

Prison records of rapists show that approximately 75 percent of them
are under age 30, and 61 percent of them single. Eighty-five percent of
these men have average intelligence as measured by standard I.Q. tests.
Most of them have a juvenile or adult criminal record of one sort or
another, including violent crimes in over 50 percent of the cases. Rapists
are more likely to be from lower socioeconomic classes than from middle
or upper ones. Fifty to 60 percent of rapists are affected by alcohol or some
other drug at the time they commit the crime. Rapists may know or even
be related to their victims — they do not have to be strangers.

Although the legal definition of rape includes mention of the woman
not being the wife of the assailant, there are efforts underway, especially
by women's groups, to remove that part of the definition. Legal reform in
that area is based on the premise that women and men who are married
must make equal, joint decisions on the conduct of their sexual life. In
addition, such a reform would strike at the heart of the age-old notion that
a wife is her husband's property and that sex is a wifely duty to be performed at the husband's demand.

Q: "What does unlawful sexual intercourse mean?"

A: "Unlawful sexual intercourse is when a man or boy has intercourse with a girl who is under the legal age of consent. In
England, Scotland and Wales, the legal age of consent is 16. In
Northern Ireland it is 17. Even if the girl herself wants intercourse, and no coercion is used, the law has set an age under
which the girl does not have the capacity to consent, so the act
is still considered a crime punishable by a prison sentence. The
sentences imposed vary enormously depending on the age of the
girl and the age of the man or boy involved."

Q: "Is it possible for a woman to get pregnant after being raped?"

A: "Yes. Sometimes ovulation occurs spontaneously under the
shock of a rape. After being raped women will sometimes take
a pill high in oestrogen called the 'morning-after pill.' This will
bring on menstruation and avoid the possibility of pregnancy.
Menstrual extraction can also be used."

Q: "A friend of mine was raped and one of the reasons she didn't
report it was because she felt she would be humiliated by the
police. Is that common?"

A: "Yes, although it appears to be changing somewhat of late.
Frequently women who have been raped report that the way the
authorities treated them made them feel more like a criminal
than a victim. Insensitive, sexist and disbelieving authorities
have made it very difficult and humiliating for women to
describe what happened, and rather than put up with that (and
perhaps worse at a trial if the criminal were caught) many

women do not report rapes and try to bear their burdens without legal support."

Q: "If a woman is raped and goes to the authorities, what kind of examination does she get?"

A: "If a woman reports a rape to the police they will arrange for the police doctor to conduct a thorough physical examination to collect evidence.

"Rape victims can request that a woman doctor and woman police officer are present during the examination. Consent must be given by the woman before the physical examination and collection of evidence can take place. The presence of a friend or family member can be helpful.

"The examination has to be thorough, and is likely to contain these elements:

* careful physical examination for redness, swelling, bruises and other evidence of restraint on the woman's body
* examination of the vagina and cervix for the presence of semen (although the absence of it does not necessarily dismiss the charge)
* examination of the rectum and mouth, if those areas were involved in the rape
* a check for semen stains on garments
* a check to see if the hymen has been torn (if appropriate) or if there is evidence of bruised tissue in the vagina
* a check for traces of the assailant — hair, blood or fibres from his garments under the victim's fingernails, for example
* blood samples are taken to determine the victim's condition prior to the rape
* a gynaecological history is taken, recording last normal menstruation, last pregnancy and whether the woman has had any sexually transmitted disease; this information will help the doctor and victim decide what medical steps to take.

"Another very important aspect of the medical–legal care and management provided for the rape victim is the taking of a complete history of the event; as with the medical treatment, this must be done with sensitivity and thoroughness. All evidence collected may ultimately be used in court. Previous sexual history may also be taken but this is no longer admissible in court as evidence against the rape victim. The woman must consent to providing this information."

Q: "I read that women have been advised to resist their attackers in order to avoid being raped. Is that good advice?"

A: "There are several ways to offer resistance in the face of a possible rape. An important rape prevention and self-defence method is for women to be psychologically prepared to ward off the possibility of an assault. Keeping the home and car safe, being continually aware of the surroundings (without being paranoid) and being verbally assertive when involved in a situation that may escalate into an attack are important aspects of self-defence for women without the necessity of physical violence.

"When confronted with a potential rapist some women pretend to go along with the situation willingly until they can flee or offer resistance at a more appropriate moment. This redirection of resistance is helpful at times.

"The use of physical force (the martial arts, for example) is recommended by some groups. However, physical self-defence is best used when the woman is reasonably sure that it will be effective in disabling or deterring the assailant long enough to allow for escape. Training for such self-defence is arduous and requires a great deal of practice. Its benefits, however, are not only physical but psychological, as a feeling of competence emerges as a result of the training. The combination of physical skills and psychological preparation enables some women to cope with an attempted rape."

Q: "Can anything be done to reduce the risk of rape?"
A: "Yes. The following suggestions are frequently given to ensure personal safety:

* women who live alone should list only their last name on doorbells and in telephone directories
* unidentified people should not be allowed into the home
* homes should be locked securely day and night
* porches and doorways should be brightly lit; leave a light on when you are away
* do not enter your home if there is evidence of a forced entry; call police from a neighbour's home
* don't hitch-hike or pick up hitch-hikers
* do not respond or react to strange men making inquiries on the street; just keep moving towards crowded areas
* avoid walking alone in deserted areas
* do not leave your car unlocked; check back seat before you enter your car
* ask drivers of taxis or cars to wait until you enter your home before they leave."

Q: "Can a woman really rape a man?"
A: "Yes. There are cases where women, by force or threat of force, have had intercourse with a man against his will. Although it is difficult to imagine, the man's penis can erect, probably as a result of a reflex mechanism. Very few cases have been reported, however, and even fewer have come to court."

Q: "Is it true that if a man has enough sex, he is not likely to rape?"
A: "No. Sexual desire and sexual gratification are not the principal

motivating factors in rape. Violence, aggression and anger are the primary operating forces being expressed by rapists."

Q: "If a woman really resisted and screamed and kicked, wouldn't that prevent most rapes?"
A: "No. The notion of a woman screaming and kicking and fighting sounds good, but the rapist controls the circumstances, using force or the threat of it to do so, with the result that the woman fears serious injury or death. Rape victims feel powerless and helpless; screaming, pleading and bargaining usually are for naught and may in fact both create more aggression in the assailant and stimulate him."

Q: "Do women rape other women?"
A: "It is rarely reported, and then usually from women's prisons. When it does occur, it seems to be less aggressive than male homosexual rape.
  "There are, however, known cases of women helping a man to rape another woman, either by restraining the victim or by acting as lookout."

Q: "Do homosexuals rape other men in prisons?"
A: "Rape in male prisons is a significant problem. There are no definite statistics about its incidence, but the few scientific studies done and the many recorded anecdotes confirm that rape is a major form of violence in prison. The assault is usually in the form of oral or anal sex and the target of the aggression is usually a weaker (by prison standards), newly arrived convict who has no friends or group support. The rapists in these cases are likely to be men whose orientation is heterosexual, but who while in prison express themselves homosexually for lack of their preferred method."

Q: "What kind of person usually commits a rape?"
A: "It is very difficult to present a profile of a typical rapist. Most rapes or attempted rapes are unreported, and in those cases that are reported only a small percentage of the assailants is ever caught, so drawing an accurate personality profile involves some degree of speculation. However, experts in the field have discovered some characteristics. Rapists:

* have a history of violent, aggressive behaviour
* are more frequently from lower socioeconomic backgrounds
* are usually under 30 years of age
* have poor ego development and low self-esteem, feel inadequate and have difficulty in establishing relationships
* do not have an unusual sex drive
* have a history of drug or alcohol use
* have impaired family relationships.

"Although these characteristics are common to quite a lot of rapists, they are also common to many people who, as far as we know, are not rapists; they are some of the characteristics of people inclined to problematic behaviour in general. Also, they derive from the records of the criminal justice system, which, we must recognize, has a bias against people who are poor or from minority groups. Some people also believe that many rapists are already felons of one sort or another who add rape to the list of their offences. It is difficult, therefore, to get a clear profile of rapists."

MYTHS There are many popular misconceptions about rape:

* women can't be raped unless they want to be
* you can tell a woman wants to be raped by how she dresses
* women who are alone in pubs or who hitch-hike are asking for it
* if a woman ever fantasized about being raped, she really wants it to happen to her
* only strangers rape
* rapists have an unusually high sex drive
* most women really like the idea of being raped
* adjusting to rape is not a problem for most women
* rape in prison is usually by homosexuals against other homosexuals
* if a woman doesn't report a rape, it's because she feels she was responsible for it in some way
* most rapes of white women are by black men
* most rapists have a look about them that is identifiable
* unmarried pregnant women usually claim they were raped.

FEELINGS The sense of violation rape brings about is a trauma of enormous proportions that is likely to remain with the victim in some degree for the rest of her life. In some women the horror of what has happened is immediately apparent, but some feel its full effects only when an initial numbness has worn off.

"My life just stopped. I had no feelings."

"I felt so disgusted that I could not eat, work or see anyone."

"At first, I felt happy to be alive, then after a while it hit me and has lasted for a long time."

"My moods have really changed since I was raped. I've lost my sense of humour, I cry a lot and get depressed easily."

"Although I was the victim, I find myself thinking what I did to cause it to happen."

"After I was raped, I felt so dirty and used. It was always on my mind and each time I felt that way, I rushed to the bath to clean myself. Then I found a group of women who had experienced the same thing;

they were enormously helpful to me. The feelings haven't disappeared but I'm much better."

"I knew I could never tell anyone, I was so ashamed."

A rape victim is quite likely to have been very close to serious injury and even death — that is one aspect of rape likely to affect the woman for a long time. Even more serious for many victims is the invasion of privacy — the violation of her body — that diminishes her self-esteem, damages her trust in others, her spontaneity and her sense of being capable of taking care of herself. Eating, sleeping and work patterns are frequently disorganized after a rape; fear of being alone is another powerful force that can change a woman's life over a long period for the worse.

Rape has always been taken seriously as a legal issue, but it is only quite recently that we have made serious efforts to help the victim as well as punish the offender. Rape counselling centres, such as the Rape Crisis Centre in London and women's health groups are becoming part of the health-care networks of many cities, providing a service that cannot be duplicated even by understanding family and friends. These support groups frequently include women who have also been raped and who are trying to live with the trauma. Their understanding and support have proved extremely helpful to many rape victims.

Rape victims who do not report their assault are, unfortunately, less likely to seek the help of available services. Many try to suppress their feelings, believing that they must accept the permanent psychological scarring of the experience because there is no way of easing it. The consequence for them is likely to be more intense suffering over a longer period and functioning at reduced levels in their daily lives.

RELATIONSHIPS There are no statistics, but there is evidence to suggest that women who have been raped are likely to suffer breakdowns in relationships with their husbands or lovers and families. Anger, fear, shame, guilt and mistrust resulting from the rape frequently get in the way of a normal continuation of close ties with loved ones.

Fear of being touched, belief that the rapist will rape again and nightmares about the experience are not uncommon reactions, and they present difficulties in maintaining what were once ordinary activities like working, going to school and shopping. From this standpoint, close family and friends are themselves victims and may require counselling to help them resolve their own feelings about the rape and give the maximum help to the victim.

Q: "My wife was raped and I'm wondering what to do to make her feel comfortable."

A: "Your wife needs your love and your comfort. Touching her and holding her are very important now; even if she appears frightened or seems to withdraw from you, it is important that she should know you are there and that you care for her and love her. Because of the assault she may be reluctant to resume sex with you right away — it is important that you understand this and be gentle and non-demanding. Usually these feelings diminish over time but she must not be rushed. Sometimes a discussion with a qualified counsellor can help a couple's awareness during the important adjustment phase following a rape.

"Rape is a *couple concern*, a *couple crisis*."

Q: "My wife has been raped, and I feel disgusted by it all. I try to control it but it is such a strong feeling. Is that unusual?"

A: "No. Husbands frequently experience disgust and mistrust and they may blame their wives for not resisting enough. But your wife is in great need of your support and understanding right now. She has to come to terms with her experience before she can do her part again in sustaining your relationship. Don't let your negative feelings get in the way of helping her. If you find this is happening, both of you should see a qualified counsellor."

Q: "How can a man rape his wife? And how can it be proved?"

A: "As the law stands, a man cannot be convicted of raping his wife (except under certain circumstances relating to legal separation agreements). If a man forces his wife to have intercourse against her will, it is described in legal terms as indecent assault, which carries a maximum penalty of two years' imprisonment and/or an unlimited fine. When the first case of rape against a wife came to court in the US the husband was acquitted. Pressure groups for women's rights are campaigning to get the current law changed.

"Obviously, it is difficult to prove rape against a wife. The court needs not only to assess the testimony of both parties, but it would also be necessary to understand the couple's relationship and its history."

CULTURE The first rapes took place when, in the earliest societies, men carried off women against their will and forced them to live with them and to bear children. This practice derived from the idea that women were property rather than individuals with basic human rights. Women could be traded or bought, so rape, meaning the stealing of a woman, came under the heading of property theft. The Babylonians therefore punished a man by death if he raped a virgin. The punishment was so severe because the woman's "market value" was significantly diminished.

In the Book of Deuteronomy it is recorded that rape was punished according to the marital status of the woman and the location of the rape. If the woman was raped in the city, she was judged not to have resisted sufficiently and was herself punished. If she was raped in the fields, it was judged her cries for help would not be heard, so she was less guilty. A man who raped a married woman was punished harder than if she was single — again, probably because the notion of belonging or personal property had been offended.

SEX EDUCATION

FACTS Sexual learning is the formal and informal, verbal and nonverbal experiences implicit in being a female or a male. All these experiences, from birth onwards throughout life, affect personality development and relationships. Sex education is the formalization of sexual learning within a programme of some kind which must explore the biological, emotional, social, spiritual and intellectual factors that comprise the total person.

Genital sexual expression can be a very important part of a person's sexuality, but it is a relatively small part of sexual learning. The other elements are: gender identity and gender role; family role and social role; body image; sexual expression, sensuousness and eroticism; affection, love and intimacy; relationships. All these together form our sexual education.

The ordinary process of living provides us with informal sex education. We develop feelings about ourselves and about other people. We acquire views on how people do and should behave from watching those around us. We learn to give and receive affection and love and we learn to form relationships.

Our experience of life may give us a good sex education if we are fortunate enough in our families, early experiences and friends. On the other hand, it is likely that certain aspects of sexual learning will be over-emphasized, certain others under-emphasized and we will not acquire a full, balanced, accurate understanding of our sexuality without the help provided by a formal programme that integrates all the issues.

Ideally, sex education deals with the whole person and elaborates information as appropriate to the understanding of the participants. Much of sex education used to deal just with the mechanics of reproduction, birth control and sexually transmitted disease, and by current standards, it was inadequate. All the information imparted may have been accurate, but it was not integrated into the vital areas of experience that constitute someone's life.

These are some of the important points about sex education that are inadequately recognized:

* recent public opinion polls in the UK show 96 percent of adults favour school sex education
* young people overwhelmingly indicate interest in and feel a need for sex education
* it is estimated that 43 percent of young people receive their initial sex information from their friends, 31 percent from teachers and only 12 percent from their parents and the rest from other sources
* sex education is becoming more common for the physically disabled and the mentally handicapped
* over 80 percent of boys and over 90 percent of girls now receive some form of sex education at school compared with ten years ago when something like 47 percent of boys and over 80 percent of girls received sex education in some form or another at school

* formal sex programmes are opposed by a small, well organized and voluble minority who too often work on the natural concern of parents for the welfare of their children by propagating the myth that sex education will increase sexual promiscuity among the young. The counter argument needs to be put. Adolescent sexuality is a fact of life and the young can only use their sexuality responsibly if they are armed with knowledge. Of course there will always be unwanted pregnancies (as there always have been in the past) but the estimated 5000 pregnancies a year in Britain among girls under 16 years of age are less likely to happen if those children are educated sexually (which is a vastly different thing to being sexually experienced, as one in four boys and one in eight girls claim to be before their sixteenth birthday). It is interesting that in a recent survey of 16–19-year-olds the withdrawal method was second to the sheath as the most common form of contraception (if it can indeed be called contraception, so unsatisfactory is it). A greater awareness of conception, contraception and the responsibility we owe one another can only help to reduce the risks some young people take

* sex education programmes show the most positive results when there is a grass roots approach including community needs assessment, involvement of religious and civic leaders and parents and young people in the development of such programmes

* many local education authorities have laid down guidelines for sex and health education in their schools and soon will be legally obliged to publish information for parents on the "ways and context" of sex education. Devon now requires every school to provide a programme of health education, including sex education, for all its pupils. Without exception all local authorities stress the importance of close liaison between parents and teachers in this area.

Q: "When is the best time to begin a school sex education programme?"

A: "Under ideal circumstances school sex education should be integrated with every subject in the school curriculum from preschool to secondary school. In this way sexuality will be taught as it naturally emerges in science, literature, art, and other subject areas in which it has a natural place, and young people will see how sexuality is integrated in all dimensions of life. Separating off sex education as a single class, expedient though it may be, produces a 'sexectomy' — that is, the separation of sexuality from the rest of life. Although there is a great deal more openness today about sexuality than there has been over the past 100 years it is still too often true to say, as did two American authors recently that 'learning about sex in our society is learning about guilt; conversely, learning how to manage sexuality constitutes learning how to manage guilt.'"

Q: "If I don't like the sex education my children are receiving at school do I have the right to take them away from those lessons?"

A: "No, there is no statutory right. There was a recent but unsuccessful attempt to change the UK law to give parents the right to know what sex education was provided at their children's school and, if they disapproved, the statutory right to remove the child from that class. The amendment was defeated in parliament because the government feared an avalanche of requests for similar rights on a whole range of subjects. At the moment, however, some local authorities do allow parents to withdraw their children from sex education classes but in practice find that few do once the parents have discussed the issue with the teachers."

Q: "Have sex education programmes shown any positive results?"
A: "Yes. Despite the fact that sex education is only now being evaluated thoroughly, there is already evidence of gains in the areas of improved knowledge, more understanding attitudes and behaviour change too.

"*Knowledge* increases dramatically after sex education. Information about the structure and functions of the male and female sexual systems, with special emphasis on issues like puberty, menstruation, reproduction and birth, all show very impressive gains. This is very important because knowledge is the foundation for behaving in a responsible fashion.

"*Attitude* changes resulting from sex education usually are in the direction of becoming more tolerant of other people's behaviour and views. Greater understanding of different gender roles, appreciating the equality of women and men and undoing socially fixed sexism are common results. A better understanding of marriage and the responsibilities of parenthood can also occur. It is also clear that there are some individuals who do not alter their own beliefs and attitudes, but who become more willing to accept diversity among others.

"*Behaviour* change resulting from formal sex education is harder to assess. There are some studies that show reduced unintended pregnancy rates, but these results are not widespread. Some data shows that sex education helped participants feel more comfortable about their bodies and know more about others' bodies, thereby making them feel more comfortable in relationships. Armed with knowledge and liberated from misconceptions they also stand a much better chance of making decisions about their own code of behaviour which will help them avoid harming themselves and others.

"It must be pointed out that some of the results of sex education will never be seen immediately; they will emerge later on in life. To me, the value of sex education is self-evident, and to look for an immediate outcome as the test of whether it should be continued is pointless. It is not a standard used to determine the value of other school subjects. If church attendance was ever taken as an indication of the efficacy of religious education then that subject would have a difficult time justifying itself. In truth, this is not a relevant criterion to apply to either religious or sex education."

Q: "Can a young person be harmed by a sex education course?"
A: "If the course is taught insensitively and judgmentally, without due respect for religious and cultural values, a young person could become confused or, worse, made to feel inadequate or in some way not normal. That would be harmful."

Q: "Are all sex education programmes alike in various countries throughout the world?"
A: "There is great similarity in the information they provide; the differences lie in local religious and cultural values and the emphasis placed on them. For example, South American countries are deeply influenced by Catholicism and their sex education reflects the teachings of the Catholic Church on issues such as autoeroticism, premarital sexual relationships and birth control. African and Japanese programmes reflect differing cultural views on male–female relationships. Programmes in Israel reflect particular national views on gender role and on marriage and the family. Swedish programmes, which became compulsory for all schoolchildren in 1956, underscore the holistic view of sexuality and emphasize relationships characterized by responsibility, consideration and concern."

MYTHS There is no truth in any of these statements:

* school sex education encourages teens to experiment with sex
* religious groups generally oppose sex education
* the majority of adults disapprove of sex education
* sexual knowledge stimulates sexual behaviour
* sex education is the leading cause of unintended pregnancies and venereal disease
* teachers of sex education seek to replace the family as chief sex educators of young people
* no positive results of sex education have been found
* sex educators and those who support such programmes usually have no religious convictions
* sex education *per se* reduces unintended pregnancies
* sex education seeks to challenge the religious and cultural beliefs of learners.

FEELINGS Feelings about formal sex education in schools and community agencies are often passionate. Some of the negative feelings about such education derive from strong convictions about the family being the proper place for sex education, while others are the results of prior experiences with poorly planned and implemented lessons. Some people also oppose sex education because they believe that in them children will be learning how to use contraceptives, how to masturbate, how to have intercourse, and will be encouraged to try homosexual relationships. Although no such advice is given in proper sex education the parental concerns are none the less real. The existence of these negative feelings is evidence that some sex educators have not fully defined their point of view.

The parents who support formal school sex education are, unfortunately, not vocal in their support, nor are they as well organized as those who wish to exclude sex education from schools. Supporters believe sex education helps their youngsters to acquire important information about themselves and others, helps dispel powerful myths about sexuality, and helps develop decision-making skills and a better understanding of relationships. Most parents do not feel that such teaching in school competes with their family and religious values since, after all, respect for self, respect for others and behaving in non-exploitive and non-destructive ways are universally accepted as important values regardless of specific religious and family beliefs. Perhaps if school sex education begins to disappear, concerned parents will seize the initiative to sustain it.

In my own work with parents from many social and economic classes holding a variety of religious beliefs, I regularly hear expressions of certain feelings about formal school and community sex education:

"I'm glad the school is helping out on this subject. We have had some good discussions as a result."

"It's nice to be innocent — life's not the same when they know the harsh facts of life."

"As long as the teacher is qualified and not way out, we feel it is an important school subject. We do our share too."

"I don't like the idea of some stranger talking to my child about those kinds of topics. I'm watching the programme very carefully."

"Sex is too sensitive to be taught in school. We want our values taught."

"After going to parent–teacher meetings, I feel much better about the school's attitude."

"Not being too sure about all the latest facts, we like the idea of our kids learning about them in school. It's better than learning about them in the street."

Q: "I never had sex education, and I'm fine and happy. Isn't it just a waste of time and money to learn about it in school?"

A: "There are other people like yourself who never had formal sex education in school, find they are happy and, like you, see the expenditure of public money on such teaching as unnecessary. Valid as this is for you, there are many other people (of all ages) who are uninformed, influenced by irrational fears and whose feelings about themselves and others are profoundly affected by their lack of genuine information in the subject. These people need help so that they can lead a fuller life, and formal sex education can provide that help. The much discussed sexual freedoms of the 1960s and 1970s have come up empty, as authentic human values were neglected. Thoughtful, sensitive sex education can help people, young and old, to see things in a proper perspective.

"Recent research shows that children themselves recognize the need for sex education and in a recent study over 50 percent felt the school to be the most appropriate place. Many children commented on the need to treat sexual matters 'normally' as part of their whole education."

RELATIONSHIPS Formal sex education has an effect on relationships. Properly conducted sex education enables young people to learn how to express themselves about sensitive topics. They learn how to communicate to people of their own and of the other sex on issues that most people think about but do not verbalize, even when it would be much better for them to do so. Learning how to express oneself without overwhelming embarrassment helps in relationships at every age. I believe this skill facilitates a more secure relationship with a partner, since guesswork is eliminated and needs can be described without any possibility of misunderstanding.

Proper sex education also allows for better communication between parent and youngster. It can become a common interest between parent and child, and many parents have commented that their relationships with their children improve in many ways when they discuss aspects of the school or community sex education. Adults who participate in sexual learning programmes frequently report improved relationships with their partners. The information gained, the opportunity for clarification of personal values, and the feeling of comfort resulting from improved understanding often lead to expanded communication and sharing of views.

CULTURE Sex education is not a product of the sexual revolution of the 1960s and 1970s. Informal sexual learning has necessarily gone on from the beginning of time, since it happens regardless of people's views about formalizing it into sex education. Religious authorities and texts have been providing pronouncements and views on sexual matters for thousands of years, so they qualify as sex education in a broad sense. Certainly the *Kama Sutra*, the writings of Ovid and many other works of literature and art can be considered sexually educational, even though their intent may not have been in accord with our current goals.

There has been (and to some extent still is) a feeling that if sex has to be discussed formally at school it should be minimal and preferably related to animals and plants rather than humans! If human sexuality was dealt with then it had to be kept to the basic facts only — the headmaster's or science teacher's often embarrassed "short, sharp talk." Sex education was permeated with a Victorian notion that sex was dirty and best learned about in the gutter. Although this attitude is not entirely dead there has been an improvement in schools thanks to such programmes as those devised for the Nuffield Secondary Science Project and the Schools Council Moral Education Project. However, there is no comprehensive review of sex education in schools and it seems to be largely a matter of luck and teachers' inclination whether our children are taught about sex. There have been government moves to make provision and set some sort of guidelines for sex education. Very often, however, the presence of an "approved" morality can be detected. The Newsom Report of 1963 declared that sex education must be based on "chastity before marriage and fidelity within it." In 1978 the Department of Education and Science published some guidelines which declared that information on masturbation, contraception and venereal disease was acceptable but that "sexual deviation" should not be mentioned unless specifically raised by pupils and that homosexuality "was best dealt with in passing if and when it arises."

In the United Kingdom, the Health Education council and the Family Planning Association have been important stimuli to sex education in the community. In Australia the Family Life movement has been responsible for many school programmes in sex education and family living, and the states' departments of education, together with the Social Biology Resource Centre, have also been instrumental in developing sex education. Japan, India, France, the Netherlands and the Scandinavian countries not only have various types of school and community based sex education but they also have their own national and regional sexology societies for professional development.

RELIGION As one might expect, some of the major religious groups have strong feelings about formal sex education in schools and in the community. In general, the views of major religious groups are supportive and encouraging. Basic to the positive position taken by many religions is the belief that sexuality is a gift from God to be received with thanks and to be expressed with joy and dignity. Many churches have their own sex education programmes, but for those to whom they are not available, secular courses implemented by qualified teachers are given support provided they meet certain criteria.

The clearest statement on sex education by representative bodies of Jews, Protestants and Catholics is an Interfaith statement on sex education, published in the late 1960s. It remains valid as the conscious position of these groups today. Here is the part that discusses secular sex education programmes:

> "In addition to parents and the religious community, the school and other community agencies can have a vital role in sex education in two particular ways:
> 1 They can integrate sound sexual information and attitudes with the total education which the child receives in social studies, civics, literature, history, home economics and the biological and behavioural sciences.
> 2 They can reach the large numbers of young people whose families have no religious identification but who need to understand their own sexuality and their role in society.

> "For those who would introduce sex education into the schools, however, the question of values and norms for sexual behaviour is a problem — indeed, the most difficult problem. It is important that

sex education not be reduced to the mere communication of information. Rather, this significant area of experience should be placed in a setting where rich human, personal and spiritual values can illuminate it and give it meaning. In such a setting, we are convinced it is not only possible but necessary to recognize certain basic moral principles, not as sectarian religious doctrine but as the moral heritage of Western civilization.

"The challenge of resolving this problem of values in a pluralistic society makes it all the more imperative that communities planning to introduce sex education into the schools not only call upon educators to become involved in decisions about goals and techniques, but also invite parents and professionals in the community to take part in shaping such a curriculum.

"To those groups responsible for developing school and community programmes in sex education we suggest the following guidelines:

a) Such education should strive to create understanding and conviction that decisions about sexual behaviour must be based on moral and ethical values, as well as on considerations of physical and emotional health, fear, pleasure, practical consequences, or concepts of personality development.

b) Such education must respect the cultural, familial and religious backgrounds and beliefs of individuals and must teach that the sexual development and behaviour of each individual cannot take place in a vacuum but are instead related to the other aspects of his life and to his moral, ethical and religious codes.

c) It should point out how sex is distorted and exploited in our society and how this places heavy responsibility upon the individual, the family and institutions to cope in a constructive manner with the problem thus created.

d) It must recognize that in-school sex education, insofar as it relates to moral and religious beliefs and values, complements the education conveyed through the family, the church or the synagogue. Sex education in the schools must proceed constructively with understanding, tolerance and acceptance of difference.

e) It must stress the many points of harmony between moral values and beliefs about what is right and wrong that are held in common by the major religions on the one hand and generally accepted legal, social, psychological, medical and other values held in common by service professions and society generally.

f) Where strong differences of opinion exist on what is right and wrong sexual behaviour, objective, informed and dignified discussion of both sides of such questions should be encouraged. However, in such cases, neither the sponsors of an educational programme nor the teachers should attempt to give definite answers or to represent their personal moral and religious beliefs as the consensus of the major religions or of society generally.

g) Throughout such education human values and human dignity must be stressed as major bases for decisions of right and wrong; attitudes that build such respect should be encouraged as right, and those that tear down such respect should be condemned as wrong.

h) Such education should teach that sexuality is a part of the whole person and an aspect of his dignity as a human being.

i) It should teach that people who love each other try not to do anything that will harm each other.

j) It should teach that sexual intercourse within marriage offers the greatest possibility for personal fulfilment and social growth.

k) Finally, such a programme of education must be based on sound content and must employ sound methods; it must be conducted by teachers and leaders qualified to do so by training and temperament."

SEXUALLY TRANSMITTED DISEASES

FACTS Sexually Transmitted Diseases — STDs — is the label for the range of diseases passed between people through specifically sexual contact. We used to talk of VD — Venereal Disease — by which was meant gonorrhoea and syphilis. We now know of so many more diseases transmitted by sexual contact, most of them less threatening than gonorrhoea and syphilis, that a broader term is needed to indicate the wider range.

There are numerous sexually transmitted diseases, each caused by a specific organism. They produce various symptoms and each requires a specific type of treatment. They are most commonly passed through:

* vaginal and/or anal intercourse
* mouth contact with the genitals or anus
* mouth-to-mouth kissing
* mouth or genital contact with infected areas on the skin.

Taken as a group, STDs can affect any part of the body; their effects are not limited to the genitals. Although most of them can be treated quickly and painlessly, the increasing worldwide prevalence of STDs suggests that a great many people are not seeking treatment often enough or soon enough. Several STDs can, if left altogether untreated, cause serious health problems. This can happen to pregnant women, for example, who can pass diseases to their babies. In such a situation, the baby can sustain serious damage before birth. Treatment is, however, relatively simple and usually highly effective.

Who Gets STDs? Almost anyone who is sexually active and has more than one partner. The age group most at risk is 15 to 30 — which is what you would expect if you consider the pattern of most people's lives. It is within that period that most people are searching for a primary partner with whom to establish a long-term relationship. The rates halve after the age of 30 and drop even more drastically after 35, by which time most people have married or established other enduring sexual partnerships.

Syphilis: percentage change in numbers of cases reported 1970–78

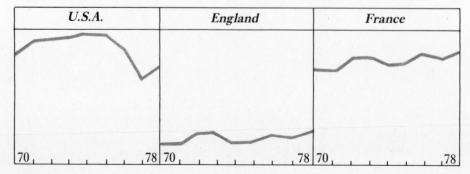

U.S.A.	England	France
70 ... 78	70 ... 78	70 ... 78

Gonorrhoea is now one of the most common infectious diseases in Europe, in fact next in importance to colds and flu. About 60,000 new cases are reported in the UK each year; 300 out of each 100,000 teenagers in the UK become infected with gonorrhoea each year compared to Scandinavia, where 2,000 per 100,000 are sufferers. In the US the incidence of gonorrhoea and herpes has increased by 140 percent in 15–19-year-olds. The rates for some other diseases are declining: in the US in 1975, for example, there were 700 reported cases of chancroid; in 1977 the figure had fallen to 455. There were 353 reported cases of lymphogranuloma venereum in 1975 and 284 in 1978. The widespread diseases are herpes, gonorrhoea and syphilis.

Why some of these rates should be rising we can only speculate. What we can be sure of is that it is a mistake to regard STDs as modern diseases: they have been around for millennia. Ramesses V, a Pharaoh in ancient Egypt 3,000 years ago, and a Roman Emperor, Tiberius Caesar, 2,000 years ago, seem both to have suffered from syphilis. Columbus probably had it and Napoleon certainly did.

Q: "But there must be some good reason for the increasing rates of sexually transmitted diseases in most countries?"

A: "The exact reasons are not clear. It seems likely though that the following factors in various combinations are responsible:

* changing values about sexual activity; casual sexual encounters are more common and frequent today than at any other time; each one of these encounters increases geometrically the chances of spreading one or more STDs
* the number of diseases now reported as sexually transmitted has grown to include many more than used to be reported; today's figures are therefore not directly comparable with those of, say, 20 years ago
* decreased use of spermicidal barrier methods of contraception, which provide some protection against STDs
* increased use of the oral contraceptive, which is said to alter women's natural immunity mechanisms; it may, in fact, create an environment that favours growth of the gonorrhoea micro-organism
* more risk-taking by people who feel the easy availability of

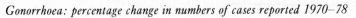

Gonorrhoea: percentage change in numbers of cases reported 1970–78

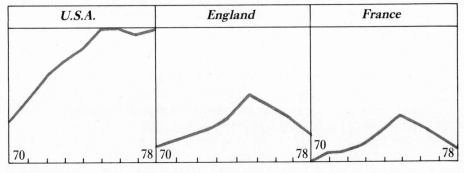

medical services will cure them if they contract a sexually transmitted disease

* the condom, a useful protection against the contraction of STDs, is being used less due to the easy availability of contraceptive jellies, creams, the oral contraceptive, IUDs and diaphragms

* the evolution of strains of gonorrhoea bacteria — the ß-lactamase producing ones — which are able to break down and neutralize penicillin completely, and due to the widespread use of antibiotics the evolution of strains of bacteria that produce fewer symptoms

* inadequate public education programmes, and insufficient expenditure of government money on research also contributes to the continuing increase in STDs in all age groups

* if all doctors reported, as they should do, all cases of STDs, follow-up on the patient's sexual contacts would reduce the total pool of people capable of spreading these diseases; it is estimated that general practitioners report fewer than half the number of patients they treat for STDs: clinics specialising in STDs are probably more punctilious

* increasing urbanization of the population and the ability of the population to be highly mobile

* increasing use of alcohol and other drugs, leading people into a false sense of security and thereby both encouraging sexual risk-taking and increasing their chances of getting an STD

* the increase in infections that have no obvious symptoms (asymptomatic infections) increases the pool of people who are potential spreaders of STDs without their knowing about it."

Preventing the Transmission of STDs. There are no vaccines that prevent the transmission of STDs. Individual care is the only effective means. These are some precautions that everyone can take:

* if squeezing the penis prior to intercourse produces a milky discharge *don't have sex* then, and go to your doctor or clinic immediately

* if a general examination of the genital area and anus shows bumps, sores, a discharge of any kind or any other suspicious or unusual condition, *don't have sex* and check with your doctor or clinic

* washing the genitals and the anal area with soap and water before and very soon after sexual contact is minimally helpful but a precaution nonetheless

* urinating after intercourse is of some help to men if an STD organism is in the urethra; the urine can flush out the organism; urinating after sex is not effective for women as the disease-producing organism is usually around the vulva or in the vagina

* a condom is partially effective in preventing the spread of sexually transmitted diseases; a condom used with a vaginal spermicide is very

effective against getting or spreading gonorrhoea, NSU, trichomoniasis and syphilis
 * contraceptive creams and jellies also help reduce risks
 * routine medical checkups to discover asymptomatic sexually
   transmitted diseases are especially useful for those who have
   multiple partners.

Q: "How is it that women seem to have bigger problems with
    sexually transmitted diseases?"
A: "Probably because more women than men are asymptomatic.
    For example, 60 percent of women who have gonorrhoea may
    not show symptoms at all, whereas 80 percent or more of men
    will quickly know they are infected. The disease can therefore
    affect women for a much longer time.
       "Some STDs are of course exclusive to women or much
    more common in women — trichomoniasis, vaginitis and PID
    (Pelvic Inflammatory Disease), for example."

Q: "Can a sexually transmitted disease cause a person to be sterile?"
A: "Yes. In women, untreated gonorrhoea can lead to sterility
    because the gonococcus bacteria can cause scarring of the Fal-
    lopian tubes, preventing the sperm and egg from meeting each
    other. In men, untreated gonorrhoea can cause scarring of the
    urethra leading to sterility.
       "In both women and men early medical treatment cures
    the gonorrhoea and leaves neither of these after effects."

Q: "What should I do if I suspect I have an STD?"
A: "Go immediately to your own doctor or straight to a clinic
    (usually called the 'special' clinic in the hospital.) Look under
    'Venereal Diseases' in the telephone directory or if you prefer
    just ring your local hospital who will tell you where the nearest
    clinic is if they do not have one. There are often lists, also, in
    public lavatories. You do not need an appointment or referral
    from your doctor. Clinics are staffed by specialists who will
    examine you and if necessary start treatment on your first visit.
    Clinics are usually split into male and female sections.
       "You may register with a false name if you wish (but
    remember to use it in subsequent visits as your case notes will
    be in that name!) and there is complete confidentiality. Your
    notes are kept separate from the main hospital records.
       "Nearly all clinics have contact-chasers and although there
    is no question of your being refused treatment for not identifying
    your sex partner(s) there is a moral obligation for you to tell your
    friend to reduce the risk of their ill-health and the spread of
    disease. The staff of the clinic are experienced, objective and do
    not make moral judgments on your sex life, nor do they treat
    homosexuality, cunnilingus, fellatio or whatever turns you on as
    perversion. The examination and treatment procedures are not
    painful nor are they in any way meant to be a 'punishment.'"

Q: "Is it true that VD germs can't live outside the body?"

A: "Yes, it is true on the whole that the organisms that cause sexually transmitted diseases do poorly outside the body. However, there are just a few cases of gonorrhoea bacteria remaining alive outside the body and causing infections without any sexual contact having taken place. It is rare, though."

Q: "Can you have sex immediately after getting treatment for a sexually transmitted disease?"

A: "No. Your doctor will advise you when it is safe for you to resume having sex once treatment for a sexually transmitted disease has begun. Some of these diseases require several negative follow-ups before sex can be resumed safely, so you could have to wait a week or more."

Q: "Can babies get VD?"

A: "Yes. Many sexually transmitted diseases can be passed on to babies in the womb, during birth or even after birth. Babies born to mothers with active herpes, for example, can even die from the complications the virus produces. Babies born to mothers with gonorrhoea can suffer damaged eyes, and syphilitic mothers can pass the disease to their babies with a variety of serious results. Early detection and treatment of infantile STDs is essential and seems to be effective. In the UK, for example, 227 infections of newborn babies were reported in 1950; 18 in 1960 and 12 in 1970."

Q: "Is it true that there is sort of a VD hotline, where a person can get free information about sexually transmitted diseases?"

A: "Yes. Many cities have a widely publicized telephone number where a caller can get free information and referral advice in an anonymous and supportive way from trained staff. The telephone directory (look under 'Venereal Diseases') or local health centre will have the current number in your area."

Q: "A friend of mine said he had two VDs at the same time. Can that happen?"

A: "Yes, certainly — in fact, you can have more than two at the same time, each requiring different treatment. Remember, too, that your friend will not be immune to these diseases even after he is cured: he could get one or both of them again."

Q: "Can someone under the age of consent get treatment for VD without their parents knowing about it?"

A: "Yes, a minor can receive treatment for STDs without prior parental knowledge. Some local health departments do, however, urge the young person to involve their parents when that can be done without creating great difficulty."

Q: "A friend of mine routinely uses antibiotics to protect himself against getting VD. Is this a wise practice?"

A: "Absolutely not. Antibiotics have wide-ranging effects on different people and the routine use you describe can lead to serious medical problems. Also, the proper treatment of STDs varies according to the specific kind of disease and the health of the individual. This self-treatment is dangerous and you owe it to your friend to make sure he understands that."

Q: "Can you get VD in the throat or rectum?"
A: "Yes. Gonorrhoea of the throat can result from having oral sex with an infected person. Gonorrhoea of the rectum results from anal intercourse with an infected person or the accidental infection of the woman's anus through vaginal intercourse (of all female gonorrhoea sufferers in the UK up to 40 percent have been known to have an anal infection.) In both cases, the treatment is antibiotics prescribed by a doctor after examination."

Q: "I heard hepatitis being referred to as a sexually transmitted disease. Is that true?"
A: "Yes, it can be. Hepatitis is a serious viral disease that affects the liver. One kind can be transmitted sexually by anal contact, either anal–oral or anal intercourse. Gay men appear to have higher rates of hepatitis than the rest of the population.

"The chief symptoms are fever, aching muscles, fatigue; urine turns coffee-coloured, faeces become grey and there is usually jaundice (yellowing) of the skin and eyeballs. An attack of hepatitis takes six to eight weeks to pass, during which time the patient has to eat a special diet, rest a lot and avoid alcohol."

Q: "I heard a doctor tell a group of women they should always carry a condom with them if they were sexually active. Why would he say that?"
A: "Women suffer more complications from STDs than men, especially from Pelvic Inflammatory Disease (PID). Condoms provide some worthwhile protection. Also, the fact that a woman carries a condom for a new partner to use tells him that she is independent, responsible and takes care of her body."

Chancroid Chancroid is caused by the bacterium *Hemophilus ducreyi*, and is more common in the tropics and subtropics than in cooler climates. Travel and migration have been largely responsible for its spread outside tropical areas.

The signs of chancroid are soft, painful chancres, pustules or sores that usually appear on the penis, on or around the labia and around the anus. The disease is passed by contact with the pus from these sores. Some women with chancroid are asymptomatic.

Untreated chancroid can cause painful swelling of the lymph glands in the groin but usually does not lead to permanent damage. Tests are required to identify chancroid and to differentiate it from syphilis; treatment is usually antibiotics and special soaks and lotions.

Gonorrhoea 60,000 new cases of gonorrhoea are reported each year in Britain and over 2,000,000 Americans contract the disease each year.

Gonorrhoea is caused by the bacterium *Neisseria gonorrhoeae* and is spread by vaginal intercourse, oral–genital and anal contact. Men who come in contact with the bacterium contract gonorrhoea less than 50 percent of the time. Women contract it more than 75 percent of the time on contact with it, although they frequently show no symptoms.

The majority of men show symptoms, which are pain and burning upon urination and a milky discharge from the penis that turns heavy and thicker after a few days. Urine may be filled with pus, and lymph glands become enlarged in the groin area. Sometimes, uncircumcized men have an irritation around the head of the penis. The symptoms may disappear without treatment, but the men remain asymptomatic carriers. Long-term untreated gonorrhoea can cause infection of the epididymes and prostate and may lead to sterility.

Up to 60 percent of women remain asymptomatic, but some have a cervical or vaginal discharge. When the urethra is infected, women feel pain on urination, and there may be some pus oozing from the urethral opening as well. Some women feel pain low down in the back and get a mushroom-like odour from their vaginas. Pelvic Inflammatory Disease (PID) is a serious result of untreated gonorrhoea. Fever, vomiting and abdominal pain are signs of PID, which may lead to sterility in the long term.

In both men and women, gonorrhoea of the throat, rectum and anus can occur after oral or anal contact with an infected person.

Gonorrhoea is easily identified by doctors and clinics and can be cured with antibiotics in a week or so.

> Q: "What are the chances of catching gonorrhoea during intercourse with an infected partner?"
>
> A: "Although it is difficult to be certain it has been estimated that there is a 50–80 percent risk, a risk which obviously increases with the frequency of intercourse and depends on whether a barrier contraceptive such as a condom was used."
>
> Q: "Is it true that penicillin doesn't work on gonorrhoea any more?"
>
> A: "There is a strain of gonorrhoea that is resistant to penicillin. This particular strain (known as PPNG) produces an enzyme called ß-lactamase that destroys penicillin. Other antibiotics are effective in curing PPNG."

Granuloma Inguinale Also known as granuloma venereum, granuloma inguinale is caused by a bacterium called *Donovania granulomatis*. It is more common in tropical climates and can be transmitted by intercourse. Granuloma inguinale may appear within a week of contact or not until several months later. Men contract the disease more frequently than women. Common first symptoms are lesions on the genitals and anus which may be red and raw looking; alternatively there may be elevated nodes of skin, which are not particularly painful. Untreated, they ulcerate and spread slowly, damaging underlying tissue. Arthritis and anaemia can result in the long term if the disease is not treated.

Sexual intercourse may not be the major method of transmission of this disease. Some authorities believe lack of personal cleanliness is more important, though at present the issue is controversial.

Tissue examination is necessary to diagnose granuloma inguinale and antibiotics are usually prescribed to treat it.

Herpes Herpes is so widespread in America and Europe that it is now considered a major sexually transmitted disease. In the UK it is the most common cause of genital ulceration. Herpes is incurable.

Herpes is caused by a virus that affects mucous membranes and skin. There are two types of herpes virus: Herpes Simplex Virus I (HSVI), which causes cold sores or fever blisters on the lips, mouth and face; and Herpes Simplex Virus II (HSVII), also known as genital herpes. In women, genital herpes causes sores and blisters in and around the labia, urinary opening, vaginal walls and cervix. In men, these sores and blisters are commonly found under the foreskin, on the penis or in the urethra. Clusters of sores may also appear on the thighs, buttocks and round the anus in both sexes.

HSVI and HSVII are caused by different viruses from the same family, but in each case the virus enters your body when you have direct skin and/or mucous membrane contact with someone who has the virus in its active state. You can then pass it on to someone else.

Herpes Simplex I is spread by mouth-to-mouth kissing or mouth--genital kissing. It can only be spread when the sores are present — they signify that the disease is active. HSVI usually remains in the mouth and lip area, but a small percentage of HSVI is transmitted to the genital region through mouth contact with the penis or vulva while the virus is active.

HSVII, though it affects primarily the genitals, can be transmitted to the mouth by mouth–genital contact with an actively infected man or woman. Herpes sores will then show on the lips or in the mouth. If contracted through intercourse, vaginal or anal, the symptoms will appear in the genital area. Symptoms occur within two to 20 days; four to six days is the average.

Although some people show no symptoms at all of HSVII (more women than men are asymptomatic), these are the common signs: the appearance of one or more groups of small, painful, fluid-filled blisters on or around the penis or the vaginal area. These blisters usually burst after a few days and ooze; they may itch or burn. In this phase the infected person may suffer general fever, muscle aches and lymph gland swelling in the genital area. After two to three weeks, the sores begin to heal and the attack ends. Once healing is complete the active phase is over and the person cannot pass HSVII on to another person.

Thereafter, some people are lucky. Either the virus remains inactive and they never get another attack or they get repeat attacks infrequently. Others have active attacks quite regularly; the blister formation, oozing, discomfort and rehealing process are repeated. Whether the virus is active or inactive, it remains in the skin of the infected person.

Why HSVII should erupt irregularly we do not know. Keeping emotional stress to a minimum, maintaining a well balanced diet and keeping fit are recommended to limit its recurrence.

Herpes cannot be cured. Treatment is usually directed toward relieving pain and discomfort and preventing secondary infections. Drying agents can help speed up drying out of the sores and relieve the irritation, but that is all that can be done at the moment.

Q: "I heard that genital herpes causes cancer. Is that true?"
A: "It has been suggested that HSVII might cause cervical cancer, but at present there is no conclusive evidence. Tests on animals have shown that the virus can change normal cells into tumorous cells, but there is no such evidence from humans. In any event, women who have HSVII should have a regular Pap smear."

Q: "What should a pregnant woman do if she gets genital herpes?"
A: "Be absolutely certain her doctor knows she has or has had herpes. Although there are differences of opinion on exactly how to handle each case, the goals are to reduce the risk of unnecessary Caesarean section, to minimize risk to the baby of contracting the virus during the birth process, and to reduce the chances of the baby getting the virus in its first few weeks after delivery."

Q: "Can genital herpes be spread in nonsexual situations?"
A: "Technically possible, but extremely unlikely."

Q: "Will using a condom prevent the spread of genital herpes?"
A: "No, a condom won't prevent your catching genital herpes, though it may help. There is no substitute for avoiding contact with anyone who has herpes sores. Remember that genital herpes can be spread by hands or any other parts of the body that come into contact with an open sore."

Q: "Is it true that taking special vitamins and minerals can cure genital herpes?"
A: "No. There is no cure. Special diets, vitamin supplements and extra minerals are not necessary if your routine diet is a healthy one. They certainly won't affect herpes. Your doctor will advise the quickest and safest way to deal with HSVII."

Lymphogranuloma Venereum (LGV) This disease is caused by a virus that probably enters the skin or mucous membrane through sexual contact. Symptoms such as fever, aches and pains in the joints and raised skin at the point of entry show within ten days. The pimplelike elevation at the point of entry of the virus may disappear without treatment but usually spreads to the nearest lymph glands, causing abscesses if untreated. Diagnosis is complicated as several types of blood and skin tests are necessary to rule out other STDs. Antibiotics are the usual treatment. Blood testing throughout a year is not uncommon while treatment continues.

Untreated long-term LGV can lead to growths around the anus of both men and women. Women also report growths on the labia and clitoral area as a result of long-term untreated LGV.

Monilia Monilia, sometimes called candidiasis, thrush or yeast infection, affects more women than men. It is caused by an excessive growth of a fungus that usually lives compatibly with other organisms in the mouth, vagina, and large intestine. The chief symptoms of monilia are itching in the vagina, cracking of vaginal tissue and the presence of a thick, white, sometimes odorous discharge. Males are frequently asymptomatic, but in some cases men with monilia complain of itching and irritation of the penis and scrotum. Sexual intercourse is not a major mode of transmission of monilia but may be responsible for some of its spread. Many women get monilia while they are taking antibiotics or other medication that alters the bacterial balance in the vagina. Women who have diabetes are prone to monilia, as are pregnant women and women who take high progesterone birth control pills and although monilia does not cause any permanent damage to internal reproductive organs, a pregnant woman with monilia may pass it on to her baby in the form of a mouth infection.

Prescribed lotions, creams and vaginal suppositories are used to treat the disease. Some women have found that eating yogurt is helpful. Yogurt contains lactobacilli, which are said to help overcome monilia. Monilia can remain in the bowel and may reinfect a woman until treated.

Nonspecific Urethritis (NSU) The latest data suggests that nonspecific urethritis has become more prevalent than gonorrhoea and is becoming an extremely common sexually transmitted disease. In England, where it is a reportable disease, NSU is more widespread than gonococcal urethritis. Nonspecific urethritis (NSU) is also known as nongonococcal urethritis (NGU).

NSU is passed during sexual intercourse. In men the signs usually include a thin, watery discharge from the penis, itching around the opening of the penis, some difficulty in urinating, and in some cases a burning sensation too. A small percentage of men with NSU have no symptoms. In women the signs are not as clear as in men, although there may be some itching around the urinary opening. Many infected women show no symptoms at all. Usually, the disease remains internal and can cause damage to a woman's reproductive system if untreated. Inflammation and irritation of the cervix (cervicitis) is also a sign of NSU, as is inflammation of the Fallopian tubes.

Laboratory tests to determine the presence of certain microorganisms are necessary to make an accurate diagnosis of NSU. Once the disease has been identified as NSU antibiotic therapy is usually successful.

> **Q:** "My boyfriend has had NSU several times lately. He says he hasn't had any sex partners but me, and I'm fine and feel good. His doctor wants to see me. Is it a good idea for me to go?"
>
> **A:** "Absolutely. Many women have NSU without showing obvious symptoms, but they are still active carriers of the disease. Your boyfriend may become reinfected by you after being cured unless you are cured too."

Pelvic Inflammatory Disease (PID) Pelvic inflammatory disease is caused by bacteria that pass through the cervix, into the uterus and infect the Fallopian tubes. It is not so much a disease in its own right as the effects of complications arising from untreated STDs.

PID can be caused by the bacteria that cause gonorrhoea or by many nongonococcal agents. Persistent pain in the lower abdomen, legs and back are common signs, as are fever, chills and prolonged bleeding. There may be some discharge and the woman may vomit.

PID can weaken a woman in such a way that she is open to other kinds of pelvic infections later on in her life. Untreated PID can lead to major complications, such as pelvic abscesses, a tendency toward ectopic pregnancy and, in some cases, infertility.

Pelvic inflammatory disease is diagnosed by a number of procedures including laboratory tests of the blood and examinations of the discharge, if any. Sometimes a laparoscopy is necessary to confirm PID. A stay in hospital may be required to treat advanced cases, but antibiotics and bed rest are usually sufficient. Intercourse should be avoided until the disease is cleared up, and the infected woman's partner should be checked medically to avoid the probability of reinfection.

Pubic Lice Pubic lice — also called "crabs" — are tiny bugs resembling crabs and contrary to popular belief, cannot jump. Pubic lice are transmitted by sexual contact with a carrier or having contact with infected clothing, towels, bedding and toilet seats. The lice live in hair — head, pubic or underarm — and their bites cause intense itching. They can be seen and felt near the roots of hairs. Treatment is with special medicated creams, lotions or shampoos that can be purchased without a prescription.

Q: "Are crabs the same as scabies?"
A: "No. Scabies are mites that burrow under the skin near hair follicles, causing itching and redness. They spread by close body contact. Scabies can be treated with scabicide lotions, which are available from chemists without a prescription."

Syphilis Syphilis, also called "the syph," is caused by the bacterium *Treponema pallidum*, is highly contagious and is transmitted through sexual intercourse or mouth–genital contact. Rates of syphilis are not rising like those of gonorrhoea and some other STDs, but it is a very serious disease. In the UK, for example, there are about 2,000 new cases each year.

After exposure to the organism, the first sign or stage of syphilis is a sore called a chancre, which appears a few weeks or months later. The chancre is usually a painless, slightly elevated crater and is commonly found on the penis, labia, anus, lips or in the throat. It is filled with the syphilis germ and the person is highly infectious during this period. Because the chancre is painless, it can remain undetected. Even without treatment the chancre disappears, but the bacteria are in the person's bloodstream, leading on to the development of the second stage over the ensuing weeks or months.

The symptoms of secondary syphilis are: rashes on the palms of the hands and soles of the feet; headache; sore throat; loss of appetite; low-grade fever, and loss of patches of hair. Sometimes chancres appear again in this stage, when they are highly infectious — just like primary chancres.

After a couple of months or so of this state an untreated person moves into the latent and then the tertiary or late stage of syphilis. These later stages are not infectious; there may or may not be symptoms.

For all these years the *Treponema pallidum* has had a chance to affect all parts of the body and even if a person looks and feels healthy a problem may be in the making and may appear at any time. The nervous system may be affected, including the brain and spinal cord, as may the heart and blood vessels; bone structure may be damaged and difficulty with reflexes may also occur.

A variety of laboratory tests may be used to confirm a diagnosis of syphilis. Then, depending on the stage, various antibiotic therapies are used. Sexual contact must be avoided, especially during the first month or two of treatment. Careful monitoring and repeated blood tests are required, especially for patients who did not have the disease treated in its early stages.

Like all other sexually transmitted diseases, syphilis can be caught more than once.

Q: "If syphilis is untreated does the person usually die?"
A: "No. Less than one third of those with untreated syphilis show physical complications that are life-threatening. However, pregnant women with latent or tertiary syphilis pass it on to their developing babies, whose lives are then at real risk. They may be born with congenital defects or even be born dead unless the mother is treated fairly early in the pregnancy."

Trichomoniasis Trichomoniasis, frequently referred to as "trich," is caused by a single-celled organism called *Trichomonas vaginalis*. The organism is usually spread through sexual contact and commonly affects the vagina, urethra and cervix in women and the urethra and prostate in men. Some women and many men are asymptomatic, but both partners must be examined even if only one partner shows symptoms. Infected women generally complain of a frothy vaginal discharge with an extremely unpleasant odour. Men may have some penile discharge and both sexes may experience painful irritation during urination. Trich can be diagnosed by examination of the discharge.

There are several drugs available which are highly effective in eliminating trichomoniasis from both sexes, and Metronidazole was both the earliest and is the most widely used. Some patients, however, have reported such side effects as intolerance to alcohol, vomiting and diarrhoea. Courses of treatment vary from one to seven days and because it is particularly difficult to diagnose in the male sexual partner of the infected woman it is sometimes justifiable to treat the man in any event. Metronidazole is not suitable for pregnant women or breastfeeding mothers.

Vaginitis Vaginitis is a general term used to describe inflammations or infections of the vagina. Chief symptoms are pain, itching and a discharge that may have an unpleasant odour. There are a number of possible causes — bacteria, irritation from unnecessary vaginal sprays and other vaginal hygiene products, and sometimes sensitivity to tampons or contraceptive cream. The usual treatments are prescribed vaginal creams or suppositories, or antibiotics.

Venereal Warts Venereal warts are caused by a virus passed between sex partners. They usually appear within one to six months of contact and grow singly or in groups around the vagina, cervix and anus of women, and around and on the anus and the glans and shaft of the penis in men. Venereal warts have a cauliflowerlike appearance and tests are not usually required for diagnosis. Treatment can include electrosurgery, freezeburning or the application of various prescribed drying lotions. Even after the warts have been removed the virus sometimes remains and may cause the warts to reappear.

Self-treatment of any kind is unwise as damage to the surrounding tissue may occur.

MYTHS The following are common misconceptions about sexually transmitted diseases:

* masturbation causes STDs
* taking the pill or using an IUD gives some protection against STDs
* men who ejaculate prematurely are less likely to get an STD
* a penicillin injection every so often will prevent STDs
* vaginal sprays and deodorants provide some STD protection
* washing with soap and hot water can cure crabs
* men always have symptoms if they get gonorrhoea
* once you are cured you cannot get an STD again
* STD tests are painful and complicated
* sexually transmitted diseases only occur among poor, uneducated people
* if you have sex with someone who has an STD you will automatically get it
* you can tell if someone has an STD by examining their genitals
* STDs can be cured by home remedies and special herbs
* teenagers get STDs more than any other age group
* you won't catch an STD unless you have intercourse
* people can treat themselves for an STD.

FEELINGS Sexually transmitted diseases carry with them a heavy social stigma. People are sometimes so ashamed that they will avoid seeking treatment rather than admit they have an infection, or they will refuse to tell their sex partners for the same reason. They believe that the disease may disappear on its own and not require medical attention that would cause them to feel humiliated. This approach can only lead to serious physical and social problems. STDs require diagnosis and treatment. Interestingly, some doctors connive at this secrecy, and are reluctant to suggest to some patients that they have an STD for fear of giving offence.

The feelings of shame come from several sources: having to name your sexual partner or partners can be uncomfortable. STDs have been associated with unclean, improper sexual relationships by society; the moralizing of some health-care workers about STDs and the problems associated with them can also lead to lessened self-esteem; having to tell your regular partner that you have an STD and that he or she may also have it is necessary, but fraught with tension and maybe risk to the relationship.

RELATIONSHIPS Sexually transmitted diseases can have a powerful effect on relationships:

* accusations about how the STD was contracted and who passed it to whom can lead to mistrust between the couple
* repeated episodes of STD cause physical distress and interfere with usual sexual activities, causing stress for both people
* STDs can lead to pregnancy and fertility problems; this places a strain on feelings of adequacy and self-worth, and sometimes creates barriers between a couple
* the ping-ponging of an STD between a couple causes mistrust and creates frustration.

Q: "When I got an STD, I was shocked. I only had sex with one person for years. Soon the shock was replaced by real anger, and it affected our relationship for a long time."

A: "Yes, STDs do tell a lot about what people really do rather than what you think they do. Many people have been caught in your situation and reacted as you did, with shock and then anger.

"It is an unfortunate way to discover what is going on in your relationship, but sooner or later you would have had to learn. Use the occasion to examine openly what you are both seeking from the relationship. Has your commitment to an exclusive sexual relationship ever been shared by your partner, for example? Anger as a reaction is understandable, but it is not a good element in a continuing relationship — much better to discuss it honestly."

Q: "My husband and I do not have VD now. How can we be sure we will never get it?"

A: "By not having sex with anyone else. The moment either of you does that, you are risking infection."

WOMEN'S SEXUAL SYSTEMS

This description of women's sexual systems is divided into three parts:

I   THE EXTERNAL GENITALS — see further down this page

II   THE INTERNAL GENITALS — women's reproductive systems, together with menstruation: page 333

III BREASTS — which, though they are not genitals, have considerable sexual significance: page 363

I   THE EXTERNAL GENITALS

The name that covers all the external female genitals — those you can see — is the **vulva**. The different parts of the vulva are: **1** the large, outer lips called the **labia majora**; they join at the top at **2** the **mons pubis**, a soft mound that is covered with hair after puberty; **3** the smaller, inner lips called the **labia minora** that are found within the labia majora; **4** the **clitoris**, which is located at the point where the inner lips join; and **5** the **vestibule**, the almond-shaped area within the labia minora where the urine passageway and the opening to the vagina appear.

1 Labia Majora

The labia majora, the outer lips, are the outermost part of a woman's

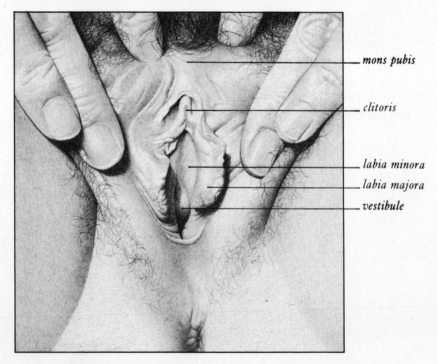

mons pubis

clitoris

labia minora
labia majora
vestibule

genitals, and they vary in size and shape from woman to woman. After puberty they are usually covered with hair.

During sexual excitation, the labia majora swell and flatten out, exposing the vaginal opening. This is caused by extra blood swelling the vessels. The labia of women who have had a child show the response a little more strongly than the labia of women who have not.

After menopause the labia majora thin out and lose most of the fat that gave them shape and prominence; they no longer swell and then flatten out as they used to.

2 Mons Pubis

The mons pubis (the "pubic mound"), also called the mons veneris (the "mound of Venus"), is the deposit of fatty tissue over the pubic bone. It becomes covered with hair during puberty.

3 Labia Minora

FACTS The labia minora, the inner folds of tissue, are not as thick as the labia majora, but they are more sensitive and can feel good when touched. When a woman reaches a certain level of sexual excitement, her labia minora change colour. This colour change is called the sex skin change and indicates that orgasm will occur if the stimulation continues. The labia of women who have not had a child become a glistening bright red; in women who have had a child, the colour changes to deep wine or amber.

At the same time as the colour change happens, the labia minora become larger through an increased blood flow that is a natural result of sexual stimulation. When there is no more stimulation, both the large outer and the smaller inner lips return to their usual size and shape within a short period of time.

CULTURE The external genitals of women often used to be referred to as the *pudendum*, which is Latin for "thing to be ashamed of." This is part of the legacy of embarrassment, fear, disgust and detachment about their bodies that women have to come to terms with. It is no wonder that women have had such a difficult time accepting their bodies in our culture, and in many others around the world, as being competent and important in themselves, and not just in the service of others.

In ancient India and Persia the labia minora of girls coming up to puberty were joined together with thread. A space was left for the passage of urine and for the menstrual flow, and the labia remained joined until marriage, when the stitches were removed. The practice is called "infibulation." In Abyssinia and Sudan too, infibulation was widely practised, though the details of the method differed. There, the labia minora of girls reaching puberty were scraped with a sharp instrument until they bled. The bleeding lips were then joined together and the feet, legs and thighs were bound together for approximately two weeks. A kind of funnel was inserted for urination and a small opening was also left for menstruation. At the appointed time, when the labia had joined, the bonds were released and the woman could shuffle about. Her labia remained attached

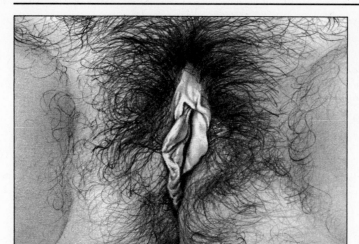

Because each woman's labia are unique, one woman's genitals can never look quite the same as another's. The variation in appearance can be very marked, as here.

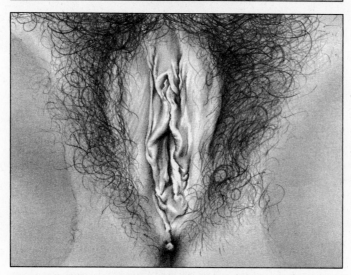

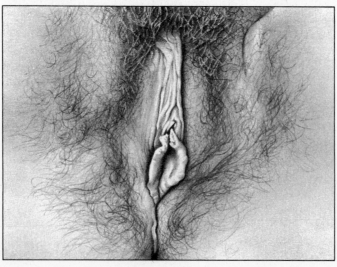

to each other until marriage, when a woman from the tribe would open the scar to permit intercourse.

In some African cultures the labia were sewn together from puberty until marriage and then drawn closed again whenever the husband left the village on an extended trip.

4 The Clitoris

FACTS The clitoris, which you can find where the labia minora or inner lips meet, has a single function — to give pleasure to its owner. It has nothing to do with having children. The innumerable nerve endings in the clitoris and the area immediately around it mean that it is very sensitive to direct or indirect contact.

The clitoris consists of a head or rounded area, called the glans, and a longer part, called the shaft or body. The body of the clitoris is usually covered by the tissue of the inner lips, which make a hood to protect it.

In its normal state, when it is not stimulated, a clitoris is about the size of a cherry stone. The normal variation in length is from an eighth to one-half of an inch. When it is stimulated, it fills with an extra flow of blood and increases in size: both the shaft and the glans enlarge — the glans can double in diameter. As stimulation continues and orgasm approaches, the clitoris retracts and moves under its hood. It moves out again when the stimulation stops.

After orgasm the clitoris returns to its normal size within about ten minutes. If the woman doesn't have an orgasm the extra blood that has flowed into the clitoris in response to her stimulation may remain there, keeping the clitoris enlarged for perhaps several hours. Many women find this uncomfortable. Orgasm leads to a dispersal of the extra blood.

Q: "Can the clitoris get damaged from too much contact?"
A: "No. The clitoris will not be damaged by intercourse or by hand or mouth contact, directly on the clitoris or indirectly on the clitoral area. If your clitoris is overstimulated it will begin to get sore and you will automatically want stimulation to stop. Take that cue, as you take cues from other parts of your body, and your clitoris won't get hurt. If it does get irritated — and this rarely happens — the irritation may not be related at all to contact. If the irritation continues, get qualified help."

Q: "What happens to the clitoris during intercourse?"
A: "During intercourse the penis does not contact the clitoris directly. The thrusting of the penis in the vagina, regardless of the position used, moves the labia minora (the inner lips), and it is this movement of the lips against the clitoris that usually creates the feeling of pleasure.

"You can, of course, have direct contact with the clitoris during intercourse by touching it with a finger or a vibrator, but many women find direct contact more irritating than stimulating; a more general contact with the area is likely to produce a more pleasurable response. This is one of those cases in which talking to your partner about what you like can produce greater pleasure for you both."

Q: "When I'm making love, I lose the clitoris. Am I doing something wrong?"

A: "You are not doing anything wrong. On the contrary, you are doing something right.

"When a woman is sexually excited, the clitoris normally retracts under its hood. The general clitoral area is still very sensitive, so continue what you are doing rather than fumble around in a vain search for the clitoris. The fact that your partner's clitoris has pulled back means she is excited, responding and moving towards orgasm. Remember too that always wondering how you are doing can take the joy and naturalness out of sex, and make you an observer rather than a partner."

Q: "What happens if a woman has her clitoris removed?"

A: "Whether it is removed for cultural reasons or because of disease or accident, she will still feel pleasure and be capable of orgasm. The tissue around the clitoris is quite sufficiently sensitive to respond fully to stimulation. This means that historical attempts to control women's pleasure by removing the clitoris were ignorantly foolish, but makes it even more outrageous that the attempt was ever made.

"The psychological consequences of removing the clitoris may be more severe than the physical if the woman is not thoroughly counselled about the operation in advance."

MYTHS There has been, and continues to be, a controversy over an alleged difference between orgasm produced by stimulation of the clitoris alone and orgasm produced with a penis in the vagina. Freud believed — and many of his followers continue to believe — that it is appropriate for a young girl to fondle her clitoris and so achieve sexual pleasure and orgasm. But, they said, in order for her to mature as a woman she should come to accept and prefer orgasm induced by a penis in the vagina — so-called "vaginal orgasm." If she fails to make this transfer, her psychosexual development is arrested. Freud and his followers therefore placed a strong positive value on "vaginal" orgasm, and a negative one (except for adolescents) on "clitoral" orgasm.

Masters and Johnson and other sex researchers and analysts have shown beyond any doubt that the physical indicators of orgasm are identical, regardless of the way the orgasm is produced — whether it's by a penis in the vagina, a hand, tongue or vibrator on the clitoral area, by breast fondling or through fantasy. Physically, what is happening to the woman at the point of orgasm is the same.

It is of course the case that women vary widely in the way they prefer to reach orgasm. Many women find that orgasm produced by direct stimulation of the clitoral area feels more intense than orgasm resulting from a penis in the vagina. Equally, a great many women find orgasm with a penis in the vagina to be more fulfilling and meaningful.

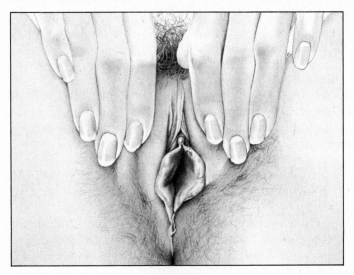

What happens to the clitoris when a woman is sexually aroused —

As the woman starts to become excited extra blood flows into the clitoris and it increases in size.

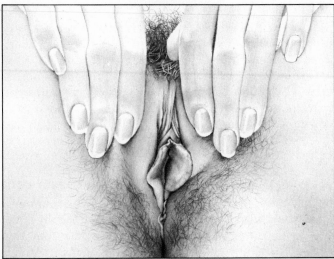

As stimulation continues, the clitoris begins to retract under its hood.

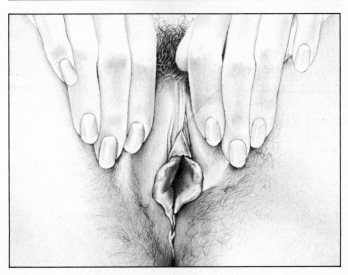

When orgasm is near, the clitoris retracts completely and can no longer be seen.

The important issue, then, is for each woman to be able to achieve the feelings she wants and finds most satisfying. To do this she has to select the right context and she probably has to be able to communicate with her sex partner to indicate what she wants and to arrive at a situation where both people may achieve the satisfaction they seek.

It used to be widely believed that masturbation would cause the clitoris to grow larger. Girls who rubbed the clitoral area to give themselves pleasure were accordingly warned off. The belief was and is entirely false: the clitoris will not grow larger through rubbing. The idea that masturbation could cause extreme growth had no basis in evidence; it was merely the work of people who believed that sexual pleasure was inconsistent with their idea of womanhood.

A woman's clitoris may become sore (as any part of any person's body may become sore) if it is rubbed a lot. The body is then issuing a simple cue to stop until the soreness ceases. That cue is entirely sufficient as a guide to individual behaviour.

CULTURE Perhaps because the clitoris is the source of so much pleasure for women it has been customary in some societies for it to be removed. The process is called clitoridectomy.

In some African civilizations and in Abyssinia, the clitoris was normally removed at puberty. The Arabs, Copts, Ethiopians, Persians and some Central African cultures removed only part of the clitoris.

In the Victorian period, in Europe and America, clitoridectomy was administered as a punishment for girls or women who touched themselves "excessively" — whatever that meant — or who showed an "abnormal" interest in sex. The Victorians also used clitoridectomy in a pseudomedical way to curb "nymphomania."

Nowadays, clitoridectomy is only performed in developed countries if cancer treatment requires radical surgery. In these countries it is no longer used with the idea of limiting women's sexual pleasure or reducing their interest in sex. Unfortunately there are many countries in which clitoridectomy is still performed, sometimes as part of an even more drastic measure known as female circumcision.

There is considerable concern among international health authorities, women's groups and ordinary citizens about the practice of female circumcision in at least 26 countries. Approximately 30 million women are affected. The World Health Organization and the United Nations itself are investigating the nature and extent of this practice, and UNICEF, an agency of the United Nations, is committed to eliminating it.

Reports from various countries — Australia, Brazil, Pakistan, Egypt, Saudi Arabia, Iraq, Jordan, Syria, Ethiopia and Sudan, among others — describe the appalling consequences of female circumcision. Massive bleeding, shock and blood poisoning are some of the physical results of female circumcision. Psychological consequences include fear of sexual contact, shame and guilt. Although sexual pleasure is not necessarily reduced, inhibition and anxiety about their circumcisions does affect some women's ability to enjoy sex fully. In these countries, circumcision is performed for local religious and cultural reasons. Interference from people outside the country, and the use of descriptive terms like "barbaric" and "primitive" usually lead to resistance and create barriers to change. Thoughtful, sensitive approaches must be made to start a movement for reform, which can only be made really effective if local political and social leaders will take the initiative. As long as female circumcision remains connected to male domination it is going to be difficult to eradicate. Rethinking sexual relationships is the only way to guarantee an effective outlawing of the mutilation of female genitals.

Q: "Just what do they do in a female circumcision?"
A: "The most common procedures are either removal of the entire clitoris (called a clitoridectomy) or the removal of the hood and tip of the clitoris (called a Sunna circumcision). In some countries it may be even worse, as the labia are removed along with the entire clitoris. Female circumcision is usually done between ages five and eight and may be associated with infibulation — the sewing up of the vaginal opening until marriage."

5 The Vestibule

The vestibule has two main parts, the urethra and the opening to the vagina. The urethra is the passageway that carries urine from the bladder out of the body. Its opening is below the clitoris and above the opening of the vagina.

Just below the urethra is the vaginal opening, which is the beginning of the vagina itself. The vaginal opening is not a large hole and can be seen best when both sets of labia are parted.

II THE INTERNAL GENITALS

Women's internal genitals are described as follows:
1 the **hymen**, the thin piece of tissue that partly blocks the entrance to the vagina; 2 **Bartholin's glands**, on each side of the labia minora, which secrete a few drops of fluid when a woman is sexually aroused; 3 the **urethra**, the urine passageway; 4 the **vagina**, the passage that leads from the vulva to 5 the **cervix**, otherwise known as the neck of the womb; then there is 6 the **womb** or **uterus**, in which a fertilized egg can grow into a fully developed baby prior to birth; if an egg is not fertilized, the lining of the womb will be shed in the process called **menstruation**; if the uterus should become diseased it may have to be removed in the operation known as **hysterectomy**; at the upper end of the uterus are 7 the two **Fallopian tubes**, along which the woman's eggs pass and where they meet a man's sperm; the eggs are stored in 8 the **ovaries**, of which there are two.

1 Hymen

FACTS Just inside the opening to the vagina is the hymen or maidenhead, a thin piece of tissue partially blocking the way into the vagina. It is named after the Greek god of marriage and has no known biological function. Although some women are born without a hymen, most have one; it varies in size and shape from woman to woman. The hymen does not cover the entire vaginal opening, since there must be a hole to allow the menstrual flow, or period, to leave the body.

The hymen can be perforated when the body is stretched strenuously, as in exercise or sports; it can be perforated during intercourse or by inserting a tampon during menstruation, and sometimes it is perforated for no apparent reason. A perforated hymen is not an indication of having had intercourse, nor can it prove a loss of virginity. As a matter of fact, some women have to have the hymen removed surgically (in a hymenectomy) prior to the birth of their first child, as it was so flexible or small that it remained intact during intercourse.

If the hymen is perforated, whether during first intercourse or at some other time, there may be some slight bleeding and a little pain. Both the bleeding and the pain are quite normal and both will stop after a short time. For some women this can occur with no discomfort at all (a common term for this is "losing your cherry").

Sometimes a woman may be nervous about intercourse, especially the first time, and this tension can produce more discomfort than the perforation of the hymen. Also, men who are clumsy or rough while having intercourse, or who try to penetrate the vagina before it is lubricated and ready for the penis, can cause pain too. Usually, however, the excitement of building up to intercourse takes care of the problem, and the woman feels minimal discomfort even if her hymen has not previously been perforated.

It is important to remember that a woman can become pregnant even if her hymen is intact and no penis has entered the vagina. If sperm comes in contact with the labia or the general vaginal area, it can move through the opening in the hymen, pass into the vagina and possibly lead to a

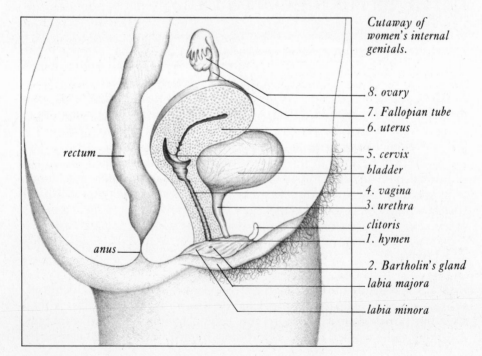

Cutaway of women's internal genitals.

8. ovary
7. Fallopian tube
6. uterus
5. cervix
bladder
4. vagina
3. urethra
clitoris
1. hymen
2. Bartholin's gland
labia majora
labia minora

rectum

anus

pregnancy. There is no substitute for an effective means of birth control.

Q: "Can a doctor tell if my hymen is thick and will give me pain when I first have intercourse?"

A: "Yes. Sometimes a sensitive and understanding doctor will instruct a woman on how to use her fingers to stretch (dilate) the hymen so it will present less difficulty during first intercourse. This kind of advice is very valuable and can result in more pleasant, painless first intercourse."

FEELINGS A woman learns about her hymen in many ways, but rarely from parents, doctors or informed adults in a supportive and sensitive manner. Rather, women learn about the hymen in ways that promote anxiety and uncertainty about their own bodies and their behaviour.

The principal message women generally get about the hymen is that it really serves no known medical purpose, but while it remains intact it indicates that they are still virgins. If the hymen is perforated before marriage they are taught to believe it will be taken as evidence of sexual activity.

This is not only unfair, but sometimes damaging too. A woman whose hymen has perforated through work, athletics, or for no apparent reason at all can become intensely anxious about having intercourse for the first time. She can become deeply disturbed at the thought that the man will think she is not telling the truth when she says that she has never had intercourse before. Should she tell him first? Will he believe her if she does? Is it better to hope he won't notice? Will he accuse her of sleeping around and so ruin what may be a very important act of giving on her part?

Another common distortion of the facts that is also damaging is that perforation of the hymen (if in fact it is there) by a penis is going to cause a lot of pain and some bleeding too. A woman may want very much to have intercourse with a man yet be afraid to do so. When she does have intercourse for the first time, she is tense and awkward, not free to respond fully. Few women suffer any considerable pain or inconvenience on first intercourse, and if that fact were generally known, far fewer women would be apprehensive and far more would be able to express themselves freely.

The old notion that the hymen existed so that a woman should suffer when she first had intercourse follows from the idea that sexual intercourse itself is wrong, evil or sinful. But it is a scientific fact that the hymen is often perforated for reasons quite unconnected with sexual intercourse. No association of an intact hymen and virginity has any factual basis, nor can there be any evidence that a torn hymen means a loss of virginity. Only when these facts are accepted will many women be freed from the seriously negative effects of popular mythology.

CULTURE In some Australian tribes, the hymen is perforated by a specially appointed older woman a week prior to marriage. If the hymen has been perforated already, the bride to be is publicly humiliated, tortured and perhaps killed.

In the Polynesian Islands of the Marquesas, the expectation was that during puberty the hymen would be perforated naturally due to vigorous work, athletics, masturbation and horseback riding.

Q: "My parents told me that it used to be the custom to show sheets to everyone after the wedding night. What's that all about and why did they do it?"

A: "In many cultures throughout the world there has been, and continues to be, a great importance placed upon virginity: that is, not having sexual intercourse until marriage. A way of proving that a girl was a virgin until her marriage was to show the marriage guests or family members the blood-stained bed sheets the couple used on their first night together. If her hymen had been intact, it would have been penetrated by her new husband and she would have bled. That, at least, was the theory of it.

"Obviously, if the girl did not have her hymen intact, either because of prior intercourse or for other reasons, this tradition could present problems. The bed sheets still had to be stained with a little blood to keep everyone happy.

"Retaining virginity until marriage is still considered as quite important by many people (mostly men). Some men look for virginity in women with whom they desire to establish a long-term relationship, while at the same time they continue to have sex with other women where a serious and long-term relationship is unimportant. This is commonly known as the double standard of behaviour."

2 Bartholin's Glands

FACTS On each side of the labia minora (inner lips) are Bartholin's glands. These glands have outlets very close to the vaginal opening and produce a small amount of fluid when a woman is sexually aroused. This small amount of fluid was thought to be important for lubricating the vagina, but the research of Masters and Johnson proved that vaginal lubrication comes from further up the vagina, so Bartholin's glands are not obviously important during sexual excitation. Quite what function they fulfil we have yet to discover.

Sometimes Bartholin's glands become irritated or infected; they can then swell and be painful. This condition can be treated successfully by a doctor.

3 Urethra

FACTS The urethra is the short tube connected at one end to the bladder and opening at the other in the vestibule. It is the passageway for the elimination of urine from the bladder. Its opening is between the clitoris and the vaginal opening.

Q: "I find that I must urinate immediately after having intercourse with my husband. Sometimes I even feel I am going to urinate during intercourse. Do I have a problem?"

A: "Probably not. Before intercourse try to urinate so your bladder will be empty, then the indirect pressure of the penis on the bladder will not trigger the need to urinate during intercourse.

A lot of people — men as well as women — find they want to urinate right after intercourse; this is because intercourse can irritate the urethra and the bladder very slightly."

Q: "My sister said she got 'honeymoon cystitis.' What is that?"
A: "Cystitis is the general name given to irritation, inflammation or infection of the bladder. The chief signs are painful, burning and frequent urination. Cystitis is not VD.

"Cystitis is caused by bacteria that invade the bladder and may get into the urethra during intercourse, especially if the amount of sexual activity increases sharply, as it might on a honeymoon. You don't, however, have to have sex to get cystitis, but intercourse often aggravates it.

"Cystitis may disappear on its own, but it is always wise to seek medical advice and treatment. Urinating after sex and drinking large amounts of fluid (especially citric juices) to cause a heavy urine flow are also helpful in avoiding the disease. If a woman contracts cystitis, soaking in a hot bath has also been found to help. Many women get cystitis at some point in their lives and some have it more than once. It is painful and it must be treated, but usually the cure is simple and speedy.

"Cystitis-like symptoms can also appear after intercourse because the woman's urethra has been bruised by being pressed between the pubic bone and the penis."

MYTHS Some people believe that urination immediately following intercourse acts as a contraceptive method. Since urination is through the urethra and not out of the vagina, sperm cannot be flushed out of the vagina in this fashion. People who practise this method of birth control are usually called parents.

AGE As a woman ages and passes through menopause, it is common for her to feel more irritation to the bladder and urethral area during and after intercourse. The reduction of oestrogen that comes with the menopause causes the tissue to thin out in and around the vagina, resulting in less cushioning during intercourse. This may lead to an urge to urinate during or after intercourse.

The situation is a common one and is not serious. Urinating before intercourse helps, and so does lubricating the vagina.

4 Vagina

FACTS The vagina begins on the outside at the vaginal opening and ends inside at the cervix or neck of the womb. The vagina varies in size from woman to woman, but is usually three to five inches long. It is shaped like a flattened tube, the walls of which touch each other. The walls of the vagina are not smooth — they contain folds or wrinkles (called *rugae*) throughout. The vagina has enormous powers of expansion and contraction. For example, it widens during the birth process, and during sexual intercourse it can adjust to any size penis.

During sexual excitement the vagina responds almost immediately to pleasurable stimulation. In a matter of a few seconds droplets of fluid appear along its walls. As sexual excitement continues, these beads or droplets join together and spread to cover the sides of the vagina completely. When a woman begins to be sexually excited what happens is this: blood vessels in the walls of the vagina quickly become swollen with blood. This engorgement continues, and as it does so the blood vessels press against the tissue in that area, forcing natural tissue fluid through the walls of the vagina. The fluid is not only a sign of sexual arousal but serves as a lubricant for intercourse if that is to follow, without which the woman would find penetration painful. The vagina, like the eye, is a self-cleansing part of the body, and does not require special attention to be kept clean. Regular douching, unless it is prescribed by a medical specialist, is not necessary and, in fact, robs the vagina of the natural substances that keep it clean.

The internal walls of the vagina itself do not have a great supply of nerves and are not overly sensitive. The innermost two-thirds of the vagina are more responsive to pressure than to touch, whereas the outer one-third, especially around the vaginal opening, has many more nerves and is much more sensitive to touch.

Q: "When I get really sexually turned on I usually feel a lot of wet, sticky stuff in my vagina. Is there something wrong — am I oversexed?"

A: "No, there is nothing wrong — rather, everything is right — and no, you are not oversexed.

"The natural result of sexual excitement is the formation

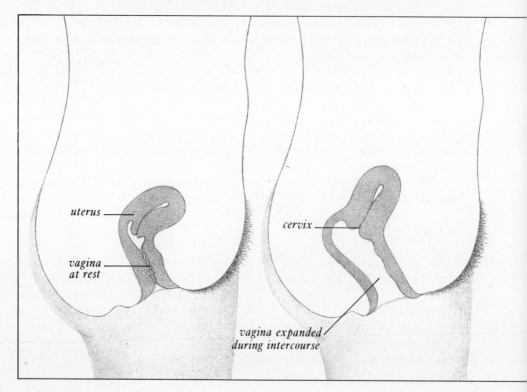

uterus

vagina at rest

cervix

vagina expanded during intercourse

of fluid on the walls of the vagina. If you decide to go on and have intercourse you need this fluid to allow your partner's penis to enter and thrust easily.

"The amount of fluid produced by the vagina and the area surrounding it varies according to your feelings about what is happening at the time, whether you are alone or with someone else and how that makes you feel, and, of course, your general physical health and well being. Usually, your vagina will produce enough fluid to meet your needs and expectations, with some normal variations occurring from time to time. Having a little more or a little less vaginal fluid need not be seen as a problem, nor should it interfere with your sexual activity."

Q: "OK, but occasionally I get hardly any wetness, and that is painful and embarrassing. What's that from?"

A: "The cause of too little vaginal lubrication leading to pain during intercourse can be physical, emotional, or some combination of the two.

"Physically, for example, you may have a hormonal problem, or an infection or cyst in the vagina that will cause pain during intercourse. Get qualified medical treatment. It is unlikely to be a difficult matter to cure. Sometimes a woman who is using a birth control pill that is high in progesterone can find she has lessened vaginal lubrication, but this can be taken care of easily by her doctor.

"Then there are emotional causes. Sometimes, too little

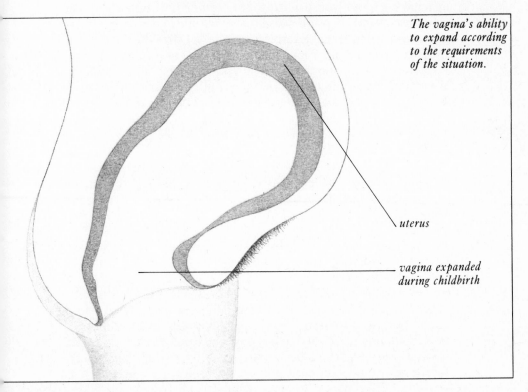

The vagina's ability to expand according to the requirements of the situation.

uterus

vagina expanded during childbirth

vaginal lubrication can be caused by your emotional problems or your anxieties about your relationship with your partner. In these cases, your feelings block the natural physical responses, and your body gives you a message about how you are feeling about yourself and your situation. Many people suffer this kind of emotional block on their physical response at some time or other. You may be able to deal with the situation on your own, but both women and men often benefit from talking with a qualified person who can help them understand their feelings and so ease the block. If you can ease it by talking with your partner, so much the better.

"Remember that lubrication gradually decreases as you get older, but that is a natural physical condition which doesn't indicate any physical or psychological problem."

Q: "My husband says my vagina has got bigger. Can that happen, and what can we do about it?"

A: "Sometimes after childbirth, and particularly after the birth of several children over a short period, the vagina may lose some of its muscle tone, loosen a bit, and feel larger. You can feel it too, as well as your husband. Therefore, during intercourse he may not contact the walls of the vagina and he may feel that he is slipping out. Also, you may not feel pleasure from the penis making contact with the walls of the vagina.

"In this situation try changing positions for intercourse to those which lead to more penis–vagina contact. Also, there are specific exercises you can do to strengthen and tighten up the muscles around the vagina and improve tone and feeling. These exercises, called Kegel Exercises (page 342) after the doctor who first prescribed them, require the woman to contract the muscles necessary to stop the urine flow. You hold the contraction for three to five seconds and do that ten times in a series. The series is usually repeated several times a day. You can also do these exercises during intercourse, contracting the vaginal muscles around the penis. Both of you can then feel the progress being made.

"In extreme cases, where exercise has not helped at all, it is possible to perform plastic surgery to tighten the vagina but this is a last resort, to be used only when all else has failed."

Q: "I was told that my vagina has a strong odour. I don't want sex to be a turn-off. What can I do?"

A: "Most people have a personal odour on all parts of their body, but especially on their genitals, since those areas are not usually exposed to fresh air. Some women have a strong genital odour which is natural to them and is not a sign of poor cleanliness or personal hygiene. If you have a strong natural genital odour and it interferes with sexual behaviour, washing, bathing or showering alone or with your partner before having sex can provide you with the reassurance and security you need: it may be an enjoy-able turn-on as well.

"A strong genital odour resulting from poor personal clean-liness can be taken care of by washing the vulva daily with soap and water. Feminine hygiene sprays are not helpful; they are, in fact, quite likely to cause allergic irritation.

"Sometimes strong vaginal odours are caused by irritations and infections that produce a smelly vaginal discharge. Usually these conditions do not go away by themselves, and medical treatment is required to clear them up. Once cared for, the discharge and the odour will disappear. Remember, also, that strong genital odours may not repel, and can be attractive to some people during lovemaking."

Q: "What is a douche and why is it used?"
A: "Douching is flushing out the vagina with water or a special solution. The douche itself is a rubber pouch with a tube coming out one end. You fill the pouch with fluid, put the tube in the vagina and squeeze the pouch to make the fluid squirt out of the tube into the vagina.

"Why is it used? The vagina is a self-cleaning part of the body. Therefore, unless medically prescribed, douching is not necessary. As a matter of fact, the regular use of douches, especi-ally those advertised as containing special cosmetic ingredients and flavours, can rob the vagina of its natural protection and balance and may lead to irritation and infection. *Douching is never to be considered a method of birth control*, regardless of the fluids used. Sperm travel through the cervix to the uterus too quickly for the douche to be useful for birth control. In fact, a douche is more likely to have the opposite effect. If the stream of fluid is strong as it enters the vagina, it may give the sperm a boost and propel them into the uterus more quickly. Although some people find douching reassuring for personal cleanliness, simple, regular cleansing of the vulva with mild soap and water should achieve maximum cleanliness and comfort. It is not ad-visable to use a douche unless it has been specifically rec-ommended by a doctor."

Q: "Is there such a thing as an artificial vagina?"
A: "Yes. Due to a congenital malformation some girls are born without a vagina. This condition is called vaginal agenesis, and these girls have vaginal plastic surgery prior to puberty whereby an artificial vagina is constructed. It functions just like a natural vagina. It is fine for intercourse, it allows the menstrual flow to leave the body in the normal way and it gets wet during sexual excitation.

"If the rest of the reproductive organs are normal, the woman can become pregnant, either naturally or through artificial insemination. In these cases, a Caesarean will usually be performed to prevent possible damage to the surgically made vagina as the baby passes through it.

"Men who have an operation to change their sex (transsexuals) have a surgically created vagina that functions for intercourse and other pleasuring only."

KEGEL EXERCISES

Kegel exercises were developed to help women who sometimes passed urine involuntarily when they sneezed, when they had sex (especially during orgasm) and at other times as well. After practising the exercises for several weeks, women reported that not only had the urination problem been eliminated, but that they had increased vaginal sensation as well. As a result, the exercises are now used by women who want to tone up their vaginal muscles for increased sexual pleasure as well as by women who have an involuntary urination problem.

There are some variations on Kegel exercises, but what follows is the basic pattern.

The muscles concerned are those which you contract to delay urination (pubococcygeal or PC muscles). Kegel exercises consist of contracting these muscles to a count of three, relaxing them for the same amount of time and repeating this contract–relax routine ten times. If the exercises are done two or three times a day for six or eight weeks, the vaginal muscles should regain proper tone. It is important not to use the abdominal muscles.

Kegel exercises can be done anytime, anywhere, sitting, standing or lying down. No-one can tell you are doing them. Progress can be checked by inserting a finger in the vagina and seeing how well the muscles tighten round it. If, once muscle tone is restored, the exercises are repeated several times a week there should be no problem with maintaining the increased level of vaginal sensation.

MYTHS It is an ancient myth that a penis can get trapped in a vagina, there is in fact no way that this can happen. The vagina cannot intentionally or unintentionally clamp up on the penis to prevent withdrawal. The anxiety probably stems from observing dogs. The male dog, while having intercourse with a female dog, can develop a knot in the penis (something human males can't do) and be unable to withdraw until ejaculation or loss of erection.

During intercourse, women can contract certain vaginal muscles (see Kegel Exercises above) to grip the penis more tightly. This does not lead to locking or clamping; on the contrary, many men enjoy the sensation.

Occasionally, women suffer from a condition called vaginismus, in which the muscles around the entrance to the vagina contract and make it impossible for a penis to enter. Vaginismus is frequently accompanied by a deep-seated phobia about intercourse, and should be treated. It cannot occur when a penis is already inside. See page 109.

There are ancient and recurrent myths that vaginas contain teeth or sharp objects that can harm a penis and even "bite it off." Freud reflected on this notion and called it *vagina dentata* — "vagina with teeth." It is a belief that is shared by only a few people, and they are usually men who have a fear of women and of forming relationships with them. They avoid any kind of intimacy because they are afraid of being emasculated. There is nothing in the vagina that can harm a penis in any way.

AGE After menopause, when the ovaries greatly reduce their production of oestrogen, the walls of the vagina thin out significantly. The vagina also becomes shorter and narrower, and it takes longer to produce a reduced amount of lubrication. The vagina also loses its ability to expand during sexual excitation as a woman ages.

These changes are natural and inevitable in all women as they age and pass through menopause, but it is clear that sexual interest, activity and fulfilment are basically unaffected and the patterns of sexual behaviour after menopause are similar to those before. Any problems resulting from reduced lubrication are eased by using K-Y or any similar safe jelly.

FEELINGS For centuries now, women have been socialized to regard their vaginas simply as places for intercourse, or as the areas which allow for the passage of children or the menstrual flow. The vagina was, and remains today, a mysterious, secret, dirty place, special in an uncomfortable way and separate from the rest of the body.

Parents, doctors and teachers have not been helpful, since few of them ever took any time to explain or answer the questions girls and women have always had about the vagina. Also, it is evident that men have always known more about the vagina than women themselves. The control of this knowledge by the other sex has put women in the undesirable position of having to go to men to learn about parts of bodies they themselves own. This situation continues today, although some efforts, spurred principally by the women's movement, have begun to help women learn more about all parts of their bodies and begin to gain a sense of control and esteem about their abilities and potentials.

The result of all this avoidance, ignorance and secrecy about the vagina is that women are often very uncertain and embarrassed about themselves whenever the topic arises during medical examinations or when making love. This very real cultural and religious influence has caused women to bear an enormous burden not of their own making, has interfered with their capacity for full self-knowledge and has inhibited them from expressing themselves freely in sex.

5 Cervix

FACTS The cervix is the narrow, bottom part of the uterus which dips into the back end of the vagina. In that area the cervix has an opening called the cervical os. This opening is very small, like the end of a small straw, and feels like the tip of a nose or a dimpled chin. Women who use IUDs for birth control have the threads of the IUD hanging down through the cervix into the vagina.

The cervix has the ability to expand and contract to allow a baby to pass through it during birth. Menstrual fluid also passes through the cervix on its way out through the vagina. Sperm once in the vagina travels up through the cervix to the uterus and Fallopian tubes. The cervix secretes a fluid called cervical mucus. The mucus varies in appearance during the menstrual cycle, and is used by those who practise natural family planning methods as an indicator of safe or unsafe times to have intercourse (this is called the Billings or cervical mucus method; see page 74).

Q: "What kind of test do they do to check for cancer of the cervix?"
A: "A simple painless procedure called a cervical smear, whereby your doctor, using a plastic spatula, gently removes some cells from your cervix. The cells are then studied under a microscope to determine the presence of abnormal cells. This test, which should be done every three years, was introduced by Dr George Papanicolaou, who discovered the cancerous changes in the cervix and developed the test."

Q: "Do you have to have an operation if the test shows abnormal cells in the cervix?"
A: "No, not necessarily. First of all, it is always wise to have another cervical smear to be certain the first results were accurate. Secondly, abnormal cells in the cervix do not always indicate the presence of disease that requires surgery. Unusual cells in the cervix are often due to infections or inflammation and may disappear on their own, or after short nonsurgical treatment.

"On other occasions, irregular cells in the cervix may be diagnosed as highly suspicious or premalignant; treatment may then be removal of the abnormal cells only. Cold cauterization (cryosurgery or freeze burning) by the specialist is one method. Cone biopsy, or the removal of a cone-shaped section of the affected area of the cervix, is another method used both for further diagnosis and for treatment of some cases of cervical disease. It requires hospitalization and anaesthesia. Hysterectomy is prescribed by some doctors as the immediate treatment when cancer cells are present to any degree in the cervix, though it is not accepted by all specialists or patients as the only treatment for cervical cancer.

"It is important for women to recognize the widespread differences of opinion among doctors about treating the cause of abnormal cells in the cervix. It might well be worth asking for a second medical opinion before proceeding with any type of cervical surgery."

Q: "Is it true that cancer of the cervix is caused by too much sex?"
A: "No. First of all, the phrase 'too much sex' is meaningless as it suggests an agreed norm that is best for all people. This idea is nonsense; no such standard exists or ever will exist. The studies showing a link between early sexual activity, multiple partners and an increased tendency to suffer from cervical cancer are not conclusive. Further, more detailed study is required. There is circumstantial evidence that some women who have had cervical cancer have also had some type of sexually transmitted disease — herpes is one candidate. Studies are far from complete though, and no conclusions should be drawn until they are."

6 Uterus

FACTS In a woman who is not pregnant, the uterus or womb is about the size of a closed fist (three to four inches long and two inches wide) and is shaped like an upside-down pear. Fully expanded in pregnancy it measures about 12–13 inches in length. The narrow end or neck of the uterus is the cervix, which dips into the back of the vagina, and ends with the cervical opening or os. The upper portion of the uterus is its larger part, in which the baby grows and is nourished during pregnancy until birth.

The uterus is very thick walled and unusually elastic, as it has to expand and hold a growing baby, and then return to approximately its usual size after the birth of the baby.

The uterus contains three special layered linings of tissue and muscle. The innermost layer of very special tissue is the endometrium. After puberty, this lines the main body of the uterus ready to provide a nesting place with immediate nutrition for a fertilized ovum at the earliest moments of pregnancy. If a woman is not pregnant this lining is not needed, so it is shed from the uterus and leaves the body as the menstrual flow or period. This process is repeated monthly. Immediately, a new lining begins to appear as a replacement in the event a pregnancy occurs during the woman's next cycle. Except during pregnancy this rather regular series of events continues uninterrupted from puberty until menopause.

The second, middle, part of the uterus is the powerful muscular

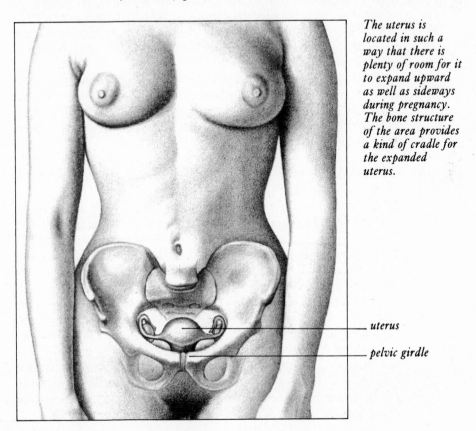

The uterus is located in such a way that there is plenty of room for it to expand upward as well as sideways during pregnancy. The bone structure of the area provides a kind of cradle for the expanded uterus.

uterus

pelvic girdle

layer called the myometrium, which gives the uterus its great strength and elasticity. This layer contracts during the birth process and forces the baby out of the uterus into the vagina. The third layer of the uterus is the peritoneum, which covers the other two layers, the myometrium and the endometrium as well as all the other organs in the abdomen.

The uterus is held in position within the pelvis by several sets of ligaments (the broad ligament, the round ligament, the anterior and posterior ligaments).

During sexual excitation, the uterus lifts itself, increases in size, and remains enlarged until orgasm or until stimulation stops. Orgasm results in a rapid return of the uterus to its usual size. The reason why the uterus expands and lifts is that much more blood flows into its walls during sexual excitement.

Q: "What is endometriosis?"

A: "Endometriosis is the growth of special womb-lining tissue in places other than the womb. The endometrium is a tissue lining the uterus that is there to nourish the fertilized egg, and for reasons not fully known this kind of tissue sometimes grows in places other than the uterus, such as the ovaries, Fallopian tubes or intestines. If that happens it is a problem because it causes pain and interferes with the fertilization and pregnancy process. Women who have endometriosis and want to have children are usually urged not to wait too long before trying to get pregnant, as the disease is usually progressive and worsens in time.

"Symptoms vary, but pain during menstruation and pain in the reproductive organs are common signs. Medical treatment is essential.

"Endometriosis is different from endometritis. Endometritis is an irritation of the lining of the uterus and may be due to many things, including the presence of an IUD birth control device. Endometritis can be treated medically without a great deal of difficulty."

Q: "A woman friend of mine told me she had a 'tipped' uterus. Is there such a thing?"

A: "Yes. Normally the uterus lies bent forward at a 90° angle to the vagina but in 15 percent of women it lies in the same plane as the vagina or is even displaced backwards. This is called a tipped or retroverted uterus. It may never cause any major problems, but it can occasionally lead to difficulties in getting pregnant and it may be the cause of lower back pain.

"A doctor after making a diagnosis, may try to tip the uterus to its correct position by inserting one hand through the vagina to the uterus, placing the other hand over the pubic area and slightly moving the uterus until it is in place. Another possibility is for the doctor to insert a special device called a pessary, which holds the uterus in its proper place. The insertion of the pessary does not require surgery and it is usually removed several months later after the uterus has been tipped back to its normal position. This straightening out procedure has enabled many women to become pregnant after years of failure; prolapse may in fact be discovered only when a woman seeks help for infertility."

Q: "I have a prolapsed uterus. Is this the same as a tipped uterus?"

A: "No. A prolapsed uterus means the uterus has moved through a supporting wall or structure into a place where it does not belong. A prolapsed uterus is caused by the weakening of the ligaments that support the uterus and hold it in place. A typical prolapsed uterus will move down into the vagina. Prolapse is generally found in older women and can occur following pregnancy which may have weakened supporting ligaments.

"A prolapsed uterus doesn't usually cause pain or interfere with general functioning, including enjoyment of sex. It can occasionally cause problems with passing urine, such as unexpected urination when coughing or laughing, but this can be treated surgically or helped by Kegel Exercises (page 342)."

MYTHS It has been suggested that during orgasm the uterus sucks up semen to help the sperm travel up to the Fallopian tubes. The only movements of the uterus during the sex response cycle are a lifting due to excitation and contractions due to orgasm. There is no sucking action to speed sperm on its way.

AGE During and after menopause, the reduced supply of oestrogen causes the uterus to decrease in size. Also, it no longer enlarges in response to sexual stimulation as it once did. This, too, is a result of the lower oestrogen level in the woman's body.

However, the feelings of sexual excitation, orgasm and fulfilment are *not* interfered with and a woman can enjoy intercourse during and after her menopause as much as she did before.

MENSTRUATION

FACTS From puberty to menopause a woman who is not pregnant will shed the lining of the uterus, the endometrium, every 28 to 30 days, although she may begin as early as every 21 days or as late as every 35 days. This process, called menstruation or the period, usually lasts three to six days, but can be more or less.

From the beginning of menstruation at puberty (the menarche) until menstruation stops in middle age (the menopause), the endometrium, the lining of the womb, prepares itself each month to receive a fertilized egg. The lining will provide the fertilized egg with a nesting place as soon as the egg comes in contact with the uterine wall. If the egg has not been fertilized by a sperm the lining is not needed, so it is shed from the uterus and passes through the cervix and out of the vagina as the menstrual flow. As the lining comes away from the womb wall the tops of the tiny blood vessels that are connected to the lining come away too. That is why the menstrual flow has blood in it.

As soon as the menstrual flow stops, a new lining starts developing to replace the one that has just left the body, in readiness for a fertilized egg in the next cycle. If no egg is fertilized by a sperm during the next cycle, the same shedding of the endometrium occurs, and menstruation takes place again. If a sperm does fertilize an egg, and if the egg does begin its growth in the uterine wall, the endometrium remains in place and the woman will not menstruate again until after the birth of the baby.

Girls who have not been told about menstruation in advance can be thoroughly frightened by the appearance of tissue and blood. It is very important that girls should know the nature and meaning of menstruation, that it is a completely normal experience, and that it signals the beginning of their childbearing years and a new stage in their lives.

Menstruation is controlled by an interplay of the pituitary gland, the hypothalamus, the ovaries, and several hormones. The exact time menstruation begins cannot be predetermined; it may be as early as nine or ten years of age, or it may not be until 15 or 16. It is no better to begin menstruation earlier or later, and menstruation does not mean a girl is more grown up than her friends if she has her period and they do not. The body decides when is the best time. The average age at which girls begin to menstruate is falling slightly in most developed countries — the reason is thought to be better nutrition and increased body weight.

The body also decides when a woman stops menstruating (the menopause), usually between 45 and 55 years of age. The climacteric, of which the menopause is part, is a gradual process, involving a number of physical changes apart from ceasing ovulation.

Q: "Can women participate in sports when they have their periods?"

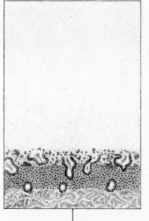

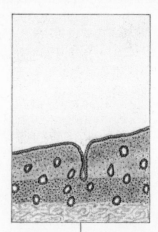

What happens to the lining of the uterus during the menstrual cycle. The inner lining of the uterus, the endometrium, is shed during the menstrual period and then grows again, achieving maximum thickness in time for the next ovulation.

endometrium at the start of menstruation

endometrium re-growing

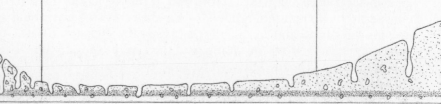

menstruation

A: "Yes, with no risk of any kind of damage. However, because of the way some women feel (and have been taught to feel), they may choose not to engage in sports during their periods."

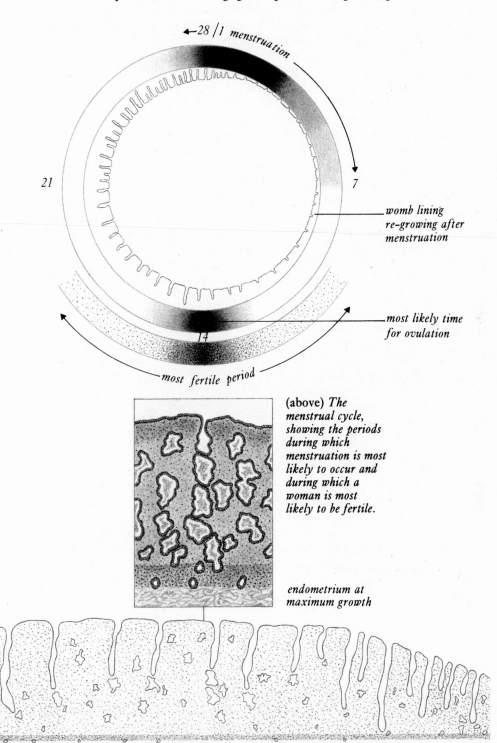

← 28 /1 *menstruation*

21

7

womb lining re-growing after menstruation

14

most likely time for ovulation

most fertile period

(above) *The menstrual cycle, showing the periods during which menstruation is most likely to occur and during which a woman is most likely to be fertile.*

endometrium at maximum growth

ovulation

Q: "Just how much blood do I lose when I have my period? It seems like an awful lot."

A: "The amount of blood lost during menstruation varies from woman to woman. It is difficult to add up the actual amount because it leaves the body mixed with tissue from the uterus, but it appears that women normally pass between one and three ounces of blood. It may be a bit more if you are using an IUD.

"The passing of this amount of blood is not in the least harmful if you are healthy and your diet is adequate."

Q: "What are those things that women use when they have their period?"

A: "Sanitary pads or tampons. Pads (often also called towels) and tampons are made of absorbent cotton and can be bought in various shapes and sizes so that every woman can choose the kind she feels most comfortable with.

"Some sanitary pads are attached to a belt that fits under the clothing and presses the pad against the vagina to absorb the menstrual flow as it leaves through the vagina. Some pads have an adhesive strip that is pressed on the undergarment so it fits gently against the vagina; no belts or pins are needed with this kind.

"Tampons are also widely used. They are tubes of cotton and come in varying sizes (small, medium, large) to fit snugly in the vagina. Some tampons have lubricated tips so that they go in easily, some are inserted with a finger and others have paper, plastic or stick applicators. Each tampon has a short string that hangs out of the vagina to allow the tampon to be removed easily and changed as necessary."

Q: "Can a virgin use a tampon?"

A: "Yes. A tampon can fit inside the vagina even if the woman has not had sexual intercourse. Even with the hymen present, the natural opening that permits the menstrual flow to leave the body usually allows for easy insertion of a tampon. Some women find that using tampons during menstruation leads them to a fuller understanding of their bodies and can help them overcome inhibitions they may have about touching their genitals. That can be a bonus."

Q: "Is there any risk in using tampons?"

A: "There may be. Small numbers of women who regularly use tampons have developed symptoms of a dangerous disease known as Toxic Shock Syndrome. The symptoms are high fever, vomiting, diarrhoea and a sudden, drastic fall in blood pressure which may cause death. The disease is apparently caused by bacteria in the vagina.

"We do not know why the majority of cases of TSS appear to be associated with tampons (in fact, five percent of reported cases are in women who don't use tampons and another five percent are reported in men). The likelihood at the moment is that the superabsorbent tampons that have been available since the late 1970s provide a breeding ground for the bacteria that cause the disease. The majority of cases of TSS have been linked to superabsorbent tampons. The probability is that the older type, less absorbent tampons are safer, perhaps because they are left in the vagina for shorter periods. Sanitary pads are likely to be safer too. Some doctors accordingly advise women to change their tampons every four hours and to use pads at night.

"TSS is not very widespread at this time, but its consequences are so serious that any woman who routinely uses tampons who gets any of the symptoms should consult her doctor immediately."

Q: "Is it safe to have intercourse during menstruation?"
A: "Yes. You can have intercourse during menstruation without any fear of discomfort or illness. There is no medical evidence to indicate that intercourse during menstruation will lead to any emotional or physical problems for either partner."

Q: "My friend says he has sexual intercourse when his wife menstruates and he never has to use any birth control. Is he right?"
A: "It is not possible to become pregnant during menstruation. However, not all vaginal bleeding is due to menstruation, so that unprotected intercourse during these times of vaginal bleeding could lead to pregnancy. Unprotected intercourse during menstruation may mean that your friend is indicating a dissatisfaction with the method of birth control that he and his wife use. This cue needs to be explored by both of them until they find and agree on a better birth control method."

Q: "Should I wash more during my period?"
A: "No. Menstruation does not cause any special odour, so daily washing with mild soap and water is quite sufficient. Undergarments may become stained with a drop of blood from time to time, but you'll be washing them anyway."

Q: "I heard a woman can have her period over within a few minutes by using some new gadget. What is that all about?"
A: "You are probably talking about a method that is known as menstrual extraction. A plastic tube is inserted through the vagina and into the uterus, and gently sucks out the uterine lining and deposits it in an attached collection bottle. Menstrual extraction is done just prior to menstruation and can be completed in a matter of minutes. It's a technique that's used in certain parts of the US, but it is not used much in Britain yet as it is a highly controversial technique. Doctors in the US do not normally perform menstrual extraction, but a small number of women in the United States do practise it as part of some self-help group activities.

"Not having to experience the discomfort of a period for several days is a major advantage — having control over your own body is also an important aspect of this procedure. However, there are several major questions that are still unanswered: How safe are multiple menstrual extractions? Can the cervix and uterus be damaged? Will it interfere with possible future pregnancy? Can nonmedical persons continually provide the sterile conditions and safety necessary?

"Until more reliable medical data become available the probable difficulties of menstrual extraction outweigh its possible advantages, so it should be avoided."

Q: "I heard about a drug that helps prevent menstrual pain. Is one available and how can I get it?"

A: "You are probably referring to a drug called mefenamic acid. It prevents the uterus from contracting and so relieves some women's discomfort during menstruation. It is available under a couple of different brand names and you should discuss with your doctor whether it might be suitable for you. Several other drugs are available, including aspirin, which have a similar effect — again, discuss their suitability for you with your doctor if you feel you need something to relieve your menstrual pain."

Q: "Is it true that women feel more sexy when they are having periods?"

A: "No. In fact, most women report that their sexual drive is at a peak around the time of ovulation."

Q: "My breasts get tender and hurt a bit just before my period. Is this normal?"

A: "Yes, quite normal. It happens because at that time in your cycle your body contains an increased amount of the hormone progesterone, and that causes some congestion of the blood vessels in your breasts."

Q: "I'm 13 and my period is very irregular. Does this mean I have a problem?"

A: "No. During the first couple of years of puberty it is common for menstruation to be irregular. Sometimes your period may last a week or two, or it may occur every two or three weeks and then not begin again for a month or more. Although this irregularity is a nuisance, it is the body's way of getting its normal cycles in order, so you will have a more regular cycle throughout your childbearing and adult years until menopause. Some doctors will prescribe a short-term low-dose hormone tablet to help make you more regular.

"Other doctors however, feel strongly that this is precisely the time to avoid such interference, including birth control pills for contraceptive purposes. Hormonal intervention at this point, they believe, only delays real regularization."

Q: "I've just started getting my period, and I always know when I'm about to get it because that is when I break out with pimples. Just what's going on?"

A: "Yes, this happens to many women. Just prior to your menstrual flow, the natural shifting of hormone levels causes your skin glands (sebaceous glands) to overproduce, and sometimes your pores become clogged with dirt and bacteria causing pimples or acne. Keeping your skin clean, especially around the time of menstruation, may be of some help. Usually, after puberty, when your body has adjusted to the presence of increased amounts of female hormone, the acne decreases."

Q: "I've just lost a lot of weight and my friend said my period will be affected. Is that true?"

A: "If your weight changes by ten percent or more in a short period of time, your cycle may well be affected. An unusual amount of tension or stress can also temporarily affect your period. The use of some drugs — especially tranquillizers or antidepressants — will also change your usual menstrual pattern, as can travel or a change of diet."

MYTHS The following are common myths about menstruation. They have no basis in fact. They are all *absolutely false*.

* hair-washing must be avoided during menstruation, as it will lead to disease
* plants wither and die if touched by a menstruating woman
* menstrual blood is damaging to a penis
* active sports must be avoided when a woman is menstruating
* women should avoid making important decisions just before and during their menstrual flow
* women cannot be trusted with important positions because of their irrational behaviour during menstruation
* you needn't use contraceptives if you have intercourse during menstruation
* by menstruating, women clear their body of dirty blood each month
* menstruation leaves a woman unclean so she should douche right after her period
* menstrual cramps are all in the mind.

FEELINGS How does menstruation make women feel? These are some typical responses: "I feel messy." "I feel generally uncomfortable." "I feel ugly and bloated." "I get all pimply." All negative. It isn't often that you hear a woman say "Oh, it's fine. I feel healthy and normal," or "It makes me feel feminine."

A lot of women suffer some real physical discomfort during their periods, but the figure for those who suffer psychological discomfort is almost certainly higher. They feel, in the biblical word, "unclean." This is because throughout recorded history menstruation has been surrounded by silence, mystery, misunderstanding and ignorance.

A great many girls grow up with the idea that menstruation is a mystery. Their parents don't tell them what it means, they don't show them that it is a natural part of growing up. When a girl has her first period she is likely to be warned "Now you must watch out for men," or "Be sure to keep your legs closed." The mystery that she is just beginning to come to terms with is thus reinforced with negatives and prohibitions. No wonder that many women carry this negative confusion about menstruation right through their lives and probably pass it on to their own daughters. If a great many women can't feel easy about menstruation it is scarcely surprising that men can't either. Hence the widespread idea that because women menstruate they are sometimes "unclean" and therefore inferior.

A major step toward full equality between women and men will be the banishing of the idea that women are inferior because they menstruate. Beginning menstruation signals the start of a new and very important stage in a girl's life; it is a sign of coming of age, and should be celebrated as such. If family and friends can show positive happiness that the girl has reached a significant stage in her growth, the negative confusion that so many people suffer from will be done away with. This is the kind of legacy that, passed from generation to generation, will help women to understand themselves fully and will help men to understand women better.

RELATIONSHIPS People respond to menstruation in all sorts of different ways. Even within a couple, the two partners may respond completely differently.

Some couples find menstruation to be a terrible interference with their sex life and can't wait for it to end. Others, take advantage of the period to have unprotected intercourse which may erode the contraceptive habit and increase the risk of an unplanned pregnancy.

Because they have been taught that menstruation is something dirty and secret, many women feel a need to apologize for their "problem" and hide it. This means no sex of any kind during the woman's period, which some people enjoy because it provides them with a good reason to avoid sexual contact without awkward explanations.

On the positive side, some couples have come to terms with menstruation and do not regard it as a matter of shame and secrecy. They find that intercourse during menstruation is particularly intimate and shows real understanding and support between them.

If menstruation means nothing in a relationship, all well and good. If it has a positive side, so much the better. The negative effect it has on some relationships is quite unnecessary.

Q: "What if you don't like to have intercourse while you are having your period?"

A: "It's entirely up to you and doesn't matter one way or the other. Some women feel crampy, bloated or just not right physically or emotionally when they're menstruating, and some men feel uneasy about putting their penis in a vagina during menstrual flow. Whether you decide to have sex or not during menstruation, as long as the choice is a relationship decision, there probably will be no difficulties. However, most couples are realistic about menstruation and have intercourse or other sexual activities as usual, if they want it, and deal with any slight messiness with little trouble."

CULTURE AND RELIGION In Orthodox Judaism, it is the practice that a man may not sleep with, have sex with, or touch his wife during the days of her menstrual flow, or for the seven clean or "white" days following the last day of her period. Following the last clean day, she takes the ritual cleansing bath, the mikvah, and can then resume her usual relationship with her husband. This ancient custom, still adhered to by Orthodox Jews around the world, is derived from Leviticus, when God instructed Moses that a man should not be near a woman during her "uncleanliness" under punishment of both of them being separated from their people.

The exact reason for this compelling law is not fully understood. There is some speculation that a physical separation and control of the sexual urge leads to a higher level of spirituality for the couple; it may be that this separation serves to sustain physical attraction between the couple; and some feel that this custom is followed to increase the chances of pregnancy, since the time the husband and wife resume intercourse is the most fertile period in her cycle.

The Islamic faithful are similarly instructed by the Koran. Men must keep away from menstruating women, and intercourse can be resumed only when the woman has taken her ritual bath of cleansing.

The ancient Greeks viewed menstruation as a negative time for women. They believed that plants, flowers and vegetables withered if they were touched or looked at by a menstruating woman. They also believed that the touch of a menstruating woman would turn linen black and blade edges dull.

Australian Aboriginal custom dictated that menstruating women were so contaminating they could not step over the head of anyone or over any useful object. Sitting in a canoe or on a chair was prohibited during menstruation. Intercourse during menstruation was also forbidden. If contamination occurred, it could be removed only if the woman was killed.

Early African and Brazilian customs provided for young women to be isolated in a special hut for girls about to menstruate for the first time. After menstruating their bodies were painted, and with ritual dances and chants they were accepted into the adult female community.

In France, if a woman commits a crime during her premenstrual time she can claim, in her defence, temporary impairment of her sanity.

It is interesting to note that women who believe in rather orthodox religious systems like Catholicism and Judaism are more likely to have menstrual difficulties such as irregularity and discomfort than women who believe in religions where menstruation, intercourse and chastity are not tied together in deeply meaningful ways. It is clear that the way a woman is socialized can have an effect on common bodily functions.

PROBLEMS *Dysmenorrhoea.* Women often feel pain or general discomfort around the time of menstruation. Dysmenorrhoea is the medical name for the cramps, back pain and breast tenderness some women experience during menstruation. Premenstrual discomfort — feeling bloated, some weight gain, headache, and so on — is properly known as molimina, but dysmenorrhoea is often used to describe both.

There is no single cause for dysmenorrhoea, but water retention, hormonal imbalance and other chemical reasons are suggested as possible factors. Menstrual pains can also be related to medical problems such as an infection, tumour or endometriosis, so discuss your symptoms with your doctor.

The discomfort and pain of dysmenorrhoea may be helped by birth control pills, eating less salt, taking extra vitamins C and B complex, exercise, sauna or steam baths or having an orgasm. Any woman who wishes to take steps to reduce menstrual discomfort should discuss what is best for her with her doctor.

Irregular Menstruation. Many women do not have absolutely regular periods each cycle. Counting from the first day of one period to the first day of the next, the menstrual flow may begin anytime between the 26th day and the 35th. Unless the menstrual flow is accompanied by extraordinary bleeding or unusual pain, irregularity is not a medical problem. Irregular periods are especially common just after puberty and just prior to menopause.

Another kind of irregularity, which is also common, is missing the occasional period altogether. Almost every woman misses some periods in the course of her life and it is no cause for alarm, as long as it does not signal an unwanted pregnancy. Unusual stress or illness can cause women to miss a period or two; the usual cycle returns once the difficulty has passed. Women who are regularly missing a period — several times a year — should have themselves checked.

Premenstrual Tension. Often known as PMT. Several days to a week before their period is to begin, many women notice a tenderness in their breasts, bloating or fluid retention, and some fatigue and irritability. Premenstrual tensions are real, and whether or not they affect any particular woman, to attribute them to emotional or psychological factors alone is to oversimplify. Premenstrual tension is obviously connected with real physical and chemical changes and may be complicated by cultural factors as well.

Amenorrhoea. When a woman does not have a period (even one) after she has reached puberty she has primary amenorrhoea. If she stops having her period after having a history of menstruation she has secondary amenorrhoea. Amenorrhoea may be due to hormonal imbalance, specific disease of the brain, ovaries or pituitary gland, extensive drug use or emotional stress. It also occurs of course when a woman is pregnant, but then it is normal and not a problem. Amenorrhoea requires a complete medical evaluation.

Hysterectomy

FACTS Hysterectomy is the surgical removal of the uterus, or womb (the Greek word for womb is *hystera*). The surgery is done in one of two ways: either the uterus is removed through an incision in the abdominal area (below the navel), or it is taken out through the vagina. If the cervix is removed along with the rest of the uterus, a total hysterectomy has been performed. If only the upper part is removed, and the cervix remains, it is a subtotal hysterectomy.

A hysterectomy is performed when there is definite evidence of disease or disorder that cannot be cured except by removing the womb. For example: when there is cancer of the cervix or cancer of the lining (endometrium) of the uterus; when abnormal tissue growths (fibroids) in the uterus interfere with normal function; when there is excessive uterine bleeding that does not respond to treatment; or when disease of the ovaries or Fallopian tubes also affects the uterus.

With the uterus removed two events are certain: the woman is sterile — she can no longer have a child — and she will no longer have her menstrual flow.

After a hysterectomy, the ovaries, which continue to produce hormones and ova, and the Fallopian tubes are still attached to structures in the pelvic area as before, so they can't move around. The ova or eggs, which continue to be released until menopause, simply break down naturally, causing no pain or unusual sensations.

There is serious controversy today both in the UK and abroad over the use of hysterectomy as an immediate way to remedy problems that possibly could respond to other nonsurgical methods of treatment. It is already the most common operation among women — in the US 20 to 25 percent of women over the age of 50 have had it done. The projection currently is that about one half of all women now under 65 will have had a hysterectomy by the time they reach that age. Yet studies suggest that a great number of the hysterectomies performed are unnecessary or very questionable. The US has a particularly high hysterectomy rate.

Hysterectomy as the only known remedy for obvious uterine disease is difficult enough for the woman concerned. But women who have had hysterectomies *without* having had severe uterine disease are referred to or seek psychiatric help *twice as frequently*. Hysterectomy as preventive medicine appears to set up serious personality conflicts.

It is always wise to consider all the alternative treatments before any woman agrees to have a hysterectomy.

Q: "Is a hysterectomy like a D&C?"
A: "No. A hysterectomy is the surgical removal of the uterus. A D&C is the spreading of the cervix (dilation), and the gentle scraping of the uterine tissue (curettage), and is a procedure that used to be used to diagnose and treat specific disorders of the uterus. Tissue from the uterus is removed by D&C and examined for indications of cancer, polyps, infertility problems, abnormal uterine bleeding and other associated difficulties.

"D&C has never been used as an alternative to hysterectomy, but it has been used as an early (during the first three months) abortion method. In this procedure, the tissue of the foetus is removed from the walls of the uterus by the curette, a metal loop on the end of a long thin handle. D&C has been largely replaced by another method, called vacuum aspiration."

Q: "Don't your hormones stop after a hysterectomy? A friend told me she got menopause after her operation."

A: "No. Your hormones do not stop after a hysterectomy. Remember, hormones are produced and released mainly by the ovaries, and the ovaries are not removed in a hysterectomy. Generally, only the uterus, or the uterus and cervix, are removed in a hysterectomy, and they do not produce or control hormones.

"It sounds like your friend had her ovaries removed in a procedure called oopharectomy. This surgery is performed when there is a major disease (like cancer) of the ovaries. When both ovaries are removed the woman no longer receives the major portion of her natural supply of the hormone oestrogen. Although other glands, like the adrenals, try to help out, the total amount of oestrogen decreases, and this often produces some of the symptoms of menopause.

"In cases where both ovaries are removed, the degree to which early menopause symptoms appear varies widely from woman to woman. The physical and mental well-being of the woman play an important, not yet fully understood role in these situations, making it very difficult to generalize about what is likely to occur after surgery of this kind.

"In order to deal with the anticipated or actual menopausal symptoms that may occur after removal of both ovaries, some doctors prescribe regular doses of oestrogen in pill form (known as HRT — Hormone Replacement Therapy). This practice is extremely controversial, as many doctors and researchers claim a relationship between the use of this drug and increasing rates

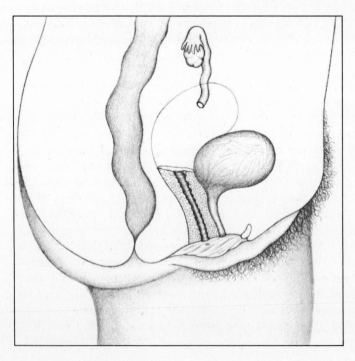

A total hysterectomy, with an indication of the position the uterus occupied before surgery. The Fallopian tubes remain where they always were because they are attached to other body structures.

of cancer in women. It may be advisable to obtain more than one medical opinion before the routine use of this drug. Women can read the available literature on this topic and prepare themselves to ask their doctors the proper questions regarding their condition, the treatment, and possible outcomes of the treatment. This will enable them to make more informed decisions."

Q: "What happens to your sex life after a hysterectomy?"
A: "Sexual interest and drive, and the ability to have orgasm, are not affected by hysterectomy. In fact, it is likely that sexual pleasure and response may increase after hysterectomy, since a source of disease or a cause of ill health has been removed, which may result in a sense of sexual reawakening. It is reasonable to assume that if intercourse and other lovemaking was happy and pleasant before hysterectomy, the same kind of enjoyment and pleasure should continue afterwards. Also, since the vagina is not seriously affected by the hysterectomy, there should be no concern or fear about the male penis hurting the vagina or internal organs. The physical sensations during intercourse remain the same for both the man and the woman. When sexual problems occur after the operation, it is very likely that they existed before surgery, so the cause is usually in the relationship, and not in the surgery.

   "Sometimes, sexual problems that are emotional in origin can occur after a hysterectomy. Not being able to have a child may make a woman feel she is no longer complete and her interest in, and responsiveness to, sexual activity may be affected by this feeling of incompleteness and loss of self-esteem. Following a hysterectomy, a male partner may have similar negative feelings about his wife or lover. Obviously, these feelings affect the relationship generally and sexual behaviour specifically, and they need to be worked through by the couple themselves or, with the help of a qualified person."

Q: "Is it true that some women use hysterectomy as a permanent birth control method?"
A: "Some women, who for religious or cultural reasons will not use any artificial birth control measures and who have found natural birth control methods unhelpful, may see hysterectomy as the only sure way to gain protection from pregnancy. This very extreme and potentially dangerous action calls attention to the real need for a better public understanding of currently available birth control techniques. It is much commoner in the US than elsewhere.

   "Hysterectomy as a birth control method is a radical and unnecessary measure. While it is true that the removal of the uterus leads to sterility, there are many birth control methods available that do not involve major surgery and the risks associated with any kind of organ removal. If a woman wishes to be made sterile, tubal ligation is just as effective and much safer."

MYTHS In a hysterectomy, the uterus and ovaries are removed. *False*. Hysterectomy does *not* involve removal of the ovaries — only of the uterus. Removal of the ovaries is called oophorectomy and is done only when there is disease of the ovaries.

Hysterectomy results in advanced ageing. *False*. Ageing is ageing, and the removal of the uterus does not stimulate the ageing process.

Hysterectomy interferes with a woman's sex life. *False*. Sexual interest, sexual desire, sexual response and sexual pleasure are not affected by hysterectomy. Just the reverse may be true, as many women report increased sexual interest when accidental pregnancy and menstruation are no longer possible.

Hysterectomy is required if a woman "has too much sex." *False*. There is absolutely no relationship between sexual activity and the sort of disease or injury to the uterus which would require hysterectomy.

Hysterectomy masculinizes a woman. *False*. Just because the uterus is removed a woman does not lose her femininity and start to take on male qualities.

FEELINGS Mild depression is common after a hysterectomy, but in most cases it soon disappears. Some women, however, find it difficult to regain their sense of self-worth. They doubt both their femininity and their ability to return to their life as it was before the operation. Stress with husband, children and friends may well result and may threaten family harmony. Professional help is needed if these symptoms persist.

It is clear that women who have had a hysterectomy as the way to manage a uterine disease or disorder, and who have been completely informed about the procedure along with their husband or partner, show the best results emotionally, both in themselves and in their relationships.

RELATIONSHIPS If a woman is involved in a relationship, it is important to the outcome of the treatment that her partner be involved from the outset in all discussions with the doctors. A full understanding of the nature of the operation and of the short- and long-term results will enable the partner to provide more support and understanding; the evidence of that care and love can speed, or at least ease, recovery.

Many women feel that a hysterectomy strikes at the very core of their femininity. Society has decreed that a woman's principal role is to bear children, and the loss of that ability can so damage her self-esteem that her relationships become difficult.

Husbands, too, sometimes react negatively to their wives' loss of that potent symbol of womanhood. Several studies suggest that husbands of women who have had a hysterectomy show evidence of emotional difficulty and are likely to seek professional help several years after the operation. This is especially true of the men who were not involved in the discussions and decision-making that preceded the surgery.

7 Fallopian Tubes

There are two Fallopian tubes, about four inches long, attached to each side of the upper portion of the uterus. Each leads to an ovary. The

Fallopian tubes (they are named after Gregorio Fallopio, the sixteenth-century anatomist who first described them) are quite narrow (one to two millimetres) and are the passageways that allow an ovum or egg from the ovary to reach the uterus or womb. The Fallopian tubes are not attached to the ovaries but surround and envelop them at their upper end. The upper ends of the Fallopian tubes are open and look like the head of a trumpet with a fringed rim (the fringes are called "fimbriae"). When it is released from the ovary, the ovum or egg is drawn or swept into the opening of the Fallopian tube and begins its movement downward toward the uterus, which is at the other end of the tube.

The walls of the Fallopian tubes are filled with hairlike structures called cilia, which contract slightly along with the tubes, and assist the ovum in moving toward the uterus. It is interesting to note that any sperm in the Fallopian tubes must move or swim against the downward tide or current of the cilia. Therefore, only the most mature, developed sperm can make the journey. This is the body's way of ensuring that if fertilization does take place, there is a good chance that a healthy pregnancy will occur.

Fertilization — that is, when a sperm and ovum meet and connect — usually occurs in the upper portion of a Fallopian tube. Occasionally Fallopian tubes get blocked — this situation is dealt with under Infertility (page 203); sometimes a fertilized ovum gets stuck in a Fallopian tube and develops there. This is called an ectopic pregnancy.

8 Ovaries

FACTS Women have two ovaries, one on each side of the upper part of the uterus. They are located well below each side of the navel or belly button, and are not directly connected to the uterus or Fallopian tubes. They are held in place by ovarian ligaments.

The ovaries are almond shaped, about $1\frac{1}{2}$ inches long, $\frac{3}{4}$ inch thick and 1 inch wide. The ovaries have two important functions: through the process called ovulation they release ova or eggs, which can be fertilized by sperm from a man; they also produce female hormones called oestrogen and progesterone. Oestrogen is crucial for sexual development, progesterone is very important for pregnancy. These hormones are passed directly from the ovaries into the bloodstream.

A woman is born with approximately 200,000 ova or eggs in each ovary (*ovum* is Latin for "egg"; *ova* is plural). Between 300 and 500 of these ova will be released during a woman's reproductive years. Each ovum is contained in a follicle, a cavity in which the immature egg can rest. When the egg matures, it rises though the cavity and is released from the ovary into the Fallopian tube on that side. Ripening of the follicles so that they can release ova starts at puberty, when one follicle from either the right ovary or the left releases an ovum into a Fallopian tube. This process is called ovulation, and occurs approximately once every four weeks from puberty to menopause. During the time a woman is pregnant, ovulation does not occur; it resumes its regular pattern though shortly after the birth of the baby.

Q: "I think I know when I am ovulating. Is that unusual?"

A: "No. You are among the women who can feel the ovum or egg leaving their ovary each cycle.

"Some women feel it as a cramp, slight pain or twinge. This event is known as *Mittelschmerz* or 'middle pain' since ovulation usually occurs at around the midpoint of each woman's menstrual cycle."

Q: "Can a young woman have a period but never ovulate?"
A: "Yes, it quite often happens for the first year or so after a girl starts to menstruate. Thereafter it is very unusual, but certain emotional or hormonal problems can prevent ovulation. Denial of her femininity, or deep dependency on her parents may trigger this reaction. Counselling with a psychologist may help, if this is the cause."

Q: "Can a doctor check my ovaries without inserting any device?"
A: "Yes. When you have your regular pelvic examination, your doctor does a bimanual examination of your ovaries. Using both hands, the doctor palpates or presses on your ovaries and feels for size, shape and any mass that may be growing there. This is a routine and desirable check."

Q: "What is an ovarian cyst?"
A: "An ovarian cyst is an abnormal growth in an ovary containing a collection of fluid. Ovarian cysts are fairly common and generally do not cause pain. They may disappear by themselves or they may need to be removed by surgery.

"Usually only the cyst will be removed; the rest of the ovary then remains healthy, and normal menstruation and reproductive functioning continue. Simple drainage of the cyst may be performed by passing an instrument up through the vagina to reach the diseased ovarian tissue. This procedure is called culdoscopy. The cyst on the ovary may also be reached through an incision in the navel (laparoscopy). Both these methods avoid the necessity for major abdominal surgery. The ovaries should not be removed unless there is a very good reason for doing so."

Q: "Is it true that breastfeeding completely stops ovulation?"
A: "No. This is a misunderstanding that has led to many unintended pregnancies. At first, breastfeeding delays the onset of ovulation, but it soon begins again, so use a contraceptive as soon as you begin to have intercourse after the birth of your baby."

Q: "What is female castration?"
A: "Oophorectomy (or ovariectomy), the removal of both ovaries, is also called female castration. It is performed only when the ovaries are diseased and cannot be treated in any other way. Oophorectomy makes the woman sterile, of course, and it also removes the main source of the hormone oestrogen. Oophorectomy does not interfere with interest in, or enjoyment of, sex."

Q: "What if only one ovary is removed?"

A: "One ovary or even a piece of one ovary is sufficient to allow a follicle to release an ovum or egg during each cycle. The egg can become fertilized by a male sperm, and lead to a natural and healthy pregnancy and birth. A fascinating and wonderful mystery of the body is how it sends messages to all organs and structures when changes need to be made. For example, when two ovaries are functioning, there is usually a pattern of one ovary releasing an egg during some cycles, and the other ovary releasing an egg during the remaining cycles. This ovulation pattern varies from woman to woman, but when one ovary is removed the other simply takes over the entire job of ovulation and releases an ovum each month, so the woman has her periods just as before. Each ovary contains about 200,000 eggs, so there can never be a shortage."

MYTHS The following statements about ovaries are false:

* ovaries do not work after abortion
* ovulation is regular and predictable
* some women are sterile because they ran out of eggs
* you are sterile if one ovary is removed
* as long as you keep breastfeeding, you can't ovulate.

Anyone who believes any of these and acts accordingly could very easily become a parent.

AGE Ovulation, the releasing of an egg each month, generally begins between the ages of ten and 14; the majority of young girls start to ovulate at 12, 13 or 14. It often happens that a young girl begins to menstruate, but doesn't ovulate for several cycles. These are called anovulatory cycles, and are quite normal in girls at puberty. Ovulation usually stops sometime between the ages of 45 and 50. There are women who stop ovulating earlier than 45 and some who continue ovulating after 50 — these are normal variations and they do not indicate a problem or disease, nor do they interfere with sexual interest or performance.

III BREASTS

FACTS There are three important aspects of women's breasts: they often give erotic pleasure, they have a large part to play in shaping a woman's self-image, and a woman can feed a baby with them. Men's breasts can give erotic pleasure, but they have little influence on self-image.

It is a normal reaction to stimulation for a woman's nipples to erect. Until menopause, if she has not breastfed a child, her breasts will increase in size too, as extra blood swells the veins. Men's breasts do not increase in size under stimulation but a little more than 50 percent of men have noticeable nipple erection. Being naked and cold may also quite often cause the nipples to stiffen.

Women's breasts are made up in the following way. On the outside there are **1 nipples**, each surrounded by **2 areolae**. Inside there are **3 milk glands**, which produce milk after delivery of a child, and **4 milk ducts**, which convey milk from the milk glands to the nipples. The remainder of the breasts is composed of fatty tissue and fibrous connective tissue that binds the breasts together and gives them shape.

1 Nipples. Nipples may point out prominently, they may have a flattened appearance, they may be set a bit deeper in the breast or they can be inverted. The normal range of variety in appearance is large. The milk ducts leading from the mammary glands in each breast converge and empty into the nipple, allowing a baby to suckle. Each nipple is supplied with nerve endings, which make it very sensitive to touch. The thin muscle fibers present in each nipple enable it to become erect during sexual excitement, and in response to other stimuli such as cold. Just as one breast is often slightly larger than the other so too some women find that when sexually aroused or cold one nipple will become more erect than the other.

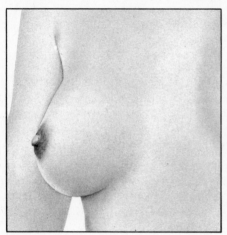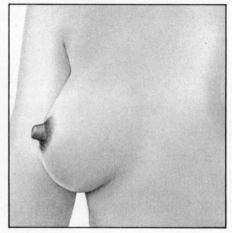

The same nipples in their normal state (left) *and erect* (right).

2 Areolae. The areola (plural: areolae) is the darker pigmented area around each nipple; its colour varies from woman to woman. It is quite normal to have small bumps in the areola — they are oil-producing glands that secrete a lubricant to make breastfeeding easier. During pregnancy the areolae become darker and remain that way to a degree after pregnancy. The size of the areolae varies from person to person.

3 Milk Glands. Inside each breast are 15 to 25 small milk-producing sacs. The milk they produce passes through ducts to the nipple, ready for the baby to suckle. Regardless of breast size, the milk glands are about the same size in each woman and they produce about the same amount of milk.

4 Milk Ducts. These ducts connect the milk glands in each breast to the nipple. The milk is produced in the glands, passes through the ducts and collects around the nipple. The baby then sucks the milk from the breast.

Milk is produced in response to the action of two hormones, prolactin and oxytocin. Prolactin stimulates the milk glands to make milk, and as a baby suckles, more prolactin is released into the bloodstream to cause more milk to be produced. Oxytocin causes the milk to move from the glands to the nipples in the process called "let down." Sometimes a newborn baby does not suckle vigorously enough during the first day or two, so insufficient amounts of oxytocin are released into the bloodstream and "let down" is inadequate. Once the mother and baby learn the breastfeeding routine, everything works out properly.

The breasts produce a further substance, colostrum. Colostrum is not milk, but it is extremely nutritious. It is thick and yellowish and is liable to drip from the nipples occasionally during the final weeks of pregnancy.

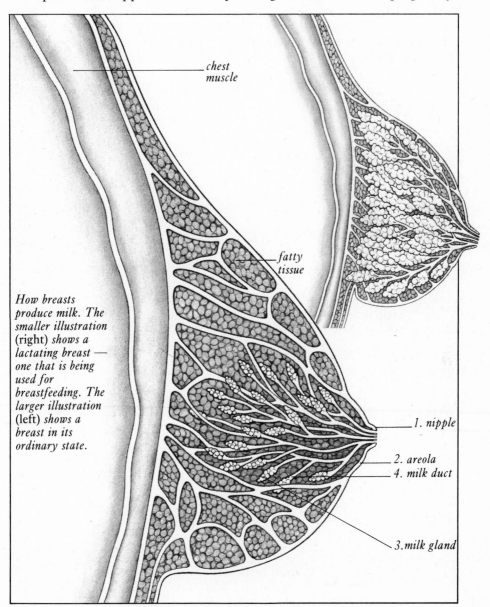

chest muscle

fatty tissue

How breasts produce milk. The smaller illustration (right) shows a lactating breast — one that is being used for breastfeeding. The larger illustration (left) shows a breast in its ordinary state.

1. nipple

2. areola
4. milk duct

3. milk gland

Babies feed on colostrum for the first few days, until the proper milk flow arrives. Not only is colostrum rich in proteins but it also contains important antibodies and the baby thereby gets protection against certain diseases to which newborn children are particularly liable.

Q: "I have hair round my breasts. Do I have a hormone problem?"

A: "No. Many women have hair around their nipples. It is a perfectly normal part of your genetic inheritance. Many women accept the appearance of hair on the nipples as they accept pubic hair or leg hair, though some women remove it for cosmetic reasons. If you decide to remove yours, do it carefully as it is easy to irritate sensitive breast tissue."

Q: "Do women produce milk all the time?"

A: "No. Milk starts to be produced only when a woman is pregnant. The milk-producing glands in her breasts respond to the particular hormone changes that occur during pregnancy, and by the time the baby is born the woman will be ready to give milk. She will continue producing milk as long as the baby is breast-feeding."

Q: "I don't get any thrills from having my breasts fondled or kissed. Am I normal?"

A: "Yes, you are. A lot of women find that they get very little erotic pleasure from their breasts, despite popular belief that all women do. It is often the case that a woman's breasts do more to turn her partner on than they do for her."

Q: "My breasts really get sore and swell up just before my period. Is that normal?"

A: "Yes, it happens to a lot of women. The shift in hormone levels and fluid build up and retention are the chief causes. If you avoid excessive salt, alcohol and refined carbohydrates, you may feel some relief."

Breast Size Because of the enormous importance we attach to breasts, their size and shape, many women worry that their breasts are too small, too large, or just the "wrong" shape. As a culture, we often think of breasts as sex objects, not as living parts of someone's body, and that gives rise to all sorts of anxieties.

The fact is that breasts vary just as much as faces — and for the same reason: that we are all unique. Occasionally — and only occasionally — surgery is desirable to reduce the size of uncomfortably large breasts. Only very rarely is there justification for surgery to increase the size of a woman's breasts. Both reduction and enlargement are dealt with under PROBLEMS on page 380.

Q: "What is the normal breast size?"

A: "There is no normal size. Breast size and shape are determined by heredity, but remember that regardless of size and shape

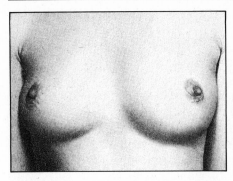
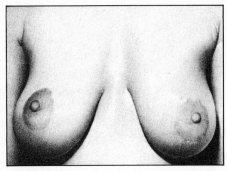

It is impossible to tell anything from the size and shape of a woman's breasts. These six pairs

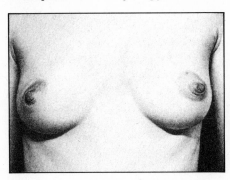
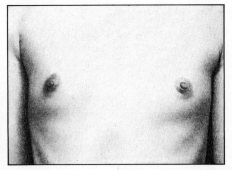

all look very different, but in fact they all belong to 24-year-old women living in the same city.

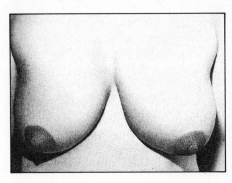
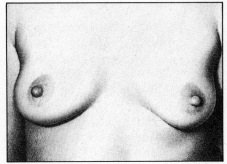

almost every woman can breastfeed, and many can be aroused by touch as well."

Q: "Can exercise increase the size of my breasts?"
A: "No and yes. No amount of exercise can increase the amount of breast tissue you naturally possess, but exercise can thicken the chest muscles (pectoral muscles) and firm up the breasts, making some change in their measurement."

Q: "A friend of mine is taking the pill to make her breasts larger. Does that work?"
A: "It may. There is a slight increase in some women who take the oral contraceptive, but any benefit she may feel from it should

not disguise the fact that she is being manipulated by 'big breast' propaganda."

Q: "My lover just started to take the pill to regulate her period, and I've noticed her breasts have enlarged, and she complains of tenderness. Is this common, or is there a problem?"

A: "It is quite common. A lot of women find that in the first few months of using oral contraceptives their breasts become tender. If the discomfort is severe, she should consult a doctor. Perhaps a different pill will overcome the problem. Slight breast enlargement is also common among women who use the pills. She should consult a doctor though if her breasts enlarge so much she needs to change bra size."

Q: "I'm 15, overweight and very busty. One of my friends in the same situation lost weight and has these terrible stretch marks around her breasts. What can I do to avoid this?"

A: "Just because your friend developed stretch marks does not mean you will too. The simple fact is that some women are born with a more elastic skin than others. Those with an elastic skin remain free of stretch marks while those unlucky enough to have less elastic skin may develop stretch marks. Fortunately, these blemishes become paler and less noticeable with time."

Q: "What is a wet nurse? I've read about them in novels."

A: "A wet nurse is a woman who breastfeeds another woman's baby. Wet nurses are no longer used as frequently as they used to be, probably because bottle-feeding is now so safe and easy. They were women who had had a baby and breastfed it, and then kept the flow of milk going by continually having someone else's baby at the breast. They were used when the real mother had difficulty producing milk, and they were also used by upper-class women who thought that breastfeeding was not for them — they handed their babies over to nurses and nannies to be brought up. In colonial America, for example, slaves often wet-nursed landowners' babies."

Q: "Can a woman have an orgasm by breast stimulation alone?"

A: "Yes. Masters and Johnson found that a very small percentage of women can do this, but it is not sufficiently arousing for most women. It seems that in general it is partners who get more turned on by breasts."

MYTHS Because breasts have achieved such enormous importance as sex symbols, there are numerous common myths about them. Each of these is totally wrong:

* larger breasts mean a woman is sexually active
* breastfeeding causes breasts to sag
* jumping rope as a teenager causes breasts to sag

* breast cancer is caused by a bruise or blow to the breast
* a "real" woman's breasts stand out and her nipples protrude
* smaller breasts are not good for breastfeeding
* women aren't really concerned about their breast size — it's only men that care
* hair around her breasts means a woman is manly
* breastfeeding changes the shape of breasts permanently
* women with smaller breasts are less interested in sex
* men are always attracted to women with larger breasts
* women do not get any feeling from touching their own breasts
* all women enjoy having their breasts stimulated
* men who enjoy having their nipples touched are homosexual.

AGE Women's breasts begin to develop at puberty; oestrogen, a hormone produced by the ovaries, causes the nipples to bud and the milk glands and fatty tissue to grow. Breast development is often uneven, in that one may start to develop before the other, and no-one can say precisely when it will happen as there is no set order in which the events of puberty occur.

Under stimulation, a woman's nipples will normally erect, though the extent of the erection varies widely from person to person. A woman who has not breastfed and who has not yet reached menopause will probably experience some increase in breast size as she becomes sexually excited. The veins will become more obvious and the areolae will enlarge too and become darker. This is due to vasocongestion, an increased blood flow — just the same thing as happens to her vagina. After menopause women still have nipple erection, but there is no increase in the size of the breasts, whether they have had children or not.

During pregnancy the areolae and nipples darken. Breast size increases rapidly during the first three months, so much so that most women have to change to a larger bra. At this time, a number of women report that their breasts feel tender when they are sexually excited.

A little over 50 percent of men report nipple erection when they are excited (but no increase in breast size), though they tend to lose this characteristic after the age of 55 or so.

Q: "My daughter's breasts started to develop a bit when she was three years old. Is anything wrong?"

A: "Probably not. Have your doctor check your daughter to see if her hormone level is proper for her age. It probably is, so don't alarm your daughter or make her feel self-conscious or abnormal. Puberty will occur as usual and development will be normal. If your daughter's hormone level is higher than it should be for her age, a hormone specialist (an endocrinologist) should be consulted.

"As a special case, it has happened that small children have eaten someone's birth control pills. Check that this is not the case with your daughter, but check with your doctor anyway."

Q: "My 11-year-old daughter's left nipple is developed and the other one hasn't. Is that a problem?"

A: "No. Sometimes one breast will begin to develop sooner than the other. We don't know why this happens but we do know that it is not unusual. The other breast will probably catch up in size by age 15 or so. Reassure your daughter if she is concerned and try to prevent her from feeling too self-conscious about it."

Q: "I'm 13 and my breasts haven't begun to grow yet. I'm ashamed to go to a doctor and I'm worried."

A: "It is natural to worry when your breasts haven't developed when you want them to. You need to be patient for a bit because your body has its own timetable that triggers breast growth, and your time will come soon. If you go to a doctor, she or he will tell you to try to relax and allow your biological clock to respond in its own way. Incidentally, many adult women will remember the time when they were younger and felt the way you do now, and soon afterwards they felt the relief you will when their breasts developed."

Q: "I'm 14 and flat chested. One of my friends told me to wear a padded bra. I just don't know what to do."

A: "Wearing a padded bra ('falsies' as they are sometimes known)

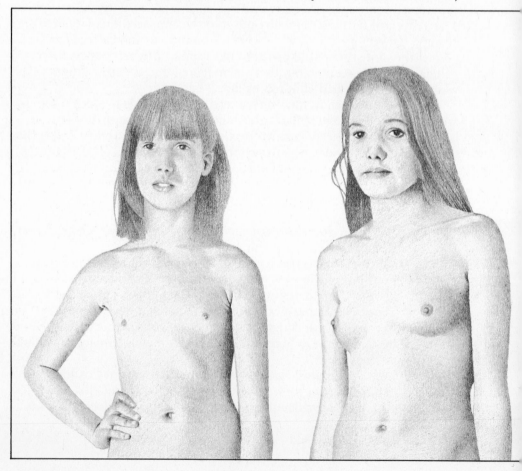

may give you some temporary comfort. Padded bras have been used by many women who weren't satisfied with their breast size. However, in your case you still have several years of development ahead of you. It may very well be that your natural breast development hasn't been triggered yet. Remember also it is important for you to accept your own unique shape. Only you can look the way you do, and becoming content with your individuality will help your growing self-image and your ability to relate to others."

Q: "My brother is 15 and his breasts look like they have grown a little. Is that normal?"

A: "Yes. Around puberty the breasts of many boys do develop slightly. This is called gynaecomastia and is probably due to very small amounts of oestrogen in their bodies. As puberty goes on, hormone levels settle down and other parts of the body grow to balance up any breast increase."

RELATIONSHIPS

"I used my breasts in relationships, they gave me power."

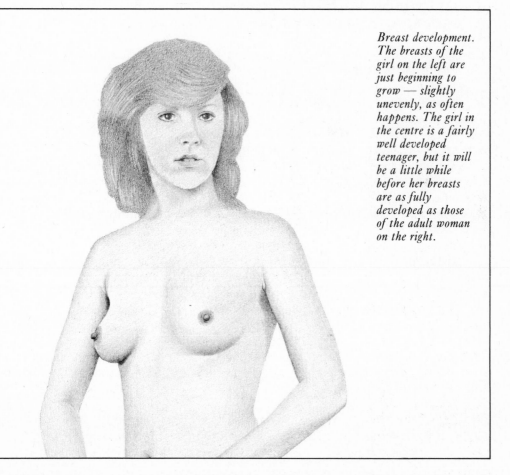

Breast development. The breasts of the girl on the left are just beginning to grow — slightly unevenly, as often happens. The girl in the centre is a fairly well developed teenager, but it will be a little while before her breasts are as fully developed as those of the adult woman on the right.

"I felt nobody would want to go out with me because I was flat chested."

"As I got older the importance of my breasts, and especially how other people felt about them, really diminished."

"I felt men liked me only for my breasts."

"I'm a breast man, so it is important for me to be in a relationship with a woman with big breasts."

"Guys really started to go out with me when my breasts developed."

"For years I didn't want to expose my breasts because I was afraid to be judged by my lovers."

"I think her breasts were more of an issue to her than to me."

"As I learned to accept myself as a woman I didn't care how others liked my breasts or any other part of me."

"Although her breasts were important to me when we were first together, our relationship has become much deeper."

"Sometimes I get a sad feeling when I look at my sagging breasts — but life goes on."

One can see from these comments how the significance of breasts varies from person to person, and from relationship to relationship. There is also a distinct connection between the significance people attach to breasts and their stage in the life cycle. It is not unusual for young women to be seriously concerned about their breast size and shape as predictors of whether they can become involved in a relationship. Some young women overcome feelings of anxiety and inadequacy by using their breasts as lures or as weapons in relationships. Men sometimes assign such importance to the size of a woman's breasts that just that one attribute may be the reason for starting a relationship — even for continuing one.

Although these values linger in some people, most are able to move beyond the simple physical aspects of a relationship. The beginning of this wisdom is the ability to accept yourself completely, recognizing that the kind of a person you are arises from the deepest parts of your personality and not from a single part of your body. This is not easy when, as now, society's messages about who is successful in relationships concentrate on superficial, cosmetic aspects and not on people's more fundamental qualities. Even if it is difficult, it is one of the keys to a mature, lasting, fulfilling relationship.

CULTURE Ours is a culture in which "tits sell." The notion has overwhelmed advertising and the media. It has also made breasts perhaps the most compelling symbol of womanhood, sexiness and desirability.

Despite the statements of many women who say they really aren't concerned about their own breast size, and similar protests from men regarding the relative lack of importance of women's breasts, the evidence is that breast size and shape matter enormously to a great many people. Breasts affect self-esteem, relationships — in fact sexuality in general — to a profound degree: "It's what's up front that counts."

"To men a man is but a mind,
who cares what face he carries or
what form he wears?
But woman's body is the woman."
      Ambrose Bierce, *The Devil's Dictionary*

Unfortunately, many women (and men) feel that breasts need to be a certain size and shape in order to fit our culture's current standards of beauty and desirability. Standards change from decade to decade, so that recently we have gone from pointed bras and the sweater look of the 1950s to bralessness or natural-look bras in the 1960s and 70s. Large breasts are sometimes in style, then smaller breasts, full looks, and understated looks, and so on. Women rush to keep in style and many men expect that the women with whom they relate will do so. Whether the need to change is commercially inspired or not, a great many people obviously feel that this is what they should do, however arbitrary it may seem.

Young girls express very strong feelings about their breast development. "When will it begin for me?" "Will I be flat chested?" "Will I have enough hormones?" "Will I look funny?"

It is natural to want to develop properly, but such self-questioning also reflects the pressures young people feel to fit in and be like the popular image of sexy women. Of course they would like their breasts to be just right, but achieving that ideal is not something many young girls believe will happen to them.

At the same time that girls are beginning to worry privately about their breasts, family members and contemporaries start to comment and show a greater interest in their general development, but especially in their breasts. Imagine the feelings of humiliation when a parent, a brother or a sister points out the 12-year-old girl's two tiny mosquito bites. On the other hand, having well-developed breasts can signal comments from peers about alleged early sexual activity and this leads some girls to overdo intellectual and academic interests as a compensation. Not being an early developer can lead to embarrassment and self-consciousness, and perhaps a withdrawal from relationships with friends. Of course, some young girls develop at their own pace without too much fuss being made about size and shape, and some young girls are very fortunate in being able to see their friends naked while changing for sporting events. This helps them to realize how varied breast size, shape and development can be.

During this period boys become very interested indeed in breasts, and sometimes obsessed with them. This comes from their own growing sexual interest but is also greatly influenced by our social and media attitudes; it is the beginning of how boys become "breast men." Around puberty boys and girls also learn the accepted synonyms for breasts — tits, jugs, boobs, knockers, bazooms, headlights, bristols. By the time they have done that, they are well on the road to absorbing the breast lore that Western cultures are saddled with.

Much breast lore says that women's breasts are singularly sensitive to erotic touch, but some women find that this is not so, which may lead them to worry about their normality. At the same time men seem to be very interested in breasts, and one must wonder who this interest is for. Men are truly shocked if they discover that all the time they may have been spending on their partners' breasts gave pleasure to themselves alone.

Some people by the time they reach adulthood are imprisoned by conventional ideas about what is normal, average, sexy. And in some cases women will have their breasts enlarged, reduced or shaped in a certain way to please someone else. It is true that this kind of surgery may positively influence a woman and her self-image, and I am sympathetic to the meaning and importance of self-esteem. But I believe it stands out as a poor reflection on the character of a culture, when any person must alter her or his physical appearance to conform to the changeable standard of a society, in order to gain acceptance from others and a sense of personal value.

PROBLEMS Problems that can occur with breasts fall into two categories. The more common, by far, is **lumps**. The less common is anxieties over **breast size** that affect a woman's mental health or prevent her from leading a fulfilling life.

Breast Lumps When a woman discovers a lump in her breast, she isn't much comforted to know that 75 to 80 percent of lumps are benign and not cancerous. She is likely to be flooded with anxiety. She may hope that it will not be there tomorrow, that it will just go away. Ultimately, though, she will see her doctor, as she should. When she does, she will probably be examined in one of the following ways:

Mammography. This is an X-ray of the breast which allows the doctor to evaluate the size, nature and depth of the lump. This test can detect breast tissue changes before they form a lump or before it spreads, but the risks of being exposed to X-rays prevent mammography from being used for routine screening.

Thermography. A temperature survey of all parts of the breast — it is quite safe. Cancer causes an increased blood flow to the area affected and therefore a higher temperature at that place. Thermography avoids the need for radiation, but it is not an absolutely accurate technique.

Needle Biopsy. Often done in the specialist's surgery with a local pain killer. The doctor inserts a needle into the breast and draws out fluid from the lump. The lump may break down or collapse immediately, indicating it was a fluid cyst. The fluid will be sent to a pathologist for examination. Usually this type of cyst is benign and soon disappears.

Surgical Biopsy. This is a surgical procedure usually done under general anaesthesia, although local anaesthesia can sometimes be used if the patient

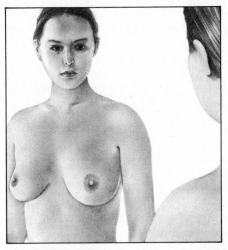
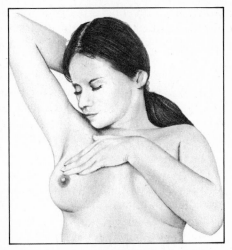

Examining your breasts for lumps: first check in the mirror for any irregularities,

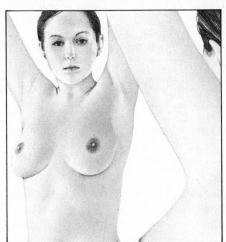
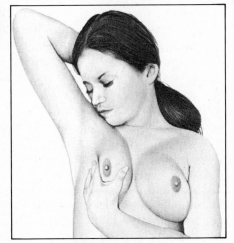

starting hands by sides, then hands raised, then hands on hips; next feel each breast

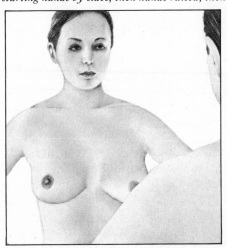
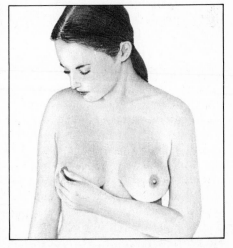

in turn in a spiral motion and finally squeeze each nipple to check for discharge.

prefers. An incision is made in the breast and the lump is removed, leaving a scar on the breast about an inch or two long. The operation does not change the shape of the breast. The tissue from the lump is then analyzed by a pathologist for the presence of any abnormal cells. If the tissue is benign, the major concern is over and a routine treatment for the lump will be conducted. If the tissue is malignant (cancerous) the woman can discuss the type of surgery and/or other treatment she requires for her situation. The short delay in scheduling new treatment after a decision does not complicate future treatment or affect the likelihood of recovery.

Frozen Section. Tissue is taken from a suspicious area, frozen immediately and examined to determine if it is benign or cancerous. This can be done in 15 minutes, but it is not as reliable as the routine pathologist's examination, which takes a day or two. When possible, the standard, longer tissue examination and diagnosis should be done.

Many women elect to have only a biopsy first and then surgery, if required, at a later date. This gives an opportunity to discuss the operation and allows the woman to prepare herself and her family for her surgery.

Noncancerous Lumps Seventy-five to 80 percent of breast lumps are not cancerous. These are the two common benign conditions:

Fibroadenoma. This is a tumour made up of gland tissue and fibrous cells. It is firm, round, painless and movable, and is common in younger women (15–40). Fibroadenomas may indicate a higher risk of cancer later in life, although this is not certain.

Fibrocystic Disease. These are painful cysts and produce a sense of fullness in the breast. The cysts contain fluid, which can be drawn off (aspirated) in the doctor's surgery if they grow large. The symptoms tend to be more obvious just before menstruation when the body generally retains fluid; they diminish after the period. As with fibroadenomas, the presence of fibrocysts may suggest a greater risk of developing cancer later in life.

Cancerous Lumps Lumps in the breast that are cancer feel solid, painless and they don't move. They may appear in any part of the breast.

Mastectomy, the surgical removal of the breast, is the most common form of treatment for breast cancer. There are several different types of mastectomy:

Radical Mastectomy. This is an old treatment for breast cancer and involves the removal of the entire breast, the chest muscles in that area, and the surrounding lymph nodes. This method has become very controversial and doctors and patients are questioning its long-term effectiveness compared with other, less severe types of surgery.

Modified Radical Mastectomy. In this operation the breast, near and superficial lymph nodes are removed, but not the chest muscles.

Total or Simple Mastectomy. This is the removal of the breast alone. Lymph nodes and muscle tissue remain untouched.

Lumpectomy. The removal of the lump and the minimum of surrounding tissue — occasionally called a tumourectomy. This is a rather new method of treating a cancerous lump and it is very controversial, as many doctors feel it is not enough to halt the reappearance or spread of the disease. The same objections are raised to:

Partial Mastectomy. In this procedure more tissue is removed than in a lumpectomy — as much as half the breast may be taken away.

Then there are three nonsurgical methods of treatment:

Chemotherapy. Chemotherapy is the use of powerful drugs that kill cancer cells. It may be used after breast surgery or later, should the cancer reappear, and should only be given at a special cancer clinic.

Radiation Therapy. Generally, this treatment is used in addition to mastectomy. Powerful X-rays are focused on the cancerous areas to kill the cells and prevent their spreading. In some limited cases doctors may decide to use radiation as the first method in an effort to avoid mastectomy.

Immunotherapy. A new technique designed to help the woman's body to use its own immune system to destroy cancer cells. This is done by using drugs to trigger the patient's immune system to combat the cancer cells.

Each of these methods has its advocates and detractors. It is clear that not enough is known about breast cancer and which kind of treatment is best for which person. However, people must think carefully and discuss fully the treatments that are recommended to them and the consequences of each. The signs are that the medical profession is trying to improve and expand nonsurgical treatment, so breast surgery may well begin to be used less.

After Surgery. A woman with breast cancer usually has surgery in order to continue to live; then she must learn to live with her surgery.

The normal medical concerns right after a mastectomy are to do with drainage of blood and tissue fluid, controlling the postoperational pain, and beginning to exercise the arm and shoulder, which is important in reducing any swelling of the arm that may have occurred. These physical aspects are painful and distressing and must be attended to, but for many women the principal distress is the emotional impact of losing such a sexually significant part of the body. In the broadest sense, mastectomy challenges a woman's sexuality because her body image, gender identity and role, her erotic possibilities and her ability to become involved intimately with a partner can be profoundly affected:

> "I always found an excuse not to have sex, but really I was ashamed — I felt disfigured."

"I felt like half a woman."

"Will a man ever find me attractive again?"

"During lovemaking I couldn't lean or take any pressure on that side of my body."

"I wondered what people were thinking when they looked at me."

"I was glad I was alive, but sometimes I wondered if I could ever learn to live with it."

This is real pain and real suffering. Not every woman experiences it, but many do, and in order to overcome the effects of these feelings understanding, continuing support and communication are essential. Women do overcome the physical and emotional effects of mastectomy, but it isn't easy and the trauma to their sexual identity can be enduring. The sooner sexual relationships can be resumed, with appropriate recognition of the surgery, the more easily problems will be avoided and overcome. And if sexual problems do occur, the quicker they are acknowledged and discussed candidly and sensitively, the more likely they are to be resolved without creating barriers.

The effects of mastectomy on longevity and on various physical aspects of functioning are being studied thoroughly, but research into the effects on sexual identity and sexual expression has just begun and is far

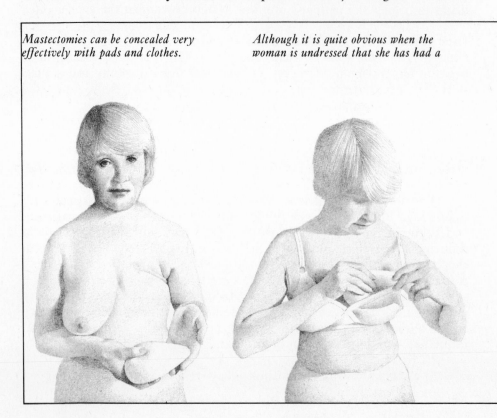

Mastectomies can be concealed very effectively with pads and clothes.

Although it is quite obvious when the woman is undressed that she has had a

from complete. Getting through the trauma of mastectomy therefore requires genuinely creative understanding from the patient's partner; we don't yet have rules to help, so each situation has to be worked through by the people concerned on their own terms. What is clear, though, is that many relationships are strengthened by the process — the effort of understanding and sharing the problem often brings two people closer together.

Q: "I heard that a discharge from a woman's nipples is a sign of cancer. Is this true?"

A: "If a discharge from a breast is bloody or brown a woman should see her doctor immediately, as she should if the discharge is heavy and continuous or if it is milky/clear and she is not pregnant or breastfeeding. A discharge is normal prior to birth, and shortly after birth if the woman is not nursing. Sometimes a watery discharge can result from manipulating the breast vigorously. Some discharges are due to hormonal imbalances, so even if a woman does have an inappropriate discharge it does not mean automatically that she has cancer."

Q: "A friend of mine said her doctor told her she should consider having a breast operation because a certain kind of tissue she has in her breast could become a problem later on in her life. Is this usual advice?"

A: "Some doctors have recently reported their view that a certain type of dense tissue in the breast is more likely to be a problem

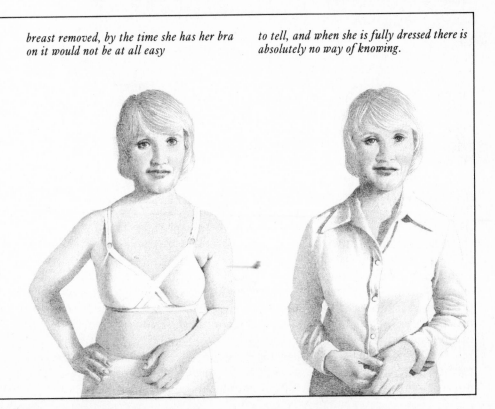

breast removed, by the time she has her bra on it would not be at all easy   *to tell, and when she is fully dressed there is absolutely no way of knowing.*

than other types. This theory has not yet been proven and is only speculation. If your friend seeks other opinions she will soon discover that most doctors are conservative about surgery and recommend it only when they are sure it is the best way to deal with a real problem."

Q: "I'm 18, and I felt a movable lump in my breast just before I got my period one month. My doctor told me to wait a month and then to see her. Is it wise for me to wait?"

A: "Usually yes. In your case your doctor probably felt that since it was so close to your period, some of the normal fluid that builds up at that time could have been trapped in the ducts of your breast. The chances are great that after your period you will notice first a reduction, then a disappearance of the cyst. But do go back and check with your doctor as she advised to allay any anxiety you might feel."

Q: "Do men get breast cancer too?"

A: "Yes, though very rarely. The forms of treatment are the same as for women. Some men who receive oestrogen to treat prostate cancer develop breast cancer."

Q: "What is mastitis?"

A: "Mastitis is an infection of the breast caused by bacteria that enter through the nipple or a crack in the nipple. Fever, tenderness of the breasts and generally feeling low are the common indicators.

"More than half the cases of mastitis occur while a woman is breastfeeding, but traumatic mastitis may follow breast surgery (this very occasionally occurs in men too). A painful swelling of the breasts may occur at puberty which is sometimes known as puberty mastitis; it disappears after a few weeks. Mastitis may also occur during the menopause because of changes in hormone levels."

Breast Size — Reduction and Enlargement Breast reduction is a serious operation requiring general anaesthesia and hospitalization for several days. The operation is done to remove excess fatty tissue and may be performed when breasts are so large that: they cause chronic backache; they interfere with ordinary movement; bra straps dig into shoulders and cause bruising or cutting; or when one breast is much larger than the other.

Breast enlargement is both serious and controversial. It is almost always done for cosmetic reasons, and tends to improve the self-image and mental health of the patient. In the past, silicone was injected directly into the breasts to enlarge them or to prevent sagging. Never, never choose this procedure as the silicone often causes infections, kills breast tissue and may cause cancer.

Lately a newer, safer enlargement procedure has been developed. A medical silicone implant is placed at the base of the breast; it does not interfere with breastfeeding, but is not appropriate in all cases.

ACTS AND FEELINGS

KISSING

FACTS Kissing is almost universal; there are few countries where it is not used. It may indicate greeting, respect, affection or desire. In some circumstances kissing is almost obligatory, in some it is inappropriate. Kissing can be affectionate — between family members and friends, for example, or it can be erotic — as between lovers. Some people kiss a lot, as a normal means of greeting or leavetaking, while others reserve kissing chiefly for lovemaking.

The variations in erotic kissing are endless — light and soft, short and intense, long, lingering. Nibbling, gentle biting and sucking can be all added for extra effect. Most people like a variety of ways of kissing to try and express as precisely as possible the way they are feeling moment by moment, for kissing is an important means of communication between lovers.

The heaviest kiss of all — the "soul kiss," "tongue kiss," "deep kiss" or "French kiss" — is the one in which partners explore each other's

mouths with their tongues. Some people are put off by this practice, some enjoy it enormously — it is just another of the options.

Some people confine kissing to their partner's lips but most enjoy some degree of kissing and being kissed elsewhere on the body. People respond to different pressures and durations of kiss on all parts of the body. There is no particular virtue in kissing someone in a particular way in a particular place if either of you does not enjoy it, but any kissing with which both partners feel entirely comfortable is appropriate.

Q: "Is kissing the same as necking?"

A: "Not exactly. 'Necking' normally means kissing for a long period of time; if in addition the two people caress each other's bodies and fondle each other's genitals, it is known as 'petting.'"

Q: "Is it true that you can tell how far you will get with someone just by the way they kiss?"

A: "I don't know the answer to that question. But I do know that if you are occupied with thinking about how far you will get while kissing you won't be enjoying the act or the moment for what it is. You will be a spectator at your own event. Thinking, planning, evaluating what will follow is intrusive to an act that is enjoyable in itself and may (or may not) naturally lead on to other mutually enjoyable acts. Kissing can be a complete and fulfilling act in itself. It doesn't have to be followed by other sexual acts nor, conversely, is it obligatory to kiss before intercourse. I suspect you may find yourself enjoying kissing and other acts more if you rid yourself of the idea that kissing is just the first part of a ritual sequence."

Q: "I'm a single person and the priest in our church still discusses long kissing as a sin. I thought that teaching had changed."

A: "You raise a very important and complex issue. Kissing that stimulates or promotes strong sexual desires (except between husband and wife) is discouraged by the Roman Catholic Church. However, recent pastoral teaching suggests that a simple sinful/not sinful label on any act — including long or tongue kissing — does not do justice to the important human considerations that should be examined before any act can be evaluated morally. This examination must focus on the values the person places on both self and others, on the conviction of conscience the person has about the act in question, and on whether the act is integrative or destructive. It is a serious task that requires a special honesty and forthrightness. You should be able to discuss this freely and without embarrassment with your priest."

Q: "When my 14-year-old goes to parties, they seem to spend most of their time kissing. That worries me a bit. Should I worry?"

A: "What they are doing is exploring their awakening sexual interests and their need for contact. By the time young people have reached the age of 14 they will have seen so many people kissing in films and on TV that they are bound to think it is an appropriate part of growing up and they will want to try it. No, don't worry — it is perfectly natural."

Q: "When I was younger, I remember kissing as a passionate hungry kind of act. The more I kissed the better lover I thought I was and when I began kissing, intercourse was soon to follow. Now that I'm in my sixties, I find myself kissing in a lighter way, and enjoying the feeling of contact more. In fact, I feel quite satisfied with kissing and caressing as a complete sexual act."

A: "This is a not uncommon expression of feelings from older people. Early, eager sexual expression, which is sometimes fueled by anxiety and feelings of compulsion to do everything possible on every occasion, frequently gives way to more integrated, meaningful sexual acts that are the result of individual choice and experience. These changes are not so much a result of ageing as of maturing.

"People of all ages can benefit from being able to express tenderness and affection without having to go on to intercourse or indeed any other acts. Many people though — and young people in particular — feel they ought to have intercourse once they start expressing sexual feelings; they feel it is expected of them, and that it is the right thing to do. Yet if you ask people their feelings they will quite often say they wish they didn't feel obliged always to go on to intercourse. This is a case where establishing your own desires and communicating them to your partner is going to result in more fulfilling sexual expression."

MYTHS There are some popular misconceptions about kissing:

* kissing always leads to intercourse
* women like kissing more than men
* men don't like kissing because they would rather have intercourse
* kissing is not a meaningful act in itself
* only heterosexual people use kissing in their lovemaking
* you can tell if a person is a good kisser by the shape of their lips
* only violent kissing is good kissing.

MASTURBATION

FACTS Masturbation is the deliberate stimulation of one's sex organs to achieve pleasure. It may or may not result in orgasm.

Masturbation comes from the Latin *masturbare*, which is itself a running together of two Latin words, *manus* (hand) and *stuprare* (to defile), giving the sense of "to defile with the hand." The built-in notion of defiling has remained with us, even though medical authorities have been in agreement for quite some time that masturbation causes no physical or mental harm. Masturbation is second only to sex with a partner as our most important source of sexual pleasure, and yet it is still surrounded by guilt and anxiety. This is partly due to ignorance of the fact that masturbation cannot be harmful and partly due to centuries of religious teaching that masturbation is sinful.

The first real facts about who masturbates were discovered by Kinsey and his associates. They reported that 58 percent of women and 92 percent of men had masturbated to orgasm at some point in their lives. By 12 years of age, 12 percent of girls and 21 percent of boys had masturbated, and by age 20, 33 percent of women and 92 percent of men had masturbated. Between the ages of 20 and the mid-50s up to 58 percent of women masturbated. The proportion of men masturbating decreased after the late teenage years.

Recent data indicate that masturbation among women has increased since the Kinsey study and that among men it has continued at over 90 percent. Morton Hunt's analysis of data collected in the 1970s shows an increase in masturbation among single males aged 18 to 24 as compared to Kinsey. Hunt's analysis also suggests more active involvement in masturbation after the teen years and into the 20s and 30s. Hunt's analysis indicates that 60 percent of women aged 18 to 24 masturbate, and by the late 20s and early 30s, 80 percent of women had masturbated. This is a large increase when compared to the Kinsey data of 30 years before. Hunt also found that 70 percent of married men and 68 percent of married women masturbated. This too is a significant increase.

The *Redbook* survey of 100,000 married American women in the mid-1970s showed that 68 percent of them masturbated, often (16 percent), or occasionally (52 percent); 80 percent of those masturbating found masturbation to be satisfactory (always 31 percent, sometimes 49 percent).

Shere Hite in the *Hite Report* reported that 82 percent of her sample of over 3,000 American women masturbated. Ninety-six percent of them had orgasm regularly.

In the Kinsey data it was indicated that masturbation was less frequent among men and women from lower socioeconomic classes, poorer educational background and higher religious devotion. Current reports indicate that it is only religious devotion that continues significantly to inhibit masturbation. Devout Catholics, fundamentalist Protestants and Orthodox Jewish believers are less active masturbators than nonreligious or less religious men and women.

Masturbation and Sex Therapy. Once masturbation was on the way to becoming medically respectable, people began to view it as a positive good. Not only, they said, did it bring harmless pleasure, but it was also a valuable way of learning about one's own sexual responses. This idea was quickly taken up by sex therapists to treat people who had problems in their sexual relationships.

The purpose of the therapy is to learn about the body, and discover in a relaxed way what is pleasurable. Understanding the facts about masturbation and how the body is aroused are important parts of this process. Learning how to have an orgasm in a comfortable way is achieved by

following guidelines offered by the therapist. Programmes vary from therapist to therapist and from clinic to clinic, but they are reported to be highly successful in teaching women how to have an orgasm more regularly, either alone or with a partner, and teaching men how to achieve and maintain an erection and control ejaculation.

Q: "Can you masturbate too much?"

A: "No. Each individual decides how much is appropriate — there are no set levels. No physical or mental harm will come to you regardless of your frequency of masturbation unless it is a compulsive behaviour. In this latter case, when masturbation is preferred over all other outlets including relationships, the person has a problem of which masturbation is a symptom not a cause."

Q: "Isn't it weird for a person sometimes to enjoy masturbation more than intercourse?"

A: "No, it isn't weird at all. Masturbation has certain advantages over intercourse: it is simple, can be done quickly and you don't have to be concerned with the desires and needs of a partner. Some people find the intensity of orgasm from masturbation greater than through intercourse. In the end, however, most people prefer sex with a partner — they find it more fulfilling.

"Masturbation becomes a problem only when a man or woman uses it exclusively and compulsively, and rejects sexual relationships."

Q: "Just what is a compulsive masturbator?"

A: "A compulsive masturbator is a man or woman whose only sexual outlet is masturbation, who feels driven to do it, and who rejects all other forms of sexual release.

"Compulsive masturbation, like all other compulsive behaviours, is a sign of an emotional problem and needs to be explored by a mental health specialist."

Q: "I have an orgasm easily when I masturbate or when my husband masturbates me. During intercourse I don't have orgasms easily. Is there something wrong with me?"

A: "No. The Kinsey study and the *Hite Report* both show that the majority of women probably reach orgasm more frequently and more quickly by masturbation than through intercourse. The reason is that generally the clitoris needs to be stimulated for orgasm to occur, and intercourse is not the most effective way to do it. After all, most women choose to masturbate by stimulating the clitoral area, not by putting something in the vagina."

Q: "I heard somewhere that women who masturbate before marriage have good sex when they get married. Is that true?"

A: "Yes. The Kinsey data suggested that married women who had masturbated to orgasm before marriage responded orgasmically during marriage more often than those women who had not. It is true that orgasmic experience prior to marriage could have been due to petting, but masturbation was identified as the biggest single source of orgasmic experience. Recent studies also suggest that masturbation to orgasm premaritally has a positive effect on sex in marriage.

"This does not mean that only those women who masturbate before marriage will have happy, responsive sex lives after marriage; it simply suggests that the chances of that happening are greater among women who were orgasmically responsive before they married."

Q: "Every once in a while, I masturbate to relieve a pressure I feel when I don't have an orgasm with my lover. Is there something wrong with me?"

A: "No, nothing at all. When you are sexually very excited, the blood vessels in your pelvis become engorged with blood. Orgasm allows the blood to flow back, but if orgasm doesn't occur in your lovemaking, you may well feel an uncomfortable fullness and tenderness. Masturbating to orgasm immediately relieves the congestion and the uncomfortable feeling it gives you.

"Men, too, feel a congestion and tenderness in their testicles when they are sexually excited and do not have an orgasm; masturbation relieves it quickly and simply."

Q: "Is group masturbation a common practice among adolescent boys?"

A: "Yes, sometimes a group of boys will masturbate at the same time as a sort of virility game to see who can ejaculate fastest. Because speed is rewarded this practice may not be too helpful later in life when a slowing down of the time it takes to reach ejaculation will lengthen pleasure and fulfilment for both partners. However, this sharing of sexuality with friends can be seen as an important and on the whole benevolent stage in the sexual education of the adolescent."

Q: "Sometimes when I masturbate I see some blood in my semen. Do I have a disease?"

A: "Probably not. A little blood in your semen occasionally (called haematospermia) is not an indication of a disease, especially if there are no urethral, prostate or bladder problems. The cause of infrequent haematospermia is not known; it is not related to masturbation, wet dreams or sexual desire and activity. But see a doctor if you regularly find blood in your semen."

Q: "I heard that women used things like cucumbers, hot dogs, artificial penises and coke bottles to masturbate. Is that true?"

A: "Some women — but very few — do use objects like those you describe. Some women also get them stuck and do themselves considerable damage."

MYTHS The following commonly held beliefs about masturbation are all false:

* masturbation causes physical illness
* married people don't masturbate
* you can get hooked on masturbation
* masturbation leads to a decrease in a person's social life
* old people don't masturbate
* masturbation is for people without partners
* masturbation is a sign of homosexuality
* masturbation is a sign of emotional illness
* masturbation causes poor eyesight
* women don't masturbate
* all religions teach that masturbation is a sin
* you can tell if a person masturbates just by looking at them
* too much masturbation causes a man to run out of sperm
* regular masturbation is a sign that a person is unable to form healthy sexual relationships.

AGE Masturbation is a feature of most people's sexual expression at some time in the life-cycle. Many people masturbate from infancy to old age.

Babies clearly derive pleasure from touching their genitals, though of course they do not masturbate methodically. Children, almost whatever they are told by adults, will fondle their genitals and derive pleasure from doing so. At around the time of puberty, both boys and girls become much more purposeful about manipulating their genitals and begin to masturbate to orgasm.

Kinsey, in the 1930s, found that male teenagers and young single men masturbated most: they masturbated more than older men and more than women at any age (whereas over 90 percent of men had masturbated by age 20, only 33 percent of women had done so). He also found that the frequency of masturbation increased in women as they got older.

In the 1970s, by contrast, the disparity between the sexes seemed to be evening itself out. Both Morton Hunt and the *Redbook* survey found that masturbation seemed to be starting earlier, continuing longer and was practised equally by adult men and women. Approximately three quarters of married men and women now masturbate.

With some gerontologists encouraging the elderly to masturbate as they used to when they were younger, it seems that masturbation is now acceptable at all stages of the life-cycle for both women and men.

FEELINGS

"When I finally was able to accept masturbation as right and good for me, I began to enjoy it."

"Masturbation has always been second best for me. Maybe if I didn't have a sex partner, I would change my mind."

"I just like the pleasurable feelings I get when I masturbate."

"I don't masturbate now, and masturbated rarely when I was a kid. With all the talk about it, I feel abnormal."

"It certainly feels good physically, but I still feel a bit of guilt."

"Masturbation has improved my sex life with my partner. I know more about my body, and I know what I like."

"It's nice to be able to satisfy myself when I want to and not have to worry about pleasing someone else too."

"When I was a teenager it was OK, but now I feel it's second best."

"I have feelings of guilt, shame and fear of being discovered. How can such a simple act lead to so much difficulty?"

"I wouldn't admit it if a friend asked me — so I guess that identifies my true feelings."

"Even though I don't masturbate often, it's important for me to feel that I am in control of my body and my pleasure."

"Sometimes I wonder what my wife really thinks about me masturbating."

Feelings about masturbation are part of the fabric of our personalities and at times can affect us deeply. They come from various sources: age-old religious beliefs have influenced us in a negative way; medical and psychological teaching used to be negative but has now become positive; parents often communicate negative messages about masturbation. The cumulative effect of these influences is usually confusion and/or guilt. The confusion may be dispelled as the person grows, but the guilt is likely to remain in some degree.

A minority of more fortunate people are either not subject to so many negative influences or they manage to rid themselves of anxiety and guilt. They learn to live with their feelings and feel entirely free to masturbate when they choose. It appears that this attitude is becoming more common today, even though masturbatory mythology remains potent in many parts of the world.

Q: "When I was a kid I used to masturbate, but now I'm not interested. There's so much fuss about it being good for you to masturbate that I'm beginning to wonder if I'm normal."

A: "I think I understand your position. A great deal has been said and written in favour of masturbation in the last few years in order to try and get rid of centuries of misinformation and debilitating guilt. Having made your decision to suit your needs I can see that you may feel on the wrong end of a barrage of propaganda.

"Responsible experts are actually encouraging people not to go and masturbate but to *feel free* to do so. You appear not to suffer guilt about masturbation and that is the best way to be, whether you choose to masturbate or not."

RELATIONSHIPS Masturbation has different meanings throughout a person's life. During early childhood the sensuousness associated with touching the genitals is a universal experience. During adolescence, learning about the body, experiencing the surging sexual feelings, the thrill and anxiety associated with private, secret and taboo acts are all part of the developing process. Much of this changes when relationships are formed.

"If my wife masturbated it would be a real blow for me."

"I know my husband masturbates when he wants sex and I don't."

"When a person has a partner, why should you need to masturbate?"

"Sometimes when my husband is away, I masturbate and think about him."

"If our relationship gets tense, I masturbate more."

"It is really exciting for me to watch my lover masturbate."

In some relationships, masturbation may be mutually acceptable. Done alone or in the presence of the partner the act is pleasing and appropriate and is not a sign of rejection. For other couples the act of masturbation may be a sign of anger, alienation or displeasure with the way the relationship is progressing. The meaning could be that the partner who masturbates values his or her own body more than the partner's. Both candour and sensitivity are required in these situations, with perhaps the guidance of a qualified therapist or counsellor.

In a great many relationships, of course, mutual masturbation plays a significant role as part of the lovemaking repertoire. It may be an end in itself or a part of the buildup to other sexual acts — either way, if both partners are at ease about masturbation it can be mutually satisfying.

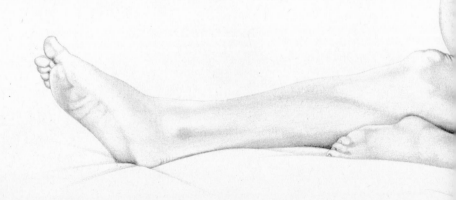

CULTURE AND RELIGION Every culture that has been closely studied has shown evidence of autoerotic behaviour, especially masturbation. The descriptions have mostly been about men masturbating, but there is usually some evidence of women masturbating as well.

In China and in Japan there is evidence that women used artificial penises of paper or clay to masturbate. The Greeks viewed masturbation as a substitute for love, a safety valve created by nature to permit the release of sexual tension; Greek women masturbated with a device called the *olisbos*. In the Marquesan civilization of Polynesia too masturbation was not believed to be harmful in any way. Men moistened their hands with saliva when masturbating and women sometimes used bananas in their vaginas. Masturbation declined in frequency once the Marquesans reached adulthood.

Our Western view of masturbation as something harmful, degrading and shameful came from our religious traditions and was powerfully reinforced by the medical profession.

In 1767 S. Tissot wrote *A Treatise on the Disease Produced by Onanism* and gave a pseudoscientific gloss to traditional religious teaching. Tissot's book, which was widely translated, attributed almost every known disease and disorder to loss of semen, either through masturbation or through intercourse. The chief disease — Batchelor's Disease or spermatorrhoea — was said to lead to destruction of the body and the mind.

Throughout the nineteenth century and until World War I the preoccupation with masturbation, its symptoms and effects, was astonishing. Physicians produced sex manuals and marriage guides that described the dread disease they called "self-abuse," "self-pollution," "the solitary vice," and "the soul and body destroyer." Women who masturbated (they said) would develop tell-tale marks on their faces, softness of the spine and hollow cheeks; they would also become highly irritable and bald. Bicycle riding for women was strongly condemned because the angle of the seat would give rise to "friction and heating of the parts where it was very undesirable, leading to dangerous practices."

Men had to be safeguarded against masturbation as it caused every disease and disability from death and idiocy to plague spots, those bluish semicircles we now call bags under the eyes. Masturbation caused muscles to weaken, blood to become diseased and nervous disorders to appear. Parents were urged to watch for the danger signs of self-pollution in their children. Pure-minded parents watched their children while they slept, bathed and played. Love of dancing, sliding down poles and wearing tight clothes were sure signs of self-polluting tendencies in young people.

The dreadful consequences of failing to protect boys from self-abuse were described by the English physician Dr William Acton in 1875:

"The frame is stunted and weak, the muscles under-developed, the complexion sallow, pasty or covered with acne. The hands are damp and the skin moist. The boy shuns society — his intellect is sluggish and enfeebled — he is on the way to becoming an idiot ..."

Treatment for self-abuse varied widely. Hand-tying at bedtime was encouraged for boys who masturbated. Cold water cures of various sorts were prescribed by doctors. One such was to get a specially made chair with a partially open seat on which the afflicted man or boy sat. Using a special pump the male could spray his genitals with a refrigerant fluid whenever he felt these "unnatural" urges.

These attitudes and some of the practices continued until the 1930s and 40s, when physiological and some psychological evidence indicated that masturbation did not cause these terrible things at all. Then in the 1950s, 60s and 70s the mythology was clearly undone, and even religions began to re-evaluate their views on this once dreaded practice. Perhaps as the years pass and fewer people are taught that masturbation is "wrong" we will as a society rid ourselves of the guilt and anxiety that many people still suffer. It is however a very deep rooted attitude that will not be eradicated easily.

Judaism. In Genesis 38: 7-11 Er died childless. His brother Onan was then bound by sacred duty to impregnate the widow and bring a child into the world to carry on the family name. Onan did not complete the sex act, spilled his seed on the ground and was killed by the Lord.

The traditional Jewish interpretation of this event is that since Onan's spilling of his seed was punished by death, all spilling of semen — and therefore masturbation — must be immoral and contrary to the wishes of the Lord. Later interpretations attribute Onan's death not to the spilling of the seed, but to his failure to fulfil his sacred duty. It has also been proposed that Onan was punished because he used a contraceptive method — withdrawal.

The strict Orthodox teaching about the immorality of masturbation is in keeping with the prohibition against touching the genitals. In the Talmud there is reference to women being allowed to examine their genitals in order to determine the onset of their periods, but for no other purpose. Men were not supposed to touch their penises at all, even when urinating (the penis had to be guided by lifting the scrotum). The absence of specific reference to women and masturbation in Jewish teaching may be attributable to the ancient Jewish belief that the male sperm was the generative seed while the woman provided only the growth place. There was also an assumption that women were sexually passive and therefore less likely to wish to masturbate.

Though the teachings of Judaism forbid masturbation, in practice the modern Jewish attitude is much more permissive. The position on autoeroticism generally and masturbation specifically is that the behaviour is acceptable as long as it is not neurotic and not harmful to a relationship. There seems to be less religious anxiety about masturbation for the majority of Jewish believers than for their traditional Catholic and fundamentalist Protestant counterparts.

Protestantism. Protestant groups take widely different attitudes to masturbation. Some fundamentalist Protestant believers see masturbation as against the Lord's will and as an immature, selfish act, indicative of poor self-control and emotional problems. Other more moderate Protestant groups see masturbation as appropriate at any age and best evaluated, if it needs evaluation at all, in the context in which it takes place. Some liberal Protestants see masturbation as normal and healthy at all ages; they do not see that it requires religious analysis and interpretation.

Catholicism. Although masturbation is not expressly prohibited in the scriptures, the teaching of the Roman Catholic Church on masturbation has been clear for centuries: masturbation is a grievous, disordered act and a mortal sin if done with knowledge and consent. A fairly recent Vatican pronouncement, the *Declaration on Certain Questions Concerning Sexual Ethics* (1975), stated that masturbation is ". . . an intrinsically and seriously disordered act." The declaration goes on to say that masturbation is a disorder in the eyes of the Church even though psychological and sociological evidence may show it to be a normal developmental phenomenon. This view is adhered to by many Catholics throughout the world, but probably many more are confused and do not follow this rigid guideline. It is clear that contemporary theologians and thoughtful Catholics are questioning whether every act of masturbation constitutes a grave offence. Catholic women and men do recognize that acts of masturbation can have many meanings, and that some of these acts are responsible and integrative, not selfish, alienating or self-destructive. Furthermore, some Catholics view masturbation as just another form of sexual expression, and sexual expression is in fact one of God's gifts to all people.

The tension within the Church and some of its adherents over masturbation is very real. Numerous believers are in conflict with themselves and it is important that discussions continue if eventually a greater understanding is to be reached.

Q: "My priest told me masturbation was a sin and must be confessed and controlled. My friend's priest asked my friend about the circumstances and how he felt about it, and he told him it wasn't a sin. How do you explain that?"

A: "This is a rather common example of the different ways priests approach the issue of masturbation. Your priest adheres to the formal Roman Catholic teaching that sexual acts are appropriate within the marital union and should be focused on procreation. Your friend's priest didn't say masturbation wasn't a sin until he understood the nature of the situation in which masturbation occurred. After doing so, he felt the occurrence was not sinful. The implication is that in a different context he might have found the act of masturbation to be sinful. A number of priests now share your friend's priest's view, but it is still counter to the Church's teaching and your friend's priest would at least be cautioned if his pronouncement came to the attention of Church officials.

"In any event, many reasonable, concerned Catholics are confused. Many of them are having to examine their consciences carefully before discussing the issue with a spiritual adviser and then trying to form their consciences in a way that is true both to their religious convictions and to their individual needs."

Q: "A friend of mine was not brought up religiously and he has no guilt problems with masturbation. Is he just lucky?"

A: "Research shows that men and women not raised within a specific religious system are less guilty about masturbation. Also, nonreligious men and women masturbate more often than religious men and women. The evidence indicates that religious beliefs generally inhibit the frequency of masturbation."

ORAL SEX

FACTS Oral sex or oral–genital sex means both mouth contact with the vagina, which is called **cunnilingus**, and mouth contact with the penis, which is called **fellatio**. Cunnilingus comes from an alternative Latin word for vulva, *cunnus*, and from the Latin word for licking, *lingere*. Fellatio comes from the Latin word *fellare*, which means to suck.

Oral sex given simultaneously by two people to each other is commonly called 69 or, from the French, soixante-neuf. This is because the body positions of a couple can resemble the numeral 69 when they are having mutual oral sex.

Cunnilingus and fellatio are common sexual behaviours both for same-sex couples and for couples of different sexes. There are various body positions for oral sex, but it is the mouth that provides the pleasure in all cases. In cunnilingus the labia, the clitoris and the vaginal area are kissed, licked and gently sucked. In fellatio the head and shaft of the penis are licked, kissed and sucked. In both cunnilingus and fellatio the feeling of the mouth and tongue on the genitals can be extremely pleasurable.

Who has oral sex? Not everyone by any means. Some people simply don't feel comfortable about it. It is as normal and proper not to have it as to have and enjoy it. It is interesting to note though that research done over the last four decades shows a growing acceptance of oral sex as a normal behaviour, this despite the historical view that oral sex was sinful and against nature, and despite some religious and legal prohibitions.

The first real evidence of how many people were having oral sex was provided by the historic Kinsey reports. These reports were published in America in 1948 (male) and 1953 (female). Since then, in the 1970s the Hunt report on sexual behaviour, the *Hite Report*, the *Spada Report*, the *Redbook Report*, the Bell and Weinberg study *Homosexualities* and others have been published in the US; all have contributed to what we currently know about attitudes to and the practice of oral sex.

A very revealing way of showing how attitudes have changed is to compare the Kinsey data on oral sex (collected in the 1930s and 40s) with

	Kinsey and Hunt Data on Oral Sex in Marriage by educational level			
	% of marriages in which fellatio is used		% of marriages in which cunnilingus is used	
	Kinsey 1930s–40s	*Hunt* 1972	*Kinsey* 1930s–40s	*Hunt* 1972
High School males	15	54	15	56
College males	43	61	45	66
High School females	46	52	50	58
College females	52	72	58	72

the Hunt data (from the 1970s). The Kinsey data were collected through interviews with 5,300 white men and 5,940 white women. The Hunt data were collected by questionnaire from 1,044 women and 982 men, ten percent of whom were black.

The increasing practice of fellatio and cunnilingus is very clear from the figures. The Hunt data if anything underestimate the level of practice in 1972, as the Kinsey researchers asked whether respondents had ever or on occasion had oral sex in their marriages, whereas the Hunt researchers asked respondents if they had had oral sex within the previous 12 months. In the *Redbook* magazine survey, which was published in 1975, 100,000 married women responded to a questionnaire about sexual attitudes and practices. The women ranged in age from the late teens to the 60s (though 84 percent were between 20 and 40) and were essentially Catholic, Jewish or Protestant — 51 percent described themselves as strongly or fairly religious, 33 percent as mildly religious and 16 percent as nonreligious. Eighty-seven percent of the women responded that they had oral sex often or occasionally and a similarly high percentage reported that they found oral sex very or somewhat enjoyable. Eighty-five percent of the women reported giving oral sex to their husbands and 72 percent reported the experience to be enjoyable or somewhat enjoyable.

Alan Bell and Martin Weinberg in their important study of homo-sexual social, psychological and sexual experience (*Homosexualities*, 1978), found in their in-depth interviews of more than 1,500 homosexual men and women that oral sex was the most frequently used sexual practice. Twenty-seven percent of the white male homosexuals said receiving fellatio was their favourite among all sexual practices; 18 percent of black male homosexuals said receiving fellatio was their favourite, while eight percent said mutual oral sex was their favoured sexual activity; 20 percent of the white homosexual females ranked receiving cunnilingus as their favourite sexual act, and 24 percent favoured mutual cunnilingus. The rankings for both men and women were from among seven common types of sexual practice.

The *Spada Report*, published in 1979, studied 1,038 male homosex-uals aged 16 to 77 from throughout the United States; 75 percent of the respondents were raised Catholic, Jewish or some form of Protestant. They were asked which acts they especially enjoyed (not which was their favourite, as in the Bell and Weinberg survey). Ninety percent especially enjoyed receiving fellatio, 88 percent indicated giving fellatio was very enjoyable, 50 percent enjoyed mutual fellatio.

In the *Hite Report* (1976) Shere Hite reported on the responses of 3,019 women aged 14 to 78 from all parts of America. Cunnilingus was consistently described as a very arousing and desirable sexual practice, leading to orgasm regularly among 42 percent of the sample.

Why has this change come about? It is difficult to identify precisely all the factors which have led to a greater acceptance of oral sex, but here are some of them:

* dispelling the myths about the harmful health effects of oral sex; scientific and medical evidence have made it clear that in and of itself oral sex does not lead to disease

* the major religions have relaxed their historical prohibitions about oral sex being sinful and unnatural; although a clear, understandable statement on oral sex being a proper means of sexual expression is still conspicuously absent from most religions, most have at least suggested that within marriage it is an acceptable practice
* since 1960 couples seem to be more willing to experiment; this is the result of more information, of issues being more openly explored, of the relaxation of rigid religious prohibitions on sexual issues generally, and of the exercise of greater freedom by couples to decide what is good and right for themselves and their relationship
* there has been an increasing acceptance by societies throughout the world of sexuality in general and of sexual expression in particular; although many repressive attitudes still exist, enormous progress has been made in extending individuals' rights to express their sexuality free from external control and in keeping with their consciences.

Q: "Is it true that oral sex is a throwback to breastfeeding and that's why some people like it?"

A: "Nobody knows for sure why so many people enjoy oral sex other than it's an exciting way to give and receive pleasure. Sexologists generally agree that what is really important about oral sex is that women and men can if they wish engage in it freely, derive enjoyment from it, and find it appropriate to their relationships."

Q: "Some friends of mine told me they went to a porno movie and saw a couple in the film having oral sex. They were both interested but had never discussed it together until that time. Now they really enjoy it. Is that uncommon?"

A: "No. It appears that some couples are learning about sexual practices from films and books more now than at any other time. Your friends are typical in that they were each interested but needed a way to get the discussion started. We all have to learn our sexual practices somewhere, after all."

Q: "Is it true that you get better orgasms from oral sex?"
A: "Some people have reported that they feel their most powerful physical orgasms when they have oral sex because the stimulation of mouth on penis or mouth on the clitoral area is so intense. Others report that intercourse gives them their most satisfying orgasms because of the feelings of closeness to their partners. Yet other people report having their most satisfying orgasms through masturbation with a partner.

   "There are no objective standards for measuring the 'best' kind of orgasm. How it feels best varies from person to person, and from occasion to occasion. Experience teaches people what they most enjoy."

Q: "Is it true that some men can have oral sex with themselves?"
A: "Yes. Kinsey reported that several men had been able to have

oral sex with themselves. This is called self-fellation (auto-fellatio), and although it would be hard to determine for sure, many sexologists believe many males at least try self-fellation at some point in their lives."

Q: "Can a man's penis be too big for oral sex?"
A: "No. Although erect penises vary in size, some form of mouth contact can be made on a penis regardless of size. A long penis may cause gagging if taken deep in the mouth, and a thick penis may stretch the mouth and lips. Under these conditions the person giving fellatio can adjust and still both give and get pleasure."

Q: "I heard that oral sex is illegal even if you are married. Is that true?"

A: "It is not true for Britain but many states in the US have had laws about unnatural acts which included prohibitions on mouth-genital intercourse or contact. Technically, these laws still remain in force in some American states, but they are rarely enforced on married couples. However, they are sometimes enforced on single homosexual and heterosexual men and women.

   "Such laws, which limit personal sexual freedoms in a rather obvious way, are a product of the centuries-old religious and cultural restrictions on sex. In the US especially, early laws were greatly influenced by repressive English attitudes toward

402 ACTS AND FEELINGS

sexual expression. The early Puritan colonists in America publically punished or jailed men and women accused of having oral sex."

Q: "I heard it's dangerous to blow into the vagina. Is that true?"
A: "Yes. Vigorous blowing into the vagina during cunnilingus is dangerous, especially if the woman is pregnant. Air bubbles may be picked up by blood vessels and create an embolism that could be fatal to the woman and the foetus."

Q: "I'm going to use contraceptive foam as a birth control method so I suppose oral sex is out for me."
A: "Not necessarily. You can have oral sex before intercourse, as long as you remember to insert your contraceptive foam before the penis makes contact with your vagina. If this is not satisfactory to you and your partner, you might consider the use of a condom instead of foam — again being certain to place the condom on the penis before intercourse."

Q: "Even though I enjoy getting oral sex and my lover seems to also, I still worry about the smell and wetness from my vagina."
A: "Women quite often have this concern; it is probably part of the larger issue of acceptance of their own genitals. Women are usually not socialized to think about their labia, clitoris and vagina as clean and beautiful. Consequently, some women have mixed feelings during cunnilingus — the feelings of arousal, stimulation and pleasure, and, at the same time, worry that part of them 'down there' is not clean enough, or attractive enough, to be acceptable to their partners.
    "The women's liberation movement has been very important in helping create a general climate in society of acceptance of women's bodies, though the issue is still not fully recognized and resolved. Parents can do a lot, too, in communicating to their daughters that their whole bodies are special and valuable. This will probably do more for women (and men) in later life than reading or than participating in body-awareness groups."

Q: "What does semen taste like?"
A: "It's hard to describe accurately something that is nearly tasteless — particularly as genital odours are part of the moment and smell and taste intermingle. The most common description is that it is slightly salty, although some people report they can taste garlic, whisky, asparagus and the like if a partner had them at a recent meal."

Q: "I feel I should douche before I have oral sex. Is that OK?"
A: "No, douching is not necessary. Your vagina is a self-cleaning organ that takes care of itself. In fact, douching probably removes the helpful bacteria that naturally protect your vagina. It is understandable that you want to feel clean when having

sex, especially oral sex, but simply washing your genitals is sufficient to prepare you for sex of any kind. Anyway, natural tastes and smells are usually more pleasant than deodorized, antiseptic ones."

Q: "I would like to have oral sex but I worry about him urinating while I'm doing it. Does this happen often?"
A: "No, he can't. When a man is sexually stimulated and has an erection he is unable to urinate. This is so because during sexual excitement and erection there is a reflex action which temporarily closes off the bladder. Men cannot ejaculate and urinate at the same time either — in fact, he won't be able to urinate until he has started to lose his erection."

Q: "Sometimes I taste a distinct sugary flavour when I'm giving cunnilingus. Other times I don't. Is that a sign of a problem?"
A: "No. This has been reported from time to time and it probably occurs when you have oral sex near the time of your partner's ovulation. Around that time she has higher oestrogen levels in her blood and that may cause the vaginal fluid to taste sweeter than in the rest of her cycle."

Q: "Is it true that some people have oral sex during menstruation?"
A: "Yes. This is not a very common practice but some people do it. Sometimes a diaphragm is used to keep the menstrual fluid from appearing in the vaginal area.
    "Because of our culture's anxieties about menstruation, many people find the idea of cunnilingus during menstruation dirty, perverse, or disgusting. It is in fact quite harmless, as menstrual fluid contains no germs. The choice of whether or not to have oral sex during menstruation is like the choice of whether to have oral sex at all — a matter of personal decision. Choosing either way does not indicate a better or worse relationship."

Q: "What is the best way to have oral sex?"
A: "There is no one best way. It seems that as soon as a practice becomes respectable in any field, a new elite emerges of the people who have perfected the skills and got all the answers. So it has been with oral sex. There are people who claim they have the perfect technique. Now it happens that there is no such thing. Each couple learns what they most enjoy, what suits them best. Any sexual act between two people is a matter of giving, receiving and sharing, not of perfect technique."

MYTHS There are many popular misconceptions about mouth–penis and mouth–vagina contact. These are some of them and they are all false.

* people who enjoy oral–genital sex are probably gay
* oral sex causes venereal disease
* real men do not have oral–genital contact

* women who give oral sex are submissive
* women who swallow semen are nymphomaniacs
* a man who gives oral sex does it because he can't satisfy a partner with his penis
* swallowing semen can cause pregnancy
* you can get hooked on oral sex if you do it too much
* oral sex can easily lead to a disease because of all the germs on the penis and in the vagina
* married people rarely have oral sex
* having oral–genital sex is a sign of being sexually immature
* men and women can get lip disease from oral sex
* oral sex is unnatural
* having oral sex is a sign of true love.

FEELINGS These are some of the feelings men and women report about giving and receiving oral sex:

"Getting it done to me is better than doing it."

"I always feel I'm doing it wrong."

"When I'm having oral sex I get lost in those wonderful feelings."

"I feel a sense of power because of the pleasure I'm giving."

"I feel alive but very vulnerable."

"With a new partner I'm worried about odours and VD."

"If it's not mutual I feel guilty or ripped off."

"I love the tastes and the textures."

"I love oral sex because it is so clear that I'm the one giving pleasure to my husband."

"When he does that to me it's really special."

"Sometimes I feel like I'm giving a performance, or like I have to do it to be with it."

"Oral sex is too impersonal."

"I feel very intimate when I have oral sex."

Many people who try it enjoy oral sex, but many have reservations about it. These reservations tend to arise from three different kinds of anxiety: first, that oral sex is unhygienic; second, that there is a taboo against it; third, that it is not a true expression of femininity or masculinity. Let us look at each in turn.

Hygiene. Neither vaginal fluid nor semen is in any way harmful. Mouth contact with genitals does not cause lip disorders. No disease is passed by oral sex that wouldn't be transmitted by any other kind of sex — if one person has a sexually transmitted disease the other is likely to catch it whatever they do together sexually. In short, oral sex between healthy people is entirely clean and safe. As to genital odour, another hygiene aspect

that people worry about, it can always be reduced by washing and is entirely natural anyway — in fact, a lot of people find some degree of genital odour stimulating.

Taboo. Oral sex has long been frowned upon and often made illegal. Underlying the legal strictures and the social disapproval there are age-old religious prohibitions on oral sex which are still powerful. People who accept and practise almost any of the major western religions can therefore be confused and made to feel guilty. On the one hand, they know the facts: that oral sex is entirely safe and that many people find it an appropriate form of sexual expression. On the other, they have grown up in an atmosphere of disapproval or prohibition. In the end, believers have to choose for themselves whether to follow the letter of their religious law or to reject it in favour of their private convictions. It is clear that the major religions are addressing more openly and humanely the morality of sexual behaviours, and this can only ease some believers' guilt. It is, however, certainly in the interest of believers to be aware of the position their religion currently takes.

Femininity and Masculinity. The age-old association between oral sex and homosexuality still threatens some heterosexual people. They feel that giving or receiving oral sex may be a sign of deep-seated or repressed homosexuality. It isn't, but heterosexual men and women who believe that the only real and proper way to express their sexuality is by having intercourse with the penis in the vagina are still affected by the idea. Women sometimes feel that in giving oral sex to a man they are giving him a service and are thereby inferior. Men sometimes feel that stimulating a partner orally reduces their masculinity because the penis is not involved. A lot of inappropriate sexual pride can be involved on both sides.

Fortunately, many people are not significantly affected by any of these negative feelings about oral sex. They feel free to accept it and enjoy it, to give, receive and share. There are also the people who feel perfectly relaxed about oral sex but choose to practise it infrequently or never; they too can gain intimacy from that shared understanding and decision.

> **Q:** "I know my feelings about oral sex are based on some really bad experiences I had. Sometimes I wonder if they will ever change."
>
> **A:** "Many people's feelings about oral sex are directly tied to their experiences. If they have enjoyed it, they will want to do it again, whereas experiences that have produced feelings of embarrassment, anxiety and guilt are not likely to be repeated. However, even when inhibitions and barriers are long-lasting they can be overcome in a trusting and tender relationship in which vulnerability can be risked without fear or shame."

RELATIONSHIPS In relationships the importance of oral sex varies from couple to couple, from person to person and from time to time. Some couples accept oral sex as a natural part of the various things they do together sexually, with each partner giving and receiving in the manner that suits them. Over time, experience with each other and communication enable them to appreciate each other's desires and pleasures and to respond to particular needs as they arise. This kind of giving can produce enormous stimulation and pleasure and is a form of receiving pleasure while giving it. It is nonmeasuring, noncompetitive and unselfish, and leads to the greatest sense of fulfilment:

Q: "All that sounds pretty good, but my wife and I just can't get ourselves to do it. It just doesn't seem right to us. I suppose we are uptight?"

A: "No, you and your wife are not uptight. The true standard of the quality of your sex life together is your mutual sexual fulfilment and happiness — not whether you practise every possible sex act. Couples who are honestly in agreement and do not have oral sex at all, or who have it occasionally, are normal too; they can enjoy just as much pleasure and intimacy as couples who have oral sex regularly.

"Problems can occur with a couple if one wants to try oral sex or have it regularly and the other doesn't. This may result in anger, conflict and guilt, and in such situations a qualified sex therapist or counsellor could be helpful in assisting the couple to sort out their feelings, attitudes and values and to understand the meaning of this issue in their relationship."

Q: "I really enjoy having oral sex with my husband, but when I do, he comes quickly, loses his erection and falls asleep. Now I don't even bother any more, and I know it makes him angry. What should I do?"

A: "This is a common situation and you need to discuss it openly. He is probably going to have to exercise some restraint. Tell him that you enjoy having oral sex with him, but when he ejaculates and falls asleep it leaves you feeling frustrated and alone. Perhaps if he told you when he is nearing ejaculation you could stop and do other things together, and then begin again — if that's what you both want — when he is not quite so excited. Be certain to discuss what gives you pleasure as well. And don't be surprised if your husband is relieved to know what you enjoy and how you feel about what you do together sexually: people individually and as couples need to be clear with each other about their sexual needs and preferences. The momentary discomfort a discussion like this may create will be outweighed by the probable long-term satisfactions and rewards that honest communication can produce."

Q: "What bothers me is my friend wants me to do it to him but he doesn't want to have oral sex with me. I want it too. How can I get him to change?"

A: "Discuss it. Don't let anger and frustration build up. It is not important for sexual activities to be exactly reciprocal and when a relationship gets a measuring, competitive dimension the issue should be sorted out as quickly as possible.

"It may be that your friend is influenced by some myth or misinformation about getting a disease or losing his masculinity. He may be embarrassed because he really doesn't know what to do and needs your help. Perhaps genital odours bother him, and it may help to bathe together and try a scented lotion. So you see it is possible for several things to be responsible for your friend's behaviour. The only way to take care of it is to work it through together so that you understand each other's needs."

Q: "I would like to have oral sex with my wife but I don't know what to do. I'm really embarrassed, and I don't want to make a fool of myself. Is there a way to learn?"

A: "Yes. Most people start off with the feelings you express, wondering if they will do it well and embarrassed by their lack of know-how, but they learn about oral sex by having oral sex. They learn what is pleasing and they take cues from their partners about what works and what doesn't.

"Reading books that show various positions and describe techniques can help. If you read them together you can discuss

what appeals to each of you. You may find that you feel more comfortable the first few times you have oral sex if you do it in the dark — this may reduce embarrassment about how you look while you're giving or receiving. Once you've got used to oral sex you can make it part of your normal range of acts and do it as freely as any other.

"Remember, there is no best way to have oral sex. The best way for you and your wife is the way you are both comfortable and fulfilled."

Q: "My boyfriend says if I really loved him I would have oral sex with him. I do love him, but I just can't. It's not for me."

A: "He's talking nonsense. One can have oral sex with someone without loving them, and one can love someone without having oral sex with them. Forcing someone to do something is rarely a good idea, and in a loving relationship it is uncalled for.

"If oral sex really is not for you, tell him so plainly. Tell him that if he coerces you, you are not going to feel good about it, and if you don't feel good about it your feelings for him are going to be put under an even bigger strain.

"It is important though that you air the subject completely.

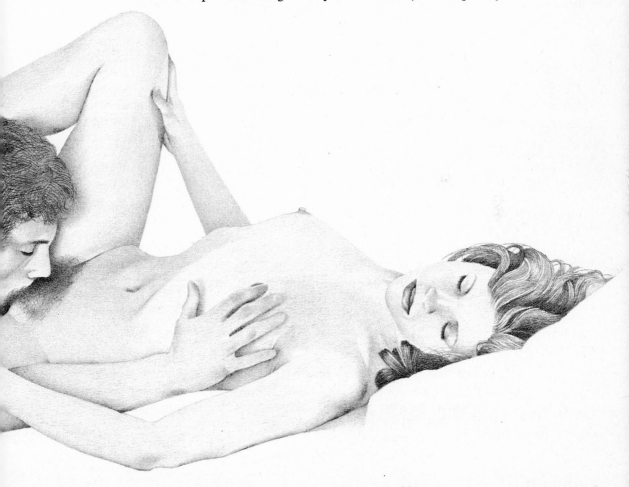

You don't want the development of your relationship to get stuck on this issue, so that it is still in the back of both your minds in the future. Both of you need to examine your motives. Why does he want you to give him oral sex? Perhaps because he wants to experiment, perhaps because he really enjoys oral sex, perhaps because other women do it to their lovers and so he feels he has a right to it. Why don't you want to do it? Perhaps you think it is unclean or unhealthy; perhaps you think that it might make you seem submissive; perhaps you think that if you give him oral sex you will have intercourse less often?

"Try and think all these things through clearly. Try and discuss them so that you can each understand the other's real position. Whether or not you decide to have oral sex, in the end your relationship will only improve by being honest with each other and replacing coercion and frustration by frank understanding."

Q: "I enjoy having oral sex with my wife, but I like to come in her mouth and she doesn't like me to."

A: "It is important to discuss this with your wife and clear up the issue before it becomes a problem. She may simply not like to swallow semen and you will have to adjust to that. Perhaps you can decide together that when you signal your wife that you are about to ejaculate, she removes your penis from her mouth.

"But there may be another side to it. After you ejaculate you may lose your erection and maybe sexual activity between you then stops. Perhaps your wife's reluctance to have you ejaculate in her mouth is a sign that she wants you to maintain your erection and carry on so that she gets satisfaction too. Perhaps you ejaculate quickly when you're given fellatio and she feels deprived of her full pleasure in that way too.

"Whatever the reason for her dislike, talk it over together; try and understand what each other wants and then see if you can't work out a way that makes you both happy."

CULTURE AND RELIGION In western civilization oral sex has always been frowned upon officially and enjoyed privately. The current mix of attitudes is our legacy from the interpretations of centuries of religious scholars and teachers, many of whom sought to prohibit oral sex as being against divine law.

Throughout history, oral sex has often been put down by heterosexuals because it was regarded as a sign of homosexuality. In ancient Greece and in classical Rome it was seen as a male homosexual activity first and as a lesbian activity second. Indeed, having or enjoying oral sex was the principal indicator of homosexuality, and if it was done heterosexually it was thought to show a tendency toward homosexuality. Women prostitutes in Greece commonly provided fellatio for men, leading a contemporary social commentator to observe that soon no female lips would be chaste enough to utter prayers.

Early Judaeo–Christian evidence of the restrictions on oral sex comes from the story of Sodom and Gomorrah. Although the Genesis (19: 4–11) account of these two cities is repeatedly used as biblical evidence against homosexuality, I believe this story is more about oral/genital contact. Because God punished by death the men of Sodom and Gomorrah and destroyed these cities, oral sex was classified as a sin; first, because of its association with homosexuality (principally male, later on female), and second as an act contrary to procreation and therefore inappropriate even within the context of marriage.

The weight of religious teaching over the centuries has had a profound effect on our legal and social rules. As the effects of religions on governments have diminished in this century, society's experience has shown that many needless prohibitions and barriers have been set up in the name of religious covenants. Some people see this as a sign of progress, others take it as an indication of the loss of important social restraints on proper feelings and proper behaviour. We shall look in turn at the attitudes of Judaism, Catholicism and Protestantism.

Judaism. There is no single teaching about oral sex in Judaism which can be called the law. Biblical interpretations, Talmudic teachings and responses from learned rabbis do not convey the attitude of Judaism in a single voice. However, it is clear that any sexual act between Jews can only be evaluated in terms of heterosexual marriage. Marriage is a duty, a mitzvah.

Some strict Orthodox Jews believe the only proper act is intercourse, and essentially for procreative purposes, but most Jews believe sex has an intrinsic worth and value beyond procreation, and each married couple may express that value in the ways they find appropriate. Oral sex can be one of the proper marital sexual expressions.

Catholicism. St Thomas Aquinas exemplified the formal Catholic opinion on oral sex. He taught that anything but face-to-face intercourse with the woman on her back was a sin against God and nature. Even if both man and woman agreed and no one was hurt, any other activity was sinful. This rigid teaching was fully in keeping with the Church's view that the passions of men and women must be controlled; when they were exercised at all, procreation must be the goal.

Throughout history, many popes have by inference argued against oral sex, expecially as an end in itself. In the Encyclical *Humanae Vitae* (1968) Pope Paul VI stated that "each and every marriage act must remain open to the transmission of life." But today the Roman Catholic Church in some of its pastoral teaching offers a more accepting (though still limiting) view of oral sex. Though not publicized by any papal teaching, oral sex is seen in the Church as an appropriate marital sexual expression as long as it is not an end in itself, but is part of an act in which intercourse occurs. This view is not uniformly accepted by all Church leaders, scholars or lay Catholics and it is clear that there exists today a real tension between the historical Catholic teachings on sexual expression and the actual sexual behaviours of Roman Catholics throughout the world. There is no simple, clear, understandable statement from the Church on oral sex. Ordinary practising Catholics are often therefore in some confusion.

It seems to me that Catholic men and women need clear guidance and reassurance by the Church's leadership that their marital sexual behaviour is proper, regardless of the way they choose to express their intimacy and love. After all, the traditional Church laws governing proper and improper sexual acts are interpretations of the Old Testament, reactions to Greek and Roman customs, and the rulings of medieval courts. Mere repetition of these moral evaluations based on sources thousands of years old is not necessarily a proper way to assess or analyze issues whose meanings are different in today's social context. This is not an argument for abandoning moral values, but a proposal that we should reassess traditional rules to be sure that they take account of current knowledge and are relevant to the contemporary world.

Protestantism. Today, most Protestant groups in Europe and America do not assign a sinful meaning to oral sex in marriage. Harmony in the marriage and the meaning of the acts to both partners in it are the standards used by most Protestant sects to evaluate sexual behaviours. Therefore, if oral sex is mutually acceptable and part of the loving relationship between a husband and wife, it is viewed positively, regardless of the procreative intentions of the couple.

Some fundamentalist Protestant sects, however, believe that the only marital act sanctioned by their religion is intercourse for procreative purposes. Their teaching derives from Calvin, Luther and the Protestant Reformation, and says that control of sexual impulses is crucial even in marriage; when they are expressed they must be for procreative purposes and not for pleasure. Oral sex is, therefore, ruled out.

The Puritans who colonized America and dominated the early legal and social system ruled that oral sex even between married couples was not only sinful but illegal and punishable. These early laws or modifications of them still remain on the statute books in many American states. As recently as the late 1970s a married couple in Virginia were prosecuted, convicted and given a jail sentence because they had oral sex in their own home and were seen by a young person who peered through their window. They won the case on appeal, but the mere fact that the case went to a criminal court is a staggering testimony to the enduring power of the ethic.

Q: "What does the Koran say about oral sex?"
A: "The Koran, which is the source of Islamic law, does not mention oral sex specifically. However, the Islamic code insists on the exercise of restraint in all marital acts, and the normal assumption is that oral sex is prohibited in the section of the holy teaching that deals with unnatural acts that are great sins."

POSITIONS FOR INTERCOURSE

FACTS Popular mythology and many manuals of sexual technique would have us believe that there are dozens, scores — even hundreds — of positions for intercourse. A profound symbolism is attached to each, and no-one may be deemed a competent lover until he or she has mastered them all. This is, of course, nonsense. There are very few basic positions (though each can be varied slightly in many many ways), no special significance attaches to any of them, and competence in lovemaking is measured by fulfilment, not by the extent of the repertoire.

People naturally seek variety, but this does not mean it is right for one partner to force choices on the other. Sharing and agreement are the routes to satisfying sex, not power plays or selfishness. This does not mean that there should be endless discussions about who should do what to whom, but that each should let the other know what he or she would like to do. If they agree, then it is fine to do it; if they don't, then one partner should not try and force the issue.

There are no hard and fast rules that can be applied to each person in every situation. The position that one person prefers above all others — what that person regards as the best position — may be one that someone else prefers not to use at all. Attitudes to sex and circumstances dictate different approaches to intercourse, with the result that some couples will use one position almost to the exclusion of all others because they mutually find it to be the most satisfying. Other couples may regularly use several positions almost every time they make love. The "best" position for intercourse is that in which a particular couple on a particular occasion finds the greatest fulfilment; one cannot say more than that.

Q: "Is 'coitus' the same as intercourse?"

A: "Yes. It comes from the Latin *coire*, which means 'to go together.'"

Q: "How frequent is it that a penis or vagina is too large or too small for intercourse?"

A: "Very rarely. Of course, people vary a lot in genital size and if there is a large disparity a couple may find they get greater satisfaction by modifying their techniques, but they can still have fulfilling sex. If a really marked difference in size leads to painful intercourse a medically qualified sex therapist should be consulted."

Q: "Is it really OK to have intercourse standing up?"

A: "Yes, it is just fine as long as you enjoy it; it cannot do any physical harm. The one area of risk is that some people believe they can safely have intercourse without contraception as long as they are standing — that is entirely wrong as a woman gets pregnant by having intercourse, not as a result of using one particular position."

Q: "What about having sex underwater?"
A: "Fine if that's what turns you on. There are no medical risks, but don't believe that the water in a pool, shower, bath or the sea will act as a contraceptive; only contraceptives act like that."

Q: "My husband and I always have sex in the dark, but sometimes I feel that we ought to be able to enjoy sex with the light on. What do you think?"
A: "I think it doesn't matter at all whether the light is on or off as long as you are both happy. If there's a difference of opinion between you, then it should be discussed. If you really want to have intercourse with the light on, suggest it to your husband, but if you feel that you ought to have the light on because other people do, forget it."

Q: "As I'm getting older, I seem to enjoy positions now I didn't like when I was younger. Is this usual?"
A: "Yes. As people age, they often find a gradual change in their preferences. This may be due to changes in mobility, energy levels or health. Incidentally, after menopause some women find that as reduced levels of oestrogen have caused their vaginas to thin out somewhat, positions that lead to more gentle penile thrusting are more suitable."

TECHNIQUES The standard techniques discussed here are: man-on-top, woman-on-top, side-by-side, rear-entry and anal intercourse. They may variously be performed lying down, sitting, standing, kneeling, indoors, outdoors — those are all areas of inventiveness that each couple can explore as they see fit.

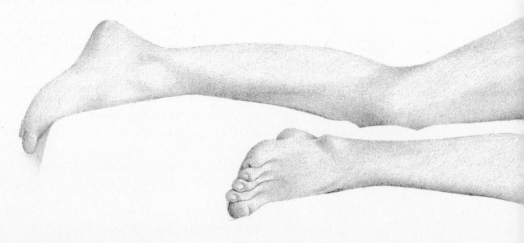

Man-On-Top This is the most common of all intercourse positions. At one time it was thought to be the most natural and proper — indeed, some people thought that any other position was unnatural and improper — but we have come to recognize that such values cannot be applied to sexual techniques.

The woman lies on her back with her legs spread. She may have a pillow under her buttocks to raise her pelvis. Either the man or the woman may guide the penis into the vagina. The man can lie flat on the woman, but this restricts movement and may be uncomfortable; he is more likely to support some or all of his weight on his elbows, hands or knees. The woman can wrap her legs around the man's hips or back if she pleases or even put them over his shoulders. The further up her legs are the deeper the penetration the man can make as he thrusts, making this a particularly good position for a couple trying for a pregnancy.

Although in the man-on-top position the man finds he is limited in the way he can use his hands to caress his partner, it is a very good position for seeing each other and kissing, both during intercourse and after. The woman can use her hands freely to caress the man or to fondle her clitoris. Some women find that the weight of the man on them restricts their pelvic movements and some do not care for the deep penetration the position encourages; it is also an uncomfortable position for women in the middle and later stages of pregnancy.

Q: "Why is the man-on-top position called the 'missionary' position?"

A: "The story goes that Christian missionaries in the last century

who believed that man-on-top was the only natural and proper position sometimes reproved their converts for the 'animal' positions they were accustomed to use and encouraged them to use man-on-top. That an intercourse position should figure in spreading the gospel and civilization may strike us now as bizarre — which is probably what the missionaries' converts thought at the time.

"The degree to which missionaries succeeded in persuading the heathen to have sex 'properly' is not recorded."

Q: "A friend of mine told me he read that the man-on-top position was not good because it lead to quicker ejaculation. Is that true?"

A: "If a man has difficulty in controlling his ejaculation, the man-on-top position is not recommended because it may lead to relatively early ejaculation. Other positions in which vigorous thrusting is less likely are more suitable until ejaculatory control is improved."

Woman-On-Top The statistics indicate that as people are becoming generally more creative and flexible about their sexual expression, so the woman-on-top position is gaining in popularity. Twice as many married couples were using it in the 1970s as in the 1940s.

Because of our traditional erroneous assumptions about men's and women's behaviour, in which the man is supposed to be vigorous and in charge, the woman passive and accepting, some men feel threatened if they adopt the "feminine" position and a woman gets on top of them. This attitude is not as common as it was, but it does still exist.

The other side of the coin is that some women feel too inhibited to try having intercourse on top. They are reluctant, probably because of the way they have socialized, to set the pace and determine the range of activities. Some women feel that if they assume the woman-on-top position it may be seen as a sign of their being "oversexed."

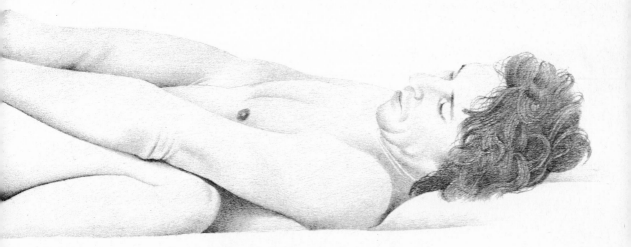

Both men and women who accept these attitudes are allowing their socialization to prevent fulfilling sexual variety. Interestingly, these attitudes are not shared by many other cultures, in which intercourse positions are not endowed with psychological significance, but only with possibilities for pleasure. Roman literature, for example, contains enough references to women "riding" men to suggest that the woman-on-top position was widely used.

The woman-on-top position is not a good one if the woman is trying to get pregnant. To encourage pregnancy, the man's semen must be able to pool deep in the vagina, so she needs to be lying on her back. If she is on top, the semen naturally tends to run out. This does *not* mean, however, that a woman cannot get pregnant in this position.

Woman-on-top is a good position for the later months of pregnancy, for it allows intercourse without the woman's growing belly getting in the way. It is also a good position for men with large stomachs: it takes the pressure off and allows considerable freedom of movement.

Older men, and particularly men with heart conditions, may have the woman-on-top position recommended to them. It is less demanding, and requires the expenditure of less vigorous energy. A waterbed is especially helpful in this context, as it reflects and repeats the couple's movements, rather than absorbing them as a conventional bed does. Another aspect of the woman-on-top position is that it allows the woman to set a gentle pace and to be symbolically caring and protective of a man with a serious medical condition.

The man lies on his back and the woman lowers herself onto his erect penis. Either the man or the woman may guide the penis into the vagina. Couples may start in this position or arrive at it by rolling over from a man-on-top or side-by-side position. The woman can remain squatting on her knees facing the man, she can straighten her legs, or she can turn around and face the man's feet. Her weight usually presents no problem.

The woman can regulate the depth of penetration of the penis and the rate of thrusting; the position also allows for maximal indirect stimulation of the clitoris by the penis, and many women report that they come more frequently when they are on top than when they are underneath. Some women though find that penetration is too deep in this position and so prefer not to use it. Also, with vigorous movements the penis can easily slip out, which is frustrating.

Woman-on-top has a number of advantages: both the man and the woman have their hands freer in this position than in most to caress each other; the man, for example, can easily stimulate the clitoris with his hands. The couple can also see more of each other than in most other positions.

Q: "Can a man's penis be damaged if the woman is on top?"
A: "No, but it can be hurt if he and his partner try it without his penis being fully erect. A semi-erect penis can be bent by the weight of the woman, and obviously this could be painful. A man can also get hurt if his penis slips out of the vagina during vigorous thrusting and she slides down onto his testicles. It is therefore desirable for the man to have a full erection before insertion and for the couple to take intercourse unhurriedly."

Side-by-Side This is a very comfortable position in which the partners have intercourse lying on their sides facing each other. A couple can start off in the position or arrive at it by rolling over from man- or woman-on-top.

Deep pelvic thrusting is difficult when a couple are side by side and some couples prefer not to use the position for that reason. On the other hand, both partners' hands are free to caress each other and they can kiss during intercourse.

Because energetic thrusting is difficult side by side, this is a particularly good position for people with heart conditions or other reasons to
avoid strenuous activity. It is also a useful position during pregnancy as the
woman's belly gets in the way less than, for example, in the man-on-top
position and the couple can feel more at ease.

Rear Entry This is *not* the same as anal intercourse. Rear entry means the man's penis entering the woman's vagina when she has her back to him. It can be done with the woman standing but bending over and supporting herself, with the woman on her hands and knees and the man kneeling behind her, or it can be done with both partners lying on their sides, her back to his front. Either partner can guide the penis into the vagina.

Rear entry allows for deep penetration and vigorous pushing if the couple want that. The man's hands are free to caress the woman and he

can reach her clitoris easily, but it is more difficult for the woman to caress the man as she has to reach behind her. Some couples greatly enjoy the sensation of the man's pelvis against the woman's buttocks.

The drawbacks of rear entry are that the penis entering from behind gives very little stimulation to the clitoris and some couples do not like the lack of face-to-face intimacy. This is a perfectly legitimate feeling and should be respected, though the other side of the coin is that rear entry is a perfectly legitimate position.

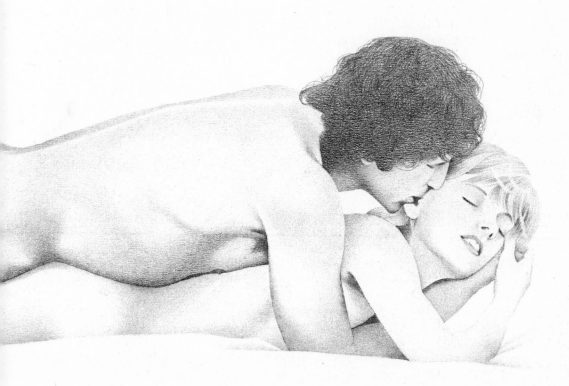

Anal Intercourse Anal intercourse is intercourse with a man's penis inserted in his partner's rectum. It is commonly thought of as a homosexual act, but many heterosexual couples enjoy it too. It is also known as "sodomy" and "buggery," and is subject to legal restriction in Britain, even between man and wife.

Anal intercourse is sometimes regarded as the ultimate in depravity and has regularly been condemned by religious and secular authorities. There is of course no way that a woman will get pregnant if a man has anal intercourse with her, and so the act is viewed as contrary to some churches' requirements that sexual acts should ultimately be open to the transmission of life. On the other hand, countless millions of people, regardless of their sexual orientation, have had and enjoyed anal intercourse without any harm resulting: they regard it as a legitimate means of sexual expression and as one of the fulfilling ways in which people can express their desire and affection for each other. It is up to each couple to decide what is best for them — if they are comfortable with anal intercourse, fine; if their consciences do not permit it or they do not enjoy the act, they should be under no compulsion to do it.

Before anal intercourse some people clear the rectum with a small disposable enema. It is also desirable to use a lubricant like K–Y Jelly or saliva to make entry easier, and it helps if the anal sphincter (the muscle on the outside of the rectum) is relaxed as well. Since the rectum contains bacteria, mouth or vagina contact with a penis after anal intercourse is unwise until the penis has been thoroughly washed.

Pain or bleeding during or after anal intercourse means that there is a problem that should be checked out by a doctor. The couple should avoid anal intercourse until this has been done.

MYTHS Mistaken ideas about intercourse positions can mean reduced satisfaction, greater risk of unintended pregnancy, unnecessary anxiety and misplaced accusations. These are some of the common misbeliefs:

* you cannot get pregnant if you have intercourse standing up
* you can get pregnant by having anal intercourse
* if the woman is on top it means she is aggressive and oversexed and the man is submissive
* the choice of positions shows who is active and who is passive
* if a woman wears a diaphragm and gets on top of the man his penis will dislodge her diaphragm
* most women prefer to have intercourse with the man on top
* contraceptive foams and jellies run out if the woman gets on top
* using different positions for intercourse is a sign of being skilled lovers
* experimenting with different positions is a sign of dissatisfaction in a relationship
* using a rear-entry position means that the two partners don't like each other
* the right way to have intercourse is with the man on top.

SEX IN PREGNANCY

FACTS Most couples find that they have sex less often once the woman has become pregnant. Sometimes the reason is physical, sometimes it is emotional and sometimes people avoid having sex because they believe, wrongly, that intercourse will damage the baby, hurt the woman or disrupt the pregnancy.

Many couples continue sexual activity throughout pregnancy in a natural way, varying the kinds of sexual expression and the frequency according to how they feel at each stage. Some couples however believe that pregnancy means they must reduce or even eliminate altogether the expression of their sexual feelings. Those who believe that sex and pregnancy don't mix are responding to ancient superstitions and myths, reinforced by age-old religious injunctions; if, as Christianity has often taught, the purpose of sexual activity is to start a pregnancy, there must, for example, be some doubt about the rightness of intercourse with a pregnant woman. Poor guidance from doctors about sex during pregnancy has also contributed to the confusion and ignorance about what can or can't be done. Also, pregnant women sometimes think they are less attractive — and on occasion men agree with them — which tends to reduce the frequency of sexual activity.

The likely reduction in activity may take the form of a decrease in all forms of sex, or it may follow a pattern that has shown up in some research in which there is a reduction of sexual activity in the first and third trimesters, and an increase to the usual or even to a higher rate during the second. Why this pattern should arise we do not know.

The nausea and discomfort some women feel during pregnancy may result in their being unable to enjoy sex. Even though this discomfort is often confined to the mornings of the first trimester, a general uneasiness is created which may cut down on the frequency of intercourse in the second and third trimesters too. The woman may be so fatigued that she lacks the energy and enthusiasm to have intercourse. Some women find that not feeling just right is enough to prevent them from initiating or participating happily in sex.

Sometimes couples are advised by doctors to avoid intercourse, at least for a short while, due to slight bleeding, vaginal or abdominal pain, or if the woman has a history of miscarriage. These are good reasons for not having intercourse early in the pregnancy, but the fear that this information produces in the couple may lead them to avoid having intercourse throughout the pregnancy. Couples should ask their doctor when it is alright to resume regular sex.

Intercourse will become more difficult as the woman's belly grows if the couple are not familiar with appropriate positions. This is a real physical factor inhibiting sex, but a little experimentation easily gets round the problem — see TECHNIQUES on page 427.

Q: "Can an orgasm during pregnancy begin labour and lead to a problem?"

A: "No. Although orgasm causes your uterus to contract, opening of the cervix, which is what is necessary for the birth process to begin, does not take place until it is time for you to have your baby. In the very last stage of pregnancy, the ninth month, your cervix may be ripe for labour, and it is possible that the contractions of orgasm may hasten what is going to occur anyway."

Q: "I read that sex late in pregnancy can in some circumstances endanger the foetus. What are the facts?"

A: "A recent study in the United States indicated that women who had intercourse during the last month of pregnancy had higher rates of amniotic fluid infection than those who didn't. Also, premature babies had more health problems, noticeably respiratory disorders, if their mothers had intercourse in the month before delivery.

"Although alarming, these results are not conclusive, as other factors that might have been responsible were not studied sufficiently. Many doctors still believe that the psychological benefits of the intimacy intercourse provides during pregnancy outweigh the possibility of any problems it may bring about. Some doctors though advise against intercourse once the cervix starts to open (dilate) during the ninth month, and other doctors are now advising their patients to reduce the frequency of intercourse during the last trimester as well. This doesn't present too much of a problem for most couples as the frequency of intercourse during the last few months tends to decrease anyway.

"Plainly, we need to know more in this area and research is under way to discover the true facts."

Q: "Is it common for men to have affairs when their wives are pregnant?"

A: "No. Although some men have extramarital sex during their wives' pregnancies it is less frequent than many people believe. Most men are able to achieve sexual satisfaction throughout their wives' pregnancies without seeking another partner. In Bittman and Zalk's book *Expectant Fathers*, only a small proportion (seven percent) of men in their study whose wives were pregnant had sex outside the marriage. The men did however report an increase in sexual fantasies about other women. The authors concluded that a temporary decrease during pregnancy in a couple's sexual contact was not a significant reason for the man to seek extramarital sex."

Q: "I'm seven months pregnant and lately I've just wanted to kiss and cuddle. Intercourse or oral sex just isn't for me right now. My husband thinks I'm turned off to him and involved only with the baby growing inside me, but I'm not. Is there something wrong with me?"

A: "No. It is common for a woman's interest in some sexual acts to decline during the last three months of pregnancy. Intercourse and oral sex may be awkward or become uncomfortable during this stage, even when they were enjoyable during the early stages. You can't expect your husband to read your mind, so share your feelings with him.

"Kissing and cuddling are important ways of expressing feelings, and if your husband understood the situation his ability to respond would be improved. There is no need for you to drift apart, misunderstand each other and lose the rewards of being close, even late in your pregnancy."

Q: "Is there any dangerous sex act during pregnancy?"
A: "Yes. Vigorous blowing into the vagina. In rare instances air bubbles may be picked up by blood vessels in the uterus and interfere with circulation in the mother's lungs and brain, resulting in the possible death of the mother and the need to remove the baby regardless of the month of development. Other than this particular kind of vigorous blowing into the vagina oral sex is safe."

TECHNIQUES All the kinds of sexual expression that couples are used to can continue during pregnancy, though as the woman's belly grows it is often desirable to adapt their customary positions for intercourse. Many couples find that the frequency of intercourse declines, but they adopt other forms of sexual expression — massage, masturbation and oral sex in particular — so that they can continue to express their intimacy fully.

We shall look in turn at each of the main ways of expressing intimacy in pregnancy: intercourse, masturbation, oral sex and massage.

Intercourse. Early in pregnancy, especially in the first three months, the man-on-top position usually presents no physical difficulty for the couple. Couples are often worried that they might hurt the baby, but there is no need for anxiety — they can't.

As the woman's belly grows larger, the face-to-face position becomes less practical — the belly presents a considerable obstacle to penis–vagina contact. People then make more use of alternatives, such as woman-on-top (page 417) and side-by-side (page 420).

The woman-on-top position, where she sits astride the man, is entirely safe and no harm can come to the baby. A side-by-side position with the man behind allows for rear entry of the penis into the vagina. Side-by-side facing each other is also favourable, as, like rear-entry, it means that both people have their hands free to caress each other.

Each couple's creativity can add variety to these basic positions. For example, the woman-on-top position can be done on a chair rather than a bed; for rear-entry the woman can be on her hands and knees to start with, rather than lying down. Pregnancy does encourage experimentation and many couples find that some of the practices they adopt during pregnancy are continued and become a regular part of their sexual expression after the birth of the baby. Intercourse is not obligatory though, and some couples find that after the first few months of pregnancy it becomes sufficiently uncomfortable that they prefer to seek their main sexual expression in other ways, such as those that follow.

Masturbation. Self-masturbation and mutual masturbation are both popular during pregnancy. Masturbation (pages 385–96) may be used as a satisfying end in itself or as part of some other way of releasing sexual tension.

Some people, of course, cannot accept masturbation as a proper practice or as part of their personal ethic, and so they reject it in pregnancy as they do the rest of the time. Masturbation is just as appropriate in pregnancy as at any other time, but if an individual or a couple feels that it simply is not right then it is best ruled off their list of options.

Oral Sex. Oral sex (pages 397–412) is popular during pregnancy — indeed, some people who used not to have oral sex before pregnancy have experimented as intercourse became more difficult, and they found it very satisfying. It can be continued safely right through pregnancy.

Sometimes, increased vaginal lubrication and a slight change in vaginal odour present a temporary difficulty, but it is nothing that cannot be overcome by bathing before sex and maybe using a scented lotion. There is one caution, however. Vigorous blowing into the vagina can lead to the formation of an air embolism that is dangerous both to the baby and to the mother.

Massage. Massage (see Touching and Caressing, pages 432-4) is an extremely sensuous and fulfilling form of sexual expression. It has the advantage of providing the opportunity for deep feelings to be communicated without a genital act. During the pregnancy period or some part of it this may be an ideal way for a couple to be in close contact with each other and not to have to worry about intercourse, oral sex or other genital practices which they may feel uncomfortable about at the time. Afterwards, massage may well remain as another way two people communicate their feelings.

You don't have to be an expert to provide pleasure through massage. Your partner can tell you what feels good and you can work out satisfying techniques together.

And then there are the small, everyday ways of showing affection. Kissing, holding and touching each other also express loving care, and are important signs that all is well in the relationship and that you are still physically and emotionally close to each other. They can provide reassurance that the two people still find each other attractive even in periods when they may be refraining from genital sex.

MYTHS Wrong beliefs about sex in pregnancy are legion. These are some:

* women lose interest in sex when they are pregnant
* men are no longer sexually interested in their wives when their bellies start to get bigger
* women cannot have an orgasm when they are pregnant
* intercourse during the first stages of pregnancy will cause the woman to miscarry
* sex during pregnancy leads the unborn to have greater sexual desires when they are adults
* frequent sex during pregnancy leaves a physical mark on the baby
* husbands usually look around for another sex partner when their wives are pregnant because they don't get enough
* from the moment of conception on, intercourse with the man on top is dangerous to the mother and baby
* masturbation is dangerous during pregnancy
* male sperm can travel up to the developing baby and be used as a source of nourishment
* intercourse during pregnancy produces labour regardless of the month
* intercourse, oral sex and sperm pass bacteria to the woman, which leads to physical problems
* babies can feel what is happening during intercourse
* the weight of the man and his thrusting can damage the baby.

FEELINGS During pregnancy many people — women as well as men — find that their feelings about themselves and their partners affect their sexual practices. These feelings range from optimism and excitement to depression and self-doubt. Not everyone feels the same way during pregnancy and feelings readily change as a pregnancy progresses.

"I feel so unattractive. I've lost my shape and I am fat."

"My breasts are finally the size and shape I've always wanted them to be. I feel so sexy."

"How can he want to look at me or touch me?"

"I couldn't believe how nurturing I felt. I thought men weren't supposed to feel that way."

"She feels ugly and I feel she is blooming. It's a real turn-on for me."

"All the attention she and the baby are getting is starting to annoy me. Frankly, I feel left out."

Some women feel deeply that they have lost their attractiveness when their pregnancies become obvious. They feel their changing appearance is bound to be a turn-off for their husbands and so they may behave defensively, without actually discovering what their husbands feel. Men may be confused and uncertain about why their wives are behaving this way — and indeed they may actually find their wives less attractive: it does happen. Either way, sexual activity diminishes to the detriment of the relationship. On the other hand, a man may find his wife just as appealing, perhaps in a different, more compelling way.

The mix of feelings can be subtle and shifting. Suspicion can breed suspicion, which is why it is important for both people to be open about their excitement as well as their anxiety, about their vulnerability as well as their optimism. Each partner is likely to need support and reassurance from the other at some stage in the pregnancy: giving and receiving it will make for greater mutuality and greater fulfilment.

RELATIONSHIPS If a couple's sexual activity is reduced during pregnancy, this can easily lead to their feeling estranged from each other. They become concerned, but are unsure whether the increased distance between them is a spontaneous effect of the woman's being pregnant or whether they can do something about it. They can, of course, change the situation for the better. The barrier that is being built doesn't have to be there, and it doesn't have to go on growing. They can discuss their concerns and come to understand each other's anxieties.

Sexual expression during pregnancy can be a very important way of keeping close, of avoiding the separateness that concerns many people. It is natural that there should be some strains on the relationship — that the baby will be alright, that the couple will successfully adapt to their imminent role as parents — but it is through continued intimacy that the couple can adjust and move together. Intimacy built during pregnancy through mutual understanding can be a positive feature of the relationship after the child is born.

CULTURE AND RELIGION Currently, the major religions do not prohibit sexual activity during pregnancy, though Catholic, Protestant and Jewish believers have all been faced with prohibitions in the past.

For centuries the Catholic Church's teaching on intercourse was that it was solely for procreative purposes. So it followed that once pregnancy occurred intercourse was not necessary and could be considered a surrender to immoral lust. In the twelfth century the Church taught that sex during pregnancy was a risk to the embryo and would cause a miscarriage. St Thomas Aquinas in the next century also condemned it, and in the fifteenth century St Bernardine wrote that it was animal-like. These attitudes persisted until recently, and were not peculiar to Catholics. The Church of England, for example, right up to the early twentieth century had similar prohibitions against sex during pregnancy. Religious prohibition was translated into social taboo: during the Victorian period intercourse during pregnancy was thought to leave an indelible mark on the baby or to cause it to suffer from epilepsy. Marriage manuals therefore taught abstinence. There have been some very strict Orthodox Jewish interpretations of Jewish law which suggest avoidance of intercourse during pregnancy, but the fundamental Jewish belief is that sex during pregnancy is a moral act, even a mitzvah for the man if his wife is desirous. The Koran, by contrast, prohibits sex during pregnancy.

TOUCHING AND CARESSING

Touching and caressing are enjoyable, fulfilling, sensuous and sexual. From earliest childhood touching is crucial to emotional development and the growth of a healthy self-image. In adulthood it is an important source of fulfilment and communication. Touching, caressing and fondling can be enriching, satisfying acts of sensual communication in themselves. Some people seem to regard them as being appropriate only when intercourse or some other sexual act is to follow, but it is devaluing this form of erotic contact to see it in such a limited context.

Touching and caressing can be enjoyably explored through some kind of massage, in which each partner takes time to touch or stroke parts of the other's body in a deliberately sensuous and relaxing way. It is not necessary to have learned the proper techniques of massage to make this kind of communication highly satisfying, but it works best when each partner lets the other know what he or she enjoys most.

Some parts of the body ("erogenous zones") are particularly sensitive to touch — the genitals are the most obvious example — but all parts if touched sensitively can bring pleasure. Everyone differs in their responsiveness in different areas and in their responses to variations in the nature of the touch.

An erotic massage can be a satisfying act in itself, whether or not it results in orgasm. It is an act that some couples enjoy particularly because it is an opportunity for one to concentrate on giving and the other on receiving, rather than both partners giving and receiving simultaneously, as in intercourse and other acts. It is a very good way both for partners to arouse each other and to prolong a sense of intimacy.

Touching (or massage or caressing) is not an obligatory act or a requirement of liberated sexuality. Nor does it have to be structured. Couples who do enjoy it however sometimes use oils and lotions (at room temperature) to increase the sensuousness of the experience (they also ensure that their hands are warm before they start).

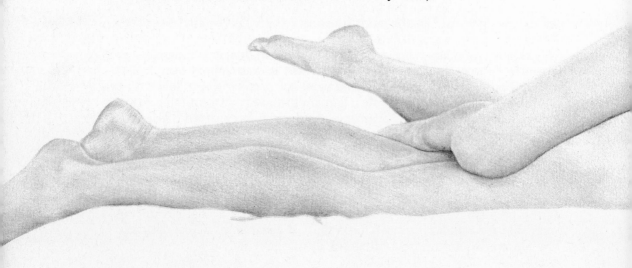

Q: "Do we need to use all those oils and lotions to get into the massage thing properly?"

A: "No. Many couples find that the use of their hands alone is sufficient. The important thing is that you and your partner should choose what you both enjoy most."

Q: "What is a massage parlour?"

A: "It is a place where men (usually) receive massage from (usually) women and frequently can have sex if they are willing to pay extra. Massage parlours tend to sell arousing massage rather than the kind that is designed to relax knotted muscles and tone up a tired body. Parlours are legal in most places because they are supposedly only providing massage; the additional sexual services are not advertised, and arrests and convictions are difficult because the woman and the man are alone in a room without witnesses."

Q: "I read where a woman became a prostitute because she needed to be touched. Can that be true?"

A: "All people need to be touched, and maybe someone who from infancy was deprived of affectionate touching might go that far to compensate. I think you would find though that there would be much more to this case if it were to be investigated."

Q: "I really like to be touched and massaged, but my partner spends all the time on my genitals. After a few minutes of touching we have intercourse and I feel cheated."

A: "At some appropriate moment discuss this situation with your partner and describe what you like and how you like it. Perhaps you can take the lead and begin the touching and massage, and indicate how you like it as you go about pleasing your partner."

FURTHER READING

General

THE ENCYCLOPEDIA OF SEXUAL BEHAVIOR, Albert Ellis and Albert Abarbanel eds, Jason Aronson Inc., New York, 1973

THE FAMILY BOOK ABOUT SEXUALITY, Mary S. Calderone and Eric W. Johnson, Harper and Row, New York, 1981

FUNDAMENTALS OF HUMAN SEXUALITY, Herant A. Katchadourian and Donald T. Lunde, Holt, Rinehart and Winston, New York, 3rd edition 1980

THE HITE REPORT, Shere Hite, Macdonald Futura, London, 1981

ON SEXUALITY, Sigmund Freud, Penguin Books, Harmondsworth, 1977

THE REDBOOK REPORT ON FEMALE SEXUALITY, Carol Tavris and Susan Sadd, Dell, New York, 1977

THE SEXUAL REVOLUTION, Wilhelm Reich, Vision Press, London, 1972

SEX OFFENDERS: AN ANALYSIS OF TYPES, Paul Gebhard et al., Harper and Row, New York, 1965

SEXUAL BEHAVIOR IN THE HUMAN MALE, Alfred C. Kinsey, Wardell B. Pomeroy, Clyde E. Martin, W. B. Saunders Co., Philadelphia, 1948

SEXUAL BEHAVIOR IN THE HUMAN FEMALE, Alfred C. Kinsey, Wardell B. Pomeroy, Clyde E. Martin and Paul H. Gebhard, W. B. Saunders Co., Philadelphia, 1953

THE SPADA REPORT, James Spada, New American Library, 1979

THE MEDICAL RISKS OF LIFE, Stephen Lock and Tony Smith, Penguin Books, Harmondsworth, 1976

Culture

HUMAN SEXUALITY IN FOUR PERSPECTIVES, Frank A. Beach ed., Johns Hopkins University Press, Baltimore, 1977

SEX IN HISTORY, Reay Tannahill, Sphere Books, London, 1981

SEX AND TEMPERAMENT IN THREE PRIMITIVE SOCIETIES, Margaret Mead, Routledge & Kegan Paul, London, 1977

SEXUAL LIFE IN ANCIENT GREECE, Hans Licht, Abbey Library, London, 1971

Religion

EMBODIMENT: AN APPROACH TO SEXUALITY AND CHRISTIAN THEOLOGY, James B. Nelson. S.P.C.K., London, 1979

HOMOSEXUAL WAY: A CHRISTIAN OPTION?, David Field, Grove Books, London, 1976

HUMAN SEXUALITY: NEW DIRECTIONS IN CATHOLIC THOUGHT, Anthony Kosnik, William Carroll, Angus Cunningham, Ronald Modras, James Schulte, Search Press, London, 1978

BIRTH CONTROL IN JEWISH LAW: MARITAL RELATIONS, CONTRACEPTION AND ABORTION, David M. Feldman, Greenwood Press, London, 1980

Ages and Stages

THE SEXUAL BEHAVIOUR OF YOUNG PEOPLE, Michael Schofield, Penguin Books, Harmondsworth, 1973

MAKE IT HAPPY: WHAT SEX IS ALL ABOUT, Jane Cousins, Penguin Books, Harmondsworth, 1980

SEX IN THE MID AND LATER YEARS, Scheingold and Wagner, Human Science Publishers, US, 1977

BOY GIRL MAN WOMAN, B. H. Claesson, Penguin Books, Harmondsworth, 1977

MENOPAUSE: A POSITIVE APPROACH, Rosetta Reitz, Harvester Press, Brighton, 1979

MY MOTHER SAID: THE WAY YOUNG PEOPLE LEARN ABOUT SEX AND BIRTH CONTROL, Christine Farrell, Routledge & Kegan Paul, London, 1978

THE SINGLE WOMAN'S GUIDE TO PREGNANCY AND PARENTHOOD, Patricia Ashdown-Sharp, Penguin Books, Harmondsworth, 1975

Birth Control

MY BODY, MY HEALTH: THE CONCERNED WOMAN'S BOOK OF GYNAECOLOGY, Felicia Stewart, Gary Stewart, Robert Hatcher, John Wiley, Chichester, 1979

THE BIRTH CONTROL BOOK, Howard I. Shapiro, Penguin Books, Harmondsworth, 1980

NATURAL SEX, Mary Shivanandan, Hamlyn, London, 1979

Desire and Response

UNDERSTANDING HUMAN SEXUAL INADEQUACY, Fred Belliveau and Lin Richter, Hodder & Stoughton, London, 1971

AN ANALYSIS OF HUMAN SEXUAL RESPONSE, Ruth and Edward Brecher, eds, New American Library, 1970

DISORDERS OF SEXUAL DESIRE, Helen Singer Kaplan, Bailliere Tindall, London, 1980

HUMAN SEXUAL INADEQUACY, William H. Masters and Virginia E. Johnson, Bantam Books, London, 1980

HUMAN SEXUAL RESPONSE, William H. Masters and Virginia E. Johnson, Bantam Books, London, 1980

THE NEW SEX THERAPY, Helen Singer Kaplan, Penguin Books, Harmondsworth, 1981

WOMEN DISCOVER ORGASM, Lonnie Barbach, Free Press, New York, 1980

Drugs
MEDICINES: A GUIDE FOR EVERYBODY, Peter Parish, Penguin Books, Harmondsworth, 1980

Disability
SOURCE BOOK FOR THE DISABLED, Gloria Hale, Paddington Press, London, 1979
ENTITLED TO LOVE, Wendy Greengross, National Marriage Guidance Council, 1976
SEX AND THE MENTALLY HANDICAPPED, Craft and Craft, Routledge & Kegan Paul, London, 1978
SEX AND SPINA BIFIDA, Bill Stewart, ASBAH, London, 1978

Erotica
OBSCENITY, Geoffrey Robertson, Weidenfeld & Nicholson, London, 1979

Gender and Sexual Orientation
BISEXUALITY, Charlotte Wolff, Quartet Books, London, 1979
HOMOSEXUALITIES: A STUDY OF DIVERSITY AMONG MEN AND WOMEN, Alan P. Bell and Martin S. Weinberg, Mitchell Beazley, London, 1978
HOMOSEXUAL DESIRE, Guy Hocquenghem, Allison & Busby, London, 1978
COMING OUT, Jeffrey Weeks, Quartet Books, London 1977
THE SEXUAL AND GENDER DEVELOPMENT OF YOUNG CHILDREN, Evelyn K. Oremland and Jerome D. Oremland, Ballinger Publishing Co., Cambridge, Mass., 1978
SEXUAL IDENTITY CONFLICT IN CHILDREN AND ADULTS, Richard Green, Duckworth, London, 1976
IS THE HOMOSEXUAL MY NEIGHBOUR? Letha Scanzoni and Virginia Ramey Mollenkatt, SCM Press, London, 1978
TRANSVESTISM, P. Brierley, Pergamon Press, Oxford, 1979

Incest
INCEST, Karen Meiselman, Sage Publications, London, 1978

Love
SEX IN HUMAN LOVING, Eric Berne, Penguin Books, Harmondsworth, 1973
IN THE NAME OF LOVE, Jill Tweedie, Granada Books, London, 1981

Male Sexual Systems
MAN'S BODY: AN OWNER'S MANUAL, Diagram Group, Paddington Press, London, 1977
MEN AND SEX, Bernard Zilbergeld, Fontana Books, London, 1980

Pregnancy
PREGNANCY, Gordon Bourne, Pan Books, London, 1975
PREGNANCY, MONTH BY MONTH, Consumers' Association, London, 1977
THE FIRST NINE MONTHS OF LIFE, Geraldine Flanagan, Heinemann, London, 1963
BIRTH WITHOUT VIOLENCE, Frederic Leboyer, Fontana, London, 1977
THE EXPERIENCE OF CHILDBIRTH, Sheila Kitzinger, Penguin Books, Harmondsworth, 1970

Pregnancy Termination
ABORTION: THE EVIDENCE, National Abortion Campaign, London, 1977
"Abortion in the USA 1978-1979," *Family Planning Perspectives* 13 (1), January-February 1981

Rape
AGAINST OUR WILL: MEN, WOMEN AND RAPE, Susan Brownmiller, Penguin Books, Harmondsworth, 1977

Sexually Transmitted Diseases
SEXUALLY TRANSMITTED DISEASES: THE FACTS, David Barlow, Oxford University Press, Oxford, 1981

Women's Sexual Systems
OUR BODIES, OUR SELVES, Angela Phillips and Jill Rakusen, Penguin Books, Harmondsworth, 1978
WOMANWISE: EVERY WOMAN'S GUIDE TO GYNAECOLOGY, Peter Saunders, Pan Books, London, 1980

Acts and Feelings
HUMAN AUTOEROTIC PRACTICES, Manfred F. De Martino, Human Sciences Press, New York, 1979
THE JOY OF SEX, Alex Comfort, Quartet Books, London, 1978
THE MASSAGE BOOK, George Downing, Wildwood House, London, 1973
TOUCHING, Ashley Montagu, Harper & Row, New York, 1979

GLOSSARY–INDEX

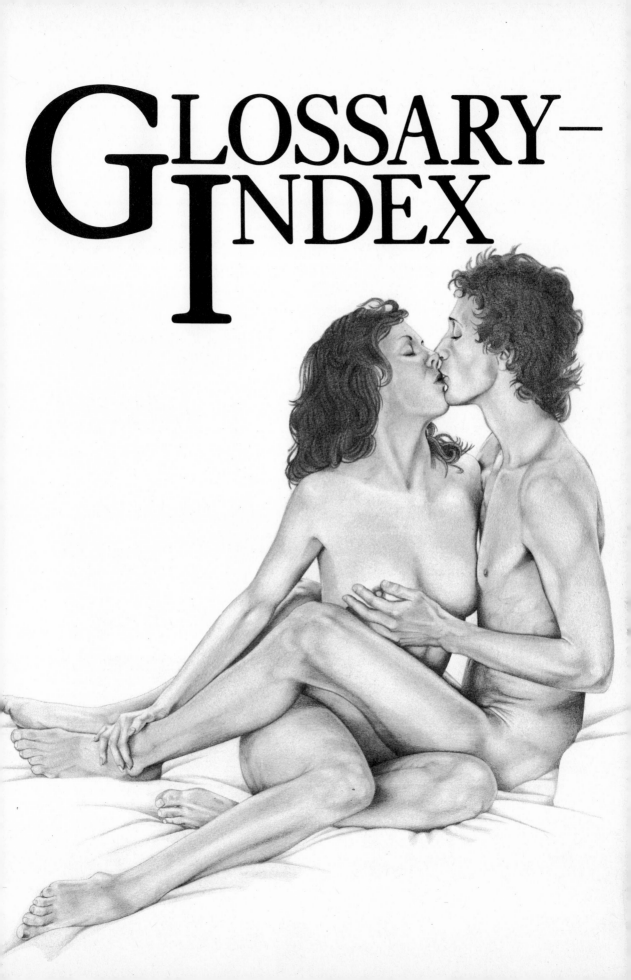

Abortion: 285–90
The termination of a pregnancy either by removing an immature foetus from the womb or by deliberately causing a miscarriage.

Afterbirth: 274
The placenta, which is delivered from the uterus after the birth of a baby.

Ambisexuality: 186–92
The capacity to express oneself sexually with a person of either sex. The realization of the capacity is called bisexuality.

Amenorrhoea: 356
The absence of menstruation in a woman after puberty.

Amniocentesis: 255
Procedure in which a small amount of amniotic fluid is withdrawn from the amniotic sac and examined to check for disorders in a developing foetus; also used to determine the sex of the foetus.

Amniotic Sac: 259, 273
Thin fluid-filled membrane that surrounds and protects the developing foetus.

Amyl Nitrite: 133
Drug that has become popular as an adjunct to sexual activity. Common names: poppers, amys.

Anal Intercourse: 424
Intercourse with a penis inserted in a partner's rectum. Common names: sodomy, buggery.

Androgens: 237
Male sex hormones, produced mainly in the testicles, though some are produced by the adrenal glands. Small amounts are produced by the adrenal glands in females.

Androgyny: 161
The integration in one personality of characteristics traditionally assigned to the other sex as well.

Aphrodisiac: 135–6
Any substance thought to arouse sexual desire or enhance sexual performance.

Areola: 364
The darker pigmented area around the nipple.

Artificial Insemination: 206–7
The placing of living sperm on the cervix in order to achieve fertilization. AIH is artificial insemination by husband and AID artificial insemination by donor.

Autoeroticism: 385–96
Sexual arousal and expression, such as masturbation and fantasy, not involving a partner.

Bartholin's Glands: 336
Glands on each side of the labia minora that secrete small amounts of fluid when a woman is sexually aroused.

Birth Control: 43–86
All forms of attempting to ensure that intercourse does not result in pregnancy.

Bisexuality: 186–92
The orientation in which a person requires sexual contact with members of both sexes to achieve satisfying sexual expression and emotional fulfilment.

Blastocyst: 259
The tiny cluster of cells which attaches itself to the lining of the uterus several days after conception and grows into an embryo.

Body Image: 87–90
The concept we have of how our bodies appear to ourselves and of how we believe others see us.

Breast Examination: 375
Routine procedures by which a woman may check her breasts or have them checked for the presence of lumps or growths.

Breasts: 363–80

Breech Birth: 283
A baby positioned to emerge feet or buttocks first.

Caesarean Section: 280–83
Surgical procedure used when vaginal delivery of a baby presents a risk to the mother or baby. An incision is made through the walls of the abdomen and uterus and the baby is lifted out.

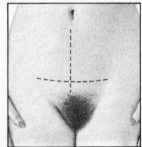

Castration: 233–4
The process whereby the testicles are removed.

Castration Anxiety: 219
Freudian theory about psychosexual development according to which small boys fear their fathers will castrate them to prevent rivalry for their mothers' love.

Cervical Cap: 60
Contraceptive device that blocks a woman's cervix.

Cervix: 343–4
The narrow, lower part of the uterus which dips into the back of the vagina.

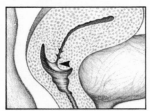

Chancre: 317, 322
Sore characteristic of both syphilis and chancroid.

Chancroid: 317
Sexually transmitted disease spread by contact with pus from sores called chancres.

Chromosome: 254
Material in the cell nucleus that contains the genes.

Cilia: 361
Hair-like structures on the inner walls of the Fallopian tubes that help move the egg towards the uterus.

Circumcision: 225–8
The surgical removal of the foreskin.

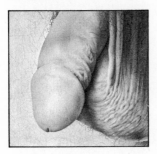

Climacteric: 36–41
Critical period in the midlife of women and men. In women menopause is a chief sign of this period. In some men psychological and emotional difficulties may be apparent.

Clitoridectomy: 332–3
The surgical removal of the clitoris, sometimes called female circumcision.

Clitoris: 329–33
Female sex organ consisting of a head called the glans,

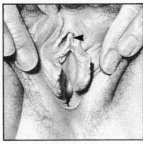

and a body or shaft. Approximately the size of a cherry stone, it is covered by a hood made up of tissue where the labia minora meet. Common name: clit.

Cohabiting 27–9
Arrangement whereby two people live together in a sexual relationship without being married.

Conception: 252
The time when a fertilized egg implants in the womb.

Condom: 51–4
Thin rubber sheath worn over the penis as a birth control method. Common names: Johnnies, rubbers, French letters.

**Contraception/
Contraceptives:**
  see Birth Control

Corona: 217, 225
The rim of the glans or head of the penis.

Couvade: 266–7
The parallel physical and psychological responses some men experience during their wives' pregnancies.

Cowper's Glands: 245
Two glands located either side of the urethra, below the prostate. During arousal but before ejaculation they secrete a small amount of fluid into the urethra which appears at the tip of the penis. This fluid contains sperm and can cause a pregnancy.

Crabs:
  see Pubic Lice

Crowning: 272–4
Point during labour at which the top of the baby's head becomes visible at the vaginal opening.

Cunnilingus: 397–412
Mouth contact with the vulva. Common names: going down, giving head.

Curettage:
  see Dilation and Currettage

Cystitis: 337
Inflammation or infection of the bladder caused by bacteria. Cystitis is not a sexually transmitted disease, though its symptoms may be aggravated by sexual activity.

Desire: 91–2, 101–2
First phase in the sexual response cycle which moves a person to seek out a sexual situation; also called libido.

Diaphragm: 54–60
Contraceptive device which is placed in the back end of the vagina to block off the opening to the uterus.

**Dilation and Curettage
(D&C):** 286
Dilation is the spreading of the cervix to allow curettage, the scraping of the inner lining of the uterus with an instrument called a curette. Used as an abortion method and to diagnose certain uterine disorders.

Dilation and Evacuation: 286
A method of terminating a pregnancy. After the cervix is dilated a vacuum pump is used to remove foetal tissue from the womb. The uterine lining may be gently scraped afterwards (curettage).

Douche: 341
Device for flushing out the vagina. Douching is not necessary unless prescribed and is not a proper birth control method.

Drag Queen: 171
A male homosexual who dresses flamboyantly in the clothing of the other sex.

Dry Come: see Retrograde Ejaculation

Dyke: 173
A negative description of a woman who seems masculine either in behaviour or in appearance.

Dysmenorrhoea: 355–6
The pain or discomfort a woman may experience during menstruation. Cramps, back pain, breast tenderness, bloated feelings, weight gain and headaches may be experienced.

Dyspareunia: 109
Condition in which a woman finds sexual intercourse painful.

Ectopic Pregnancy: 267–8
Pregnancy in which the fertilized egg implants and grows in a Fallopian tube rather than in the uterus.

Ejaculation: 245
The release of semen from the penis. Common names: coming, shooting, popping off, getting off.

Ejaculatory Ducts: 245
Located within the prostate, the passages where the seminal vesicles join the vasa deferentia.

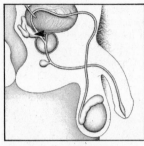

Electra Complex: 17
Freudian theory describing part of a girl's psychosexual development from three to five or six years of age, according to which a girl feels cheated by not having a penis and competes with her mother for her father's affection. The Electra complex parallels boys' Oedipus complex.

Embryo: 258–9
A developing baby from the third to the eighth weeks of pregnancy.

Endometriosis: 346
The growth of womb-lining tissue in places other than the womb, such as the ovaries, Fallopian tubes or intestines.

Endometritis: 346
An irritation of the lining of the uterus.

Endometrium: 345
Innermost layer of the uterus. It leaves the body as part of the menstrual flow unless pregnancy occurs, when it provides a place for the fertilized egg to grow.

Epididymes: 238
Tightly coiled tubes which adhere to the surface of each

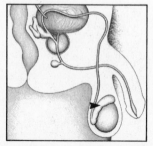

testicle and act as maturation and storage chambers for newly developed sperm as they move out of the seminiferous tubules.

Erection: 220–23
Process whereby the soft

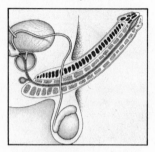

spongy tissue in the shaft of the penis is filled with blood, causing the penis to enlarge and stiffen. Common names: hard-on, stiff.

Erectile Difficulty: 104–5
A problem of sexual response in which a man is unable to achieve an erection. The difficulty may be occasional or regular. Common name: impotence.

Erogenous Zone: 432
Any part of the body that is particularly sensitive to sexually arousing touch.

Erotica: 139–49
Any written or visual material or device that arouses sexual interest or is used to enhance a sexual experience.

Ethinyl oestradol: 67
Synthetic oestrogen used within 72 hours of unprotected intercourse. Common name: morning-after pill.

Exhibitionism: 151–2
Compulsive act of inappropriately exposing the genitals to the other sex for the purpose of sexual arousal and gratification.

Fallopian Tubes: 360–61
Two thin tubes,
approximately four inches
long, which extend outward
from the sides of the uterus
toward the ovaries and
convey eggs from the ovaries
into the uterus.

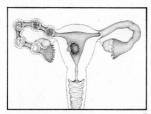

Fellatio: 397–412
Mouth contact with the male
genitals. Common names:
giving head, going down,
blow job.

Fertilization: 251
Penetration of an ovum by a
sperm; it usually occurs in a
Fallopian tube.

Fetishism: 150–57
Fixation on an object or
body part and a compulsive
need for its use in order to
obtain sexual gratification.

**Foetal Alcohol Syndrome
(FAS):** 264–5
Name given to a dangerous
physical and mental disorder
affecting babies born to
women who are alcoholics or
heavy drinkers.

Foetus: 258–62
The name given to a
developing baby from the
eighth week after fertilization
until birth.

Fimbriae: 361
The finger-like structures at
the end of each Fallopian
tube that enclose the ovary
and aid the passage of the egg
into the tube.

Forceps Delivery: 284
The use of special tongs
when complications make it
necessary to help move a
baby quickly through the
vagina.

Foreskin: 218
Tissue that covers the glans
of the penis. It can be rolled
back to expose the glans.

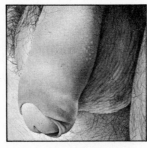

Frenulum: 217
Sensitive area on the
underside of the penis where
the glans meets the shaft.

Gay: 164
Man or woman having a
homosexual orientation.

Gender: 158–63
The definition of a person's
sex as male or female.

Gender Identity: 158
A person's private conviction
of his or her maleness or
femaleness.

Gender Roles: 158–63
Society's norms of masculine
and feminine behaviour.

Genes: 254
Chromosome components
that define our biological
characteristics.

Gestation: 257–72
The period after conception,
also known as pregnancy,
during which a baby develops
in the womb.

Glans Penis: 217, 225
The head of the penis, often
known just as the glans.

Gonorrhoea: 317–18
A sexually transmitted
disease spread by a variety of
sexual acts. Painful urination
and discharge from the
urethra are some common
symptoms. Common names:
clap, drip, dose.

Granuloma inguinale:
318–9
A sexually transmitted
disease which commonly
occurs in tropical climates.
Painless skin lesions in the
genital area are common
signs.

Hepatitis: 317
Infection characterized by an
inflammation of the liver
among other symptoms; one
form of it can be transmitted
by sexual contact.

HCG: 253
Human chorionic
gonadotrophin, a hormone
associated with pregnancy.

Herpes: 319–20
Major sexually transmitted
disease caused by a virus
which affects the skin and
mucous membranes. Both
types, Herpes Simplex Virus
I and II, are spread through
direct contact with the sores
or blisters which are present
when the disease is in its
active state.

Heterosexual: 165–6
A person whose primary or
sole means of obtaining
sexual fulfilment with a
partner is through sexual
activity with members of the
other sex. Common name:
straight.

Homophobia: 173
Fear of and revulsion toward
homosexuals and
homosexuality.

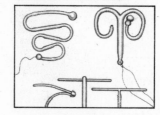
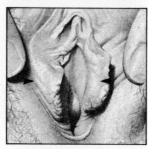

Masturbation: 385–96
The deliberate stimulation of
one's sex organs or of a
partner's sex organs.
Common name: wanking.

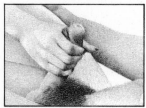

Menarche: 347–8
The beginning of
menstruation at puberty.

Menopause: 36–9
The cessation of a woman's
menstruation.

Menstrual Extraction: 351
Method of evacuating the
uterine lining to minimize the
duration and inconvenience
of normal menstruation. Not
widely used, tested or
recommended.

Menstruation: 347–56
The monthly shedding of the
lining of the uterus mixed
with blood. Common names:
period, curse, having the rag
on.

Milk Ducts: 364
The tubes in the breast
which convey milk from the
glands to the nipples.

Milk Glands: 364
The 15 to 25 milk-producing
sacs in each female breast.

Miscarriage: 268–9
The spontaneous separation
of a developing foetus from
the womb before it is ready
to be born.

Monilia: 320–21
Vaginal infection caused by
an overgrowth of a yeast
fungus normally found in the
vagina.

Mons Pubis: 327
Soft mound that forms the

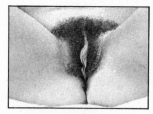

upper end of a woman's
external genitals.

Morning-after Pill: *see*
Ethinyl oestradol

Morning Sickness: 252
Symptoms such as nausea
and vomiting which may
occur early in pregnancy as a
result of changes in the
body's hormone levels.

Multiple Orgasm: 94–5
Several orgasms within a
short period of time and
during one sexual experience.

Myometrium: 346
The muscular middle layer of
the uterine lining that gives
the uterus its strength and
elasticity.

Natural Family Planning:
72–6
Group of birth control
methods, including Billings,
calendar, temperature, using
a knowledge of women's
ovulatory cycles alone.

Nocturnal Emissions: 18
Involuntary ejaculation of
semen while a man is asleep.
Common name: wet dream.

**Non-Specific Urethritis
(NSU):** 321
Sexually transmitted disease
of which the symptoms are
irritation of the urethra and
discharge. In women it may
be asymptomatic. It is also
known as non-gonococcal
urethritis.

Oedipus Complex: 17
Freudian theory describing
part of boys' psychosexual
development between the
ages of approximately three
and five–six, according to
which boys fear their fathers
will castrate them for
competing for their mothers'
affection.

Oestrogen: 361
Sex hormone produced by a
woman's ovaries that
stimulates the growth of a
girl's sex organs and helps
regulate the menstrual cycle.

Oral-genital Sex: 397–412
Term that embraces both
cunnilingus and fellatio.

Oral Phase: 13
According to psychoanalytic
theory, a stage in a young
child's development during
which the mouth is the
principal site of pleasurable
fulfilment.

Orgasm: 93–9
Peak experience during
sexual response for both
sexes. Common name:
coming.

Orgasmic Difficulty: 106–9
Problem of sexual response in
which a woman fails to
achieve orgasm.

Ova: 361
The eggs produced by the
ovaries; ovum is the singular
form.

Ovarian Cyst: 362
An abnormal growth in an
ovary; it may disappear by
itself or may need to be
removed surgically.

**Ovariectomy
(Oophorectomy):** 362–3
Removal of one or both of a
woman's ovaries. If both
ovaries are removed the
woman will be sterile.

Ovaries: 361–3
Organs on each side of the upper part of the uterus that produce ova (eggs) and the female hormone oestrogen.

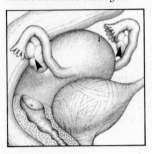

Oxytocin: 365
Hormone involved in the production of breast milk. When released into the bloodstream, it causes the milk to move from the milk glands to the nipples.

Pap Smear: 344
Test for cancer in which mucus from the cervix is removed with a cotton swab and examined to detect the presence of abnormal cells.

Pelvic Inflammatory Disease (PID): 321–2
Condition that may result if sexually transmitted diseases are left untreated; it can adversely affect a woman's internal reproductive system.

Penis: 217–28
The male sex and reproductive organ, consisting of a head, called the glans, and the shaft or body. The shaft is made up of soft spongy tissue into which extra blood can flow causing the penis to erect. Common names: dick, prick, cock, shaft, peter.

Peyronie's Disease: 221–2
Abnormal curvature of the penis making erection painful and sex difficult to enjoy.

Pill: 65–8
Chemical method of birth control for women, taken orally. Synthetic hormones prevent the ovaries from releasing an egg so that pregnancy cannot occur.

Placenta: 258
The organ that develops after conception to act as a nutritional exchange and filtering system between mother and foetus.

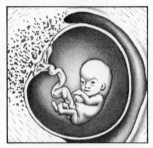

Plateau Phase: 93
Masters' and Johnson's term for the peak level of excitement after which orgasm will occur if appropriate stimulation continues.

Pornography: 139–43
Written or visual material in any medium whose primary objective is to arouse people sexually.

Premature Birth: 283
A baby born significantly before the full thirty-six weeks of development in the womb.

Premature Ejaculation: 102–4
Sexual response problem in which a man consistently has little or no control over the timing of his build-up to orgasm and ejaculation.

Pre-menstrual Tension (PMT): 356
Symptoms such as breast tenderness, bloating, and fatigue which many women experience several days before the beginning of their menstrual period.

Prepuce: *see* Foreskin

Priapism: 222
Disorder whereby a male's erect penis will not return to its flaccid state.

Prolactin: 365
Hormone involved in the production of breast milk. As an infant suckles, prolactin is released into the mother's bloodstream causing the milk glands to produce more milk.

Prolapsed Uterus: 347
Condition in which the uterus sags or slips into the vagina due to a weakening of supporting structures.

Prostaglandin: 287
Substance that causes uterine contractions and is used in some abortion procedures.

Prostate Gland: 240–45
Gland located near the bladder that produces the majority of the fluid which, combined with sperm and other secretions, constitutes semen.

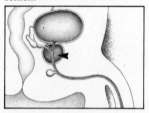

Prostatectomy: 242–3
The surgical removal of part or all of the prostate gland.

Prostatitis: 241–2
Condition in which the prostate gland enlarges leading to frequent urination and a slowing of the urine stream.

Prostitution: 291–4
The exchange of sexual services for money or other reward. Common names: the life, the game.

Puberty: 19–21
The phase of adolescence during which boys and girls develop the sexual characteristics of adults.

Pubic Lice: 322
Tiny bugs that cause intense itching near the roots of head, pubic, or underarm hair. They are spread by sexual contact or by contact with infected clothing and objects. Common name: crabs.

Quickening: 261
Stage of pregnancy when the foetus is first felt to move in the womb.

Rape: 295–302
Assault in which a person uses force or the threat of force to have sexual contact.

Refractory Period: 93–4
The length of time following orgasm and ejaculation in the male during which he is unable to achieve another erection.

Resolution: 93
Masters' and Johnson's term for the phase during which the body returns to its sexually unexcited state after orgasm.

Retarded Ejaculation: 103
Sexual response problem, also referred to as ejaculatory incompetence, in which a man is unable to ejaculate even though he is highly aroused.

Retrograde Ejaculation: 243–4
Condition whereby semen is ejaculated backward into the bladder. Common name: dry come.

Rhythm: 73–4
Natural family planning method based on avoiding intercourse during a woman's fertile period.

Rh Factor: 263
Rhesus factor – a description of one aspect of the constituents of blood; Rh factors have to be checked in pregnant women as certain combinations can cause problems.

Sadism: 152–4
A form of fetishism in which a person (a sadist) is sexually aroused and gratified by threatening or inflicting pain.

Sadomasochism: 152–4
A form of fetishism which combines sadistic and masochistic roles in sexual interaction.

Scabies: 322
Mites which are spread by close body contact, burrow under the skin near hair follicles and cause itching and redness.

Scrotum: 228
A soft muscular pouch, containing the testicles; also called the scrotal sac.

Semen: 239
The fluid that leaves a man's penis when he ejaculates. It is made up of fluids from the prostate gland (95%) and the seminal vesicles (4%). Only about 1% of semen is sperm.

Seminal Vesicles: 239
Two pouches located on either side of the prostate gland that contribute a fluid to semen.

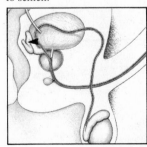

Seminiferous Tubules: 230
Structures within each testicle where sperm is produced.

Sex Education: 303–11
The entire process of conscious and unconscious learning about the sexuality of oneself and others from birth onwards; also the formalization of such learning within a programme.

Sexism: 158–63
The conscious or unconscious assumption that the members of one sex are on the whole inherently superior to the members of the other in certain attributes by virtue of their sex.

Sex Surrogates: 101
Men and women who act as sex partners in the treatment of sexual problems, usually under the supervision of a sex therapist.

Sex Therapy: 99–109
The treatment of individuals' or couples' sexual problems whether of physical or psychological origin.

Sexually Transmitted Diseases (STDs): 312–25
Label given to the range of diseases normally passed between people only through close body contact. Some can also be passed through contact with towels etc. used by an infected person. Common name: venereal disease or VD.

Sixty-nining: 397
Mutual oral-genital sex.

Smegma: 226
A natural secretion under the foreskin. Without regular washing, smegma may collect and cause odour, discomfort and possibly infection. Common name: cheese.

Sodomy: 424
Anal intercourse.

Spanish Fly: 132–3
Preparation made from dried, crushed beetles, mistakenly thought to be an aphrodisiac.

Sperm: 234–7
Microscopic cells produced in the testicles and ejaculated as a very small proportion of semen. If a single sperm unites with an ovum fertilization occurs and a pregnancy may follow.

Spermatic Cords: 228
The cords that connect each testicle to the abdominal cavity.

Sperm Count: 205–6
Medical test used in cases of infertility in which a complete ejaculate is examined to determine the number and mobility of the sperm.

Spermicides: 68–73
Sperm-killing products placed in the vagina before intercourse as contraceptives. They are available as foam, cream, tablets, and pessaries.

Sterility: 203
The permanent inability to father or conceive a child.

Sterilization: 76–86
Surgical procedure used as a permanent method of birth control. For a man it is called vasectomy; for a woman tubal ligation.

Stillbirth: 284
A baby born dead.

Swinging: 31
The practice, usually among married couples, of openly exchanging partners for sexual activity. Also called "wife swapping" and "mate swapping."

Syphilis: 322–3
A highly contagious and serious disease transmitted through sexual contact and characterized initially by the presence of a chancre in the genital area. Common name: syph.

Tampon: 350–51
A cotton tube inserted into the vagina to absorb the menstrual flow; used as an alternative to a sanitary towel or pad.

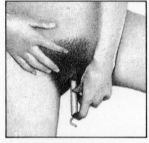

Test tube baby: 208
A baby that develops after a woman's egg has been fertilized by sperm outside her body and placed in the womb to grow as in a normal pregnancy.

Testes: 228–34
Alternative name for testicles.

Testicles: 228–34
The two small balls in the scrotum; they produce sperm and hormones. Common names: balls, nuts, family jewels.

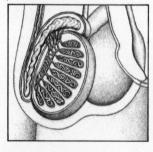

Testosterone: 237
The most important androgen or male hormone, produced in the testicles.

Toxaemia: 269–70
Disease thought to be caused by inadequate nutrition that affects some women during the middle and later months of pregnancy.

Toxic Shock Syndrome: 350–51
Serious bacterial disease linked in some cases by recent research to vaginal infections associated with some superabsorbent tampons.

Transition: 273–4
The shortest but often most uncomfortable period of labour between contractions and the actual birth of the baby.

Transsexual: 192–8
Person who though biologically of one sex is convinced that he or she really belongs to the other.

Transvestite: 154–7
Person, usually a heterosexual male, who gets sexual pleasure and relief from using a garment commonly reserved for the other sex.

Trichomoniasis: 323
Infection of which the symptoms in women are an itchy, odorous discharge; men may have a slight discharge but often have no symptoms. Usually, but not necessarily, transmitted by sexual contact.

Tubal ligation: 80–83
Sterilization procedure for women in which the Fallopian tubes are cut or sealed off. This prevents egg and sperm from meeting and starting a pregnancy.

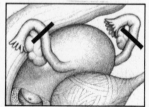

Umbilical Cord: 258, 274
Flexible cord which connects the foetus to the placenta and transfers oxygen, nourishment and wastes.

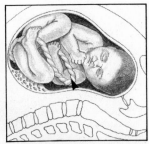

Undescended Testicles: 233
A quite common condition in infant boys, usually resolved easily. In certain cases the testicles cannot be enabled to descend – this is known as cryptorchidism.

Urethra: 245, 336-7
The passageway that links the bladder to the urethral opening in both sexes and is used for urination. In men it is also used for the ejaculation of semen.

Urethritis: 321
Inflammation or infection of the urinary opening and/or the urethra.

Uterus: 345-7
The organ which holds a growing baby during pregnancy. Shaped like an upside-down pear, it consists of layers of muscle and tissue. At the upper end are the Fallopian tubes and at the lower end the cervix. Common name: womb.

Vacuum Aspiration: 286
Abortion method using a vacuum pump inserted through the cervix to remove foetal tissue; frequently used for first trimester terminations.

Vagina: 337-43
An organ approximately three to five inches long at rest and shaped like a flattened tube which extends from the outer opening in the vulva to the cervix. It is capable of considerable expansion during sexual intercourse and the birth process. Common names: pussy, cunt, fanny, hole.

Vaginal Lubrication: 338-40
During sexual arousal, the fluid which collects on the walls of a woman's vagina.

Vaginismus: 109
Condition in which the muscles around the opening to the vagina lock tight.

Vaginitis: 323
An inflammation, infection or irritation of the vagina.

Vasa Deferentia: 238-9
Two narrow tubes, conveying sperm to the point where it can mix with the other constituents of semen. Each vas deferens is approximately 16 to 18 inches long.

Vasectomy: 83-6
The operation in which a man is sterilized by having both vasa deferentia sealed

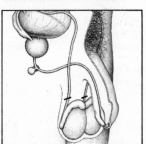

off. Usually irreversible. The parallel female sterilization technique is tubal ligation.

Vasocongestion: 220
The increased blood flow to certain parts of the body that accompanies sexual arousal; it shows as erection in men and as vaginal lubrication in women.

Venereal disease: 312-25
Term that used to be used to describe gonorrhoea and syphilis only. Now on the whole replaced by the term "sexually transmitted disease," which covers all diseases spread by specifically sexual contact.

Vestibule: 333
The area around the opening to the vagina and the urethra.

Virginity: 336
The state of not having had sexual intercourse.

Voyeurism: 154
The fetish of deriving sexual satisfaction from watching people undressing or nude, or observing them during sexual acts without their knowledge or consent.

Vulva: 326
The name for a woman's external sex organs.

Wet Dreams: *see* Nocturnal Emissions

Womb: *see* Uterus

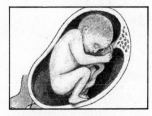

Yohimbine: 133
Crushed tree bark believed erroneously to be an aphrodisiac.

HELP

Some national organizations which can offer advice, information or referral to a local resource to help with particular sexual difficulties.

Birth Control
Family Planning Association,
27-35 Mortimer Street,
London W1N 7RJ,
01 636 7866

Well Woman Clinic,
108 Whitfield Street,
London W1,
01 388 0662

Brook Advisory Clinic for Young People,
233 Tottenham Court Road,
London W1P 9AE
01 323 1522/01 580 2991

Pregnancy Termination
The British Pregnancy Advisory Service,
Head Office: Guildhall Buildings,
            Navigation Street,
            Birmingham B2 4BT,
            021 643 1461

Pregnancy Advisory Service,
40 Margaret Street,
London W9,
01 409 0281

Release,
1 Elgin Avenue,
London W11,
01 289 1123

Homosexuality
Campaign for Homosexual Equality,
PO Box 427,
33 King Street,
Manchester M60 2EL,
061 228 1985

Gay Switchboard: 01 837 7324

Lesbian Line: 01 794 2942

Disability
Physically Handicapped and Able Bodied,
42 Devonshire Street,
London W1N 1LN,
01 637 7475

Sexual Problems of Disabled People,
25 Mortimer Street,
London W1N 7RJ,
01 253 9433

Rape
Rape Crisis Centre,
PO Box 42,
London N6 5BU,
01 340 6145

Infertility
National Association for the Childless,
Birmingham Settlement,
318 Summer Lane,
Birmingham B19 3RL,
021 359 4887/2113

Health & Sex Education
The Health Education Council,
78 New Oxford Street,
London WC1A 1AH,
01 637 1881